MW00611755

Linguistic Luck

Linguistic Luck

Safeguards and Threats to Linguistic Communication

Edited by
ABROL FAIRWEATHER
and
CARLOS MONTEMAYOR

OXFORD
UNIVERSITY PRESS

OXFORD
UNIVERSITY PRESS

Great Clarendon Street, Oxford, OX2 6DP,
United Kingdom

Oxford University Press is a department of the University of Oxford.
It furthers the University's objective of excellence in research, scholarship,
and education by publishing worldwide. Oxford is a registered trade mark of
Oxford University Press in the UK and in certain other countries

© Oxford University Press 2023

The moral rights of the authors have been asserted

All rights reserved. No part of this publication may be reproduced, stored in
a retrieval system, or transmitted, in any form or by any means, without the
prior permission in writing of Oxford University Press, or as expressly permitted
by law, by licence or under terms agreed with the appropriate reprographics
rights organization. Enquiries concerning reproduction outside the scope of the
above should be sent to the Rights Department, Oxford University Press, at the
address above

You must not circulate this work in any other form
and you must impose this same condition on any acquirer

Published in the United States of America by Oxford University Press
198 Madison Avenue, New York, NY 10016, United States of America

British Library Cataloguing in Publication Data
Data available

Library of Congress Control Number: 2023930843

ISBN 978–0–19–284545–0

DOI: 10.1093/oso/9780192845450.001.0001

Printed and bound in the UK by
Clays Ltd, Elcograf S.p.A.

Links to third party websites are provided by Oxford in good faith and
for information only. Oxford disclaims any responsibility for the materials
contained in any third party website referenced in this work.

Foreword

Duncan Pritchard

Analytical philosophy is notorious for many traits, one of which is the tendency to define every term that could possibly be of philosophical interest. With this in mind, it is odd that, until relatively recently, luck was not itself a topic of direct philosophical analysis. This is especially puzzling given that it has always been crystal clear, going right back to antiquity, that luck is a deeply important philosophical concept. Think, for example, of how luck figures in metaphysical debates about causation and free will, in political debates about just deserts, in epistemological debates about the nature of knowledge (e.g., Gettier-style cases), and in ethical debates about moral luck. And yet nonetheless analytical philosophers, so often caricatured as being unable to resist a conceptual analysis even when it is unnecessary, tended to treat luck as an undefined primitive, or at least only offered partial accounts of it.

I don't know why philosophy took this detour around the analysis of luck (this is probably more of a topic for sociologists), but whatever the reason, we do now finally have a thriving debate about the nature of luck and how it impacts philosophical questions. This has, in turn, re-energized those philosophical discussions, such as those concerned with moral and epistemic luck, where the notion of luck is prominent. The contemporary concern with the nature of luck and its import to specific philosophical questions has also spawned new topics of interest.

The present volume nicely illustrates this last point by bringing together a rich body of chapters concerned with the emergent debate about linguistic luck. In its most general form, the topic of linguistic luck is concerned with the relevance of luck to questions of meaning and communication. As such, it brings the luck debate squarely into the terrain of philosophy of language and linguistics. As the editors to this volume note in their introduction, the discussion of linguistic luck has lagged behind parallel debates in other areas of philosophy. I think we can locate one obvious explanation for why this might have occurred in the lack of a philosophical treatment of luck itself. As the analysis of luck has come to the fore of philosophical discussion, so there has been a renewed impetus to reconsider how luck might be relevant to a range of philosophical topics.

The chapters in the present volume demonstrate the wide array of ways in which luck can be relevant to linguistic topics. Despite the varied approaches, however, one can discern an overarching philosophical concern when it comes to linguistic luck: how successful communication depends on the implementation of luck-reducing measures, at both the individual and the social/structural level. When one starts to ponder the potential for such luck to undermine human communication, it can seem miraculous that our language use is as seamless as it is (or that, for example, we are able to systematically make confident judgements about whether a sentence is meaningful, much less what it means). Most of the chapters in this volume engage with this fundamental issue regarding linguistic luck in some form, whether by considering its implications at the level of linguistics, or by considering particular cases where specific communicative attempts, such as an assertion, fail to hit their target due to luck.

So construed, the debates about linguistic luck mirror the concerns about luck that appear elsewhere, in that luck tends to undermine conditions that demand not only success but also that the success is due to a particular kind of relationship obtaining. In cases of causation, for example, luck undermines genuine causation when the success in question (the obtaining of the target effect) is not brought about by the relevant causal factors but is rather due to luck. Or think about the notion of achievement. It does not suffice for achievement that one is successful, since it also needs to be the case that the success is appropriately attributable to one's relevant exercise of agency, and the latter can be undermined by luck. We see the same structure at work in the core debates about linguistic luck, in that communication demands more than just the relevant successful outcome (e.g., that a string of words is correctly heard), but also that certain other conditions that relate to the parties involved also obtain. These latter conditions can, however, be obviously subject to luck, just as they are in parallel debates about causation and achievement.

With this structural point about debates about luck in mind, we should start to see common features emerging in how luck relates to specific areas of philosophy. One such common theme is the evaluation of particular accounts of luck—such as modal, probabilistic, and lack of control accounts—when it comes to accommodating the relevant phenomena within that field. Another common theme is whether a particular notion might be more compatible with luck—perhaps even to the extent of being compatible with it—than one might have hitherto supposed. This last issue looms large in discussions about moral and epistemic luck, for example, where there are positions that hold, controversially, that luck is entirely compatible with certain kinds of moral and epistemic standing. Could there be analogous standings with regard to linguistic concerns which, it turns out, can happily coexist with the presence of luck in bringing about the relevant successful states that underlie those standings?

Of course, we may also discover, as the luck debate moves into new territory, that there are important disanalogies to its application across different domains. (Indeed, it is usually with disanalogies of this kind that philosophical progress is made.) This new volume on linguistic luck promises some interesting avenues in this regard, as several of the chapters note differences in how luck plays out in the linguistic realm when compared to other domains like ethics and epistemology. For example, the anti-luck condition imposed on linguistic understanding may well be importantly different to the anti-luck condition usually imposed on knowledge. If that's right, then this would be a significant result.

As with all emergent debates, it will take time for the fruits to show. But the beauty of this volume is that it brings together, for the very first time, a sophisticated body of literature on this new topic in order to turbo-charge the debate. As such, it represents the excitement of being part of a discussion at its inception, when new tools are being brought to bear, and one is not yet confident of where the consensus might eventually lie. Moreover, the quality of the work makes a compelling case for the philosophical importance of the topic. There will, I'm sure, be much more philosophical debate about linguistic luck in the coming years, but the foundation for this debate will be the excellent chapters assembled here.

University of California
Irvine
September 2022

References

Pritchard, D. H. (2005). *Epistemic Luck*, Oxford: Oxford University Press.

Pritchard, D. H. (2014). 'The Modal Account of Luck', *Metaphilosophy* 45, 594–619.

Pritchard, D. H., & Whittington, L. (Eds). (2015). *The Philosophy of Luck*, London: Routledge.

Pritchard, D. H., Millar, A., & Haddock, A. (2010). *The Nature and Value of Knowledge: Three Investigations*, Oxford: Oxford University Press.

Contents

Acknowledgements

We thank Kent Bach, who helped us identify some of the key problems surrounding the phenomenon of linguistic luck. Anand Vaidya deserves recognition for especially valuable conversations at our Wednesday coffee shop meetings in Berkeley, California. We are grateful for his demanding philosophical engagement and ongoing friendship. Many conversations with Adam Morton made this volume possible for us. Regrettably, Adam will not be able to see its final form, because he passed away in 2020, when the project was still in its infancy. We are saddened to be without him, but grateful for his collaboration and friendship over the years. Barry Stroud also deserves special mention, though he was not here to see our project develop either. His influence on some of the early ideas that led to the thematization of the volume was fundamental.

Audiences and participants at the Invited Symposium on Linguistic Luck at the Pacific Meeting of the 2021 American Philosophical Association were invaluable and provided a great opportunity to provide early comment and criticism to some of the essays. Many thanks to the organizers and participants. Thanks to audiences at San Francisco State University and Thammasat University for opportunities to reflect on and improve the project, and also to examine cross-cultural aspects of the issues.

Other people we would like to thank that have directly or indirectly inspired the project include: Carlotta Pavese, Josh Armstrong, Erna Nishime, Charington Nongbua, Sumalee Ma, Teerabhat Ruensiri, Muanmard Mukpradit, Tomas Marconi, Ernest Lepore, Bradley Armour-Garb, Mikkel Gerken, and Jodi Halpern. We thank Lauren Wong and Jordan Woolsey for their help proofreading the text.

List of Contributors

John Collins (University of East Anglia)

María de Ponte (University of the Basque Country)

Michael Devitt (CUNY)

Imogen Dickie (University of Toronto)

Abrol Fairweather (San Francisco State University)

Elizabeth Fricker (Oxford University)

Georgi Gardiner (University of Tennessee)

Samia Hesni (Boston University)

Justin Khoo (MIT)

Jeffrey C. King (Rutgers University)

Kepa Korta (University of the Basque Country)

Carlos Montemayor (San Francisco State University)

Andrew Peet (Lektor at Umeå University)

John Perry (Stanford University)

Georges Rey (University of Maryland)

Claudine Verheggen (York University)

1

Introduction

Abrol Fairweather and Carlos Montemayor

I. What Is Linguistic Luck?

Despite the considerable attention the topic of luck has received in ethics and epistemology,[1] very little has been published in the philosophical literature overtly on linguistic luck.[2] The essays collected here provide the first sustained examination of the diverse forms of linguistic luck, the mechanisms available to reduce the impact of linguistic luck and to cope with residual luck not eliminated by the causal, inferential, and intentional mechanisms which aim at its eradication. Of primary interest is not some, hitherto unnoticed, widespread prevalence of luck in the determinants of meaning and communication, but rather the impressive extent to which luck is reduced or eliminated therein. Whether through causal, inferential, or intentional means, the determinants of meaning and communication are impressively independent of luck and chance. In fact, it is difficult to imagine a world with human language where efforts to communicate succeed no better than chance.[3] Linguistic communication is only possible because robust luck reducing variables are at work. The essays collected here seek to understand the diversity, scope, and mode of operation of luck reducing mechanisms in language.

So, how do we do it? How do we reduce the impact of chance and luck to make communication in language so reliable and trustworthy? While it is not possible to cover here the full range of linguistic phenomena affected by luck, a wide range of issues in linguistics and philosophy of language are investigated, including syntax processing, demonstrative reference, conversational implicature, testimony, lexical innovation, joint attention, communicative value, conventionalism vs. anti-conventionalism, metasemantic safety, and semantic skepticism, to name a few. Some key questions examined here, and for future research on the topic, include: What is the nature and significance of linguistic luck? How much luck can be tolerated in language and how do we avoid it? What are the primary luck

---

[1] Nigel (1979); Williams (1981); Statman (1991); Zagzebski (1996); Riggs (2007); Pritchard (2015).
[2] Loar (1976); Buchanan (2014); Dickie (2015); Peet (2016); Unnsteinsson, (2018).
[3] While it is beyond the scope of this introductory chapter, classical skeptical arguments considered by Wittgenstein, Quine, and Davidson are plausibly seen as advancing such arguments. See Verheggen (Chapter 9, this volume); Myers and Verheggen (2016).

Abrol Fairweather and Carlos Montemayor, *Introduction* In: *Linguistic Luck: Safeguards and Threats to Linguistic Communication.* Edited by: Abrol Fairweather and Carlos Montemayor, Oxford University Press.
© Oxford University Press 2023. DOI: 10.1093/oso/9780192845450.003.0001

reducing mechanisms in linguistic theory and practice? How do we cope with ineliminable remainders of luck despite our best efforts to eradicate it? What areas of linguistic theory and practice are most impacted by linguistic luck?

Fortunately, some linguistic luck reducing mechanisms do not depend solely on conscious attention or acquired skill. Many are due to genetic endowment[4] and nomological connections between human beings and their environment (including other human beings). Other luck reducing mechanisms will be more closely tied to forms of conscious attention, motivation, and linguistic convention. Because they are so important to our form of life, many luck eliminating measures in language are familiar and can seem even trivial—pointing (ostension), "do you mean that...?" questions, reframing, grammars, Gricean maxims, etc. We first examine some nomological luck reducing mechanisms below, and then more intention and convention dependent mechanisms, followed by a summary of the essays to follow.

In addition to furthering the aims of linguistic theory, our inquiry is important because trust is important. Luck is generally no friend of trust, the two typically trend in opposing directions. The more a given outcome or state of affairs depends on luck, as opposed to skill or necessity, the less trustworthy people will appear in relevant respects. Linguistic trust is especially important because highly reliable, non-luckily successful linguistic capacities underlie so much of the trust essential to our moral, epistemic, social, and personal lives. It's difficult to imagine forming rational trust in any human being or institution without the mutual trust that speakers and interlocutors reliably manifest in a host of reliable linguistic processes, such as properly projectable (non-grue) predication, successful identification of speaker intentions and speech act types, native syntactic capacities, etc.[5] The widespread possession of capacities for non-lucky linguistic success is essential to preserving a wide range of important human activities supported and sustained by trust.

II. Nomological Luck Reduction

Perhaps the most distinctive and important aspect of being a member of our species, homo sapiens, is the remarkable fact that it makes us automatically (in standard circumstances) members of a linguistic community. This means three things. First, we are members of a species that distinguishes itself by large-scale cooperation based on the universal capacity to learn a language that can be symbolically, morphologically, and behaviorally expressed. Second, by having a human genome, very young members of our species are capable of quickly

---

[4] Especially relevant for syntax and human uniqueness, Berwick and Chomsky (2016).
[5] For forms of trust constitutive of membership in linguistic communities, see Bach and Harnish (1979) and Clark (1996).

learning a spoken language with unbound possibilities for meaning construction, without any conscious reflection on the complex rules of syntax and their application in grammatical articulations of meaning, quickly generalizing rules for well-formed sentences with very little exposure to all the correct instances of sentences in a natural language. Third, the human capacity for meaningful symbolic manipulation is used in contexts and settings that generalize and transcend the environments in which our species evolved, from music notation to mathematics. This immediate and constitutive kind of membership inclusion is itself a major feat of risk and luck reduction, but what is even more notable is how many types of luck reduction it involves.

In terms of communicative luck reduction, meaningful signals need to be picked up through different types of patterns and behavior. At the receiver's end, infants, for instance, need to parse contents through gestures concerning joint attention for *de re* reference, vocalizations, and sounds, associated with mouth patterns, hand gestures, etc. But the generalizations that are the most critical aspects of language learning are not merely dependent on the association and projection of meanings and utterances. By far the most critical inferential generalizations concern the nature of well-formed sentences, the possible number of grammatical rules for the formation of sentences, and the reduction of possible grammars governing expressions (see the contributions by Rey and Collins, Chapter 5, and Devitt, Chapter 6, this volume).

Justified true belief with a safety condition above average (say 60% or 70% of truth production) cannot account for these kinds of luck reduction. Besides a very high rate of success, there has to be robust and widespread agreement among speakers regarding what constitutes a well-formed sentence. As will be explained below, cases which Rey and Collins call "WhyNots" include not only completely exotic or aberrant cases, which make no sense and cannot be adequately called a sentence of a specific language; but also cases that are only slightly incorrect and, more importantly, are semantically clear, but can still be easily recognized by speakers as erroneous. Such a fine grained recognitional capacity so prevalent in a population of speakers cannot depend on belief formation regarding piecemeal amounts of linguistic evidence. As Norbert Hornstein says:

> Theoretically, this perspective leads one to develop formal systems embodying universal principles that are responsive to the acquisition problem. These principles come in two varieties: structural universals, which limit the range of configurations in a natural language, and substantive universals, which limit the kinds of formatives a natural language may have. Both act to restrict the variety of grammars available for language acquisition.   (Hornstein, 1990, 3)

Two kinds of generalization are involved in grammatical luck reduction. First, there is luck reduction with respect to possible grammars available to articulate the compositional rules of a language. This is fundamental for the community to be on the same page with respect to grammaticalness, sentence structure, and meaning entailment. Second, luck reduction also concerns the number of possible expressions that are available to speakers, delineating the scope of what is acceptable. On the one hand, the set of formal rules determining grammaticalness needs to be constrained and made uniform. On the other hand, expressions need to be hierarchically organized in terms of the possible meanings that can be assigned to them given their syntactic structure. These are all nomologically dependent, biologically instantiated constraints on grammar and meaning.

Ambiguity based on qualifier position is an excellent example of the need for luck reducing attention that is formally guided by this hierarchical structure. If we merely learned associations between symbols and their referents, the way some species are capable of doing, we would not understand the ambiguity behind the expression "deep blue sky." This is because qualifiers can be hierarchically related in a way that meanings are altered simply by being so organized, irrespective of their associated referents. Thus, the expression "deep blue sky" has two possible meanings (rather than only one or four or five). The term "deep" could qualify either the color blue or the depth of the sky, entailing two different kinds of truth-maker for the meaning of a sentence containing this expression. Without the hierarchical rules of syntax this would not be possible (for a discussion of why this hierarchically driven attention to content might be a uniquely human feature of linguistic communication, see Berwick and Chomsky, 2016).

This is such a unique skill, so robust and widespread in human communication that researchers were expecting to find at least some traces of it in our closest evolutionary cousins with whom we share recent ancestors. But after training, investigating, and studying chimpanzees, bonobos, and gorillas for years, nothing like the capacity to structure meanings hierarchically has been found. In fact, even more striking, researchers found that while human communication is almost entirely determined by this kind of hierarchical embedding, what Tecumseh Fitch (2014) called "dendrophilia," the opposite is found in our cousins (bonobos). This capacity to organize contents has been identified even in visual tasks in humans. The "dendrophobia" of our genetic relatives seems hard to explain, but whatever the explanation, we are not "dendrophilic" on the basis of our justified true beliefs about syntax. We are not "responsible" for being members of the human linguistic community. We are born into it.

What does this mean for linguistic luck? The fact that humans are non-luckily and remarkably dendrophilic gives them an initial communal homogeneity that allows them to pay attention to content in unlimited and complex ways while having principled means of reducing the possibilities for acceptable grammars and formal expressions. This type of nomological luck reduction is clearly an important component of our epistemic agency. But the luck reduction is not done by our activities alone. Our close cousins, bonobos and chimpanzees, seem to be helplessly dendrophobic, even after years of intensive training. Our agency is a cause of luck reduction but there is something more important happening here, besides our agency. Our genetic endowment homogenizes our skills and allows for substantial agreement about the formal aspects of language.

Joint attention, joint action, and joint commitment, without this non-lucky agreement, would never transcend the level of associative communication found in many animals. We could be non-lucky at jointly attending to red objects, infer that they are dangerous, and create common ground and joint salience regarding the fact that red is associated with danger. But our communication would not scale up and generalize the way it does without the initial boost we get from syntax competence, which grounds much of our trust in other speakers. With such a high degree of success, much higher than any epistemic or moral standard would require, luck at the syntactic level would prevent other metasemantic or linguistic anti-luck mechanisms to operate. However, while Loar and related cases show that luck at the referential level has cumulative negative impacts (discussed below), some accidents at the syntax level can be tolerated (such as Rey and Collins' WhyNots), raising doubts about the role of explicit knowledge in linguistic communication (see Pettit, 2002).

The examples that Rey and Collins call "WhyNots" (which Chomsky initially called "perfectly fine thoughts") are based on the extremely sensitive capacities we have to detect syntactic errors that, nonetheless, still allow us to understand contents. Speakers can understand the semantic content (truth-making relations, implications, etc.) of expressions that are not quite exactly syntactical, and yet clearly recognize the correct form from the incorrect one. "Who did Max and Kat kiss?" versus "Who did Max and kiss Mary?," as Rey and Collins show, can quite easily be contrasted as grammatical and ungrammatical, yet the mistake does not lie simply in lack of grammaticalness (e.g., she goes to the park) or incapability to understand the meaning of the sentence. These cases show how picky and obsessive we humans are about positional rules, or strictly formal features of language. An important question, raised by Devitt in his response to Rey and Collins, is to ask what the psychological, as well as social or conventional, contributions are of luck reduction for learning grammatical rules (see his distinction between r-luck and i-luck; Chapter 6, this volume).

The contributions to this volume discuss anti-luck mechanisms not only at the formal stage of processing, but also at the semantic, pragmatic, and even at the lexical-innovation level. They also go beyond documenting and examining sources of anti-luck by showing the complex interconnections between linguistic luck and various kinds of social, political, and practical engagement (see, for instance, the chapters by Dickie (Chapter 3), Hesni (Chapter 11), and Gardiner (Chapter 12), in this volume) We provide a brief illustration, in what follows, of the diverse sources of luck reduction in linguistic communication that are analyzed in this volume.

III. Luck, Trust, and Losing Common Ground

Membership in a linguistic community enables human beings to share parts of the world with one another, thereby enabling complex forms of coordination essential to human communal life. One fundamental mechanism for so doing is accessing contents held (and accrued) in common ground.[6] However, luck often impedes the accrual of common ground. Below, a slight modification to a well-known case of referential luck described by Brian Loar (1976) shows the destructive potential of undetected linguistic luck. One-off cases of referential luck, as in Loar's original, can appear deceptively innocuous if the effect on communication downstream is not considered. Diachronically extended cases bring out the threat to fundamental forms of trust and cooperation presented by lucky recovery of referents. Non-lucky cases reliably sustain extended linguistic cooperation and trust.

In Loar's original case (1976), the exchange below has neither Smith nor Jones believing 'the man on TV = the man on the train', so it is not in common ground between them. In our slight modification below, Smith, but not Jones, knows (or believes) the identity, and this is precisely what prompts Smith's remark 'He is a stockbroker', as this was previously unknown to either. Just as before, 'the man on TV = the man on the train' is not in common ground and it is still by luck that Jones recovers the same referent.

The stockbroker: Suppose that, whilst watching the television, Smith, but not Jones, becomes aware that the man being interviewed on television is someone they see on the train every morning and about whom, in that latter role, they have just been talking. Smith says 'He is a stockbroker', intending to refer to the man on television; Jones takes Smith to be referring to the man on the train. Now Jones, as it happens, has correctly identified Smith's referent, since the man on television is the man on the train; but he has failed to understand Smith's utterance.

Extending the case to include communication downstream about the stockbroker, suppose Smith, who believes 'the man on TV = the man on the train', now regularly refers to him as 'the man on TV', playfully drawing attention to his newly discovered public stature, while Jones remains ignorant of the identity. Upon seeing the mood, mode of dress, facial expressions, etc., of the man on the train, Smith will regularly ascribe these properties to the man on TV—"The man on TV is awfully sullen today," "The man on TV is dressed for success today," etc. Jones has not caught on that the man on TV is the man on the train, so the identity is still not in common ground and the lucky recovery of the same referent in the original case has not been detected.

---

[6] Stalnaker (1972); Grice (1989); Clark (1996).

Smith's assertions will now strike Jones as unjustified, random, and downright weird. Smith will be attributing reasonable predicates to the man Jones is looking at on the train, but for some reason attributing the properties of the man on the train to 'the man on TV', whom Jones remembers seeing with Smith previously. To Jones, Smith appears to be violating a conversational norm of relevance by consistently changing the subject of their conversation, attributing 'is awfully sullen', 'is dressed for success today', etc., to 'the man on TV' while the subject of their conversation is the man in front of them on the train. To Jones, Smith also appears to violate conversational norms for truth or justified belief. Smith appears to be in no position to know the mood or attire of the man on TV.

Due to undetected linguistic luck, Smith appears to be an increasingly uncooperative interlocutor from Jones' perspective, regularly violating Gricean maxims for relevance and truth.

The problem is not linguistic malice or incompetence on Smith's part, but that he and Jones did not increment common ground when Smith uttered "he is a stockbroker" while looking at the man on TV. To make matters worse, Jones will appear an equally problematic interlocutor to Smith, as he refuses to make appropriate conversational contributions to his (Smith's) perfectly evident assertions about the man on the train when he (Smith) reports the mood and attire of the man on TV. As communication about the stockbroker breaks down, so too will their trust in each other. Each would appear to have good grounds for harboring mistrust in the linguistic competence or intention to cooperate of the other (see de Ponte, Korta, and Perry, Chapter 2, this volume).

This unwelcome situation would be avoided by a clarificatory question by Jones—"Do you mean the guy we see on the train?" or "Who are you talking about?" Such questions are common devices for reducing the impact of luck.[7] There are many such remedies available to reduce undetected luck in communication, many of which are familiar and unremarkable. Others are non-conventional and biologically grounded. The case above shows how quickly and in how widespread a way trust and communication easily break down without some mechanism in place to eliminate merely lucky recovery of reference.

IV. Some Unique Features of the Linguistic Form

Causation, inference, and agency are amongst the primary vehicles of linguistic luck reduction, each having greater or lesser salience in a given domain of

---

[7] There are, of course, many familiar linguistic devices that aim to monitor, identify, and eradicate luck. An interesting case is noted by Donnellan (1966) for safeguarding potentially unclear uses of definite descriptions where the speaker's intention might be unclear to hearers between attributive and referential use—when a speaker intends to use a definite description referentially they often utter descriptive content that the intended referent satisfies well enough to be picked out if the hearer happens to interpret the description descriptively.

linguistic theory (syntax, semantics, pragmatics) and particular linguistic events. Since the products of each are controlled by the processes that bring them about, links between luck reduction and control found in many discussions of moral and epistemic luck are broadly retained in theorizing about linguistic luck. However, while much normative theorizing in ethics and epistemology emphasize volitional powers of individual human agents, as is fitting to their subject matters, individual volitional powers are thus less central to the full range of phenomena of interest in linguistic theory. For example, in syntax processing, twin earth cases, and truth conditional semantics, the primary luck reducing controls are human genomes, the structure of the external world, and entailment relations respectively. Different levels of linguistic analysis will make different demands on an adequate account of linguistic luck reduction and this diversity will be reflected in any complete account of linguistic luck reduction.

The standards for a sufficiently non-lucky linguistic success are typically less luck tolerant than for epistemic or moral cognates. While "getting things right more often than not" or "performing with a high rate of success" can provide an acceptable standard for epistemic and moral accounts of non-lucky success,[8] consider the rate of accuracy required for syntax processing, which registers precise formal articulations from many possibilities in an automatic way. Similarly high rates of accuracy are required for word comprehension and speech act identification. Instances of linguistic luck easily metastasize to cumulative and communal effects that threaten the foundations of communication and speaker trust (as seen between Smith and Jones). For example, lucky guesses identifying word meaning could lead to misidentifying the type of speech act a speaker is uttering. Lucky guesses in speech act recognition would themselves lead to communal trouble among speakers.

In addition to issues concerning permissive success rates, linguistic competence depends thoroughly on common ground, public cooperation, and mutual trust (Verheggen, Chapter 9, this volume), each of which is threatened by robust luck dependence. One non-luckily fixes reference by cooperating with other speakers (see Dickie, Chapter 3, this volume), a collective action that Davidson called "triangulation." Davidson thought that this non-lucky form of cooperation was so fundamental that the notion of objectivity depends on it—otherwise we would only have our private standards for belief without securing reference or communication (Myers and Verheggen, 2016). This form of non-lucky linguistic success is necessary to create, preserve, and increment common ground in communicative exchanges of any kind—moral, epistemic, or otherwise. Problematic forms of

---

[8] For debates on how high or low success rates for justification should be set, see Stich (1988); BonJour (2001, 2010); Hetherington (2006); Turri (2016). For empirically based debates on success rates for character traits, see Doris (2002).

linguistic luck easily erode trust and thus constitute a threat to many important human practices.

Given the fundamentality of linguistic phenomena, that agential controls are less essential to linguistic phenomena than moral and epistemic phenomena, and the variability of relevant notions of success within linguistic theory, a certain kind of methodological independence from theorizing about luck in ethics and epistemology is warranted while investigating linguistic luck.[9] The essays to follow highlight a diverse range of luck reducing mechanisms that are relevant to different areas of linguistic theorizing. While our inquiry into the nature and significance of linguistic luck will proceed autonomously, connections with moral and epistemic luck are always held in mind.

V. Summary of Chapters

In "Language and Luck," **María de Ponte**, **Kepa Korta**, and **John Perry** consider three cases of luck. One is historically relevant, but not philosophically problematic; another is a case of lucky necessity, originally presented by Stephen Hales (2016); and another, a well-known case of linguistic luck presented by Brian Loar (1976). In all three cases, a phrase of the form "It was lucky for A at t that S" is a natural description. This suggests that being lucky is a relation an agent has to a proposition at a given time, just as "propositional attitude" reports suggest that believing, hoping, or saying are relations an agent has to a proposition at a given time. They have defended an alternative explanation of propositional attitude reports, the "reflexive-referential" account (Perry [2001] 2012; Korta and Perry 2011). Here, they apply it to luck and the natural way of describing it. They use this account to show that, contrary to appearances, lucky necessities do not pose a problem for standard views of luck. Also, they use it to explain Loar's example and, by doing so, they provide a referentialist view that allows us to appreciate the insights of Frege's theory of names without accepting his theory of sense and reference.

In "Specificity and Resolution in the Communicative Use of Singular Terms," **Imogen Dickie** examines what is required if speakers are to count as understanding one another's uses of singular terms, especially in cases of 'felicitous non-specificity', i.e., cases of successful communication using a singular term where, given the context of utterance, it is not determinate which particular individual the speaker's 'intended message' is about. The speaker, it seems, is operating at a level at which the distinction between candidate target entities just does not matter for what they are attempting to get across. Such cases can appear to be so saddled with indeterminacy that successful communication could only come down to luck, as

---

[9] However, see King, Chapter 4, this volume.

there is no determinate aboutness conveyed. Dickie's 'cognitive focus' model shows how communication can non-luckily succeed even when using non-specific singular terms. She argues that ordinary thinking about ordinary things is a joint information-marshalling activity directed at achieving and sustaining relations of cognitive focus, and thus it does not rely on luck for mutual understanding to be achieved. Speakers understand one another's uses of a singular term in a conversation iff, in using it as they do, they are exercising competence at sustaining a relation of joint cognitive focus.

Jeffrey C. King proposes a Coordination Account Metasemantics (CAM) that depends on an Anti-Luck Linguistic Mechanism (ALLM). In "Luck and Metasemantics," he argues how, given Duncan Pritchard's account of luck, a metasemantic approach eliminates luck in ways that no other account can. King proposes that coordination occurs among speakers and their utterances, not in terms of a set of events arranged according to similarity across possible worlds, but in terms of the actions of agents with expectations. King's approach appeals to a variety of abilities that speakers must have in order to reduce luck, such as attentiveness and linguistic competence. Especially, satisfying the conditions for coordination requires attentive hearers in conversation, as well as their communicative intentions. King's metasemantic account easily engages with other accounts in this volume that appeal to cooperation and attentiveness, for instance Dickie's and Hesni's.

In "Laws and Luck in Language: Problems with Devitt's Conventional, Commonsense Linguistics," **Georges Rey** and **John Collins** argue that intuitive verdicts to "WhyNots" are not luck dependent insofar as they are fairly directly caused by representations of syntactic structure produced by the I-language, analogous to reports of visual illusions. They contrast this view to Devitt's, which they find frailer and objectionably subject to luck. In particular, Rey and Collins defend a more innate and causal source of luck reduction for the acquisition of syntax, while Devitt proposes a socially mediated source of luck reduction, which includes conventions.

In his response, "Linguistic Luck: A Response to Rey and Collins," **Michael Devitt** proposes that expressions of thought by members of a linguistic community are typically, to some extent, governed by the rules and principles (briefly, rules) of a shared language. Rey and Collins argue that relative to the system of rules that constitute a language, an expression of thought that is not governed by the rules is a matter of linguistic "luck": the linguistic rules are luck reducing mechanisms. To what extent are the semantic and syntactic properties of the linguistic tokens in expressions of thought, in utterances, not governed by the rules of the language and hence "lucky"? What is the source of those rules? Are they innate or learned? Insofar as the rules are lucky, so too are the expressions governed by them. Devitt answers this question by distinguishing two sorts of linguistic luck: linguistic tokens that are accidental relative to linguistic rules are "r-lucky"; and linguistic rules, hence expressions governed by them, that are accidental relative to human nature are "i-lucky." This exchange between Rey and Collins and Devitt offers a wide variety of arguments and observations in favor of their views, which should help advance this important debate concerning the acquisition and development of syntactic abilities.

Vagueness provides another source of potential linguistic luck, with epistemicists like Timothy Williamson arguing that borderline cases of vague predicates have precise cutoffs which we can only guess as a matter of luck. It is such ineliminable luck that prevents us from knowing whether some borderline bald person is bald or not. In "Epistemicism without Metalinguistic Safety," **Justin Khoo** argues against this epistemicist thesis, which appeals to metalinguistic safety: we can know that *p* only if our true belief that *p* is not metalinguistically lucky. Khoo proposes instead that epistemicists should avoid appealing to metalinguistic safety by adopting a diagonalized version of their view. However, in a twist, Khoo argues that we should in fact not be diagonalized epistemicists either.

Assertion is the paradigm vehicle for acts of testifying. The speaker gives her word to her audience that the presented content is true, allowing them to gain knowledge via a distinctive mechanism: believing in the speaker's say-so. This is made possible by the conventions and norms that govern the social practice of making assertions, encapsulated in the norm that: one must assert that *p* only if one knows that *p*. In "Testimony, Luck, and Conversational Implicature," **Elizabeth Fricker** examines whether other means of conveying a message also amount to testifying, and how they would be different with respect to luck and trust. She first examines presupposition and conversational implicature, which are shown to be epistemically fragile means of conveying a message, and not governed by a social norm, as is the robust communicative means of assertion. We see that only explicit assertion of a conveyed message amounts to testifying to it.

In "Linguistic Luck and the Publicness of Language," **Claudine Verheggen** examines the connection between Wittgenstein's views on rule following and Davidsonian triangulation. It might appear that if one's meaning something by one's expressions (and thus one's expressions, being subject to conditions of correct application, are based essentially on the ways one uses those expressions and not on there being any things in the abstract, natural, or social world that could by themselves determine those conditions), then one's success in communicating with others might be thought to be dependent on luck. Verheggen argues to the contrary. If, as Wittgenstein's writings on rule following and Davidson's writings on triangulation suggest, one has to play an active role for the meaning of one's expressions to be determined, the amount of luck, if any, needed for communication is significantly reduced. The conditions for determining meaning are less luck dependent if meaning is *use*, than if determined by things in the world, independent of patterns of use.

Does utterance understanding require reliable (i.e., non-lucky) recovery of the speaker's intended proposition? In "Understanding, Luck, and Communicative

Value," **Andrew Peet** argues that there are good reasons to answer in the affirmative. The role of understanding in supporting testimonial knowledge seemingly requires reliability, and in communicative analogs of Gettier cases luck precludes the audience's understanding of an utterance despite recovering the intended proposition. He proceeds to specify the precise sense in which understanding precludes luck—the anti-luck condition attached to linguistic understanding is importantly different than anti-luck conditions typically applied to knowledge. However, assuming understanding precludes luck, we get a communicative analog of the value problem for knowledge—i.e., why is it better to meet the other conditions for understanding in a reliable way than in a lucky way? Due to the difference between epistemic and communicative luck, we cannot simply apply solutions to the epistemic value problem to handle the communicative value problem. Peet argues that the epistemic and communicative value problems will require different solutions, and he sketches the beginnings of an alternative answer to the value problem for communication.

In "Luck-Reducing Features of Lexical Innovation," **Samia Hesni** explores the difference between two kinds of lexical innovation: (i) lexical innovation as it pertains to lexical items that are already in use in a given linguistic community (for example, the evolution of the term 'unicorn'); and (ii) lexical innovation that involves the creation of new linguistic items. Hesni considers a potential tension between treating the two the same way and whether the two differ in their respective degrees of luck dependence, drawing on Josh Armstrong's dynamic account of linguistic conventions. In a novel turn, Hesni develops a procedure for updating the common ground with new linguistic items, as opposed to facts or states of the world. She argues that views that treat these two in tandem (Davidson 1984; Armstrong 2016) do so at the expense of overlooking certain luck reducing features of linguistic innovation.

Georgi Gardiner's essay "We Forge the Conditions of Love" is not about what love is, but rather what self-ascriptions of love do. People typically self-ascribe romantic love when a nexus of feelings, beliefs, attitudes, values, commitments, experiences, and personal histories matches their conception of romantic love. But what shapes this conception? And (how) can we adjudicate amongst conflicting conceptions? Self-ascriptions of love do not merely describe the underlying nexus of attitudes and beliefs. They also change it. Her essay describes how conceptions of love affect romantic experience, limning distinctions between love and obsessive infatuation and ways language can cultivate queer romantic preferences. Since conceptions of love are shaped, often implicitly, by terms available in one's linguistic community, the resulting nexus of concepts and conceptions manifests linguistic luck. Gardiner suggests ways we might sculpt the language of love to better understand—and change—ourselves. Love can help us flourish and so can our "love" language.

References

Armstrong, J. (2016). "The Problem of Lexical Innovation," *Linguistics and Philosophy*. 39: 87–118.

Bach, K. and Harnish, R. (1979). *Linguistic Communication and Speech Acts*. MIT Press.

Berwick, R. C. and Chomsky, N. (2016). *Why Only Us: Language and Evolution*. MIT Press.

BonJour, L. (2001). "The Indispensability of Internalism," *Philosophical Topics*, 29(1/2): 47–65.

BonJour, L. (2010). "The Myth of Knowledge," *Philosophical Perspectives*, 24(1): 57–83.

Buchanan, R. (2014). "Reference, Understanding, and Communication," *Australasian Journal of Philosophy*, 92(1): 55–70.

Clark, H. H. (1996). *Using Language*. Cambridge University Press.

Davidson, D. (1984). "Convention and Communication," *Synthese* 59(1): 3–17.

Dickie, I. (2011). "How Proper Names Refer," *Proceedings of the Aristotelian Society*, 111(1): 43–78.

Dickie, I. (2015). *Fixing Reference*. Oxford University Press.

Donnellan, K. (1966). "Reference and Definite Descriptions," *Philosophical Review*, 75(3): 281–304.

Doris, J. M. (2002). *Lack of Character: Personality and Moral Behavior*. Cambridge University Press.

Fitch, W. T. (2014). "Toward a Computational Framework for Cognitive Biology: Unifying Approaches from Cognitive Neuroscience and Comparative Cognition," *Physics of Life Reviews*, 11: 329–64.

Grice P. (1989). *Studies in the Ways of Words*. Cambridge University Press.

Hales, S. D. (2016). "Why every theory of luck is wrong," *Noûs*, 50(3), 490–508.

Hetherington, S. (2006). "Knowledge's Boundary Problem," *Synthese*, 150: 41–56.

Hornstein, N. (1990). *As Time Goes By: Tense and Universal Grammar*. MIT Press.

Korta, K. and Perry, J. (2011). *Critical Pragmatics: An Inquiry into Reference and Communication*. Cambridge University Press.

Loar, B. (1976). "The Semantics of Singular Terms," *Philosophical Studies*, 30(6): 353–77.

Myers, R. H. and Verheggen, C. (2016). *Donald Davidson's Triangulation Argument: A Philosophical Inquiry*. Routledge.

Nagel, T. (1979). *Mortal Questions*. Cambridge University Press.

Nigel, T. (1979). *Mortal Questions*. Cambridge University Press.

Peet, A. (2016). "Referential Intentions and Communicative Luck," *Australasian Journal of Philosophy*, 95(2): 379–84.

Perry, J. ([2001] 2012). *Reference and Reflexivity*. 2nd edition. CSLI.

Pettit, D. (2002). "Why Understanding Does Not Require Knowledge," *Mind*, 111(3): 519–50.

Pritchard, D. (ed.) (2015). *The Philosophy of Luck*. Wiley-Blackwell.

Riggs, W. (2007). "Why Virtue Epistemologists Are so Down on Their Luck," *Synthese*, 158: 329–44.

Stalnaker, R. (1972). "Pragmatics," in D. Davidson and G. Harman (eds.), *Semantics of Natural Language*. D. Reidel, 380–97.

Statman, D. (1991). "Moral and Epistemic Luck," *Ratio*, 4: 146–56.

Stich, S. (1988). "Reflective Equilibrium, Analytic Epistemology and the Problem of Cognitive Diversity," *Synthese*, 74(3): 391–413.

Turri, J. (2016). "A New Paradigm for Epistemology: From Reliabilism to Abilism," *Ergo: An Open Access Journal of Philosophy*, 3(8): 189–231.

Unnsteinsson, E. (2018). "Referential Intentions: A Response to Buchanan and Peet," *Australasian Journal of Philosophy*, 96(3): 610–15.

Williams, B. (1981). *Moral Luck*. Cambridge University Press.

Zagzebski, L. (1996). *Virtues of the Mind*. Cambridge University Press.

2

Language and Luck

María de Ponte, Kepa Korta, and John Perry

1. Introduction

In this chapter we consider three cases of luck, only one of which deserves the title "linguistic luck." In all three cases a phrase of the form "It was lucky for A at t that S" is a natural description. This phrase suggests that being lucky is a relation an agent has to a proposition at a time, just as "propositional attitude" reports suggest that believing, hoping, or saying are relations an agent has to a proposition at a time. We have argued that this picture is too simple in the case of propositional attitude reports, and put forward what we call the "reflexive-referential" account, or "critical referentialism" as an improvement. Here we argue this account is very helpful in dealing with luck and the natural way of describing it.

The first case is historically important but not philosophically problematic in any obvious way. We use it to motivate our working definition of "luck." Consider:

When he crossed the Delaware early in the morning of December 26, 1776, in order to mount a surprise attack on the British garrison of Hessian soldiers near Trenton, George Washington was lucky that most of them were not awake.

This tells us quite a bit about a lucky incident (A). We elaborate a little.

(A) 1. What was lucky: That most of the Hessians were not awake;

2. Who was lucky: George Washington;

3. What he was trying to do: To mount a surprise attack on the Hessian garrison;

4. When he was lucky: The morning of December 26, 1776;

5. Why he was lucky: Because most of the British were not awake, Washington was able to destroy a garrison of over 1,000 Hessian soldiers, weakening the British and having a positive effect on the morale of his own troops.

The *Oxford English Dictionary* (*OED*) offers many definitions of "luck," including

María de Ponte, Kepa Korta, and John Perry, *Language and Luck* In: *Linguistic Luck: Safeguards and Threats to Linguistic Communication*. Edited by: Abrol Fairweather and Carlos Montemayor, Oxford University Press.
© Oxford University Press 2023. DOI: 10.1093/oso/9780192845450.003.0002

> The chance occurrence of situations or events either favourable or unfavourable to a person's interests. (*OED*)

The term "chance" suggests "random." We think this narrows things too much and prefer:

> The occurrence of situations or events, either favorable or unfavorable to a person's interests, which are contingent, and not completely under that person's control.

Washington had good reasons to think it likely that the Hessians, or most of them, would be asleep fairly late the morning after Christmas, for he had good reasons to believe that like good Hessians they would have done a lot of celebrating the day before, probably ingesting significant amounts of alcohol. He wasn't just relying on chance. But, of course, he couldn't be certain, and had no control over how late they would sleep. Indeed the British were warned of his attack, but the Hessian in command thought the Americans were pretty feeble, and that it wouldn't be necessary to wake all of his troops to defeat the Americans.

Here is our working definition of luck:

> An agent *A* is lucky at *t* that *S*, if *S* is a contingent fact, uncertain and favorable to *A*'s interests, and the contingencies are not under *A*'s control.

> An agent *A* is *un*lucky at *t* that *S*, if *S* is a contingent fact, uncertain and *un*favorable to *A*'s interests, and the contingencies are not under *A*'s control.

This is a broad definition, which accords more or less with plausible accounts of luck available in the literature. In what follows, we first discuss a case of a lucky necessity, which allegedly contradicts our working definition (and other common accounts of luck). We argue, using the "reflexive-referential" account, that it does not. We then apply this account to a well-known case of linguistic luck presented by Brian Loar (1976).

2. Lucky Necessities

In "Why Every Theory of Luck is Wrong," Stephen Hales (2016) offers a short and clear presentation of the most common accounts of luck: in terms of probability, in terms of modality, and in terms of the agent's control over the events leading to the bit of luck. It seems that if it is lucky for *A* that *S*, then *S* must be a truth that is improbable, or at least not certain; contingent, rather than necessary; and the sort of thing an agent might control, but in this case does not.

But then Hales gives several examples where the bit of luck in question seems to be a necessary truth. According to him, such cases are a threat to all three accounts of luck. If this is so, they would also challenge our working definition. We will focus on this example:

> Jack the Ripper is terrorizing the neighborhood. There's a knock on your door, which you promptly and thoughtlessly open. It is your friend Bob (who is not Jack the Ripper). Bob rolls his eyes at your carelessness and says, "You're lucky I'm not Jack the Ripper." It is metaphysically necessary that things (and people) are self-identical. Given that Bob is not Jack the Ripper, it is metaphysically impossible for him to be Jack the Ripper. Bob cannot be other than what he is.   (Hales, 2016, 495)

On our working definition, a bit of luck must be a contingent fact, and this requirement is explicitly or implicitly shared by the three accounts. So it seems such accounts are defective.

Let us modify some details of the example. We'll let Enid answer the door instead of you. We'll move the example back a bit more than a century, to June 12, 1888, and locate it in London's East End, where Jack the Ripper, Enid, and Bob were all living. Bob says to Enid, "You are lucky that I am not Jack the Ripper." The embedded sentence, "I am not Jack the Ripper" identifies the bit of luck: *that Bob is not Jack the Ripper*. If he had been Jack the Ripper, he would have likely killed her. This is what this example (B) seems to tell us about this lucky incident:

(B) 1. What was lucky: That Bob is not Jack the Ripper;

2. Who was lucky: Enid;

3. What she was trying to do: To answer the door (without getting killed);

4. When she was lucky: June 12, 1888 (when Jack the Ripper was alive and terrorizing London neighborhoods);

5. Why she was lucky: Because had Bob been Jack the Ripper, she would have been painfully killed.

In (B), like in (A), the bit of luck is identified with a sentence embedded in a "that"-clause. This suggests that bits of luck can be propositions. But the proposition that Bob is not Jack the Ripper is necessarily true. How can something that is necessarily true be lucky?

If luck is a matter of something with relatively low probability happening, metaphysical necessities are not matters of luck. The modality explanation doesn't fare better. Luck, according to this view, involves modal fragility, that is, a lucky event is one that happens but could easily have not happened. It doesn't happen in many "close possible worlds." But Bob being Jack the Ripper, given that he is not, simply could not have happened. It's not a contingent fact; we won't find it in any world in which either of them exists, however distant.

Finally, the control explanation claims that lucky events are those over which we have little control. Enid certainly has no control over whether Bob is or is not Jack the Ripper. But, clearly, this case isn't what the defenders of the control explanation have in mind. An extra element is needed: a lucky event is a contingent event we cannot control. That is, an event that might or might not happen, and about which we can do little or nothing. But we cannot control whether or not something impossible happens.[1]

It seems to us that the problem comes from a wrong understanding of Bob's utterance of "I'm not Jack the Ripper." This, in turn, results in a wrong understanding of what is *the piece of luck*—what Enid is lucky for and why. We suggest that this case can be handled by using the reflexive-referential account of the contents of utterances and thoughts, which we now explain.

3. The Reflexive-Referential Account

The account focuses on contentful *episodes*: utterances, thoughts, perceptions, actions, beliefs, desires, intentions, etc. These things occur in space and time and have causes and effects. They involve cognition; we'll call them "cognitive episodes." In so doing we stretch the phrase. As we use the term, an episode can be very brief, as one's perception of a bolt of lightning, or very long, as one's subsequent fear of lightning might be. Beliefs and desires are states one may be in for a long time, but we'll include them as episodes.

Cognitive episodes have *contents*. The truth-conditions of a statement or a belief are the paradigm case, but orders have fulfilment-conditions, desires have satisfaction-conditions, and so forth. We use "contents" for all such conditions. We think of contents as propositions that encode the conditions of truth for statements, conditions of satisfaction for expressions of hopes and desires, conditions of compliance for orders, and so forth. We take propositions to be abstract objects that are useful for classifying episodes in terms of their conditions of truth, etc. We agree with Frege that propositions (his "Thoughts") are not mental or physical episodes or states and so have no causes or effects. We don't, however, accept everything Frege says about propositions.

We do not regard episodes of belief, desire, etc., as consisting of relations to propositions. These episodes have causes and effects. We think propositions are

---

[1] In "Luck and Risk and the Lack of Control" (2015), Fernando Broncano-Berrocal develops a plausible account of luck that incorporates ideas from the probability, modality, and especially the lack of control accounts, and emphasizes the element of risk. But risk doesn't seem to provide an answer to Hales challenge either. Enid was not at any risk that Bob would be Jack the Ripper, since it was metaphysically impossible.

abstract objects that have been designed to be useful in classifying events in the causal realm, but not themselves as causes and effects. To be useful, such propositions need to be well-behaved and well-understood abstract objects, usually sets. The language that is used for propositions needs to be correlated with the elements of utterances and thoughts that determine their truth-conditions. Sentences play a major role in identifying these elements in the case of utterances and thoughts that can be expressed with sentences.

We repeat, with emphasis: propositions, in our account, are tools to keep track of the contents of cognitive episodes. Saying, believing, hoping, and other "propositional attitudes" do not consist in relations of a speaker or thinker to propositions, although they induce such relations. One of the authors is 79 years old. This fact puts him into a relation to the number 79 and the numeral "79" because they are the number and numeral used to classify and refer to his age. But being 79 years old doesn't consist in having these relations to numbers and numerals. It involves living for a long time, however we measure or refer to lengths of time. Similarly, having the belief that the Canary Islands are beautiful induces a relation to the proposition *that the Canary Islands are beautiful.* The belief induces the relation to a proposition, just as a person's height induces a relation to the number assigned to that height by some system of measurement. But the belief does not consist in the relation to this abstract object. It consists in having memories and images of the Canary Islands and a concept of beauty that these memories and images fit.

On the reflexive-referential account such cognitive episodes have multiple consistent layers of content that can be classified with propositions.[2] As we said, the time is June 12, 1888, and the place is East End of London, where Bob, Enid, and Jack all reside. Bob knocks on Enid's door. Bob and Enid are old friends, but today he has just moved into a flat near hers in Whitechapel. Before uttering the remark about luck already quoted, Bob says to her, "Today you and I are neighbors." We'll call this utterance **u**. Then, on many accounts, Bob said the proposition:

P: *that Bob is Enid's neighbor on June 12, 1888*

On a simple account this proposition is a set consisting of the relation of x being a neighbor of y at t, and the sequence of Bob, Enid, and June 12, 1888. One might take it to be the set of possible worlds in which Bob is a neighbor of Enid's on that day. Or perhaps the set of worlds w in which Bob's counterpart in w be a neighbor of Enid's counterpart in w on that day, or perhaps on that day's counterpart. Indeed, there are many kinds of abstract objects philosophers have taken to be

---

[2] For more about the reflexive-referential account, see Perry ([2001] 2012) and Korta & Perry (2011, 2013).

propositions. We'll stick with the simple account, and assume that the reader gets the general idea.

We agree that the proposition P is *a* truth-condition of Bob's utterance. But we don't agree that it is *the* truth-condition. On our account, the truth-conditions of an utterance are *relative* to a set of facts that are taken as *given*. The truth-condition of an utterance, relative to a set of facts g, is *what else* has to be the case for the utterance to be true, *given g*.

Suppose we start with the fact that u is "Today you and I are neighbors," and that the sentence is in English. Given that, do we have truth-conditions for u? Of course we do:

> P_{ub}: *There is a day* d *on which* u *occurs, a day* d' *to which "today" in* u *refers, persons* x, y *to whom the utterances of "you" and "I" in* u *refer, a relation R to which the utterance of "are neighbors" in* u *refers, and on day* d', x, *and* y *stand in relation R.*

We call P_{ub} an *utterance-bound* truth-condition of u.[3] The references of the expressions are identified only in terms of the utterance u. P_{ub} is certainly not what Bob said, as we ordinarily use "said." To get at what Bob would ordinarily be taken to have said, we need information about u that allows us to instantiate on the variables, so that we can free the identification of the referents from their dependence on u. In this case:

> d = June 12, 1888, and, given the conventions of English for the utterances of "today," "you," "I," and "are neighbors": $d' = d$, x = Enid, y = Bob, and R = the relation of living close to.

To get to what Bob said, ordinarily construed, we need to identify referents independently of u. So, given, in addition to P_{ub}, the information that u occurs on June 12, 1888, that "today" refers to the day of utterance, that "I" refers to the speaker and Bob is the speaker, that "you" refers to the person spoken to and Enid is the person spoken to, so x and y are Bob and Enid, and that "are neighbors" refers to the relation of being neighbors, *what else* has to be the case for u to be true? Just our old friend P:

> P: *that Bob is Enid's neighbor on June 12, 1888*

P_{ub} gave us an utterance-bound truth-condition for u. To get from there to what we would normally regard as "the proposition expressed" or "what was said," we

---

[3] We do not call P_{ub} "*the* utterance-bound truth-conditions." We started by giving the language and expressions of u. At an even more utterance-bound level these might only be identified relative to the utterance. For example, the language might be identified as "the language of u" rather than as "English."

need the instantiating information. But P does not encode or entail all of the information we need to get to it. For example, P does not entail that Bob is the speaker of **u**, or that Enid was the audience of **u**, or even that **u** occurred.

P doesn't put any conditions on **u**. The conditions can be met even if **u** doesn't happen. It puts conditions on Bob, Enid, the relation of being a neighbor of, and June 12, 1888. That is, it gives us conditions on the referents of the expressions in the utterance, but not on the utterance itself. So it is the *reference-bound* content, or simply the *referential* content.

Suppose for instance we didn't bother to tell you *when* this all happened, that is, what day "today" referred to. Would you know conditions of truth for Bob's utterance? Of course you would. Bob's utterance is true iff

P_h: *there is some day* d *during which the utterance* **u** *occurred, and Bob and Enid were neighbors on* d

P_h, like P_{ub} is utterance-bound. But not every referring term in P_h is utterance-bound, only "today." We'll call such a content *hybrid*. There are many hybrid contents on the way from P_{ub} to P, which might be relevant in variations on the case.

P_{ub}, P_h, and P are different propositions. The first two are independent of the third. But they are consistent with it. P_h follows from P_{ub} when we add the meanings of "I," "you," the reference of "are neighbors" and the facts that the speaker was Bob and the audience was Enid. P follows from P_h when we give the date of **u**.

Our claim is that utterance-bound contents can be used by theories of luck to handle Hales' lucky necessities. We'll now recycle **u** for Bob's utterance of "You're lucky I'm not Jack the Ripper," in the original example. We'll use **u'** for the sub-utterance of "I'm not Jack the Ripper." Given the details we supplied, the referential content of **u'** is the necessary truth:

Q: *that Bob is not Jack the Ripper on June 12, 1888*

The date is irrelevant and we'll usually ignore it. We agree that it is hard to see the necessary truth Q as a matter of luck. But consider the hybrid content of **u'** given everything except the identity of the speaker:

Q_h: *Someone* x *is the speaker of* **u'***, and* x *is not Jack the Ripper*

Enid knows, before opening the door, that the person knocking on her door is on her porch. She knows that when she opens the door, she will be face to face with this person, with at most a screen door between them. She realizes, or would if she thought about it, that it would be dangerous to be in that situation with Jack the

Ripper. She opens the door, sees Bob, hears his utterance **u'** and believes it. The speaker doesn't look like a deranged killer, and isn't doing anything threatening towards her. So when she opens the door and hears Bob's utterance **u'** she learns that Jack the Ripper is not the person on her front porch, she is not face to face with him, and is in no danger. So Q_h conjoined with something obvious to Enid, that the speaker of **u'** is the person on her front porch, gives us the contingency that Enid was lucky about: That the person on her front porch is not Jack the Ripper.

Looking at things this way, what the example tells us about the lucky incident is:

(B')   1. What was lucky: That the speaker of **u'** (the person on the porch) is not Jack the Ripper;

2. Who was lucky: Enid;

3. What she was trying to do: To answer the door without being killed;

4. When she was lucky: June 12, 1888 (when Jack the Ripper was alive and terrorizing neighborhoods);

5. Why she was lucky: Because had Jack the Ripper been the speaker of **u'** (the person on the porch), she would likely have been killed.

There is nothing particularly problematic here, nothing that differentiates this case from any other lucky episode, such as (A) above. What is more, looking at things this way, the three approaches to luck seem to at least contribute something to understanding Enid's luck:

- Most of us, not living in London's East End in the late nineteenth century, don't have to be lucky to open our front door and not be face to face with Jack the Ripper. That scenario would be extremely improbable, occurring only in possible worlds very remote from our own. For Enid, living in London's East End in 1888, the probability that the person knocking on one's door was Jack the Ripper was still low, but not negligible; and the consequences would likely be terrible for Enid. So Enid is lucky that the person on her front porch is not Jack the Ripper, and probability seems at least part of the story.
- It is metaphysically impossible that Bob is Jack the Ripper. But it was not metaphysically impossible that the person on Enid's front porch that afternoon was Jack the Ripper. Suppose Knute says to Mary, as she goes to answer the front door, in Donostia in the twenty-first century, "If that's Jack the Ripper, you are in trouble." She might reasonably reply, "Well, perhaps the antecedent of your weird remark isn't metaphysically impossible; maybe Jack has been in Hell all these years and has somehow escaped. But that's a very remote possibility at best. So I'm not going to worry about it." But Jack the

Ripper being on the front porch knocking on her door would not have been a remote possibility for Enid in London's East End in 1888. Given the likely consequence, Enid was lucky it wasn't him, and modality has a role in the explanation.

- It wasn't under Enid's control whether Bob was or was not Jack the Ripper. Since he is not, Enid is lucky. But the issue of control seems irrelevant. No one can do anything to control whether Bob is Jack the Ripper. Metaphysics settled that. But it was under her control whether she opened the door without further investigation of who was there. That was stupid on her part. Given the likely consequences, she was lucky that Jack the Ripper wasn't on her front porch and control seems relevant.

So, in our view, a proper account of cases of "lucky necessities" does not require giving up otherwise plausible accounts of luck. What is needed is a proper understanding of the truth-conditions of luck-utterances (of the type "X is lucky that S").

Of course, one might object: What Bob *said* was *that he was not Jack the Ripper*. He did not say anything about the front porch or who was standing there. We agree, pretty much. The default choice for "what is said" by an utterance is the referential content of the utterance. But a proper understanding of how this works makes it clear that what is said does not exhaust the information that an utterance can convey, and be intended to convey, to a semantically competent hearer. Any of the information of the utterance-bound or the hybrid contents can be conveyed, and often, the intent of the speaker is to do so.

In this case it seems clear that the utterance-bound content that Bob wants to convey to Enid is a hybrid one with all the references unbound except "I." Regardless of what Bob *actually* said, a topic on which philosophers of language might engage in long discussions, it seems clear that what he meant to convey was not that Enid was lucky that he was not Jack the Ripper, but rather that the speaker on the porch could have been Jack the Ripper, and Enid was lucky because he was not. This is actually a quite common sort of case, not in any way restricted to lucky necessities or to luck-utterances. Let us look at a couple more examples:

Fred puts a big platter of kale before his young children and says "You will love this kale."

He knows his children have never seen this ugly vegetable before. But he thinks they will learn the name for it from his utterance. They will realize that his utterance is true iff there is some stuff Fred is referring to with "this kale" and they will love it. They realize that "kale," in the singular "this kale," is most likely a name of the kind of stuff he is pointing at. That is, they know how English works. They don't know this in the way people who have taken a linguistics or even a philosophy of language class know it. They may not know what an utterance is, or what referring is, or what a singular term is. But they are *attuned* to these facts about English, and are capable of making inferences from them, without being able to articulate the premises of their reasoning. What explains their inference is an utterance-bound content of Fred's utterance, given the meaning of the sentence and the fact, conveyed by glance and gesture, that he was referring to the green stuff on the platter. Given all of that, *what else* had to be the case, for Fred's utterance to be true? That "kale" is a name for the ugly green stuff. Note that in this case Fred succeeds in teaching his children something, that "kale" names kale, even though what he says is almost certainly false.

> John tells Frenchie that he is going to San Sebastián in the Basque Country for a week. She looks at the map of the Basque Country in John's office for "San Sebastián" but can't find it. He says, "San Sebastián is Donostia." Frenchie finds "Donostia" on the map, points to it and says, "That's where you are going?" and John says "yes."

John has conveyed to Frenchie that "Donostia" and "San Sebastián" are names for the same city. But what he said was simply that San Sebastián was Donostia, a necessary truth, which is the same thing he would have said with "San Sebastián is San Sebastián" and "Donostia is Donostia," if what is said is always to be identified with referential content. But those utterances would not have been helpful. A philosophical rule of thumb should be that the information conveyed by utterances of identity sentences can almost never be understood simply in terms of their referential content. If you insist on doing that, you will be lucky to get much of anything right.

4. Linguistic Luck

So far, this hasn't been a philosophy essay on linguistic luck, but rather a linguistic philosophy essay on luck. Now, we will use the reflexive-referential account to address a well-known issue concerning a possible case of linguistic luck, according to our working definition. Consider Brian Loar's example:

> Suppose that Smith and Jones are unaware that the man being interviewed on television is someone they see on the train every morning and about whom, in that latter role, they have just been talking. Smith says "He is a stockbroker," intending to refer to the man on television; Jones takes Smith to be referring to the man on the train. Now Jones, as it happens, has correctly identified Smith's referent, since the man on the television is the man on the train; but he has somehow failed to understand Smith's utterance. It would seem that, as Frege

held, some "manner of presentation" of the referent is, even on referential uses, essential to what is being communicated.   (Loar, 1976, 357)

Suppose the man on the train and on television is Peters. In the standard interpretation of Loar cases, Smith intends to communicate the singular proposition P, that Peters is a stockbroker, by uttering "He is a stockbroker." Jones grasps P, but "it turns out to be merely a matter of luck that both interlocutors entertained the same proposition" (Peet, 2017, 381). Either that or direct reference theories of demonstratives are wrong and they must be replaced by a Fregean theory, or at least supplemented with Fregean "manners of presentation."

Briefly, what Loar's example shows, in our view and terminology, is that the referential content is not enough to correctly explain linguistic understanding and communication, and failures of such endeavors. In particular, when singular terms are involved, communication is not merely a matter of correct referent assignment by whatever means. We agree with Loar that there is some communicative mismatch between Smith and Jones, but we wouldn't just say that Jones "has failed to understand Smith's utterance." It is a bit more complicated than that.

To understand the misunderstanding, we need something in addition to the expressions Smith and Jones both use and the entities that they both refer to. For that purpose, we bring in *notions*. Here is the explanation of this concept from *Critical Pragmatics*.

We think the ideas we have of particular objects—we call them "notions"—are in many ways like files. They are relatively stable, more or less concrete structures in our minds. We establish them, when we meet people, or see buildings, or read about them, or hear about them. We use them to store information, some accurate, some inaccurate, about those things. This information is in the form of ideas of properties, relations, and notions of other things that we associate with the notions. Each association is a cognition—a belief, a desire, a hope, an expectation, a memory perhaps. The notion is a *component* of the cognition. We use that information when we interact with the objects, or engage in conversations about them. A notion is *of* the object it was introduced to keep track of, however poorly or well the associated ideas may fit [the object].

(Korta & Perry, 2011, 38–9)

The reference of an utterance of a personal pronoun is typically determined, in part, by the intentions of the speaker and the notions that are part of that intention. We are standing at a corner, looking at a pair of women across the street. I nod in their direction and say "She looks like Kamala Harris." You ask, "Who?" or perhaps "To whom are you referring?" "The one on the right," I answer. In this case, I acquired two notions when I observed the scene across the street. When I added the information picked up visually to my stock of memories and beliefs, and after thinking a little I concluded that one of the women, whom we'll call X, looks a bit like Kamala Harris. I formed the intention to call this to your attention, and fulfilled that intention by uttering a sentence, by referring to X with "She" and predicating the resemblance with "looks like Kamala Harris." My notion of this woman plays a causal role in my action. X is a cause of my perception, which is a cause of my notion, which is a part of the intention that caused my utterance of "She." Given those facts, our identification of the referent of "She" no longer needs to be utterance-bound. It can be *notion-bound.* The referent of my utterance of "She" is the person the notion that motivates that utterance is of.

Now that notion will have content. It may be part belief (There is a woman across the street who looks like such and such...), part memory (I think Kamala Harris looked such and such when I met her at a campaign event...), or part conjecture (I don't think, even being vice-president, she would have changed that much...). The content may add up to something that doesn't fit X at all. But it is *of X*, because X was its origin, regardless of the fact that the machinations of an aged mind may have made it one that doesn't fit her all that well.

In natural language, the intentions of the speaker are often crucial in determining reference. Suppose I say, "George Bush was from Texas." You might reasonably ask, "Which George Bush, the father or the son?" Both are equally salient, so it seems that it is up to me to decide to whom I refer with my use of "George Bush." Of course I may be confused, absent-minded, or plainly wrong, but paradigmatically, it is the job of the speaker to resolve such "nambiguities."[4] Further, the notion involved can outweigh the meaning: "That wolf is going to eat your golf-ball." "That's not a wolf, it's a fox." "Well whatever it is, it's chasing your golf ball."

Notions might be compared with Frege's "modes of presentation." Fregean modes of presentation have two roles. First, they help in explaining recognition and reasoning about things. This is also a role that notions have. But for Frege modes of presentation also have the job of *determining* reference, and this is where modes and notions differ. Names and other forms of reference are associated with modes of presentation, their "senses," and are *of* the object that the mode of presentation identifies, the one that has the properties and stands in the relations. This is not how we regard notions. They don't do the second job. The reference of names (or other forms of reference) is determined by their causal source, by the thing they were introduced to organize information about, and not by their satisfying the conditions that the images and descriptions in the notion identify.

---

[4] See (Korta & Perry, 2011, ch.7) for more on names and ambiguities.

We regard notions as crucial parts of the sorts of historical/causal chains that many philosophers plausibly take to establish reference. These may be short, as the one that goes from your sighting of X to your use of "That person." They may be longer, thousands of years longer, as the one that stretches from Aristotle's parents giving him a name to Chris Bobonich's use of "Aristotle" in a lecture to refer to him. The chains will involve many persons with many quite different notions of Aristotle, a great many of which may be mistaken in the properties attributed to him. Information can be passed along such chains, but also misinformation.[5]

The term "direct reference" employs a rather odd use of "direct." It basically means the connection does not involve Fregean senses. The paradigms of direct reference are not very direct in the ordinary sense of the word. The path from Aristotle's parents' use of some Greek precursor of "Aristotle" to a contemporary use of "Aristotle" in a Stanford classroom is not very direct. And it involves many notions in the many heads that have passed on information and misinformation about Aristotle. It involves many "manners of presentation," but they don't serve as Fregean senses, fixing the reference of use of the name. They are the information and misinformation passed along the historical chain, from one person thinking and talking about Aristotle to another.

Indexicals and demonstratives are paradigms of "direct reference." But again, there is nothing very direct about them in the ordinary sense of "direct." An utterance of "you" by B is determined by the character of "you"; it is the person B is addressing. But B may have an audience of dozens. Does his use of "you" refer to all of them, to some of them, to one of them? This is determined by all sorts of facts, but they pretty much boil down to the intentions of the speaker. Perhaps he is lecturing in classroom at UCLA, but "you" is directed at an Asian spy he takes to be listening in via a chain of events that goes from the classroom to a satellite and then to another and then to a listening base in Beijing or Vladivostok. Again, pretty non-Fregean, but not direct in any other sense.

Returning to Loar's example and to Smith's utterance **u**: "He is a stockbroker." A personal pronoun like "he" can be used deictically or anaphorically. If deictic, the referent is something that the speaker is thinking of—"has a notion of," in our lingo—and to which he is (typically) trying to draw the audience's attention. Anaphorically, the pronoun picks up the reference of an earlier use of a singular term, possibly by a different speaker, even if the speaker of the anaphor has no idea what or who that is. But there is still a weak and fleeting notion involved: The speaker intends to refer to whatever the earlier utterance referred to. For this essay, however, we'll simply assume that Smith's use of "he" is deictic.

On the reflexive-referential account, Smith's utterance **u** has at least three different relevant contents or truth-conditions. The referential content, which is

---

[5] See Perry ([2001] 2012) and Korta & Perry (2011).

a singular proposition involving the individual—Peters—and the property of being a stockbroker.[6] An utterance-bound content, or the content that is determined by the rules of English and the fact that utterance **u** has been made. And the notion-bound content, which includes the notion or mental file—call it N_{TV}—that is motivating the speaker's use of "he," and that in the example is perceptually created by the image on the TV screen.

What we call "pure referentialists" will take the only content of Smith's utterance to be the referential content, identified as "what is said." But what we call "critical referentialists," while recognizing singular propositions and referential content, and the fact that this content is usually the default candidate for "what is said," will insist that other contents, with less taken as given, must be recognized for referentialism to be viable. With regard to the case under discussion, these other contents must be recognized for referentialism to be a plausible explanation. In this case, three contents of Smith's utterance **u** are crucial to understand what is going on:

- P_u: *That the person referred to by the utterance of "he" in* **u** *is a stockbroker*
- P_h: *That the origin of* N_{TV} *is a stockbroker*
- P: *That* **Peters** *is a stockbroker*

With these contents at hand, we can see where the communicative (mis)match in Smith and Jones' exchange lies. Assuming that Jones is a competent English speaker, alert and with no hearing problems, he can certainly identify the utterance-bound content of **u**. He correctly identifies the sentence uttered and its meaning. For **u** to be true, "he" has to refer to a male person and that person has to be a stockbroker. That is not what the speaker said, but assuming that Jones' understanding process has not completely failed him, P_u is a content he can easily identify. Also, by hypothesis, Jones also identifies **u**'s referential content P correctly. He correctly identifies Peters as the referent of "he" and understands that the property of being a stockbroker is being attributed to him. So, the mismatch must take place at the notion-bound content P_h.

Jones does not identify N_{TV}, the type of perceptual notion that both minds instantiate as they watch TV, and the one that motivates Smith's use of "he." Rather, he takes the notion that motivates Smith's use of "he" to be N_{Train}, the detached notion that both have of the person they see every day in the train but don't attach to any present perception.[7] Now, both notions do in fact correspond to the same person, and that's the source of the alleged luck in Smith's and Jones's convergence onto the same referential content.

---

[6] We will leave time issues aside, since they are not relevant for our argument.

[7] We could also track the difference to a kind of *refined* utterance-bound content that distinguishes between anaphoric and deictic uses of demonstrative pronouns. Smith uses the pronoun deictically, and Jones takes him to be using it anaphorically, and that's what lead Jones to a different notion-bound content.

When he introduced the example of Smith and Jones, Loar suggested that it seems to show that "[as] Frege held, some 'manner of presentation' of the referent is, even on referential uses, essential to what is being communicated." We agree. But, as we have argued, that doesn't mean we agree with Frege's theory of sense and reference. We agree with Frege that senses, or at least manners of presentation, and references are a crucial part of semantics. But their relation is more complicated than his theory envisages.

We claim to be referentialists, but critical referentialists, not direct referentialists. Does that mean we think the semantical views about names and indexicals and demonstratives and such espoused by "direct referentialists" are incorrect? No, mainly we think it is misleading—extraordinarily so—to call this "direct reference." There are many steps between utterance and reference, and these are systematically exploited to convey all sorts of information other than referential content—what we sometimes have called "official" content.

So, given all this, where is the luck in Loar's example? It is not lucky or unlucky that the man they see every morning in the train is the same as the man on TV—that Peters is Peters. That Peters is Peters is as necessary as that Bob was not Jack the Ripper. But it is a matter of luck that they both identify the same content as **u**'s referential content, given that they are making use of different notions. Again, the identity that Smith and Jones ignore is not the trivial fact that Peters is Peters, but the non-trivial identity that can be rendered as

(*) *The origin of* N_{TV} = *The origin of* N_{Train}

In other words, there is a true identity relevant to the coherence of the conversation, the referents of the two uses of "he" are the same. They both believe this. But they each believe it on the basis of a mistake. Jones thinks Smith is thinking of the referent of his use as the man on the train, but he is not. Smith thinks Jones is thinking of the referent of his use as the man on TV, but he is not. An interesting case, but is this a matter of luck? Good luck? Or bad luck?

It seems there is linguistic luck involved in this case and that it is due to the fact that Smith and Jones did not know that the identity (*) above is true. Taking this into account, what the example tells us about luck and lucky referential convergence is something like:

(C) 1. What was lucky: That Jones identified the referential content of Smith's utterance correctly;

  2. Who was lucky: Smith;[8]

---

[8] Perhaps a better answer would be "both," since Jones was also lucky in having understood what Smith said, that is, he correctly identified the referential content of Smith's utterance. We will focus on Smith, just to keep things simpler. Adding Jones to this schema would not modify it significantly.

3. What he was trying to do: To refer to the origin of N_{TV}—Peters—and to state that he is a stockbroker;

4. When he was lucky: At the time of the utterance;

5. Why he was lucky: Because Jones identified the reference of Smith's use of "he," even if he, unknowingly, employed a different notion, and neither knew that and, hence, that the origins of both notions were the same.

There is nothing exceptional here. Nothing to differentiate this episode from any other lucky one, like (A) and (B') above. Also, like in (B'), the three main approaches of luck can contribute to understanding it. The probability of Smith and Jones' referential convergence onto Peters, taking that they were both associating different notions to their uses of "he" and that they didn't know this, is quite low. Also, the outcome, although not dramatically important for their lives (as it was for Enid in the previous example), is still relevant. It is not clear, however, whether it is a positive or a negative outcome, and this is why it is not clear if this is a case of good or bad linguistic luck. The fact that they converge onto the same referential content of Smith's utterance is a good outcome. The fact that they did this on the basis of a mistake might cause further complications along the line.

Referring is an action. People perform the same action in different ways, and different actions in the same way. Smith performs the action of referring to Peters with "he"; Jones performs the action of identifying Peters as the referent of Smith's action. But they do what they do in different ways, relying on different circumstances. Smith refers to Peters in virtue of Peters having been on TV, and so the historical/causal source of the notion that motivates his utterance. Jones identifies Peters in virtue of Peters having been the man seen on the train, and so being the causal/historical source of the notion he employs. Given this, referential convergence is a matter of pure luck, being good or bad and for whom depending on how we continue the story.

Suppose that the man they see on the train wears bib overalls while on the train, because he fears spilling coffee on his shirt and tie while on a moving train. He changes into a suit when he gets to work at the brokerage or the television studio. So he doesn't look much like a stockbroker while on the train. The conversation continues, after Smith's utterance **u**, "He is a stockbroker."

JONES: I doubt very much that what you just said is true.
SMITH: I can't imagine why. It's obvious. I'm sure of it.
JONES: I can't imagine why you think so. I'll bet you $10 that he isn't a stockbroker.
SMITH: I accept.

Eventually they figure things out and Smith wins the bet. It is good luck for Smith that neither realized they were using different notions of the same man; if Jones, in particular, had realized that (*) was true he would have realized that what Smith said was likely true, and wouldn't have offered the bet. Smith didn't control this; he didn't even realize that (*) was relevant until after the bet was made. It was a bit of bad luck for Jones that their notions were of the same person. Otherwise, he could have declared the bet moot, since he would think they were talking about different people. Or at least he could put off paying until they had done a thorough study of the notion Smith was employing in such a case, and its relation to his own notion of Peters. Smith clearly intended to refer to the man he saw on TV. But didn't he also intend to refer to the man they were both thinking of? Well, they were thinking of the same man, but they didn't know they were thinking of him in different manners, and, Jones at least, didn't know that these manners had the same origin, so, was there really a proposition to serve as the basis of the wager? Perhaps in another year or so they could agree on this. Our point is simply that our critical referentialism would be the best framework in which to debate the question. Also, that probability can contribute to understanding the luck element.

On the other hand, although it is not metaphysically possible for Peters not to be Peters, the identity (*) is non-trivial. It is a contingent fact that the origin of N_{TV} is the same as the origin of N_{Train}. So this is a modally fragile situation. There are many possible situations where the mismatch could have not ended in referential convergence.

Finally, it is not under Smith's control that Jones identifies the intended notion-bound content. It is quite normal for him to assume that Jones would identify it, and would also make use of N_{TV}; after all, they are both watching TV together. But, since he doesn't realize that the man on TV is the man they see on the train, it is not under his control to anticipate Jones identifying N_{Train} instead. Had he been aware of the fact that the man on TV is the same as the man they see on the train, then, maybe, he should have made this connection explicit, to avoid possible complications and to make sure Jones understands he is talking about Peters by his use of "he."

In any case, what is most relevant for us is not what "luck" is, but rather how to account for this lucky incident from a linguistic perspective. Critical referentialism can easily account for this and similar cases, where two (or more) people refer to or think of the same object in different ways or, conversely, where they refer to or think of different objects in the same way. In most, if not all of them, luck will surely play an important role. Just as it does here. But these are not unusual or particularly complicated situations. Quite the contrary. These are cases where the speaker and the hearer identify different notions as motivating different uses of the same demonstrative. But that is not an extraordinary feature in communicative exchanges, by itself a matter of good or bad luck. It certainly does not justify the claim that Jones does not understand Smith. Jones actually understands quite well Smith's utterance. He identifies the utterance-bound content and, most importantly, the referential one. So he understands quite a lot of what Smith is saying.

Loar's claim was that his example posed a problem for direct referentialist theories: "It would seem that, as Frege held, some 'manner of presentation' of the referent is, even on referential uses, essential to what is being communicated" (Loar, 1976, 357). We agree. Fregean modes of presentations, or something along their lines, is needed. Direct or "pure" referentialists are in trouble. Critical referentialism introduces the idea of notions, similar to modes of presentation, but not quite the same thing as Fregean senses. With it, we can explain how the misunderstanding occurs and why; the amount of things Jones actually understands; referential convergence; and the role luck plays in it.

We don't claim to have provided a theory of luck in language, or an account of what we assume when we believe we have good reason to suppose we are talking or thinking about the same person. But we hope to have shown that critical referentialism provides a promising framework for further development. It allows us, as referentialists, to discard Frege's theory of sense and reference, without discarding the insights that made it plausible enough to be the accepted theory of names for most of a century.

Acknowledgments

We are grateful to the members of the Zoom group. The first two authors benefitted from grants by the Spanish Government (PID2019-106078GB-I00; MCI/AEI/FEDER, UE) and the Basque Government (IT1612-22). We are particularly grateful to the editors of this volume, Abrol Fairweather and Carlos Montemayor, for their invitation and their help and patience during the process.

References

Broncano-Berrocal, F. (2015). Luck as risk and the lack of control account of luck. *Metaphilosophy*, 46(1), 1–25.

Hales, S. D. (2016). Why every theory of luck is wrong. *Noûs*, 50(3), 490–508.

Korta, K., & Perry, J. (2011). *Critical pragmatics: An inquiry into reference and communication*. Cambridge: Cambridge University Press.

Korta, K., & Perry, J. (2013). Highlights of critical pragmatics: reference and the contents of the utterance. *Intercultural Pragmatics*, 10(1), 161–182.

Loar, B. (1976). The semantics of singular terms. *Philosophical Studies: An International Journal for Philosophy in the Analytic Tradition*, 30(6), 353–377.

Peet, A. (2017). Referential intentions and communicative luck. *Australasian Journal of Philosophy*, 95(2), 379–384.

Perry, J. ([2001] 2012). *Reference and Reflexivity*. 2nd edition. Stanford, CA: CSLI.

PART I

NOMOLOGICAL, FORMAL, AND COGNITIVE LUCK REDUCTION

3

Specificity and Resolution in the Communicative Use of Singular Terms

Imogen Dickie

1. Introduction

This chapter is about what is required if speakers are to count as understanding one another's uses of singular terms. Extant discussions of this issue are dominated by what I shall call the 'standard picture'. This picture has three components:

(i) In central cases, a speaker using a singular term is expressing a thought about a specific particular.

(ii) Understanding requires that the hearer respond by forming a thought about the same particular.

(iii) Understanding also requires that (ii) be secured in an appropriately non-lucky way.

For example, according to the standard picture, when I say (in a commonplace situation, with no funny-business) 'Agnes needs her dinner', I am expressing a belief about my dog. You understand my remark only if you respond by forming an attitude about this same individual (maybe a belief about the dog; maybe a belief as to what I believe about the dog), and doing so in a way that meets an appropriate non-luckiness condition.

With the standard picture more-or-less assumed, the debate has focussed on what is involved in each of (i)–(iii), and on how to stretch the account to cover non-central cases, for example, those where there is, by accident or because speaker and hearer are engaged in a pretence, no object the exchange is about.

Variants of the standard picture address these questions in their own ways. For example, a 'Fregean' variant will treat speakers as associating singular terms with 'modes of presentation' of (ways of being presented with) objects, and gloss (iii) as a requirement for an appropriate non-lucky (or luck-eliminating) relation

Imogen Dickie, *Specificity and Resolution in the Communicative Use of Singular Terms* In: *Linguistic Luck: Safeguards and Threats to Linguistic Communication*. Edited by: Abrol Fairweather and Carlos Montemayor, Oxford University Press.
© Oxford University Press 2023. DOI: 10.1093/oso/9780192845450.003.0003

between the modes of presentation associated with a term on the speaker's and hearer's sides of a communicative transaction.[1] A 'Stalnakerian' variant will look very different. Stalnaker argued that a conversation can be modelled as a shared activity directed at enhancing the agreed-upon record of how the world is (the 'common ground'), where this is a matter of narrowing down the set of possibilities that are 'live' as ways the world might be. In a Stalnakerian framework, a speaker making an utterance is proffering a move in this activity; understanding requires that the hearer's linguistic competence generate recognition of the proffered move.[2] So (i) becomes the claim that in a central case of assertion containing a singular term, the speaker is proposing, for non-lucky recognition by the hearer, an update about some specific thing. (ii) and (iii) become requirements on how rich the common ground must be if the speaker is to count as making this kind of proposal, and the hearer as achieving non-lucky recognition of what is being proposed.[3]

But for the purposes of this chapter, the differences between these variants will not matter. I am going to argue that the standard picture—ubiquitous as it is; intuitive as it seems—is wrong. The chapter has three phases. §1 lays out an initial puzzle for the standard picture. §§2–5 develop the alternative model that I want to propose. §6 shows how this alternative model accommodates the standard picture as a limiting case.

2. An Initial Puzzle—Dynamic Non-Specificity

Some months before his death in 1982, German *auteur* Rainer Werner Fassbinder rang Jane Fonda to solicit her participation in his next project. Jane Fonda answered the phone with the words 'This is Jane Fonda herself'. So delighted was Fassbinder that, in the remaining months of his life, he would sometimes answer the phone Jane Fonda-style: 'This is Fassbinder himself', he would say.[4]

We can, of course, see Jane Fonda's point. Taking a clear-headed view of her fame, she anticipates that a caller will be expecting somebody else—a member of her entourage—to answer the phone for her. She is (helpfully) setting the matter straight. Even as Fassbinder said 'I'm ringing Jane Fonda', he almost certainly was

---

[1] Frege's own view was that genuine understanding requires speakers to associate the singular term with *the same* mode of presentation of the referent (Frege 1984 esp. pp. 357–60). The central question for subsequent attempts to develop Fregean models has been how to motivate a weaker 'appropriate relation' condition. I take Fregean proposals to include Evans 1982; Heck 1995; Pagin 2008; Dickie and Rattan 2010; Peet 2019. Kaplan's account of communication becomes 'Fregean' in this sense if supplemented with a solution to the interpersonal version of his 'problem of cognitive dynamics' (Kaplan 1989 pp. 537–8).

[2] Stalnaker 1989a pp. 79–80, and many other places.

[3] Compare Stalnaker 2009.   [4] Katz 1987 p. xiv.

not expecting to talk to Jane Fonda herself. Rather, he was announcing the making of a call in Jane Fonda's general direction; a call he expected to be answered maybe by her, but more likely by one of her people.

Fassbinder's (imagined) utterance here, 'I'm ringing Jane Fonda', illustrates the phenomenon of 'felicitous non-specificity' in our ordinary uses of singular terms: there are cases of successful communication using a singular term where, given the context of utterance, it is not determinate which particular the speaker's 'intended message' is about.[5] Here are two other cases of this kind (let us count Fassbinder-Fonda as Case 1):

Case 2: Walking past a row of parked cars, S points to one and says to H 'That's a beautiful car'.

Case 3: H arrives home. S points at a parcel in the corner and says 'This came for you'.

Was S in Case 2 talking about the car token or the car type? Given the utterance and the situation, we (and H) are in no position to answer this question. And it is easy to imagine the situation as one where S herself has neither token-not-type nor type-not-token in mind. Suppose H asks 'Did you mean that car in particular, or that make and model?' S might reply one way or another, but is equally likely to say something like 'Either, both, I don't know. I hadn't made up my mind'. Something similar holds of Case 3: S has not done enough to pin down either the parcel or the contents as referent for her use of 'that': she might mean either or (somehow) both.

On the face of things, in each of Cases 1–3, neither the speaker's side nor the hearer's side of the transaction involves identification of a specific object. Yet, on the face of things, each is a case of communication: the speaker's utterance does not register as infelicitous or in need of correction; the hearer is in a position to understand the utterance and move on with the conversation. The speaker, it seems, is operating at a level at which the distinction between candidate target entities just does not matter for what is attempted to be got across.

Now, the standard picture was initially introduced as applying only to a 'central' range of cases: those where, on the face of things, the speaker is rightly regarded as attempting to communicate about one specific object. So Cases 1–3 do not yet generate grounds for an objection to this picture. Rather, they generate a challenge: an adherent to the standard picture needs to extend it to explain them.

And it might seem obvious what the required extension should be. Every account of communication must deal with cases where linguistic competence

---

[5] I adapt the term from King 2018. The observation that there are such cases is old—see Dummett 1981 pp 73–80; as well as King 2018; more recent discussions include Dickie 2020, Szabo 2020, Charlow 2022.

and contextual factors leave the hearer with competing verdicts as to what the speaker is attempting to get across. Often such ambiguity is a barrier to communication. But this is not always the case. For example, as used by residents of Toronto, the name 'London' might refer to either London, England, or London, Ontario. Suppose I say 'Why is X walking their dog—do you think he's decided to change his ways?', and receive the reply 'No, it's just that Y is in London today'. (Suppose that it is almost invariably Y who walks X and Y's dog.) I might ask 'London here, or London over the sea?', but I might well not bother seeking the clarification: just knowing that X is walking the dog because Y is out of town tells me not to take X's behaviour as a sign of a new regime. (In linguists' terms, the ambiguity between two referents for 'London' does not block communication in this instance because it does not matter to the 'question under discussion'.) So— we might ask, on behalf of the standard picture—why not treat Cases 1–3 as cases of harmless ambiguity?[6]

To see the answer to this question, and the puzzle that I want to raise for the standard picture, we need to look more closely at how patterns of specificity and non-specificity evolve in a conversation as it unfolds over time.

It is an old observation[7] that specificity-or-not for an $\ulcorner \alpha$ is $\Phi \urcorner$ sentence used in a context depends on the predicate as well as the singular term. For example, consider this trio of 'Jane Fonda' utterances:

(1) I'm ringing Jane Fonda.
(1a) Jane Fonda was born in 1937.
(1b) Jane Fonda's sitting in all of those seats.

(1) is the initial utterance—Fassbinder might mean Jane Fonda herself, or her entourage, or both. In contrast, somebody uttering (1a) in an ordinary context can be talking only about Jane Fonda herself. (1b) goes the other way—each seat is occupied by a member of Jane Fonda's entourage.

In many cases, non-specificity is eliminated when a subsequent utterance contains a predicate whose presence forces a choice between candidate referents. For example, keeping the backdrop the same, we can imagine an utterer of the initial, non-specific (2) continuing with either (2a) or (2b):[8]

---

[6] This would take us to an account of non-specificity commensurate with recent proposals to the effect that 'what is said' by an utterance is sensitive to the question under discussion. See for example Stokke and Schoubye 2016. King's 2018 proposal is along these general lines. The idea of a question-sensitive account of representational content goes back at least to Lewis 1988. Yalcin 2018 explores the proposal for the case of belief.
[7] Dummett 1981 p. 76.
[8] Szabo 2020 p. 68 points out that the fact that a speaker uttering the initial sentence might continue with either the a or b alternative cements the diagnosis that the initial utterance is not specific.

(2) That's a beautiful car.

(2a) That's a beautiful car, but it's a bit dinged up.

(2b) That's a beautiful car—the last one they made is on display in the British Motor Museum.

The (2a) continuation closes off the 'car type' reading of the non-specific (2); the (2b) continuation goes the other way.

There is, again, an obvious move that suggests itself here for a proponent of the standard picture. If non-specificity is a kind of ambiguity, resolution of non-specificity is just . . . resolution of ambiguity: (2) is ambiguous between a car-token claim and a car-type claim; (2a) resolves this ambiguity in one direction, (2b) in another.

But now consider another variation, keeping the backdrop the same:

(2c) That's beautiful. It's a bit dinged up. It's fantastic to drive though—it's the car I learned in.

If the account of non-specificity we have pursued on behalf of the standard picture is right, this pattern should be impossible. According to this account, the first sentence is ambiguous between car-token claim and car-type claim. The second resolves this ambiguity in favour of the car token. So—if the account is right—the third sentence should also register as making a claim about the car token: 'it' in the third sentence should pick up the disambiguated referent from the sentence before. But this is a wrong result. In uttering the third sentence in (2c), the speaker might be making a claim about the car token (the claim that she learned to drive in that very car), but might be making a claim about the car type (the claim that she learned to drive in a car of that make and model).

It is not hard to think of examples that replicate the pattern. Consider these variations on Cases 1 and 3:

SPEAKER₁: Look, Jane Fonda's arrived.

SPEAKER₂: I thought she was taller than that. Let's go over there—it'll save us having to ring her next week.

SPEAKER₁: This arrived today.

SPEAKER₂: It's for his birthday. He's coveted one for ages. I ordered it from Italy.

SPEAKER₁: It's been shipped from New York.

In each of these cases, we start with an utterance that displays felicitous non-specificity. An initial subsequent remark eliminates the non-specificity; another brings it back.

I have suggested that this is a pattern the standard picture cannot explain. To consolidate this diagnosis, let us walk through the details for a Stalnakerian version of the standard view.

Recall that in Stalnaker's framework a conversation is a shared activity directed at enhancing the common ground, narrowing the set of live possibilities. A speaker making an utterance is proffering a move in this activity. In intuitive terms, if the utterance is an assertion that p, the proffered move is addition of p to the common ground, which is elimination of all not-p possibilities from the set of live options. What a speaker is using an expression to stand for is just one fact among others as to what the actual world is like. So, for example, if I tell you that 'Agnes' is my dog's name, I am proposing the addition of this claim to the common ground. A conversational situation where a hearer is in a position to understand an ordinary (specific) use of a singular term is one where the common ground already contains enough detail to pin down which object the speaker is using the term to talk about.

Against this background, the obvious suggestion about Cases 1–3 is that these are cases where the common ground is not sufficiently rich to determine a single referent for the singular term. In Case 1, the set of worlds left live by the common ground includes some where Fassbinder is using 'Jane Fonda' to refer to the film star; others where he is using the name to refer to the entourage. In Case 2, the set of live worlds includes some where the demonstrative is being used to talk about the car token, others where it is being used to talk about the car type. In Case 3 it includes some worlds where the demonstrative refers to the contents, others where it refers to the parcel.

Stalnaker's framework already has an account of how a speaker's utterance can be both in good order and understood by the hearer, in situations involving such indeterminacies. When the set of live worlds includes some where an expression is used to talk about X and others where it is used to talk about Y, the speaker's utterance is in good order iff the indeterminacy is treated as internal to the message the utterance conveys. Treating Case 2 like this, we get the result that the sentence 'That's beautiful', uttered in the Case 2 situation, proposes the update that could also have been proposed by saying 'Either I'm using "that" to refer to the car token, and the token is beautiful, or I'm using "that" to refer to the car type, and the type is beautiful'. The worlds the speaker is proposing be eliminated as live options are those where neither disjunct holds.[9] The continuations in (2a) and (2b)—'It's a bit dinged up' and 'The last one is on display . . .'—eliminate, respectively, worlds where the referent is the car type and worlds where it is the car token.[10]

But this explanation will not stretch to cover the pattern in (2c). If we treat the utterance of 'It's a bit dinged up', as eliminating 'car type' worlds from the set of live options, we are left with no account of the non-specificity in the subsequent

---

[9] In Stalnaker's terminology (1989a p. 82), the proposal is to explain felicitous non-specificity using 'diagonalisation' and the 'dagger' operator.

[10] This will be a matter of 'presupposition accommodation' (Stalnaker 1989b pp. 102–4): since it is part of the common ground that only tokens can satisfy 'dinged up', the utterance is in good order only if the anaphoric pronoun is being used to refer to the car token. The speaker exploits this fact to use the utterance to propose addition of this point to the common ground.

continuation 'It's fantastic to drive though—it's the car I learned in'. Both predicates in this sentence ('fantastic to drive'; 'the car I learned in') are 'neutral' in that they could be used to characterize either the token or the type. So there is nothing in the sentence to re-introduce worlds where the demonstrative refers to the type rather than the token into the set of live options. If the Stalnakerian version of the standard view is right, the utterance should read as making a specific claim about the car token. But this is not the case.

This is what I shall call the 'puzzle of dynamic non-specificity'. I have walked through the details for Stalnaker's version of the standard picture. But the puzzle arises for standard pictures across the board. If the standard picture is assumed, the only obvious move available to explain felicitous non-specificity is to treat it as a variety of harmless ambiguity. But once ambiguity is resolved, it is not re-introduced by a neutral utterance. So we are left with no account of the puzzle-raising pattern. (Compare: 'There's a bat in the cupboard. It's asleep with its wings tucked in. It's hanging upside down'. 'Bat' in the first sentence is lexically ambiguous (mammal or piece of sports equipment). The ambiguity is removed by the presence in the second sentence of predicates applicable only to living things. If we had just the first and third sentences—'There's a bat in the cupboard. It's hanging upside down', the ambiguity would remain: there is nothing in 'It's hanging upside down' to resolve things one way or another. But once the ambiguity is gone, it stays gone: the 'neutral' third sentence does not re-introduce the possibility that the bat at issue is something used in cricket.)

The next three sections motivate an account of the thoughts we standardly express using ordinary singular terms that predicts and explains dynamic non-specificity phenomena. Here is what I am going to propose in intuitive terms. Thinking about a particular is maintaining a kind of focus on it. Speakers communicating about a particular are maintaining a kind of joint focus. But focus relations have degrees of resolution: increase the resolution, and what looked like one object resolves into two; decrease the resolution, and the effect is reversed. Shifting patterns of specificity in our uses of singular terms are the predictable results of increases and decreases in resolution—zooming in; zooming out—of shared focus-maintaining activities.

Though I have used a puzzle to approach this alternative picture, the central motivation for it that I shall present starts from first principles. For this reason, I shall not tarry to consider undignified contortions that might solve the puzzle while keeping—on paper—the standard picture. I shall return to the comparison between the standard picture and the alternative proposal in §6.

3. Cognitive Focus (I)—The Aboutness of *Ordinary* Thoughts

The next three sections motivate what I shall call the 'cognitive focus' model of thought and speech about ordinary things. This section and the next argue that ordinary thinking about ordinary things[11] (hereafter '*ordinary* thought') is engagement in information-marshalling activity directed at achieving and sustaining relations of cognitive focus. §5 shows how this view generates an accompanying model of communicative use of singular terms.

The first step towards the cognitive focus model is to emphasize a point that is easily overlooked. Though one functional role of *ordinary* beliefs is as inputs to decisions on how to act, they are themselves the upshots of information-marshalling activity: activity in which we marshal incoming information-signal—from perception and from other people's testimony—into bodies of beliefs that we treat as 'about' ordinary things. This point is easily overlooked because it is concealed by the tendency to focus on states of the subject's mind—beliefs—rather than the processes that underpin these states.[12] But it surfaces whenever philosophers are talking about the 'aim' of belief, by which they really mean the aim of belief-formation. To say that belief has an aim just is to treat belief-formation as an exercise of agency—something we do, rather than something that happens to us.

Philosophers exploring this aspect of the nature of belief have argued that belief-formation aims at truth;[13] that it aims at knowledge;[14] that it aims at narrowing the set of epistemically live possibilities. The cognitive focus model takes off from a different suggestion about the aim of *ordinary* belief-formation: *ordinary* belief-formation is an activity part of whose aim is to secure and maintain relations of aboutness to particular things. I argue for this claim elsewhere.[15] To keep this chapter to a manageable length, I shall rest with giving it a preliminary and broad-brush motivation.

Note first that empirical findings compel the conclusion that the information-processing that generates our *ordinary* beliefs—uptake from perception; uptake from testimony—is in some sense 'looking for' objects. For example, it is widely agreed that formation of perceptual demonstrative beliefs—the beliefs standardly formed by uptake from perception, and expressed using demonstratives like 'this' and 'that'—requires an attentional perceptual channel which at least seems to the subject to be locked to a particular thing. You do not just stare unfocussedly into the distance and form beliefs you would express using 'that'; formation of perceptual demonstrative beliefs requires a perceptual experience that registers as an instance of attention to an object.[16] Similarly, it is widely agreed that following what someone is saying involves keeping track of what linguists call 'discourse referents'—bundling together utterances as delivering information treated as

---

[11] I mean to exclude both non-ordinary subject matters (numbers, bosons) and non-*ordinary* thoughts about ordinary subject matters.

[12] Though it is not possible to explore this matter here, my own view is that the right metaphysical story will relate occurrent beliefs to belief-forming (and retrieving) activity in terms of the model of 'stative processes' motivated at Soteriou 2013 pp. 45–50.

[13] Velleman 2000.   [14] Bird 2019.   [15] In Dickie 2015 ch. 3, 2020.

[16] This point was first explored in depth in Campbell 2002, but is now widely accepted in accounts of perceptual demonstrative thought.

being about the same thing.[17] So if it is to be denied that the securing of aboutness relations is part of the aim of *ordinary* belief-forming activity, the claim will have to be that, though the means by which we seek to fulfill the aim of belief-formation involve looking for objects, whether we find them is incidental to whether this aim is fulfilled.

There is nothing incoherent about the suggestion that a factor that plays a role in a subject's attempts to fulfil an aim might have no place in the characterization of what she is aiming for. Consider driving on a country road using the white line that marks its edge to maintain appropriate road position. Your use of the line is embedded in the information-processing story that generates your behaviour, but is merely instrumental to the aim of your activity: the fact that you are using the line releases no motivational pressure; in cases where it is absent—of which there are many, and many nearby—you do things in another way without really noticing.

It is, however, implausible that a right account of the aim of *ordinary* belief-forming activity will relegate the fact that this activity involves looking for objects to this kind of mere instrumental role. For the fact that it involves looking for objects does appear embrangled with the motivational story of *ordinary* belief. Consider how it is often the storyline of an individual that will stay with you out of a whole narrative; how we like to explain even very general points in terms of their significance for individuals; how the wandering mind gravitates towards thought about particular people, places, and things; how it is the particular thing in a scene, rather than any general aspect of the scene itself, that is the more typical magnet to curiosity. These aspects of cognitive life at least strongly suggest that we do not just end up thinking about particular objects on our way to fulfilling some non-object-involving aim. Rather, the mind needs to think about things, and it needs things to be thinking about: part of what we are trying to do in *ordinary* belief-formation is to lock onto particulars as subject matter for thought.

Note that this claim carries no suggestion that the securing and maintaining of aboutness relations is either the sole or a fundamental aim of *ordinary* belief-forming activity. It is compatible with all of the following: *ordinary* belief-forming activity also aims at truth; it also aims at knowledge; it also aims at delivery of representations which will enable reliable fulfilment of the subject's practical goals; it aims at aboutness only as a means to one or more of these other ends.[18]

So far in this section, I have suggested that *ordinary* belief-forming activity is (partly) driven by the mind's need to secure and maintain relations of aboutness to things in the world. I shall now show that this initial claim generates a specific

---

[17] This is part of 'Discourse Representation Theory'. See for example Guerts, Beaver, and Maier 2020.

[18] I intend the last clause here to accommodate Heck's suggestion that aboutness might be an 'emergent' goal of *ordinary* belief-forming activity: Heck 2017.

view of what these aboutness relations are—an aboutness relation is a relation of cognitive focus.

The argument requires two further premisses, which I shall treat as basic:

ABOUTNESS AND TRUTH—If a belief that <α is Φ> is about object o, it is true iff o is Φ.[19] (If my belief that Agnes is asleep is about my dog, it is true iff she is asleep.)

TRUTH AND JUSTIFICATION—(approximate version)—Justification is truth-conducive: the factors that secure a subject's justification for a belief also secure the result that the subject will be unlucky if the belief is not true.

The view of aboutness relations that I am going to propose is reached by taking these two principles—the first connecting aboutness and truth, the second truth and justification—and cutting the intermediate terms to deliver a third principle which brings out the significance for accounts of aboutness of the fact that justification is truth-conducive:

ABOUTNESS AND JUSTIFICATION (approximate version)—A body of beliefs treated by a subject as about a particular thing is about object o iff its associated pattern of justification is conducive to getting o's properties right, so that the subject will be unlucky if beliefs justified in this way do not match what o is like.

Here is an analogy to consolidate what ABOUTNESS AND JUSTIFICATION says. Consider an astronomer (hereafter 'A') compiling a report from the signal delivered by a telescope focussed on object o, where A has no reason to doubt the telescope's reliability. The telescope delivers a stream of data; A compiles her report: 'It's moving. Its temperature is fluctuating between such-and-such values…'. The fact that the telescope is focussed on o obviously does not guarantee that A's report will match what o is like. A's overall situation might involve some unlucky spoiler: a concealed fault in the workings of the telescope; a rare data-distorting anomaly in o's part of the sky. But the fact that the telescope is focussed on o does guarantee the following: A's report will match what o is like unless some unlucky spoiler intervenes.

ABOUTNESS AND JUSTIFICATION treats the aboutness of our *ordinary* beliefs as a kind of focus—what I call 'cognitive focus'. In a case where you are attending to an ordinary thing and forming beliefs you would express using 'that', your beliefs are about the thing because the associated means of justification (uptake from your attentional perceptual channel) will deliver beliefs that match what the attended object is like unless an unlucky spoiler intervenes. A parallel story holds for

---

[19] 'Belief that <α is Φ>' abbreviates 'belief the subject would express by saying ⌜α is Φ⌝', where 'α' ranges over ordinary singular terms and 'Φ' over ordinary predicates. 'Φ' ranges over properties and is braced to 'Φ': o is Φ iff o has the property introduced by Φ.

aboutness relations secured by grasp of ordinary proper names: when you are competent with a proper name, you associate it with a pattern of potential justification; in cases where competence with a proper name puts you in a position to think about a particular, it does so because, unless your situation is unlucky, beliefs justified in this way will match what the particular is like.

Why should ABOUTNESS AND JUSTIFICATION be accepted? The principle is a biconditional: aboutness iff cognitive focus. I shall argue for each direction in turn.

Here is an argument for the left-to-right direction—if aboutness then cognitive focus.

Suppose

(1) S's belief that <α is Φ> is about o.

Add aboutness and truth:

(2) If S's belief that <α is Φ> is about an object, the belief is true iff that object is Φ.

(1) and (2) entail

(3) S's belief that <α is Φ> is true iff o is Φ.

Add truth and justification:

(4) If a belief is justified, the subject will be unlucky if it is not true.

(3) and (4) entail

(5) If S's belief that <α is Φ> is justified, she will be unlucky if o is not Φ.

So we have the left-to-right direction of the ABOUTNESS AND JUSTIFICATION biconditional:

(6) If S's <α is Φ> belief is about o, if the belief is justified, S will be unlucky if o is not Φ.

The argument for the other direction of the biconditional requires a little more detail on the connections between motivational states, behaviours guided by them, and the notions of 'unlucky' failure and 'not merely lucky' success. Drawing on elements of the extant philosophical discussion of action and activity, I shall say that a behaviour is an 'exercise' of competence at fulfilling a motivational state iff it is guided by the state, and is a non-lucky generator of this state's fulfilment. I shall gloss the notion of 'non-luckiness' in terms of success across relevant circumstances: the 'relevant' circumstances are those across which a behaviour guided by a motivational state must generate success if it is to count as an exercise of competence at fulfilling the state; an exercise of competence might fail to deliver success, but only if some unlucky spoiler intervenes, in which case the circumstance is irrelevant. Finally, I shall say that a behaviour 'manifests' a competence iff it is an exercise of the competence in relevant circumstances, in which case the result will be success secured by the subject's exercise of the competence. (Consider a craftsman engaged in some skilled task. He is 'exercising' his competence iff everything goes well with respect to his information-processing, so that he will be unlucky not to end up with the intended result. He is 'manifesting' his competence iff he is exercising it in a relevant circumstance, in which case the intended result will be secured by the fact that he is exercising his competence in a circumstance in which exercise of competence is guaranteed to generate success.)[20]

Stepping from the case of action in general to that of belief-forming activity, I shall take it that a belief is justified iff formed by an exercise of belief-forming competence, and that a belief counts as knowledge iff formed by a manifestation of belief-forming competence. I shall say that a circumstance that is relevant from the point of view of belief-formation is 'rationally relevant' (so the rationally relevant circumstances are those across which the means of justification for a belief guarantees its truth).[21]

With this backdrop in place, we can argue for the right-to-left direction of the biconditional (if cognitive focus then aboutness) like this:

(1) It is not sufficient, for S's <α is Φ> beliefs to be about o, that the cognitive focus condition be met with respect to o. [Supposition for *reductio*.]

Given (1), the following is coherent:

(2) S is forming <α is Φ> beliefs by a means that is tracking what o is like: there is no spoiler interfering with any 'detection of Φ-instantiation' aspect of S's path to these beliefs; there is an object, o, upon whose Φ-ness or not S's Φ-detecting procedures are picking up. But the case is, nevertheless, one of aboutness-failure.

Now add the claim about the aim of *ordinary* belief-forming activity from earlier in the section:

(3) Part of the aim of *ordinary* belief-forming activity is to secure and maintain aboutness relations.

---

[20] I adopt the terms 'exercise' of a competence and 'manifestation' of a competence from Sosa 2015. Compare also Kelp 2017. But I take this general way of looking at activities and non-lucky success to trace to Anscombe 2000.

[21] I take these equivalences to be common across a range of views in virtue epistemology. But I intend no commitment to the priority of the 'virtue-theoretic' notions—exercise and manifestation of belief-forming competence; rational relevance—over the notions of justification and knowledge.

Given (3), we have (4):

(4) In the situation described at (2), S's belief-forming activity does not fulfil its guiding motivational state.

But a situation in which the behaviour guided by a motivational state fails to fulfil the state is either a case of unlucky failure (the subject is exercising competence in securing fulfilment of the goal, but in a circumstance outside the range across which competence secures success), or it is a case where the subject is not exercising competence. So (4) entails (5):

(5) In the situation at (2), either S's circumstance is rationally irrelevant (it is a circumstance in which exercise of competence at formation of <α is Φ> beliefs does not guarantee success at this activity) or S is failing to exercise competence at formation of <α is Φ> beliefs.

But now suppose we keep things as described at (2), and imagine S forming a <Something is Φ> belief instead. It is part of the description of the situation at (2) that S's Φ-detecting procedures are picking up on whether or not Φ is instantiated. So there are good grounds for (6):

(6) If S were to move to a <Something is Φ> belief in the situation at (2), this belief would be a case of knowledge.

And given (6), neither disjunct at (5) is acceptable. We shall show this for each in turn.

(7) In the situation at (2), S's circumstance is not rationally irrelevant to her belief-forming activity. (The first disjunct at (5) is false.)

For a belief is knowledge iff formed by a manifestation of belief-forming competence. So given (6), we are taking it that in forming a <Something is Φ> belief in the situation at (2), S would be manifesting competence at <Something is Φ>-belief-formation. And a circumstance where formation of a belief manifests belief-forming competence just is a relevant circumstance in which the belief is formed by exercise of the competence. So to affirm (6) and deny (7) is to endorse the possibility of the following combination:

A circumstance rationally irrelevant to formation of the belief that <α is Φ> may be rationally relevant to formation of the belief that <Something is Φ>.

And to endorse this possibility is to suppose that it is harder to know <Something is Φ> than it is to know <α is Φ>. For example, it is to suppose that a <That is square>

belief formed by uptake from a perceptual link might count as knowledge while the <Something is square> belief formed on the same justification does not (because knowing <Something is square> requires a means of belief-formation that eliminates extra 'nothing square there' circumstances—circumstances that must be guarded against if a <Something is Φ> belief formed on the basis of perception is to count as knowledge, but which may be ignored in moving to <That is Φ>). Now consider the standard introduction rule for the existential quantifier:

Existential Generalization	α is Φ
	————————
	Something is Φ

If it is harder to know <Something is Φ> than to know <α is Φ>, this move is illegitimate. Obviously this is not the beginning of a discovery ('Existential Generalization is invalid!'). It is reduction to absurdity of the combination that generates it: (6) and the first disjunct of (5).

(8) In the situation at (2), S is exercising competence at formation of <α is Φ> beliefs. (The second disjunct at (5) is false.)

For consider the standard elimination rule for the existential quantifier:

Existential Elimination	Something is Φ	β is Φ [arbitrary β]
(From ⌜Something is Φ⌝ and a		:
derivation of *p* from ⌜β is Φ⌝ for		*p*
arbitrary β, conclude *p*.)	————————————————	
	p	

Use of this rule is legitimate only if ⌜Something is Φ⌝ and ⌜β is Φ⌝ require the holding of the same kind of object-property relation for their truth: affirming ⌜Something is Φ⌝ has to be affirming that some member of the domain is Φ; otherwise it is not legitimate to let a claim that some arbitrary member of the domain is Φ go proxy for the quantified sentence in working out its consequences. And now suppose we deny (8), maintaining that in the situation at (2) S is failing to exercise competence in formation of <α is Φ> beliefs. In the situation at (2), S's Φ-instantiation-detection proceeds as it does because S is taking the incoming signal and using it as input to <α is Φ> belief-formation. So if we suppose that S is not exercising competence in forming this kind of belief, we have no right to the claim that her Φ *is instantiated!* verdicts are picking up on the same object-property relation as holds in cases where she knows that <α is Φ>. But given (6), we are taking it that S's path to her Φ *is instantiated!* verdict in the situation at

(2) does sustain knowledge that <Something is Φ>. So if we keep (6) but deny (8), we are taking it that the conditions for knowing <Somethings is Φ> fall short of those for knowing that some member of the domain is Φ. And in that case we must give up the claim that Existential Elimination is valid in the realm of *ordinary* thought. Again, this is (obviously) not the beginning of a discovery. It is reduction to absurdity of the second disjunct.

The (1)–(8) argument gets us the conclusion that a situation where there is cognitive focus is one where there is aboutness. But we do not yet have the right-to-left claim that we want—the claim that where a stream of belief-forming activity is focussed on o, the resulting beliefs are about o. For nothing so far rules out the following possibility: S's cognitive-focus-sustaining information-marshalling activity is focussed on both o and some $o^* \neq o$; the resulting beliefs are about o but not o^*.

How is this gap to be closed? That is the question I shall address in the next section. The answer will also bring into view the initial details of the cognitive-focus-based solution to the puzzle from §2.

4. Cognitive Focus (II)—Fineness of Grain

The end of the previous section brought out what is, in hindsight, a predictable wrinkle in the cognitive focus framework. A focus relation has a degree of resolution: increase the power of your telescope, and what registered as one object at coarse resolution may resolve into many. This does not entail that coarse-grained focus is not genuine focus: it is genuine focus; but it is coarse-grained. The parallel claim holds for cognitive focus. A strand of belief-forming, aboutness-seeking activity is focussed on o iff, across the range of properties the subject is in the business of deciding, it will generate beliefs that match what o is like unless an unlucky spoiler intervenes. This condition may be met by both o and some $o^* \neq o$, in which case the subject is sustaining a relation of cognitive focus at a degree of resolution that does not distinguish o from o^*. So there is nothing in the notion of cognitive focus to rule out the possibility that a strand of belief-forming activity is cognitively focussed on more than one thing.

What should we make of the relation between aboutness and cognitive focus given, on the one hand, the connection uncovered in the previous section and, on the other, the fact that a stream of belief-forming activity might be focussed on more than one thing? I suggest that what we have here is a deeper anchor for a familiar point. Consider this from Quine:

In general we might propound this maxim of the identification of indiscernibles: Objects indistinguishable from one another within the terms of a given discourse should be construed as identical for that discourse. More accurately: the references to the original objects should be reconstrued for the purposes of the discourse as referring to other and fewer objects, in such a way that indistinguishable originals give way each to the same new object.   (Quine 1953 p. 71)

Suppose we want an account of what the speakers of some language are saying. And suppose we have a candidate account which treats them as ascribing some array of properties to some domain of objects, where the domain divides into (non-singleton) subsets whose members instantiate all the same properties (members of the same subset are 'indistinguishable from one another within the terms of [the] discourse'). Then, according to Quine, we should move to a new, coarser-grained account: where the old account treats speakers as talking about distinct objects $\{o_1, \ldots, o_n\}$ converging in their properties, the new account treats them as talking about a single, coarse-grained object. This move is dictated by demands of simplicity. For every Φ the speakers might ascribe, and every o_i and o_j in the same subset, o_i is Φ iff o_j is. So the distinction between o_i and o_j is idle in the assignment of sentences in the language to situations in which they are true.

The cognitive focus framework generates a deeper anchor for a parallel constraint. A toy case will help bring out how this is so. Suppose you fire a laser-pulse at a target. And consider these two questions:

Question 1—What did you hit?
Question 2—What were you aiming at?

In answering Question 1, the constraints on fineness of grain come from metaphysics, and from pressures towards answering a question in a way that respects the reason it was asked. From the point of view of metaphysics, the account of which object (exactly) you hit could be as precise as the boundary between the region burned by the laser-pulse and the region left unscathed. So, from this point of view, we might distinguish a case where you hit some very fine-grained object from one where you hit another that is identically shaped but displaced by a few microns. This level of fineness of grain in the answer to Question 1 is metaphysically coherent as long as we allow the existence of the fine-grained objects in the first place. Whether it is appropriate depends on why we were asking the question. If all we wanted to know was whether you hit some coarse-grained target which could be hit by hitting any one of a range of fine-grained objects, a fine-grained answer to Question 1 fails to respect the reason the question was asked.

The constraints from metaphysics and the pragmatics of question-answering also apply to Question 2. But here there is an additional factor. The fineness of grain of an answer to Question 2 is also constrained by the level of resolution of your aim-and-fire mechanism. If o and o^* are objects so similar that you would use the same parameter settings to aim 'at' o as 'at' o^*, the suggestion that you were aiming at one rather than the other dissolves into incoherence. Taking (competent) aim at a target just is setting parameters that will generate a hit on the target unless the situation is unlucky. The facts of the matter as to what you are aiming at cannot be finer-grained than the distinctions between parameter settings that determine them.

Quine-type invocation of the match-in-grain constraint mirrors what we have said about Question 1. According to philosophers making this kind of move, preference for the coarse-grained account is generated by an appeal to simplicity. An account of which objects thinkers or speakers are representing should be no finer-grained than it must be to explain their behaviour; an account which treats subjects as thinking or speaking about objects indistinguishable relative to the properties they ascribe (or the predicates they apply) fails this simplicity criterion.

In contrast, the cognitive focus framework generates a match-in-grain constraint that mirrors what we have said about Question 2. In this framework, thinking about an object just is sustaining a relation of cognitive focus upon it: it is maintaining a body of <α> beliefs in such a way that, given how they are justified, you will be unlucky if these beliefs do not match what the object is like, and not merely lucky if they do. So the question 'What are your beliefs about?' is a disguised version of a direct parallel to Question 2: 'What is your belief-forming activity focussed on?' If o and o^* are sufficiently similar, relative to the range of properties you are in the business of deciding and accessibility to your means of justification, that (in intuitive terms) the means of justification generates beliefs that tend to match both of them, the suggestion that you are focussed 'on' o rather than o^* is incoherent. You are focussed at a resolution at which o and o^* are not distinct.

A second difference between Quine's treatment of fineness of grain and the cognitive-focus-based parallel concerns the range of cases across which the respective constraints bite. Quine's constraint is triggered by duplication: if o and o^* coincide with respect to satisfaction or not of all the predicates deployed (or deployable) in a discourse, an account of the subject matter of the discourse should be framed in a way that does not distinguish them. In the cognitive focus framework, in contrast, the constraint is triggered iff the means of justification associated with a single stream of <α is Φ>-belief-forming activity converges on both o and o^*. This is a stronger condition than mere duplication. To see this, suppose I am maintaining a body of <that> beliefs justified by uptake from an attentional perceptual link with a particular ball being kicked around in the park. My means of justification for the beliefs converges on this particular ball—I will be unlucky to get its properties wrong and not merely lucky to get them right. For all I know, the ball might have an exact duplicate elsewhere in the universe. But my means of justification—uptake from my perceptual attentional link with this particular ball—converges on this ball, and not on any distant duplicate: as far as my means of justification is concerned, the existence of a duplicate ball being attended to by a duplicate of me is a mere matter of chance.

Though non-unique justificatory convergence is a stronger condition than mere duplication, it is relatively widespread in our cognitive lives. In fact, there are views of the metaphysics of ordinary objects which—if accepted—entail its ubiquity in *ordinary* thought. Suppose we say that an ordinary object just is an appropriately causally unified parcel of matter, and accept what is often held to be a consequence of this claim: each ordinary object is 'really' many almost-but-not-quite identical objects, differing very slightly at the microscopic level. (The point is that if we grant that the dog just is an appropriately unified parcel of matter, we will find no grounds for identifying her with one specific such parcel, rather than many others that are equally unified, macroscopically the same, but microscopically different.[22]) If we allow this conclusion, every case of cognitive focus on an ordinary object is really a case of non-unique cognitive focus. Consider ordinary object o (for example, my dog), and the corresponding set of almost-identical objects differentiated at the microscopic level, $\{\omega_1,\ldots,\omega_n\}$. At the level of grain at which we usually operate, the level of ascription of macroscopic properties, the ω's are indistinguishable: for each such property Φ and each ω_i, ω_i is Φ iff all the other ω's are too. And ordinary means of justification for an $<\alpha$ is $\Phi>$ belief that converge on one microscopic ω converge on all the ω's corresponding to the same macroscopic ordinary thing. So if we start from a background metaphysics which recognizes the existence of a cloud of ω's for every o, even a flat-footed case—a case where you are attending to an ordinary thing and forming beliefs you would express using <that> by uptake from your attentional perceptual feed—is a case where explaining what the beliefs are about will involve an appeal to coarse-grained cognitive focus: your cognitive focus is at the level of resolution of o rather than the underlying ω's, so it is in terms of o not the ω's that we explain what your thoughts are about.

Coarse-grained cognitive focus obtains wherever the range of properties the subject counts as in the business of deciding, and the means of justification she would deploy in deciding them, entail that the subject's paths to justification for $<\alpha$ is $\Phi>$ beliefs converge on more than one thing. In some cases—most obviously that of thought about ordinary objects—we are happy to allow the existence of coarse-grained objects as the things subjects' thoughts are about. In others, the issue is more vexed. There are many cases where the means of investigation actually or potentially available to a subject will sustain only conclusions that apply to all members of a group. For example, consider an historian discussing some event so ancient that it is impossible to draw conclusions about its participants 'as individuals', but trying to make the story vivid for an audience. 'Consider the average participant of the battle', says the historian. 'Let's call him "Bob". He

---

[22] This is the 'problem of the many.' For a canonical discussion, see Lewis 1999. For a general introduction and survey of responses, see Weatherson 2014. I discuss the problem in more detail at Dickie 2015 pp. 27–34.

would have been between 15 and 35 years old. He spoke Common Brittonic. He probably ate some beef and pork, and a lot of barley...'. Assuming that the historian is suitably competent, the investigation sustains a focus relation at a degree of resolution that does not distinguish one participant in the event from another. Is there a specific coarse-grained (abstract) object—the average participant in the battle—upon which the historian is sustaining coarse-grained focus? If there is, the case sits alongside what we have said about an ordinary object and its underlying cloud of ω's. If there is not, the historian's situation must be described with additional care: she is sustaining an aboutness relation, but at a level of resolution too coarse to license the claim that she is thinking about some particular thing.

The solution I want to propose to the puzzle from §2 is now visible in the middle distance. Felicitous non-specificity in our uses of ordinary singular terms is a predictable consequence of the kind of thought we use such terms to express: thoughts the thinking of which involves engagement in cognitive activity directed at securing and sustaining cognitive focus. Patterns of specificity and non-specificity in our ordinary uses of singular terms rest on shifts in the resolution of the underlying cognitive activity.

But to bring out the details of this proposal, I must first extend the cognitive-focus-based story about thought into a story about linguistic communication. That is the task of the next section.

5. Communication

The last two sections have argued for an account of ordinary thinking about ordinary things built around what I have called 'cognitive focus'. I shall now extend this proposal into an account of the communicative use of ordinary singular terms. Let us suppose that communication involves some kind of 'sharing' of thoughts (exactly what this 'sharing' comes to is part of what is at issue). I have argued that thinking a thought of the kind standardly expressed using an ordinary singular term is engagement in a cognitive-focus-directed information-marshalling activity. This suggests that we should be looking for an account of the communicative use of singular terms built around the notion of a corresponding shared activity: speakers understand one another's uses of a singular term in a conversation iff, in using it as they do, they are exercising competence at sustaining a relation of joint cognitive focus.

This section argues for a more precise version of this rough proposal. The final section compares the resulting view of mutual understanding of singular terms to the standard picture.

I shall join many others in taking it that a hearer's cognitive response to the speaker's utterance is determined by two kinds of calculation, which I shall call 'update calculations' and 'uptake calculations'. In intuitive terms, 'update calculations' determine what the hearer's cognitive response would be if she were to go along with the speaker's utterance. 'Uptake calculations' determine whether she will go along with it—whether she will make the move that her update calculations register the utterance as proposing. For example, if I form a belief by taking what you say at face value, my update calculation determines which belief I form, but it is only because my uptake calculation registers you as speaking sincerely and reliably that I actually form it. Similarly, if your utterance is an imperative, my update calculation determines the intention that I take you to be proposing I form, but whether I form this intention depends on my uptake calculation. In the case of an imperative, this will involve weighing your sincerity; whether you are in an appropriate position to direct an imperative to me; and whether the proposed intention is consistent with my existing attitudes.

I shall also suppose some backdrop connecting the notion of linguistic competence with what it takes for speakers to express themselves and hearers to understand. In any case of conversation, we can regard participants as using language to do something—that is, as harnessing linguistic competence to the furtherance of the goals that guide their participation. Obviously many things might go wrong with respect to each participant's pursuit of these goals. I shall take it that the speaker succeeds in expressing herself by making an utterance iff, whatever else might go wrong on the speaker's side of the transaction, nothing linguistic goes wrong: the speaker's production of the utterance is a manifestation of linguistic competence. (Recall that an outcome 'manifests' a competence iff it is secured by an exercise of the competence.) I shall suppose the mirror-image claim for the hearer's side of the transaction: the hearer understands the utterance iff, whatever else might go wrong for the hearer, nothing linguistic goes wrong. I shall suppose that whether a hearer's response to an utterance is an instance of understanding (a manifestation of hearer's side linguistic competence) depends on her update calculations, not her uptake calculations: understanding an utterance is one thing; going along with it another. And I shall take it that linguistic communication just is what happens when a speaker expresses herself by making an utterance which the hearer understands. It follows that a case of communication just is a case where, if something goes wrong in participants' attempts to fulfil their goals, it is not something linguistic: if you are expressing yourself and I understand you, but one of us is not getting what we want out of the exchange, some non-linguistic factor is to blame.[23]

---

[23] I am treating language understanding as requiring recovery of what Gricean frameworks call the 'total signification' of an utterance, and remaining neutral on what role (if any) there might be for a notion of knowledge of 'what is said' where this is regarded as a purely semantic achievement. This notion retains a role in contemporary 'minimalist' frameworks (Borg 2012) but is left behind by contemporary contextualists (Recanati 2010).

Finally, I shall make a supposition connecting what is involved in understanding an expression across utterances made with different illocutionary force: differences in the illocutionary force with which a token sentence is uttered (whether it is being used to ask a question; issue an imperative; or make an assertion) do not impact what is involved in understanding a lexically simple expression occurring within it.[24] So, for example, though you calculate different updates in response to my utterances 'Agnes has had dinner', and 'Has Agnes had dinner?', the 'Agnes' parts of your update calculations are the same. You deploy your competence with the name as used by me in generating one kind of update when you register me as making an assertion and another when you register me as asking a question, but these are distinct deployments of the same competence embedded in different overall calculations.

I shall now argue for a conclusion about what is required to understand a stream of assertions containing an ordinary singular term, and use the last supposition to upgrade this conclusion into a requirement on communicative uses of these terms in general.

I shall start with what I shall call 'no-suspicions' cases of response to a stream of assertions containing an ordinary singular term: cases where the hearer is treating the assertions as inputs to *ordinary* belief-forming activity in a situation which trips no sincerity or reliability alarm, so that in forming the beliefs the hearer is going along with the updates she takes the speaker to be proposing. (For example, I say, 'Agnes is 2 years old. She's medium-small. She's very athletic and affectionate, but a bit prone to over-excitement and afraid of other dogs'. You form the corresponding beliefs.) Given materials already in place, we can argue as follows:

(1) Part of the hearer's aim in a no-suspicions case is to respond to the incoming stream of assertions in a way that secures and sustains a cognitive focus relation. (This follows from the facts that the hearer's response involves ordinary belief-forming activity; part of this activity's aim is to secure and sustain aboutness relations; and aboutness relations are cognitive focus relations.)

(2) Where a hearer understands a speaker's utterance, the hearer's calculation of the proposed update is a manifestation of linguistic competence, so that any failure to fulfil her aims in engaging in the conversation traces to non-linguistic factors.

Therefore

(3) In a no-suspicions case, the hearer understands the incoming assertions only if her update calculations secure the result that, unless some non-linguistic

---

[24] I intend this claim to be read consistently with Recanati's 'semantic flexibility' thesis (Recanati 2010 pp. 43–6), according to which the 'standing meaning' of a lexical simple is constant, but its contribution to the update carried by a token sentence containing it is its 'modulated meaning', where this is determined by various features of the context, including the illocutionary force of the token sentence.

factor intervenes, in forming beliefs as she does, she is sustaining a cognitive focus relation. [From (1) and (2)]

For example, (3) says that if you both understand and go along with my 'Agnes' assertions, your update calculations secure the result that, as long as you are also exercising competence at assessing my sincerity and reliability, you will be unlucky if there is not an object whose properties your resulting beliefs get right. In other words, if you understand me and form beliefs by uptake from my utterances, but the beliefs you form fail to be about anything, something other than your linguistic competence is to blame.

(3) is a conclusion about no-suspicions cases only—cases where a hearer is forming a body of beliefs by uptake from a series of assertions containing a singular term. But we are supposing that understanding depends on update calculations not uptake calculations. If you and I both understand an assertion, but you go along with it and I do not, our uptake calculations are different but our update calculations are the same. This lets us generalize (3) to a condition on understanding across all cases where a suitable backdrop could lead a hearer to move from calculation of the update to a belief formed by going along with it.

(4) A hearer's update calculations secure understanding of a stream of assertions only if, in any situation where she moves to belief by uptake from the same update calculations, and which differs from the actual situation as little as is consistent with this condition, her update calculations meet the require-ment at (3).

For example, suppose you do not go along with my 'Agnes' assertions: perhaps you have registered them as insincere. (4) entails that you nevertheless understand them only if nearby cases where you make the same update calculations but do go along with my assertions are cases where, if you are exercising competence at assessing my sincerity and reliability, you will be unlucky if there is not some object whose properties you are getting right by responding to my utterances as you do.

We are also supposing that understanding an expression is a manifestation of the same competence regardless of whether it is being used to ask a question, make an assertion, or perform an illocutionary act of some other kind. So (4) generalizes to (5):

(5) A hearer understands an utterance containing an expression only if the part of her update calculation concerned with this expression proceeds the same way it does in situations where she calculates updates in response to a stream of assertions containing the expression which she understands, and which otherwise differ from the actual situation as little as is consistent with this condition.

For example, (5) says that you understand my use of 'Agnes' in 'Have you seen Agnes?' only if, in calculating an update from my utterance, you treat the name the way you would treat it in a nearby situation in which you understood a stream of assertions containing it.

Combining (3)–(5), we get a necessary condition on understanding a token ordinary singular term:

(6) If a hearer understands ordinary singular term α as used in context c, the part of her update calculations concerned with α meets the following requirement: in all c^* where her update calculations treat α the same way while she is engaged in no-suspicions uptake from a stream of α-containing assertions, and which otherwise differ from c as little as is consistent with this condition, as long as she is exercising competence in tracking the speaker's sincerity and reliability, she will be unlucky if there is no object whose properties she is getting right by forming beliefs as she does.

I shall abbreviate the result at (6) by saying that a hearer understands an ordinary token singular term only if her update calculations involving it 'tend towards' cognitive focus. This note[25] considers some points of detail.

Given (6), if you and I understand one another's uses of a singular term, each of us is making update calculations that tend towards cognitive focus. But there is no requirement that either of us be achieving focus on anything. (This is the starting-point for a cognitive-focus-based treatment of understanding of empty singular terms.) Nor is there a requirement that, in a situation of mutual understanding where each protagonist is sustaining cognitive focus, there is some one object upon which both are focussed. But (6) does combine with a cognitive-focus-based characterization of assertions containing ordinary singular terms to entail a nearby claim. In the cognitive-focus framework, an ⌜α is Φ⌝ assertion is a report from inside the speaker's own focus-directed information-marshalling activity. But if I am forming beliefs by careful uptake from your assertions, and these assertions are reports from inside your focus-directed belief-forming activity, my belief-forming activity can be focussed on object o only if yours is: if your belief-forming activity is not focussed on o, then even if you are sincere and reliable, if I form beliefs by careful uptake from your utterances, it will be merely lucky if these beliefs match what o is like. So, though we do not have the claim that speakers who understand one another's uses of a singular term are using it to talk about some one thing, we do have a nearby but weaker claim: where speakers understand one another's uses of a singular term, each speaker is using it to talk about o iff the other is.

I have argued that a hearer understands a speaker's uses of an ordinary singular term only if her treatment of it in making update calculations tends towards

---

[25] (a) (6) applies only to *ordinary* singular terms, not to, for example, names for numbers. (b) If there are no c^* in which S engages in no-suspicions updates while treating α in the same way, the requirement in (6) is met trivially. But the requirement is only a necessary condition on understanding of *ordinary* singular terms, so nothing follows as to whether S understands α in such a case. (c) Usual issues about the identification of processes across situations arise, but nothing in this chapter depends on which among the usual pathways through these issues is to be preferred. (d) A full discussion would precisify the notion of the 'part of' an update calculation concerned with an expression, but I cannot pursue this matter here.

cognitive focus. If this is a right result, it should be possible to point to various features of our update calculations, and explain how they contribute to meeting this requirement. I shall consider one such feature—a familiar feature of our update calculations whose importance the cognitive focus framework shows in a new light.

In forming beliefs by careful uptake from other people's utterances, we make constant adjustments to allow for the fact that these utterances are made from perspectives other than our own. For example, if I describe NN as 'short' and you take me at my word, you will not just update your body of <NN> beliefs by adding <NN is short>, where the standards for shortness are your own or some ambient standards. Your update will tether the standards for shortness to those I am likely to be counting as appropriate—taking into account factors like how tall I am; whether I have just been discussing, or habitually discuss, basketball players; whether I live among taller-than-average people; and so on. If you are not in a position to reach an 'appropriate standards' calculation as part of your update verdict, you will leave the standards for shortness that you take to be carried by the update I am proposing appropriately imprecise. Similarly, if I say that NN is 'probably' going to show up for some event, your update will treat the appropriate standards of likeliness as sensitive to factors that might impact my threshold for application for 'probably', for example, how much I take to be at stake for myself and for you in whether or not NN shows up. If I, broken-record-like, deliver a stream of utterances concerning just one aspect of NN's narrative arc, you will not update your body of <NN> beliefs in a way that supposes that this is the most important aspect of what NN is like: you will adjust for the fact that I am telling you what is, at the time, uppermost from my point of view. In these and many other ways, when you use my NN utterances as a source of input to your body of <NN> beliefs, your language-understanding information-processing is making automatic adjustments to take account of the fact that my NN utterances are coming from my perspective.

In exchanges involving perceptual demonstratives, we engage in an extra layer of adjustments to allow for the speaker's perceptual point of view. If you are listening to me describe something I can see and you cannot (perhaps we are talking on the phone), you update the body of beliefs you are maintaining in response to my utterances in a way that is adjusted to what you know of the basic aspects of my perceptual perspective. Suppose I say 'It's really near'. How near you take 'near' to be will depend on (among other things) whether you take me to be outside looking across some reasonably open scene, or in an average-sized room. And in the case of perceptual demonstratives, a factor that is also present in our uses of proper names emerges more prominently: often, speakers express their beliefs in ways that minimize the difficulty of the adjustments the hearer must make. An ordinary adult speaker using a perception-based demonstrative to talk about something visible to both speaker and hearer will not usually describe the thing as 'moving away' when it is moving away from the speaker and towards the hearer, or as 'to the left' when it is on the speaker's left but the hearer's right.

This general point is familiar from discussions of what it takes to be competent with ordinary predicate expressions.[26] But in the cognitive focus framework, it emerges as central to an account of our understanding of singular terms. Without this kind of adjustment for the speaker's perspective, even if the speaker is sincere, reliable, and talking about some particular thing, it will be a matter of luck if the hearer, forming beliefs by uptake from the speaker's utterances, ends up with beliefs that match what this thing is like. It is only where each participant's update calculations include adjustments for the other's perspective that careful uptake from the other's utterances is a cognitive-focus-sustaining means to belief-formation.

And in recognizing this point, we have arrived at the aspect of the cognitive-focus-based view of communication using singular terms that it is the main burden of this section to establish. Communicative use of singular terms involves joint cognitive focus. Participants in a communicative assertion exchange incorporate elements of one another's perspectives into the calculations which determine the updates each takes the other to be proposing: to understand you I must let elements of your perspective determine aspects of my calculations of the updates associated with your utterances; to understand me, you must do the same. (Compare the structure of a 'relational' account of joint perceptual attention.[27] According to this kind of account, when you are engaged in joint attention, the presence of someone else, also attending to the object, and responding to the fact that you are doing so, is part of the story of the information-processing that generates your perceptual attentional experience. I am suggesting a parallel structure for understanding of singular terms. Understanding someone's uses of a singular term is not a matter of processing their utterances against a background in which the speaker figures as one among other aspects of the scenery. It requires incorporating aspects of the speaker's perspective into the parameter settings that determine how your update calculations go.)

There are many points at which questions might be raised about this proposal; many details requiring further development; and many applications to explore. Though I cannot embark on a full discussion here, I hope to have explained the proposal in sufficient detail to enable the reader to see one application: the solution to the puzzle from §2.

The puzzle was raised by cases like this:

(2c) That's beautiful. It's a bit dinged up. It's fantastic to drive though—it's the car I learned in.

---

[26] See for example, Szabo 2001; Recanati 2010 pp. 49–76.

[27] As developed in Campbell 2002 pp. 157–76.

In §2, we saw the problem this kind of case raises for the standard picture of communication using singular terms. Within that picture, the resource available to deal with non-specificity in the first sentence is to say that 'that' is used ambiguously—it might refer to the car token or the car type. The second sentence can then be treated as resolving the ambiguity in favour of the token. But this leaves us with no account of how the third sentence is bringing non-specificity back.

I have already sketched the solution to this problem that I want to propose. Communication using a singular term involves joint cognitive focus. And a focus relation has a degree of resolution which can vary as focus-sustaining activity proceeds. So (2c) illustrates a pattern that the cognitive focus framework predicts: speaker and hearer start at a coarse resolution; zoom in to a finer one; then zoom out again.

With the discussion of this section in place, it is possible to add some detail. In the cognitive focus framework, when speakers engaged in a no-suspicions to-and-fro of assertions understand one another, each is engaged in an information-marshalling activity which takes the other's utterances as inputs, incorporates aspects of the perspective from which they are being made, and generates beliefs treated as expressible using the singular term, where part of the aim is that all this happen in a way that sustains a relation of cognitive focus. One aspect of the speaker's perspective of which the hearer must be keeping track to fulfil this aim is the resolution at which the speaker is operating. For example, suppose that your $\ulcorner \alpha$ is $\Phi \urcorner$ utterances are reports from within an activity that is tracking the microscopic properties of some fine-grained ω. So when you say 'It's changed a lot in the last while', you mean that there has been a change that is large in microscopic terms. If I treat your utterance as input to an activity that is focussed at macroscopic resolution, I will form a belief that ascribes a large macroscopic change: because I have failed to adjust for resolution, my means of belief-formation is not tracking what the thing you are focussed on (or anything else) is like.

But we saw in §4 that the resolution of a cognitive focus relation is explained in terms of the range of properties treated as up for decision in the associated information-marshalling activity: shifts in resolution are shifts in this parameter. So we now have an account of the predicate-sensitivity of non-specificity phenomena. Felicitous non-specificity arises when, given the range of properties treated as up for decision in the phase of joint-focus-directed activity in which the speaker is soliciting the hearer's participation, this activity is focussed on more than one object. The availability of a non-specific reading of a token singular term depends on the predicate with which the term is combined because this is part of what determines the relevant range of properties. Given only the first sentence of (2c), the speaker has done nothing to expand the range of properties beyond some comparatively impoverished set carried in by the use of 'beautiful': properties that might be instantiated either by a car token or a car type. The second sentence expands the range of properties, thereby increasing the resolution of the focus relation. At the third sentence, the range is restricted again: speaker and hearer are zooming out.

The barrier to an ambiguity-based account of (2c) was that if we treat the shift from non-specificity in the first sentence to specificity in the second as resolution of ambiguity, we will have no account of why there should be a shift back to non-specificity in the third. So it is important to see how the current proposal does better in this regard. According to the cognitive focus framework, part of what guides a hearer's cognitive response to an assertion containing an ordinary singular term is a motivational state directed at securing and sustaining cognitive focus. Though we will almost always be attempting to fulfil other goals as well, to say this much is to acknowledge a role for cognitive focus in an account of why our language-understanding information-processing proceeds as it does. But, in general, the higher the resolution of a focus relation, the more work required to secure and sustain it. So one way to restrict the expenditure of information-processing resources in language understanding is to avoid trying to focus at a higher resolution than you must. The cognitive-focus-based model of understanding of singular terms therefore predicts that, unless there is something to prevent our doing so, we will tend to drift from finer-grained focus to coarser-grained— staying focussed without expending unnecessary effort to do so. (2c)-type cases emerge as supporting the model by matching this prediction.

6. The Standard Picture as a Limiting Case

I shall close by considering how far the proposal of this chapter really departs from the standard view.

The suggestion I shall make takes its shape from a point commonplace in discussions of theory change in the history of science.[28] Consider a case where a theory with reasonable-looking foundations and considerable predictive success encounters phenomena it seems unable to explain, prompting a search for, and move to, a new theory. Though it would, notoriously,[29] be over-reaching to uphold a universal version of this claim, in many instances the move from the initial theory to its successor conforms to a satisfying pattern. Taking the successor theory, and restricting some parameter values, we recover the laws of its

---

[28] This proposal is an instance of the kind of model of how views in philosophy of language that step away from various idealizations might relate to their predictively successful predecessors floated in Stanley and Beaver 2019.

[29] 'Convergent realism' in the philosophy of science is built around the suggestion that a strong version of this claim (according to which we recover not only the generalizations but also the referential relations of the predecessor theory) holds across a sufficiently wide range of cases. This is the target of the famous attack in Laudan 1981. Even the weaker claim in the text cannot be held to apply to *all* cases where what looked for a while like a good theory is supplanted by a successor.

predecessor: the new theory 'contains its predecessor as a limiting case'. For example, applying the Theory of Relativity to comparatively massive objects moving at speeds much slower than the speed of light, we 'recover' Newton's laws of motion.

It is perhaps not hard to see how this general pattern might apply to the discussion of this chapter. We have an initial family of theories, grouped under the label 'the standard picture' of the communicative use of singular terms. Each of these theories has foundational principles that appear plausible when approached from a suitable direction. And each enjoys considerable predictive success. But there are phenomena, for example, the dynamic specificity pattern described in §2, that theories in this initial family seem unable to explain. The cognitive-focus-based proposal is a candidate successor theory that does explain this phenomenon. It remains to show how the standard picture re-emerges from the new proposal as a limiting case.

What comes next will depend on which version of the standard picture we are trying to recover. And perhaps it will turn out that there are distinct, but equally compelling, stories to tell for different versions of the standard view: restrict the new proposal's parameters one way and get Frege's story; restrict them another and get Stalnaker's. Obviously it is not possible to explore the options here in detail. I shall rest with gesturing towards a rough-cut of what I want to propose.

Recall that the 'update' associated with an utterance is the cognitive move the hearer will make if she both understands it and goes along with it: if you understand my utterance but do not go along with it, you recognize but reject the update I am proposing. In the cognitive focus framework, a speaker making an assertion containing a singular term is offering the hearer an update that has two components:[30]

(a) The speaker is either proposing or endorsing participation in an information-marshalling activity associated with the singular term, and directed at securing and sustaining a relation of joint cognitive focus.

(b) The speaker is proposing a move within this activity.

So, for example, if I make an assertion containing a proper name that is new in the conversation, I am (a) proposing that you join me in associating the name with

---

[30] Compare the following proposal about gradable adjectives (Charlow 2022): when I say 'John is tall' I am proposing an update which has a prescriptive component (I am proposing that we treat only thresholds which include John as acceptable thresholds for tallness) and a descriptive component (I am saying that John meets every contextually acceptable threshold for tallness). This proposal makes fully explicit the prescriptive aspect of the update proffered by the utterance which is trying to come to the surface at, for example, Ludlow 2014 p. 113. Similarly, compare Charlow's account of imperatives (Charlow 2014, 2018): If I utter an imperative ('p!') I am proposing an update with a prescriptive component (I am proposing that you adopt a plan P (relative to which p is to be preferred) and a descriptive component (I am saying that, relative to P, p is to be preferred)).

an information-marshalling activity which takes utterances containing the name as input, delivers beliefs expressible using it as output, and is directed at securing and sustaining a relation of joint cognitive focus; and (b) proposing a move within the activity. (If the proper name is already in play in the conversation, the (a) part of the update involves endorsement of continuation in an existing activity, rather than proposed initiation of a new one.)

This aspect of the cognitive focus framework foregrounds its continuity with the tradition of 'expressivist' views, opposed to the suggestion that characterization of the proposed update associated with an assertion must be built around an account of an associated representational content (the 'proposition' that the speaker is proposing the hearer accept). The cognitive focus framework allows us to recognize that there are uses of singular terms that are in no way defective— they are perfectly understandable by the hearer—even though there is no specific representational content that the speaker is attempting to communicate. Non-specificity cases like those discussed in this chapter are one example. Another is the introduction of singular terms into a conversation when the work of getting a focus-directed activity up and running is still to be done. ('What's that?' you say, pointing to some 'thing' visible only as a speck on the horizon—a 'thing' which might turn out to be nothing at all, without rendering your use of the demonstrative defective.) In cases like these, according to the cognitive focus framework, the speaker is proposing that the hearer join (or continue in) a focus-directed information-marshalling activity associated with the singular term, but the focus relation will be established as the activity unfolds.[31]

But in many cases, a speaker using a singular term is associating it with an information-marshalling activity that is (already) focussed on a specific object. In these cases, from the theorist's point of view, it is a harmless shorthand to say that that speaker is using the term to communicate a message about this specific thing. If we consider only fragments of conversation where relations of cognitive focus are fixed at the outset, the standard picture of communication using singular terms emerges from the cognitive-focus-based proposal as a limiting case.

References

Anscombe, G. E. M. (2000) *Intention*. Cambridge, MA: Harvard University Press.

Bird, A. (2019) 'The aim of belief and the aim of science'. *Theoria* 34(2): 171–93.

Borg, E. (2012) *Pursuing Meaning*. Oxford: Oxford University Press.

Campbell, J. (2002) *Reference and Consciousness*. Oxford: Oxford University Press.

[31] I discuss cases like this involving descriptive names at Dickie 2019 pp. 29–33.

Charlow, N. (2014) 'Logic and semantics for imperatives'. *Journal of Philosophical Logic* 43(4): 617–64.

Charlow, N. (2018) 'Clause type, force, and normative judgement in the semantics of imperatives', in D. Fogal, D. Harris, and M. Moss (eds.), *New Work on Speech Acts.* Oxford: Oxford University Press.

Charlow, N. (2022) 'Metasemantic quandaries', in B. Dunaway (ed.), *Meaning, Decision, and Norms: Themes from the Work of Allan Gibbard.* Michigan: Michigan Publishing.

Dickie, I. (2015) *Fixing Reference.* Oxford: Oxford University Press. 2015.

Dickie, I. (2019) 'The subtle lives of descriptive names', in E. Lepore and D. Sosa (eds.), *Oxford Studies in Philosophy of Language*, vol. 1. Oxford: Oxford University Press.

Dickie, I. (2020) "Understanding singular terms', *Aristotelian Society Supplementary Volume New Series* XCIV: 19–55.

Dickie, I. and G. Rattan. (2010) 'Sense, communication, and rational engagement', *Dialectica*, 64(2): 131–151.

Dummett, M. (1981) *Frege: Philosophy of Language* (second edition). London: Duckworth.

Evans, G. (1982) *The Varieties of Reference.* Oxford: Oxford University Press.

Frege, G. (1984) 'Thoughts', trans P. Geach and R. Stoothoff, in *Frege: Collected Papers on Mathematics, Logic and Philosophy.* Oxford: Blackwell, 351–32.

Geurts, Bart, David I. Beaver, and Emar Maier (2020) 'Discourse representation theory', *The Stanford Encyclopedia of Philosophy* (Spring 2020 edition), ed. Edward N. Zalta <https://plato.stanford.edu/archives/spr2020/entries/discourse-representation-theory/>.

Heck, R. (1995) 'The sense of communication', *Mind New Series*, 104 (413): 79–106.

Heck, R. (2017) 'Cognitive hunger', *Philosophy and Phenomenological Research*, 95 (3): 738–44.

Kaplan, D. (1989) 'Demonstratives', in J. Almog, J. Perry, and D. Wettstein (eds.), *Themes from Kaplan.* New York: Oxford University Press.

Katz, R. (1987) *Love Is Colder than Death: The Life and Times of Rainer Werner Fassbinder.* New York: Random House, 481–563.

Kelp, C. (2017) 'Knowledge first virtue epistemology', in J. A. Carter, E. C. Gordon, and B. Jarvis (eds.), *Knowledge First: Approaches in Epistemology and Mind.* Oxford: Oxford University Press.

King, J. (2018) 'Strong contextual felicity and felicitous underspecification', *Philosophy and Phenomenological Research* 97 (3): 631–57.

Laudan, L. (1981) 'A confutation of convergent realism', *Philosophy of Science* 48 (1): 19–49.

Lewis, D. (1988) 'Relevant implication' *Theoria*, 54(3): 161–174.

Lewis, D. (1999) 'Many, but almost one', *Lewis: Papers in Metaphysics and Epistemology.* Cambridge: Cambridge University Press.

Ludlow, P. (2014) *Living Words*. Oxford: Oxford University Press.

Pagin, P. (2008) 'What is communicative success?', *Canadian Journal of Philosophy* 38 (1): 85–115.

Peet, A. (2019) 'Knowledge-yielding communication', *Philosophical Studies* 176: 3303–27.

Quine, W. v. O. (1953) 'Identity, ostension, and hypostasis', *Quine: From a Logical Point of View*. Cambridge, MA: Harvard University Press.

Recanati, F. (2010) *Truth Conditional Pragmatics*. Oxford: Oxford University Press.

Sosa, E. (2015) *Judgment and Agency*. Oxford: Oxford University Press.

Soteriou, M. (2013) *The Mind's Construction*. Oxford: Oxford University Press.

Stalnaker, R. (1989a) 'Assertion', *Stalnaker: Context and Content*. Cambridge, MA: MIT Press, 78–95.

Stalnaker, R. (1989b) 'On the representation of context', *Stalnaker: Context and Content*. Cambridge, MA: MIT Press, 96–113.

Stalnaker, R. (2009) 'What is de re belief', in Joseph Almog and Paolo Leonardi (eds.), *The Philosophy of David Kaplan*. Oxford: Oxford University Press, 233–45.

Stanley, J. and D. Beaver. (2019) 'Toward a non-ideal philosophy of language', *New School Graduate Faculty Philosophy Journal* 39 (2): 501–45.

Stokke, A. and Schoubye, A. J. (2016) 'What is said?', *Noûs* 50 (4): 759–93.

Szabo, Z. G. (2001) 'Adjectives in context', in I. Kenesei and R. Harnish (eds.), *Perspectives on Semantics, Pragmatics, and Discourse: A Festschrift for Ferenc Kiefer*. Amsterdam: Benjamins, 119–46.

Szabo, Z. G. (2020) 'The goal of conversation', *Aristotelian Society Supplementary Volume New Series* XCIV: 57–86.

Velleman, J. D. (2000) 'On the aim of belief', *Velleman: The Possibility of Practical Reason*. Oxford: Oxford University Press, 244–81.

Weatherson, B. (2014) 'The problem of the many', *The Stanford Encyclopedia of Philosophy* (Winter 2016 edition), ed. Edward N. Zalta <https://plato.stanford.edu/archives/win2016/entries/problem-of-many/>.

Yalcin, S. (2016) 'Belief as Question-Sensitive'. *Philosophy and Phenomenological Research*, 97(1): 23–47.

4

Luck and Metasemantics

Jeffrey C. King

In a series of works, Duncan Pritchard has defended a modal account of luck.[1] On this account, events are the things that are lucky or not. For an event to be lucky is for it to occur in the actual world but, keeping the initial conditions for the event fixed, for there to be close possible worlds in which the event doesn't occur.[2] So, for example, on this view the event of one's winning a lottery that is fair with long odds is lucky, since there are nearby possible worlds with the same initial conditions for the event of winning the lottery where the numbered balls fall in a slightly different way such that one loses. Here the initial conditions to be held fixed are that one buy the lottery ticket, that the lottery is fair with the same long odds, and so on. The justification for these initial conditions is that we don't want to say that the event of winning the lottery was lucky because there are nearby worlds in which one fails to buy a lottery ticket or in which the odds of winning are far lower and one loses. As usual, Pritchard's talk of closeness of worlds to the actual world is to be understood in terms of similarity: a world *w* that is more similar to the actual world than *w'* is closer to the actual world.

Pritchard's interest in luck stems from his idea that knowledge is incompatible with luck in the following sense: if the event of forming a true belief is lucky, the true belief can't count as knowledge. Here is one of Pritchard's (2014) examples illustrating this point. A subject buys a lottery ticket and, on the basis of learning the long odds of her ticket winning, forms the belief that it is a loser. In fact, it is a loser. The event of forming the true belief is lucky because there are close by possible worlds in which she formed a false belief that her ticket is a loser (and so the event of forming the true belief didn't occur) and in which the initial conditions are held fixed. Such worlds are close by because all that would have to change is that the balls would have to fall in a slightly different configuration so

---

[1] See Pritchard (2005, 2007, 2012, 2014) and citations therein.

[2] Pritchard (2014) p. 599. In Pritchard (2007), he puts the idea of a lucky event a bit differently. He says a lucky event is one that obtains in the actual world but does not obtain in *a wide range of nearby possible worlds* in which the initial conditions are held fixed. The difference in these formulations is not relevant for our purposes.

Jeffrey C. King, *Luck and Metasemantics* In: *Linguistic Luck: Safeguards and Threats to Linguistic Communication.* Edited by: Abrol Fairweather and Carlos Montemayor, Oxford University Press. © Oxford University Press 2023. DOI: 10.1093/oso/9780192845450.003.0004

that her ticket won.[3] The initial conditions here again are that the subject buys the lottery ticket as she did in the actual world and that "the lottery retains many of its salient features": it is free and fair, the odds are the same as in the actual world, etc. Because her forming the true belief that her ticket is a loser is lucky, she doesn't know that her ticket is a loser. In this case, the false belief formed in the relevant possible worlds is a belief in the same proposition that the subject forms a belief about in the actual world: the proposition that her ticket is a loser. However, in other cases this won't be so. Consider the following example from Pritchard (2012). Mathema uses a calculator to find 12×13. As a result, she forms the true belief that $12 \times 13 = 156$. Unbeknownst to Mathema the calculator is broken and is giving random answers. Here intuitively she doesn't know the target proposition, but there is no world where the proposition she believes, and so her belief, are false. This means that we cannot read Pritchard's safety principle— If S knows that p, then S's true belief that p could not have easily been false[4]—as saying that the agent's belief that p in similar circumstances would not easily be false. If we said that, Mathema's belief would be safe, not lucky and she would know that $12 \times 13 = 156$.[5] What we are interested in is how the agent forms her beliefs in similar circumstances in response to the same stimuli. So though Mathema could not form the belief that $12 \times 13 = 156$ in other circumstances and believe falsely, there are lots of possible worlds in which she forms her belief on the same basis (broken calculator) and ends up with a false belief because the calculator generates a different result. Hence Mathema's true belief is unsafe and lucky and so not an instance of knowledge.[6] I'll follow Pritchard in holding that lucky true beliefs do not constitute knowledge.

Three other features of Pritchard's account of luck are worth mentioning. First, I have thus far talked about whether an event was lucky or not. But Pritchard's account yields a continuum of lucky events with different degrees of luck being determined by the closeness of the worlds in which the relevant event fails to occur. The further away such a world is from the actual world, the less lucky the event. At some point when the relevant world is sufficiently far away, we regard the event in question as not lucky since its degree of luck is not significant. In any case, because of these differing degrees of luck, we can talk of one event being luckier than another. To illustrate this point, Pritchard gives the example of the event of not being hit by a sniper's bullet. In scenario A, the bullet misses by a few millimeters and in scenario B it misses by a meter. Intuitively, the event of not

---

[3] There is a worry that on this account *losing* the lottery will be lucky, since there are nearby worlds with the same initial conditions where the numbered balls fall in a slightly different way such that one wins. It may be that the different formulation of what constitutes a lucky event in note 2 can address this worry. Because of considerations of space, I cannot pursue these issues here.

[4] Pritchard (2012) p. 253.

[5] I'll say that a belief is lucky (or not) just in case the event of forming it is lucky (or not).

[6] Pritchard (2012) takes his safety principle so understood to be an anti-luck condition on knowledge (p. 257).

being hit by a sniper's bullet in scenario A is luckier than the event of not being hit by a sniper's bullet in scenario B. Pritchard's account gets this result since the worlds in which one is hit by the bullet are closer in scenario A than they are in scenario B. Second, Pritchard's account is intentionally silent on the question of whether a lucky event is good or bad luck. That is because Pritchard thinks that our judgments about good and bad luck are subjective responses to lucky events and that lucky events are not intrinsically good or bad. Third, there are cases of events that Pritchard's account will deem lucky, but that we would be unlikely to call lucky. He gives the example of a lucky small avalanche in a remote unoccupied region of the South Pole. Pritchard thinks that only significant events are labeled lucky by us: only events that we care about or make a difference to us are called lucky. But he thinks that insignificant events like the small avalanche are still lucky (or not). A metaphysics of lucky events should not try to pronounce on our subjective responses to lucky events such as how much people have to care about a lucky event to regard it as lucky or whether we regard a lucky event as good luck or bad luck.

I intend to take on Pritchard's modal account of luck here without argument. I do so because it is the best account of luck known to me. Above I talked about Pritchard's applying his account of luck in epistemology. Other areas of philosophy have literatures discussing luck, most notably in ethics with the notion of moral luck.[7] However, the question that concerns me here is whether the notion of luck has significant application in philosophy of language: is there a significant notion of linguistic or even syntactic, semantic, or pragmatic luck or lack thereof? *Prima facie* it seems likely that there is. After all, intuitively in normal instances of successful communication it doesn't seem as though that the communication occurred was a matter of luck. However, there are unusual cases of successful linguistic communication that are lucky. Here is one. I am looking at a picture of Ernie that I think Michael can see as well. It turns out he can't see it but he can see the back of the frame of the picture. Pointing at the picture, I say 'He is a philosopher.' intending to refer to Ernie with my use of 'He'. Unbeknownst to me, there is a picture of Ernie on the back of the frame holding the picture I am pointing to that Michael can see and that has been recently placed there temporarily by someone who temporarily placed a number of pictures in different locations. Michael wrongly thinks that I am pointing to the picture on the back of the frame. Intuitively, communication succeeds in this case. As a result of my utterance, Michael grasps the proposition I intended to convey in uttering as I did.[8] Now consider the event of Michael grasping the proposition I intended to convey:

---

[7] See Nagel (1979) (especially chapter 3) and Williams (1981) (especially chapter 2).

[8] Though this is what makes the present case a case of successful communication, I don't think that in every case in which a hearer grasps the proposition that a speaker intends to convey in uttering as she did the result is successful communication. Consider this famous case from Loar (1976): "Suppose that

the proposition that Ernie is a philosopher. There are nearby worlds in which that event doesn't occur because the additional picture of Ernie wasn't placed behind the frame and either a picture of someone else was placed there instead or no picture was placed there. Hence, Michael grasping the proposition I intended to convey, and hence the successful communication, was lucky. However, there should be mechanisms for avoiding even *successful* lucky linguistic communication. After all, if luck were a common feature of successful communication, it seems unlikely that successful communication would be reliable. And yet successful linguistic communication does seem reliable. Hence, we should expect there to be a variety of broadly linguistic mechanisms that eliminate luck in cases of normal linguistic communication. Let's call any such mechanism an *anti-linguistic luck mechanism* (ALLM).[9]

Following Stalnaker (1999, 2002), I'll assume that at every point in a conversation, there is a set of propositions that conversational participants accept for the purposes of conversation, believe that they all accept for the purposes of conversation, believe that they all believe that they all accept for the purposes of conversation, etc. Stalnaker calls this the *common ground*.[10] Stalnaker models the common ground by the *context set*: the set of worlds in which all common ground propositions are true. Such worlds are the live options at a given point in the conversation for being the actual world for the purposes of the conversation.

The first question that now confronts us is: what events involved in successful communication must generally fail to be lucky in order that successful communication be reliable? Three types of events immediately come to mind. First, there is the event of a hearer in the usual way correctly representing the syntax of an uttered sentence belonging to a language the hearer speaks. Presumably the ALLM underwriting such events not being lucky is the hearer's language faculty encoding

---

Smith and Jones are unaware that the man being interviewed on television is someone they see on the train every morning and about whom, in that latter role, they have just been talking. Smith says 'He is a stockbroker', intending to refer to the man on television; Jones takes Smith to be referring to the man on the train. Now Jones, as it happens, has correctly identified Smith's referent, since the man on television is the man on the train; but he has failed to understand Smith's utterance" (p. 357). Contrary to what Loar claims, I think here Jones grasps the proposition Smith intended to convey in uttering as he did. There are nearby possible worlds in which the man on television and the man they see on the train are distinct, so that Jones grasping this proposition is lucky. But communication does not succeed here. My own view is that the reason communication breaks down here is that both Smith and Jones believe that the man they see on the train and the man on TV are distinct. Since Smith was trying to talk about the man on TV and Jones took him to be talking about the man on the train and both think these are two different men, communication fails (Unnsteinsson 2018 seems to suggest this too). That this is so is supported by the fact that if we change the example by making Smith and Jones both truly believe that the man on the train is the man on TV, intuitively communication succeeds luckily.

[9] Abrol Fairweather and Carlos Montemayor raise the question whether all linguistic luck is bad luck. It seems to me that if we communicate luckily in a situation in which it is very important to us that we succeed in communicating, that is good luck. But it is true that it would be bad to have lots of luck in successful communication, since that would render successful communication unreliable. So it isn't that linguistic luck is always bad luck. It's that it is bad (not a good thing) to have lots of luck (good or bad) in communication. So we need to distinguish good or bad linguistic luck in particular instances from it being bad for there to be lots of luck in successful communication.

[10] Stalnaker (2002) p. 716.

the correct syntax for the language to which the sentence uttered belongs.[11] I will have nothing more to say about these events. Second, there is the event of a hearer forming true beliefs about the semantic values in context of the expressions (words) in an uttered sentence belonging to a language she speaks in the usual way by attending to the speaker and the common ground.[12] Finally, there is the event of a hearer forming a true belief in the usual way about the proposition expressed in context by an uttered sentence belonging to a language she speaks. Events of this third type not being lucky are presumably underwritten by the corresponding events of the first two types not being lucky and the hearer's language faculty encoding a compositional semantic theory for the language to which the uttered sentence belongs.[13] Again, I will have nothing further to say about events of this third type.

This leaves us with events of the second type: the event of a hearer forming true beliefs about the semantic values in context of the expressions (words) in an uttered sentence belonging to a language she speaks in the usual way by attending to the speaker and the common ground.[14] Here I want to focus on the case in which the expressions in question are contextually sensitive. More specifically, I want to focus on contextually sensitive expressions that are not pure indexicals like 'I'. This class of expressions includes tense, gradable adjectives, quantifiers (by way of quantifier domain restriction), expressions that take implicit arguments like 'ready', deictic pronouns, simple and complex demonstratives, 'only', modals and possessives, among others. I believe expressions in this class differ from pure indexicals like 'I' in that their context independent meanings do not by themselves suffice to secure semantic values for them in context, whereas the context independent meaning of 'I' precisely does suffice. Hence, I claim expressions in this class require some sort of supplementation in context to secure semantic values in context. For this reason, I call these expressions *supplementives*. I call an account of the mechanism by means of which a given supplementive secures a semantic value in context a *metasemantics* for the supplementive in question. In a series of papers, I have defended a metasemantics that I claim applies to all supplementives.[15] I call my metasemantics the *coordination account* and it can be stated as follows:

---

[11] If one follows Chomsky, as I do, in believing that each of us has her own I language and believing that to say that two people whose I languages differ both speak the same language is to say that their I languages are sufficiently similar to each other, then what I said in the text is only approximately correct. Instead, we must say the hearer's language faculty encodes a syntax that is sufficiently similar to the syntax encoded by speaker's language faculty that generated the syntax of the uttered sentence.

[12] It seems that in normal cases the hearer must attend to the common ground, since she usually knows who the speaker is (when she does), and so who she should attend to, because it is common ground.

[13] As before, if we follow Chomsky on I languages, we have to complicate this claim a bit.

[14] I won't keep adding that the hearer speaks the language in question but I will continue to assume she does.

[15] King (2020, 2013, 2014a, 2014b).

Coordination Account Metasemantics

A speaker S's use of a supplementive δ in context c has o as its semantic value iff (1) S intends o to be the semantic value of δ in c; and (2) a competent, reasonable, attentive hearer H who knows the common ground of the conversation at the time S utters δ and who has the properties attributed to the audience by the common ground at the time S utters δ would know that S intends o to be the semantic value of δ in c.[16] I sometimes abbreviate the second condition by saying that an idealized hearer would know that S intends o to be the semantic value of δ in c; and, more generally, I'll talk of the idealized hearer posited by the second condition.

Assuming the coordination account, let's return to the events we will be concerned with: a hearer forming a true belief in the usual way about the semantic value in context of a supplementive in an uttered sentence by attending to the speaker and the common ground. I assume any such hearer has the properties mentioned in condition (2) of the coordination account: she is competent, reasonable, and attentive, knows the common ground of the conversation at the time of utterance and has the properties attributed to the audience by the common ground at the time of utterance. The assumptions that the hearer is competent, reasonable, attentive, and knows the common ground at the time of utterance are required to insure that the hearer formed the true belief about the semantic value in context of the supplementive in the usual way by attending to the speaker and the common ground.[17] Obviously, the hearer must be competent, attentive, and know the common ground to form the true belief about the semantic value in context of the supplementive by attending to the speaker and the common ground. If she isn't competent, she can't form the relevant true belief by attending to the speaker and the common ground; and if she is attending to the speaker she is attentive. Finally, she can't attend to the common ground at the time of utterance if she doesn't know it. An additional reason for requiring our hearer who forms a true belief about the semantic value in context of an utterance of a supplementive to know the common ground is that very often knowledge of the common ground plays a central role in forming a true belief about the semantic value of a supplementive in context. For example, suppose it is common ground between us that John John Florence is the best surfer in the world. We have been watching a surf contest in which he is competing and has been surfing better than anyone else. Before the results are announced, we mutually recognize that we are looking down at the contestants, including Florence, shaking hands. Without pointing or anything else, I say 'He is so much better than the other surfers.'

---

[16] This is a version of the coordination account I call *Bad Intentions* in King (2013). I actually now favor the version of the coordination account I there call *Best Laid Plans*, but the latter is more complex and the additional complexity won't be relevant to the examples in the present chapter.

[17] I'll henceforth drop 'in the usual way' in talking about forming these beliefs but will assume the beliefs are formed in the usual way.

Due to your knowledge of the common ground, you form the true belief that Florence is the semantic value in context of my use of 'He'.

Further, that the hearer be reasonable is also required to insure that she forms such a true belief by attending to the speaker and the common ground in the usual way, since an unreasonable hearer could well form such a true belief in a bizarre way. We are interested in cases in which a hearer forms the relevant belief in the usual way. Finally, we can assume that the hearer in question possesses the properties the common ground attributes to her at the time of utterance of the supplementive in question. For the only such properties that are relevant here are the properties attributed to her by the common ground at the time of utterance that are relevant to recognizing the speaker's intentions. These will be things like being physically situated with respect to the speaker in a certain way, being a young child, not being deaf, etc. It would be hard for the common ground to get such things wrong. Alternatively, we could restrict condition (2) by saying that the idealized hearer possesses the properties truly attributed to the audience by the common ground at the time of utterance and so require here only that our hearer possesses these properties. Hence, we assume that in the cases we consider of a hearer forming a true belief about the semantic value in context of a use of a supplementive, our hearer is a competent, reasonable, attentive hearer who knows the common ground of the conversation at the time of utterance and who has the properties attributed to the audience by the common ground at the time of utterance.

With this much in place, I intend to argue that there is a sense in which the coordination account is an ALLM. In particular, in a case where the hearer forms a true belief about the semantic value of a supplementive in context by attending to the speaker and the common ground and the coordination account determines that semantic value, there are no nearby worlds that share the initial conditions of the actual world of utterance where that true belief is not formed. That is, the event of forming the true belief is not lucky. The first question that confronts us is: what are the relevant initial conditions that must hold in the nearby worlds we consider? It seems to me that a natural answer to this question is that the nearby worlds must be very much like the actual world with respect to all central features of the actual conversation including the features that the metasemantics under discussion claims fix the semantic value in context of the supplementive in question. In particular, the following conditions must hold in the nearby worlds we consider: (1) The conversation up to the point of the relevant utterance of the sentence containing the supplementive proceeds in very much the same way it did in the actual world; (2) At the time of the utterance, the speaker and the hearer are positioned as they are in the actual world and behave more or less as they did in the actual world in respects relevant to communication (e.g. if the hearer was carefully attending to the speaker in the actual world, she is doing the same thing in the nearby possible world; but perhaps she takes a sip of coffee at the time of utterance in the actual world but not in some relevant nearby possible worlds); (3) The speaker in uttering the sentence had the same intention regarding the semantic value in context for the supplementive in question as she did in the actual world; (4) That intention satisfies the conditions of the coordination account in the same way it did in the actual world. For example, if the speaker makes his intention recognizable to an idealized hearer with a pointing gesture in the actual world, he does so with that same gesture in the possible worlds we consider. Notice that the first two conditions insure that the conversations in possible worlds under consideration closely resemble the conversation in the actual world. The final two conditions insure that the features of the conversation that the coordination account claims fix the semantic value in context of the supplementive in question in the actual world are the same in the possible worlds we consider. Hence, when we consider other metasemantic accounts, the first two conditions will be the same and the second two will change to reflect the metasemantic account under consideration.

Note that this means that at a certain level of abstraction, the initial conditions will be the same for each metasemantic account we consider. Conditions (1) and (2) will be exactly the same for each account we consider. Additional conditions for each metasemantic account we consider will insure that the features of the conversation and its context that the metasemantic account claims fix the semantic value in context of the relevant supplementive remain unchanged. That means that when I argue, as I will, that if the coordination account is the correct metasemantics, the formation of a true belief about the semantic value in context of a supplementive is never lucky, whereas it is can be on rival accounts, one cannot respond that I built too much into the initial conditions when considering the coordination account. In the relevant sense, the initial conditions used in considering all metasemantic accounts are the same: the conversation proceeds pretty much as it did in the actual world and the features that the metasemantic account under consideration claims fix the semantic value in context for the supplementive remain unchanged.

Let me say a few words in defense of our four initial conditions here. In defense of condition (1), we don't want to say that the formation of a true belief about the semantic value in context of a supplementive was lucky because there are nearby worlds in which the conversation prior to the utterance of the sentence containing the supplementive proceeds differently and in which the true belief wasn't formed. For example, often the common ground will play a role in the hearer forming a true belief about the semantic value in context of a supplementive on virtually any metasemantics for supplementives. We don't want to say that the formation of the true belief in such a case was lucky because there are nearby worlds in which the common ground is different and the true belief wasn't formed. With respect to condition (2), we don't want to say that the formation of a true belief about the semantic value in context of a supplementive was lucky because there are nearby worlds in which the hearer is behind the speaker or out of earshot and so failed to form the belief. Assuming the coordination account, we need condition (3) because we don't want to say that the formation of a true belief about the semantic value in context of a supplementive was lucky because there are nearby worlds in which the speaker had a different intention and the relevant true belief wasn't formed. Similarly, we need condition (4) because we don't want to say that the formation of a true belief about the semantic value in context of a supplementive was lucky because there are nearby worlds in which the speaker had an intention that failed to satisfy the conditions of the coordination account or satisfied those conditions in a very different way such that the hearer would not have recognized it and so failed to form the relevant true belief.

Now let's walk through a case of a hearer forming a true belief about the semantic value in context of a supplementive by attending to the speaker and the common ground, where we assume that the coordination account determines that semantic value in context. Suppose I point to Ernie and say 'He is a philosopher.' where the coordination account determines Ernie as the semantic value in context c of 'He'. That means that I intend Ernie to be the semantic value in the context c of 'He'; and a competent, reasonable, attentive hearer H who knows the common ground of the conversation at the time I uttered 'He' and who has the properties attributed to the audience by the common ground at the time I uttered 'He' would know that I intend Ernie to be the semantic value of 'He' in c. Presumably, in a case like this the latter condition is satisfied because of my clearly pointing at Ernie, which makes clear that I intend him to be the semantic value in context of my use of 'He'. In other cases, e.g. the John John Florence case discussed earlier, the second condition of the coordination account is satisfied in large part because of the common ground at the time of utterance. Now recall that we are assuming that the actual hearer, H', is competent, attentive, and reasonable, knows the common ground at the time I uttered, and has the properties attributed to her by the common ground. But since Ernie is the semantic value in context of my use of 'He' and the coordination account determines that he is, the latter entails that a competent, attentive, reasonable hearer who knows the common ground at the time of utterance and possesses the properties attributed by the common ground to the audience at the time of utterance, would know that I intended Ernie to be the semantic value of my use of 'He' in context. That means that my actual hearer H' knows that I intend Ernie to be the semantic value of 'He' in context, since H' is competent, attentive, reasonable, knows the common ground at the time of my utterance and possesses the properties attributed by the common ground to my audience at the time of utterance. But then H' knows that Ernie satisfies the coordination account conditions for Ernie being the semantic value of my use of 'He' in c. Since H' tacitly knows the coordination account (I assume this is part of the linguistic competence of H'), it follows that H' knows that Ernie is the semantic value of my use of 'He' in c. Since knowledge has an anti-luck safety condition, it follows that there are no nearby worlds satisfying the relevant initial conditions in which the true belief of H' that Ernie is the semantic value of my use of 'He' in c is not formed. Hence, H' forming the true belief that Ernie is the semantic value of my use of 'He' is not lucky. So if the coordination account is the correct metasemantics for supplementives, when a hearer forms a true belief about the semantic value in context of a supplementive, there are no nearby worlds in which the hearer fails to form that true belief. Hence, the formation of that true belief is not lucky. As a result, I'll say that the coordination account is an *anti-luck metasemantics*.

In previous work, I have given arguments in favor of the coordination account and against rival metasemantic accounts.[18] I believe the fact that in a case where the hearer forms a true belief about the semantic value of a supplementive in context by attending to the speaker and the common ground and the coordination account determines that semantic value, there are no nearby worlds that share the initial conditions of the world of utterance where that true belief is not formed—that is, the forming of this true belief is not lucky—is an argument in favor of the coordination account. As I've indicated, since we have an interest in linguistic communication being reliable, we should expect there to be mechanisms in place in language, ALLMs, that insure that events that are crucial to successful communication are not lucky. Surely, one type of event that is crucial to successful communication and so we would want not to be lucky is a hearer forming a true belief about the semantic value of a supplementive in context. Hence, we should expect a metasemantics for supplementives to render such events non-lucky. As we have seen, the coordination account does this. But then that is an argument in favor of it. Similarly, that a metasemantics for supplementives *doesn't* insure that such events are non-lucky is an argument against it. I now wish to argue that such arguments can be given against some rival metasemantic accounts. In discussing them we can assume that in the cases of hearers forming true beliefs about the semantic value of a supplementive in context, where we assume one of these rival metasemantic accounts is correct, the hearer is competent, attentive, and reasonable, knows the common ground at the time of utterance, and has the properties attributed to her by the common ground at the time of utterance. We do this so that the assumptions made in discussing the coordination account and those made in discussing rival accounts are the same. However, these assumptions really play no role on rival accounts. As suggested above, we'll also have to consider what initial conditions to keep fixed in other possible worlds in discussing rival accounts. We'll do that for each rival account we consider.

First, consider the view of Kaplan (1977) according to which an associated demonstration fixes the semantic value in context of demonstratives and

---

[18] King (2013, 2014a, 2014b, 2020).

deictically used pronouns. Following Kaplan, I'll use 'demonstratives' in such a way that it applies to demonstratives narrowly construed ('that'; 'that woman') and to deictic pronouns in discussing him. Kaplan writes:

> Some of the indexicals require, in order to determine their referents, an associated demonstration: typically, though not invariably, a (visual) presentation of a local object discriminated by a pointing. These indexicals are the true demonstratives, and 'that' is their paradigm. The demonstrative (an expression) refers to that which the demonstration demonstrates. I call that which is demonstrated the 'demonstratum.'
>
> A demonstrative without an associated demonstration is incomplete. The linguistic rules which govern the use of the true demonstratives 'that', 'he', etc., are not sufficient to determine their referent in all contexts of use. Something else—an associated demonstration—must be provided. The linguistic rules assume that such a demonstration accompanies each (demonstrative) use of a demonstrative.[19]

Call this account of how demonstratives secure semantic values in context the *demonstration account*. The initial conditions we need to keep fixed in the possible worlds we consider in discussing this account are: (1) The conversation up to the point of the relevant utterance of the sentence containing the supplementive proceeds in very much the same way it did in the actual world; (2) At the time of the utterance, the speaker and the hearer are positioned as they are in the actual world and behave more or less as they did in the actual world in respects relevant to communication; (3) The speaker performs the same demonstration as she did in the actual world and the demonstrated thing, the speaker, and her audience are located as they are in the actual world. Here the first two conditions insure that the conversation proceeds as it does in the actual world; and the third condition insures that the mechanism that the demonstration account claims fixes the semantic value in context of the supplementive is the same as it is in the actual world.

It is easy to see that this account will allow events of forming true beliefs about the semantic values in context of demonstratives to be lucky. For example, suppose we are at school and you are looking for a philosophy major to talk to about the philosophy department. I know this and I point down a hallway where two males are standing in fairly close proximity to each other talking. I say 'He is a philosophy major' clearly pointing at the student on the left and walk away.

---

[19] Kaplan (1977) pp. 490–491. Obviously, this metasemantics does not apply to all supplementives but only to demonstratives, which include deictic pronouns for Kaplan. Also, Kaplan takes simple ('that') and complex demonstratives ('that man') to be devices of direct reference, whereas I take them to be quantifiers as argued in King (2001). Here I am using the expression 'demonstrative' in a non-Kaplanesque way so that it does not apply to deictic pronouns, by contrast with the way I use 'demonstrative' in the main text when discussing Kaplan.

Unfortunately from your angle you can't tell which male I demonstrated. However, you notice that the student on the left is holding a book and he turns slightly allowing you to see the following lettering which you recognize is only part of what is on the book cover: 'Aristo'. You can't make the other letters out. On the basis of the fact that you think the word 'Aristotle' is on the book cover, you form the true belief that I demonstrated the student on the left. Assuming that the demonstration account is the correct metasemantics for supplementives, you tacitly know that it is in virtue of your linguistic competence. Hence, you form the true belief that the student on the left is the semantic value in context of my use of 'He'. In fact the student on the left is holding a novel with the title 'Aristocrats' on its cover. Suppose that it is a fact about you that had you not seen the letters on the book cover you did or had you seen all of the letters, you would not have formed the belief that the student on the left is the semantic value in context of my use of 'He'. Obviously, then, there are very nearby worlds in which you didn't form the true belief about the semantic value in context of my use of 'He'. Such worlds include ones where the student turned just a bit more so that you could make out the title of the book he was holding and those in which he didn't turn enough for you to make out the letters you did make out. Hence, the event of your forming the true belief about the semantic value in context of the pronoun was lucky.

Suppose now that the correct metasemantics for supplementives is that the semantic value of a use of a supplementive δ in context c is the object o that the speaker S intends to be its semantic value in c.[20] Call this the *intention account*. This differs from the coordination account in lacking its second condition. Here the initial conditions to keep fixed are: (1) The conversation up to the point of the relevant utterance of the sentence containing the supplementive proceeds in very much the same way it did in the actual world; (2) At the time of the utterance, the speaker and the hearer are positioned as they are in the actual world and behave more or less as they did in the actual world in respects relevant to communication; (3) The speaker has the same intention as she does in the actual world, it is as recognizable as it is in the actual world and it is recognizable in the same way. The same scenario that we used to show that the demonstration account allows for luckily forming true beliefs about the semantic value of demonstratives in context shows the same thing for the intention account. So consider that scenario where I say 'He is a philosopher' pointing at the student on the left and intending that he be the semantic value of 'He' in context. In this case, your guide to who I intend to

---

[20] Kaplan (1989) p. 582 adopts a version of this view for what he calls *perceptual demonstratives* by which I believe he means a demonstrative used to refer to an object the speaker is perceiving. He talks of the *directing intention* determining the referent in such a case by which I think he means the intention to point at the perceived object in using the demonstrative. I believe this is a version of the present view because in intending to point at the perceived object in using the demonstrative one is intending to refer to it with the demonstrative.

be the semantic value in context is my pointing gesture. So again, given your orientation, you can't tell who I am pointing at and so who I intend to be the semantic value in context. But since I did intend the student on the left to be the semantic value in context of my use of 'He', that student is the semantic value of 'He' in context according to the intention account. As before, you form the true belief that the student on the left is the semantic value of my use of 'He' in context based on glimpsing the lettering on the book cover. As before there are nearby worlds in which you failed to form that belief. So as before, the formation of that belief is lucky.

Due to difficulties with both the demonstration and intention accounts,[21] Kaplan (1978) suggests combining the demonstration and intention accounts. Call this the *hybrid account*. Kaplan suggests allowing the intended demonstratum to play a role in securing the semantic value of a demonstrative in context "within limits." Kaplan doesn't make clear exactly what those limits are, but he does make clear that he wants to allow speaker intentions to play a role in securing the semantic value of a demonstrative in context in cases in which the demonstration mounted is too vague to do the job itself (e.g. I wave my hand in the general direction of the intended object, where there are other objects in the vicinity). He also wants to invoke intentions to make it the case that when I say 'That is a nice dog' pointing at Fido, his coat, and a flea on his coat, it is Fido who gets to be the semantic value in context of my demonstrative in virtue of my intention that Fido be the semantic value in context of my use of 'That' and not his coat or the flea.[22] Finally consider Kaplan's (1978) famous case of pointing behind himself at a spot on the wall long occupied by a picture of Carnap without turning to look at it and saying 'That is a picture of one of the greatest philosophers of the twentieth century', where unbeknownst to Kaplan the Carnap picture was replaced by a picture of Spiro Agnew. Kaplan does not want the intention to refer to the picture of Carnap to overrule the demonstration with the result that the referent of 'That' in context is the picture of Carnap. The initial conditions to keep fixed in discussing the hybrid account are: (1) The conversation up to the point of the relevant utterance of the sentence containing the supplementive proceeds in very much the same way it did in the actual world; (2) At the time of the utterance, the speaker and the hearer are positioned as they are in the actual world and behave more or less as they did in the actual world in respects relevant to communication; (3) The speaker's demonstration and intention are just as they are in the actual world and the intention is just as recognizable in the same way as it is in the actual world.

---

[21] See King (2014b) for discussion.

[22] For ease of exposition, in the present work I assume that individuals are the semantic values of demonstratives in context even though, as I've indicated, on the account of demonstratives in King (2001), which I endorse, they are not.

Supposing the hybrid account is the correct metasemantics for demonstratives, we can again use the same case we used in the case of the demonstration account and the intention account to show that the hybrid account allows for the formation of lucky true beliefs about the semantic value in context of a demonstrative. Simply consider the case again changing only that this time the semantic value in context of my use of 'He' is determined by both my demonstration and my intention to have the student on the left be the semantic value in context of my use of 'He'. As before, you are not sure which student I am demonstrating and intending to refer to, but you form the true belief that it is the student on the left based on the glimpsed lettering. Hence, you form the true belief that the student on the left is the semantic value in context of my use of 'He'. Again, the event of forming this belief is lucky since in nearby possible worlds you don't form that belief.

Let me now turn to a metasemantics defended by Michael Glanzberg (2007, 2016, 2020). Glanzberg thinks there are two kinds of covert contextually sensitive expressions, which he calls *hidden contextual parameters*. These expressions are among the supplementives in my terminology. Glanzberg calls one kind of hidden contextual parameter a *thematic parameter* and sometimes an *implicit thematic argument*. These parameters are arguments to the relevant predicates. Glanzberg gives the following examples:

1   (a) She promised.
    (b) I tried.
    (c) He insisted.[23]

In each case the relevant predicate has a second covert argument that gets assigned a semantic value in context. For these thematic parameters, as well as demonstratives and deictic pronouns, Glanzberg is willing to accept the coordination account or at least does not challenge it.[24] Hence, thematic parameters won't concern us here. However, Glanzberg claims that his second type of hidden contextual parameters—*functional parameters*—require a different metasemantics. Glanzberg calls these *functional* parameters because they occur in functional syntactic categories (unlike thematic parameters) as opposed to lexical categories like Noun, Verb, etc. Examples include quantifier domain restriction parameters (Determiner phrase is a functional category), the hidden parameter in modals (Modal phrase is a functional category), the hidden parameter in gradable adjectives that get assigned degrees on the relevant scale (Degree phrase is a functional category), and the hidden parameter in 'only' that gets assigned an alternative set. Glanzberg claims that these functional parameters require what he calls an

---

[23] Glanzberg (2016) p. 12.   [24] Glanzberg (2020) p. 41.

indirect metasemantics. Here is what Glanzberg (2007) says about his indirect metasemantics:

> I have argued for contextual parameters which require highly indirect metasemantics. What fixes their values will be complicated combinations of such factors as what is salient in the environment, speakers' intentions, hearers' intentions, coordinating intentions, linguistic meaning, general principles governing context, discourse structure, etc. From these resources, values will have to be computed.[25]

He also says:

> A contextual parameter with an indirect metasemantics must be set by the various pieces of information context provides, but context does not simply hand us a value for such a parameter, nor does it hand us a uniform rule for computing the value from a specific piece of contextual information. Rather, a range of contextual information and computational rules must be taken into account and weighed in working out the value from context.[26]

In Glanzberg (2020) he makes similar remarks in discussing the application of his metasemantics to gradable adjectives on a Kennedy (2007) style account of them:

> The point of the indirect metasemantics is that these competing features have to be combined, and combining them is itself something that takes place in context. There are general rules that might be invoked. Kennedy suggests an interpretive economy principle that asks us to maximize the use of lexical content over contextual factors. But like most contextual rules, this is defeasible. A contextual parameter with an indirect metasemantics must be set by the various pieces of information context provides, but context does not simply hand us a value for such a parameter, nor does it hand us a uniform rule for computing the value from a specific piece of contextual information. Rather, a range of contextual information and computational rules must be taken into account and weighed in working out the value from context.[27]

So on Glanzberg's view, a variety of factors including what is salient (including salient comparison classes in the case of gradable adjectives—see Glanzberg 2020), speakers' intentions, hearers' intentions, coordinating intentions, linguistic meaning, general principles governing context, discourse structure, previous discourse, presuppositions (see Glanzberg 2020 on the latter two factors), and more can

---

[25] Glanzberg (2007) p. 25.   [26] Glanzberg (2007) p. 19.
[27] Glanzberg (2020) pp. 35–36.

figure in determining the semantic value of a functional parameter in context. Further, Glanzberg also says that there is no uniform rule for combining these various factors to yield the semantic value in context of a functional parameter. Apparently, these factors can combine differently in different cases. So far as I can see, Glanzberg never explains what determines how they in fact combine to determine a semantic value in context in a given case. Finally, an important feature of Glanzberg's view is that conversational participants can be ignorant of the semantic value of a functional parameter in context with the result that they can be ignorant of the propositions they express in uttering sentences: 'One point that is made vivid by parameters with indirect metasemantics is that speakers can wind up in significant error or ignorance about what they have semantically expressed.'[28] The initial conditions to keep fixed in discussing this metasemantics are: (1) The conversation up to the point of the relevant utterance of the sentence containing the supplementive proceeds in very much the same way it did in the actual world; (2) At the time of the utterance, the speaker and the hearer are positioned as they are in the actual world and behave more or less as they did in the actual world in respects relevant to communication; (3) Whatever factors fix the semantic value in context of the supplementive in question on Glanzberg's account in a given case are as they are in the actual world. In the case we will consider, condition (3) requires us to hold a salient comparison class fixed.

To see that Glanzberg's metasemantics allows for lucky true beliefs about the semantic values in the context of supplementives, consider the following case. We have just boarded a plane and we have brought headphones and sleep masks that we are starting to put on. Just then a passenger slips in the aisle and knocks into your arm. You remark that this always happens to you on planes and I reply that it happens often to me too. A brief discussion ensues. Just as we finish it, the pilot announces that the Los Angeles Lakers basketball team is on today's flight and is now boarding. The pilot then says "You probably noticed the Lakers as they are very large men wearing Lakers team jackets. In case you were wondering, the average height of a Laker is 6'7". We smile and put our headphones and masks on. Sometime later, we remove our masks and headphones. At that point, Laker's guard Russell Westbrook, height 6'3", appears wearing his Laker team jacket. I say 'He isn't tall' and you agree. Assume we have both formed the true belief that the threshold for being tall / the semantic value for 'tall' in this context is 6'8". On Glanzberg's view, what makes this the threshold is the salient comparison class: the Los Angeles Lakers, together with the pilot's announcement. Now consider a nearby possible world in which the passenger does not slip and we put our headphones and sleep masks on before the Lakers begin boarding and the pilot's announcement. So we don't know that the Lakers are on our flight. As in the

---

[28]   Glanzberg (2007) p. 26 note 22.

previous case, we take off our headphones and masks at the later time and Russell Westbrook appears as before in his team jacket. The other Lakers are seated in such a way that we can't see them or how tall they are. I say 'He is tall' and we both think that the threshold for being tall in our context is 6'2". In this case, on Glanzberg's view we are just wrong: the salient comparison class of the Los Angeles Lakers still fixes the threshold at 6'8".[29] So here, my true belief in the actual world that the threshold for being tall in our context is 6'8" is lucky. In the nearby world just described, I don't form that belief.

As I said above, the fact that all the rival metasemantic accounts considered allow for the lucky formation of true beliefs about the semantic value in context of a supplementive is an argument against them.

Let's now turn to some consequences of the coordination account. First, what does it predict about the case we used above to argue that the demonstration, intention, and hybrid accounts all allow for the lucky formation of true beliefs about the semantic values of supplementives in context?[30] Recall that in that case two male students are standing in close proximity to each other talking. I say 'He is a philosophy major' clearly pointing at the student on the left and walk away but unfortunately from your angle you can't tell which male I demonstrated. I was intending that the student on the left be the semantic value of my use of 'He' in context, so the first condition of the coordination account is satisfied. However, the second condition is not: it is not true that a competent, reasonable, attentive hearer H who knows the common ground of the conversation at the time I uttered 'He' and who has the properties attributed to the audience by the common ground at the time I utter 'He' would know that I intend the student on the left to be the semantic value of 'He' in c. In particular the idealized hearer in question would have to be physically situated with respect to me the way you actually are, since the common ground attributes that property to you. Hence since due to your physical relation to me you can't make out which student I am pointing at, neither could the idealized hearer. But then even if she came to truly believe that I intend the student on the left to be the semantic value in context of my use of 'He' as you did, she wouldn't know it since in close by possible worlds she doesn't form that true belief. Hence, condition (2) of the coordination account isn't satisfied here and we predict that my use of 'He' does not have a semantic value in context. Further,

---

[29] What makes the Lakers the salient comparison class that fixes the threshold for being tall in this context on Glanzberg's view is the physical presence of the Lakers in the context and the pilot's announcement. Thanks to Michael Glanzberg for helpful discussion.

[30] I won't consider what the coordination account would say about the Russell Westbrook case that was used to show that Glanzberg's metasemantic account allows for the lucky formation of true beliefs about the semantic value in context of a supplementive. This is because the example hasn't been sketched clearly enough for the coordination account to render a verdict on whether the use of 'tall' in that example has a semantic value in context. In particular, nothing was said about the speaker's intentions and whether an ideal hearer would know what they are. Considerations of space militate against filling such details in and discussing this case.

your forming the true belief that I intend the student on the left to be the semantic value in context of my use of 'He' is lucky. In nearby possible worlds where the student turns far enough for you to see the whole title of the book he is holding or in which he doesn't turn far enough for you to see 'Aristo' on the cover, you don't form that belief.

The motivation behind the coordination account is that to secure a semantic value in context for a supplementive a speaker must do enough to insure that an idealized hearer knows what he intends the semantic value in context of the supplementive to be. That in turn insures that his actual hearer *could* know. In fact, she may not because, e.g., she refuses to attend to the speaker. But if the actual hearer is like the idealized hearer in being competent, reasonable, attentive, knowing the common ground at the time the speaker utters, and possessing the properties the common ground attributes to the audience at the time of utterance and the speaker's intention in using a supplementive satisfies the conditions of the coordination account, the hearer will know what the speaker intends the semantic value in context of the supplementive to be. So the coordination account requires the speaker to do all that is required to put the hearer in a position to know the speaker's intention in order to secure a semantic value in context for a supplementive. If one buys into this motivation, then the prediction that the coordination account makes in the present case seems correct: the speaker did not do all that is required to put the hearer in a position to know his intention. Let me briefly say something about why one *should* buy into this motivation. If we are constructing a semantic theory for a language with supplementives and we want to define the notion of a use of *a supplementive having* o *as its semantic value in context c*, it seems reasonable to require in that definition that the speaker did what was required on her part to insure that successful communication with the supplementive could occur. That is, it seems reasonable to require that the speaker did what was called for on her part to enable successful communication with her audience. After all, the purpose in using a supplementive is to communicate something about its semantic value in context. It seems plausible to say that a speaker *succeeded* in securing a value for her supplementive in context just in case she did what is required to insure that it could serve its purpose and will serve its purpose if the audience does its part. And that in turn is a matter of doing enough to allow her audience to know what she intends to be the semantic value in context, since this is what is required for the speaker to insure that her audience is in a position to receive information about the semantic value by means of her supplementive. But this is just what the coordination account requires for a speaker to secure a value for her supplementive in context. In this way, the coordination account's notion of *a use of a supplementive having* o *as its semantic value in context c* can be seen as characterizing what must happen on the speaker's side to insure that successful communication is enabled. That seems to me to be a theoretical virtue. At any rate, it at least shows the point of the coordination account's notion of *a use of a supplementive having* o *as its semantic value in context c.*

Turn next to the case of Ernie and Michael discussed earlier. Recall that I was looking at a picture of Ernie that I thought Michael could see as well. It turns out he couldn't see it but he could see the back of the frame of the picture. Pointing at the picture, I say 'He is a philosopher.' intending to refer to Ernie with my use of 'He'. Unbeknownst to me, there is a picture of Ernie on the back of the frame holding the picture I am pointing to that Michael can see and that has been recently placed there temporarily by someone who temporarily placed a number of pictures in different locations giving little thought to where the pictures are placed and which are placed where. Michael wrongly thinks that I am pointing to the picture on the back of the frame and so truly believes that I intend Ernie to be the semantic value in *c* of my use of 'He'. However, the event of forming this true belief is lucky: in nearby worlds where the picture of Ernie is not placed on the back of the picture frame, Michael does not form this belief. Nonetheless, intuitively, communication succeeds in this case. However, condition (2) of the coordination account isn't satisfied here since a reasonable, competent, attentive hearer who knows the common ground at the time I uttered, and who possesses the properties that the common ground attributes to my audience would not *know* that I intended Ernie to be the semantic value in context of my use of 'He'. For such a hearer would be situated relative to me as Michael is since it is common ground that Michael is so situated. Hence, her forming the true belief that I intend Ernie to be the semantic value in context of my use of 'He' is lucky just like Michael's doing so is.[31] Hence, her true belief that I intend Ernie to be the semantic value of my use of 'He' in context isn't knowledge. So, the coordination account predicts that my use of 'He' does not have a semantic value in context here. Despite that, communication succeeds since on the basis of my utterance Michael comes to entertain the proposition I was hoping to express by my utterance.

Again, given the motivation for the coordination account this seems to be the intuitively correct account of the case. Since the speaker did not do what was required to insure that his hearer was able to know his intention, we claim the speaker failed to secure a semantic value in context for his use of 'He'. Despite that luckily communication succeeds.

Let me consider a final case that John Hawthorne and David Manley (p.c.) formulated that they thought might be problematic for the coordination account. Suppose we're both listening to a male lark, call it *o*, sing, we are mutually aware that we are, and I say 'He is a happy lark' intending (*de re*) that *o* be the semantic

---

[31] Notice that I am now talking of a true belief an idealized hearer *would* form as being lucky. We have to understand this as follows. In a possible world *w* in which the idealized hearer does form the belief, there are worlds near to *w* where she does not form this belief.

value in context of 'He'. Suppose that just before the lark sang a scamp was getting ready to play a fake (synthesized, not recorded!) lark song, but stopped because a real lark actually sang. Now would a competent, attentive, reasonable hearer who knows the common ground of the conversation at the time of utterance and who has the properties attributed to you, my hearer, by the common ground know that I intend o to be the value of 'He' in c? In a world exactly like the actual world in which o sang except for containing such a hearer, the hearer would truly believe that I intend o to be the semantic value in context of my demonstrative. But in the close possibility in which the synthesized song is played, the idealized hearer presumably would believe the gappy proposition that I intend __ to be the semantic value in context (or perhaps the proposition that I intend the synthesizer or the person playing it to be the semantic value in context). Hence, the true belief the idealized hearer would form in the world like the actual world where the lark sang would not be formed in nearby possible worlds in which the real lark didn't sing and the fake lark song was played. But then, it might be claimed, the idealized hearer would not *know* that I intended o to be the semantic value of my use of 'He' in context since the formation of her true belief that I intend o to be the semantic value in context of 'He' is lucky. That would mean that condition (2) of the coordination account fails and my use of 'He' has no semantic value in context. Hawthorne and Manly thought that it is very counterintuitive to claim that o is not the semantic value in context of 'He' in this case. Finally, one might argue, the true belief you form to the effect that I intend o to be the semantic value in context of my use of 'He' is lucky. In nearby worlds in which o doesn't sing and the fake lark song is played you don't form that belief.

The problem with this case and the above reasoning about it is that the world in which the fake lark song is played, call it w, doesn't preserve the initial conditions that possible worlds must preserve in order to be considered when we are deciding whether the event of forming a true belief about the intended semantic value in context of a supplementive is lucky. Consider condition (3) of our initial conditions: The speaker in uttering the sentence had the same intention regarding the semantic value in context for the supplementive in question as she did in the actual world. This condition is not satisfied by w since in that world the object of the speaker's *de re* intention is not o, whereas the object of the *de re* intention in the actual world is o. But then these are different *de re* intentions. That means that w is not relevant to the question of whether the formation of the hearer's true belief that the speaker intends o to be the semantic value in context of 'He' is lucky. Once worlds like this are eliminated from consideration, it appears that there are no nearby worlds satisfying initial conditions in which the hearer fails to form the true belief that the speaker intends o to be the semantic value in context of 'He'. Hence, the formation of that belief is not lucky. Further, an idealized hearer would know that I intend o to be the semantic value in context of 'He'. For in the world like the actual world in which o sings, the idealized hearer will form the true belief that I intend o to be the semantic value in context of 'He'. But there is no nearby world satisfying initial conditions in which she fails to form that belief. Hence, her formation of that belief is not lucky. But then her true belief is safe and so is an instance of knowledge.[32] That means that both conditions of the coordination account are satisfied and o is the semantic value in context of 'He' contrary to what was claimed above. Hence, this case presents no problem for the coordination account.[33]

References

Glanzberg, Michael, 2007, 'Context, content, and relativism', *Philosophical Studies*, 136, 1–29.

Glanzberg, Michael, 2016, 'Not all contextual parameters are alike'. Unpublished manuscript.

Glanzberg, Michael, 2020, 'Indirectness and intentions in metasemantics', in *The Architecture of Context and Context Sensitivity*, Ciecierski, Tadeusz, Grabarczyk, Paweł (eds.), Springer Nature, Berlin, 29–53.

Kaplan, David, 1977, 'Demonstratives', published in *Themes from Kaplan*, Almog, Perry, Wettstein (eds.), 1989, Oxford University Press, New York.

Kaplan, David, 1978, 'Dthat', *Syntax and Semantics*, vol. 9, ed. Peter Cole., Academic Press, New York. Reprinted in *Contemporary Perspectives in Philosophy of Language*, French, Uehling, Wettstein (eds.), University of Minnesota Press, Minneapolis, MN.

Kaplan, David, 1989, 'Afterthoughts', in *Themes from Kaplan*, Almog, Perry, Wettstein (eds.), Oxford University Press, New York.

Kennedy, Chris, 2007, 'Vagueness and grammar: The semantics of relative and absolute gradable adjectives', *Linguistics and Philosophy*, 30, 1–45.

King, Jeffrey C., 2001, *Complex Demonstratives: A Quantificational Account*, MIT Press, Cambridge, MA.

King, Jeffrey C., 2013, 'Supplementives, the coordination account and conflicting intentions', *Philosophical Perspectives 27 Philosophy of Language*, Wiley-Blackwell, Oxford, 288–311.

King, Jeffrey C., 2014a, 'The metasemantics of contextual sensitivity', in *Metasemantics: New Essays on the Foundations of Meaning*, Burgess and Sherman (eds.), Oxford University Press, New York, 97–118.

King, Jeffrey C., 2014b, 'Speaker intentions in context', *Noûs* 48(2), 219–237.

---

[32] Recall that we are understanding safety as an anti-luck condition on knowledge.

[33] Thanks to Sam Carter, Abrol Fairweather, Michael Glanzberg, Annie Papreck King, Ernie Lepore, Carlos Montemayor, and Diego Arana Segura for helpful comments and/or conversations about issues discussed herein.

King, Jeffrey C., 2020, 'Speaker intentions and objective metasemantics', in *The Architecture of Context and Context Sensitivity*, Ciecierski, Tadeusz, Grabarczyk, Paweł (eds.), Springer Nature, Berlin, 55–80.

Loar, Brian, 1976, 'The semantics of singular terms', *Philosophical Studies*, 30, 353–377.

Nagel, Thomas, 1979, *Mortal Questions*, Cambridge University Press, New York.

Pritchard, Duncan, 2005, *Epistemic Luck*, Oxford University Press, Oxford.

Pritchard, Duncan, 2007, 'Knowledge, luck and lotteries', in *New Waves in Epistemology*, Pritchard, Hendriks (eds.), Palgrave Macmillan, London, 28–51.

Pritchard, Duncan, 2012, 'Anti-luck virtue epistemology', *Journal of Philosophy*, 109, 247–279.

Pritchard, Duncan, 2014, 'The modal account of luck', *Metaphilosophy*, 45(October), 4–5.

Stalnaker, Robert, 1999, *Context and Content*, Oxford University Press, New York.

Stalnaker, Robert, 2002, 'Common ground', *Linguistics and Philosophy*, 25, 701–721.

Unnsteinsson, Elmar, 2018, 'Referential intentions: A response to Buchanan and Peet', *Australasian Journal of Philosophy*, 96(3), 610–615.

Williams, Bernard, 1981, *Moral Luck*, Cambridge University Press, Cambridge.

5

Laws and Luck in Language

Problems with Devitt's Conventional, Common-Sense Linguistics

Georges Rey and John Collins

1. Laws, Luck, Convention, and Common Sense

A scientific explanation renders its target phenomena to be in some way non-accidental. Just what this amounts to is contentious, but the rough idea is that a phenomenon is explained by showing that it is an instance or a consequence of underlying general laws or principles.[1] Of course, the phenomena that are ordinarily observed are invariably an admixture of the effect of principles and accident. For example, that the Moon is gravitationally attracted to the Earth is due to principle, but just how high the tide rises as a result is due to multitudinous accidents of the terrain, wind, temperature, currents, etc. One could say that much of what ordinarily happens is in this way a matter of "luck," to varying degrees, as fortuitous as the roll of dice or toss of a coin. This does not credit the universe with pure chance, but only identifies the accidental relative to a certain principled system. In this sense, we might think of science as developing many partial systems of explanation with actual phenomena being due to the interaction of different principled systems in specific, often accidental, circumstances. Only under idealized or highly artefactual situations may we "directly" observe such principles in action.[2]

Our concern in this chapter will be with the different roles of law and luck in linguistics, and specifically how much and in what ways various phenomena of language depend upon accidental or "lucky" facts that are not sufficiently stable to feature in laws, and so should not be the focus of linguistic theory. We take this to be obviously true of most episodes of ordinary speech: what words people utter

---

[1] For brevity, we shall use "laws" as a cover term for what good explanations ought to provide, and prescind from adjudicating the many issues concerning the nature of laws. Of course, some explanations are concerned with particulars, such as the Earth, specific species, or the Big Bang, but we submit they enjoy their force by their reliance on background laws.

[2] Of course, the explanatory distribution between laws and luck may be a matter of degree. That the universe exists at all might have been a matter of luck, as probably was the emergence of law-like systems of chemistry and biology within it.

Georges Rey and John Collins, *Laws and Luck in Language: Problems with Devitt's Conventional, Common-Sense Linguistics* In: *Linguistic Luck: Safeguards and Threats to Linguistic Communication*. Edited by: Abrol Fairweather and Carlos Montemayor, Oxford University Press. © Oxford University Press 2023. DOI: 10.1093/oso/9780192845450.003.0005

depends upon their audience, beliefs, intentions, attention, mood, habits, available energy, etc., at the moment. But, on reflection, this would also seem to be true of groups of people, societies, even whole nations of people speaking "the same language" over varying stretches of time. Communication is a mix of luck and law. Sharing a language affords interlocutors a great deal of information as to what each other intends to communicate, but it hardly suffices: they likely also need a shared background of practices, beliefs, and expectations, all of which are notoriously difficult to specify.

Regularities, of course, emerge. Speakers known to each other will share certain phraseology, pronunciations, presumptions of politeness, and shared beliefs, and the persistence of such regularities invites the widespread, commonsensical idea that language is largely a conventional affair. As David Lewis expressed it at the very start of his famous (1969) study of convention:

> It is a platitude that language is ruled by convention. Words might be used to mean almost anything; and we who use them have made them mean what they do because somehow, gradually and informally, we have come to an understanding that this is what we shall use them to mean. We could perfectly well use these words otherwise—or use different words, as men in foreign countries do. We might change our conventions if we like.... The platitude that there are conventions of language is no dogma of any school of philosophy, but commands the immediate assent of any thoughtful person—unless he is a philosopher.
>
> (Lewis 1969:1–2)

Certainly many of the differences between what are commonly called "languages" (English, French, Swahili) appear to be conventional in the sense that we can easily imagine many of their linguistic properties being different, much of their character reflecting no natural cause or rationale, but instead being due to shared habits and cooperative inclinations of members of a group.[3] After all, isn't it just such conventions that dictionaries, ordinary "grammar books," and "manuals of style" set down, much as rule books might set down the conventional rules of chess and Go? All this would seem to be just plain common sense. But common-sense surface differences can often mislead.

For starters, dictionaries and manuals of style are relatively unstable, much of their content being driven by the wide variation and changes in speakers' purposes, interests, and knowledge. This seems an area of massive interaction effects—of "luck" on our understanding—and so is unlikely to be a domain of serious explanation in terms of laws (think of the wonderful diversity in

---

[3] For our purpose here, we will understand "conventions" along more modest lines than Lewis proposed: a regularity in action satisfying some community end that is (i) arbitrary—other regularities would serve—and (ii) not explained by any underlying natural system.

etymologies of words, which are unlikely to reflect deep explanatory principles). To be sure, what seem to be the basic rules of *grammar* seem to change much more slowly: most modern readers can (with a few exceptions) understand the grammar of Shakespeare and Milton. But perhaps these involve simply slower changing conventions. Or perhaps not.

The conventionalist view of grammar has been seriously challenged by work in generative linguistics from the late 1950s to the present, work pioneered and shaped by Noam Chomsky (1957, 1965, 1981, 1995a). For our purposes, the fundamental claim of this work is that underlying the great diversity in the ways people speak, there is a set of innate principles of grammar that both limit and make possible the kind of languages we may acquire. This psycho-biological endowment is relatively free of the vicissitudes of social conventions, and so is a more appropriate domain for lawful linguistic explanation. In terms Chomsky (1965) famously introduced, it is speakers' underlying linguistic "competence" that is likely to be law-like, not their complex and highly variegated "perform-ance," which appears to be largely a matter of varying degrees of (what we are calling) "luck."

Michael Devitt (1996, 2006a, 2006b, 2008a, 2008b, 2020) has been the foremost philosophical sceptic of this shift in the explanatory locus of linguistics, and we will focus on his views as representative of conventionalist presumptions that pervade a great deal of philosophy of language that we think is concerned largely with "lucky" performance issues at the expense of a concern for underlying competence.

We should stress that neither Devitt nor many recent philosophers of language question that human languages may well be innately constrained. Devitt allows that, insofar as it is so constrained, "a great deal of syntax is . . . not conventional" (2006a:180). However, he insists:

> Still, the syntactic differences between public languages show that *much* syntax is not innate. (Devitt 2006a:181; emphasis ours)

Indeed:

> What most linguists . . . are *mostly* doing is theorizing about the largely conven-tional syntactic and semantic properties of expressions. (2006a:182; emphasis ours)

Chomsky's innate rules and constraints simply form a background against which, in Devitt's view, linguistics properly theorizes about the more central conventional aspects of language. Indeed, Devitt (2008a:218) explicitly endorses Lewis's con-ventionalist platitude; and in his (2020) writes:

> An idiolect is shared in a community . . . to the extent that the members of the community are disposed to associate the expressions of the idiolect with the

appropriate meanings. This sharing...probably partly comes about because of some innate syntax. It is *largely* the result of the community participating in the same linguistic conventions.

(Devitt, 2020b:425; emphasis ours; see also p. 391)

And he pursues a vigorous defence of the importance of linguistic convention in his most recent (2021), *Overlooking Conventions: The Trouble with Linguistic Pragmatism*.

It is important not to draw the differences between Devitt and Chomsky in this regard too starkly. Not only is Devitt not denying the existence of innate constraints on grammar, but (despite occasional hyperbolic moments, e.g. Chomsky, 1980:81–3, 1996:47–8) Chomsky is not committed to denying a role for convention in any conceivable descriptive or explanatory task; he simply thinks any such role will be far less significant than is commonly supposed, and certainly less than the role of innate constraints that shape acquisition and mature maintenance of language. In terms of the distinction we are drawing, Chomsky claims the laws of linguistics are to be found in a nativist psychology, and he regards social conventions as largely a matter of luck, and so not what linguistic theory targets. We take Devitt to be denying this (cf. §2.3 below).

It was *inter alia* Devitt's defence of his conventionalist conception against the more purely psychological views of generative linguistics that led one of us in a recent article (Rey, 2020a) to defend a maxim of "Explanation first!," against Devitt's (2010) maxim of "Metaphysics first," which, as we'll see below, Devitt understands to include much "common sense,"—or, anyway, its "posits" (see fn 8 below)—which Rey argued doesn't reliably accord with good linguistic explanation.

Devitt (2020:429–432) protested, claiming no cases had been cited where he was in fact relying on common sense. In §2 below, we shall set out Devitt's general views about the role of common sense in metaphysics (§2.1), proceeding to indicate in detail how it seems to be the basis of his disagreements with current scientific linguistics. We shall provide a brief sketch of the project of generative grammar, and the reasons for it (§2.2), followed by a discussion of Devitt's alternative conception both of it (§2.3) and then of phonology (§2.4).

But perhaps the most philosophically interesting divergence between Devitt's and many other philosophers' conception of linguistics and a Chomskyan one is with regard to semantics, to which we turn in §3. Devitt is part of now more than a generation of philosophers that, influenced by the work of Kripke (1972/82) and Putnam (1975c), began to advocate various "externalist," e.g., causal strategies with regard to theories of meaning and mental content, a strategy that Chomsky thinks might be apt for terms in natural sciences, but finds hopelessly ill-defined for natural language. Some of the problems are vividly exhibited by "defective" phenomena, such as (what we call) "the quotidian queer" and the widely noted problems of polysemy and co-predication, some of which we set out in §3.3 and

which seem to undermine any metaphysical import of a truth-conditional semantics of a sort Devitt and others seem to presume (§3.4).[4]

A theme that will run throughout our whole discussion is our scepticism about
one common-sense platitude which we suspect underlies Devitt's and many other
philosophers' conception of language. Expressed concisely, and of course subject
to qualifications, it might be put most simply as:

(R)   Words refer to things in the world.[5]

(R) seems to us an important part of the conventionalist conception of language
that we oppose. It relates to our general theme of eschewing luck in a number of
ways, but two are most significant. First, Devitt and most philosophers are inclined
to presume that words are the sorts of real objects that are conventionally entokened
in speech, a presumption that we'll see in §2.4 phonological theory provides strong
reason to doubt. Secondly, reference has been the central concept of semantic
theorizing in philosophy, many philosophers presuming that it constitutes the
core explanans of language and our use of it, a presumption we will challenge in
§3. On our best take of what constitutes a lawful understanding of language,
reference, understood extensionally, plays no role, but is an uncritical importation
into a theory of natural language of a notion that has its home in formal logic.

To be sure, philosophers have usefully worried about how to specify "reference"
as a technical term for purposes of logic, concerns we don't mean to disparage.
But, as just intimated, the key notions in (R) involve problems that current
linguistics is often at pains entirely to avoid: it is very doubtful that either the
"words" that people take themselves to hear and produce,[6] or many of the "things"
that they take themselves to be "referring" to actually exist in the world—or even
that "reference" is as clear and useful a notion as logicians and philosophers
influenced by them have sometimes taken it to be. Rather, speakers seem to be
variously "talking about" phenomena they take to be real enough for the purposes
at hand, but which may not be as well-defined or coherent as Devitt and other
philosophers seem to suppose.

On the other hand, we don't want to dismiss one of Devitt's and other
philosopher's motivations for subscribing to some version of (R), which has

---

[4] Chomsky (1996:52) goes further and suggests that it's a mistake to think that a linguistic semantics
determines truth-conditions at all, a view Pietroski (2005, 2010, 2018) has developed in some detail, as,
in different ways, have Jackendoff (1990); Pustejovsky (1995); and Asher (2011). We won't press this
issue here.

[5] (R) seems to us implicit in many passages of Devitt that we'll discuss in §3, especially in his defence
of "most" common-sense posits (1984/97:18, 23, 73), which we presume are what are referred to in
common-sense talk. Since we doubt (R), we'll also allow intensional uses of "refer," permitting
"reference" to non-existent things like Zeus, cf. fns 24, 25, and 27 below.

[6] As is customary in linguistics, we set aside issues about orthography and "words on the page."
Literacy is by no means universal, and is not acquired in nearly the automatic way characteristic of
speech that interests linguists.

often been to resist various versions of anti-realism (or "constructivism"). We shall argue in §4 that Devitt's general antipathy towards anti-realism, which is often animated by a denial of (R), is perfectly correct. None of what we defend here should suggest a *general* idealism or "constructivism." We are sympathetic with at least Devitt's "scientific realism" according to which many objects and phenomena referred to in our best scientific theories *do* exist, and that at least some of these may include what are in fact ordinary objects, such as tables, chairs, and trees. Our moral is in a way similar to Devitt's: one shouldn't put semantics first before metaphysics. But nor, we will argue, should we adhere to the "lucky," often peculiar "metaphysics" or apparent posits of common sense. It's serious explanation that comes first.

2. Devitt's Common-Sense Linguistics

2.1. "Realism"

As we said, one of Devitt's primary concerns throughout his career has been with defending a general doctrine of realism about the external world. This he characterizes several times as the view that:

> Tokens of most common-sense, and scientific, physical types objectively exist independently of the mental. (Devitt, 1984/97:23; see also 2010:33)

In his defence of the common-sense component of such realism, Devitt deploys a "Moorean" strategy:[7]

> From an early age we come to believe that such objects as stones, cats and trees exist. Furthermore, we believe these objects exist even when we are not perceiving them, and that they do not depend for their existence on our opinions or on anything mental. This realism about ordinary objects is confirmed day by day in our experience. *It is central to our whole way of viewing the world, the very core of common sense.* A Moorean point is appropriate: Realism is much more firmly established than the epistemological theses [regarding under-determination of theory by data] that are thought to undermine it.
>
> (Devitt 2010:62; emphasis ours; see also p. 104)

---

[7] After G. E. Moore (1925/59), who famously claimed he was more certain of the existence of his two hands than of any of the philosophical arguments for scepticism about such facts. Devitt (1984/97:109) does distinguish "entity" from "theory" realism, and claims to be defending only common-sense *posits*, not *claims*. But common-sense posits are based on existential claims ("There are witches"), which are actually often more problematic than mere hypothetical ones ("If x were a witch, then x would cast spells"), so it's hard to see how Devitt's distinction matters.

Of course, Devitt (1984/97:18) recognizes that "[w]e certainly do not want to say that all common-sense and scientific physical entities exist," and so exceptions should be made for "flying saucers and phlogiston." He adds, however:

> it is not enough to say that only *some* common-sense and scientific entities exist. The realism that is worth fighting for ... is committed to the existence of *most* of those entities. (Devitt 1984/97:18; emphasis original; see also pp. 23, 73)

We shall return to the Moorean point and the general realist issue in §4. But we should note that, while Devitt endorses the Moorean stratagem, in his (2020:430) he endorses a defence of common sense based more on Quine and Ullian (1978:43–53), who understand "conservativism"—altering as few prior beliefs as possible—to be a theoretical virtue. Such a status allows for common sense to often give way to science, a point Moore didn't stress. We'll discuss common-sense conservativism in §2.3.

We should stress that, for present purposes, we are not challenging Devitt's brand of realism vis-à-vis scientific theories: a well-confirmed theory is the best reason to be had for committing to the entities the theory posits. It is only his insistence upon "common-sense entities," specifically *words* and many of their supposed "referents," that we find problematic, precisely because, as we shall argue, it frequently conflicts with what a scientific linguistics proposes. We should also stress that, while Devitt endorses common sense both broadly and with particular respect to language, he doesn't always endorse these positions *because* they are common sense; he simply thinks that common sense happens to be correct across a range of cases. Our intent is to dispute this.

In the remainder of this §2, we shall consider Devitt's challenge to the psychological hypotheses first developed by Chomsky and others that have become foundational for generative linguists. Devitt's attitude is somewhat of an echo of earlier positions, like those of Katz (1981) and Soames (1984), that view generative linguistics as conflating language as an entity unto itself with our cognitive relation to it. Devitt differs only in identifying language as consisting of spatio-temporal particulars playing a certain role, rather than as abstract objects like numbers and sets. His attitude reflects broader currents in philosophy of language, which conceive of language along the familiar lines captured by Lewis's common-sense conventional platitude.

2.2. Generative Grammar

Generative linguistics is an immensely complex project. The only component that shall concern us here is its core psychological hypothesis (Chomsky 1965, 1981):

(PSY) The acquisition and maintenance of linguistic competence is explained by a specialized, mostly innate, cognitive faculty that computationally (recursively) generates a set of interpretable structures usable in wider cognition and which therefore provides the proper nomologically explanatory focus for linguistics.

In essence, this is a scientific hypothesis that gives empirical substance to the simple idea that language is some system internal to a person's mind/brain (what Chomsky calls an "I-language") that underlies our capacity systematically to pair signs with meanings. The hypothesis is supported by many convergent lines of evidence, but we think one of the most intuitively compelling arguments is that there seem to be peculiar constraints on which strings of words qualify as sentences that are hard to explain from any perspective other than (PSY).

The point can be made vivid by considering strings that could be understood to express a perfectly fine thought that speakers feel simply can't legitimately be put that way. The question linguists are asking is: why not? Some very simple examples of (as we call them) WhyNots are ("*" indicates unacceptability):

(1)　a.　*John$_i$ thinks Paul likes himself$_i$ (where himself = John)
　　　b.　*I know he has ever spoken French (cf. I doubt he has ever spoken French)
　　　c.　*She's as likely as he's to get ill (cf. She's as likely as he is to get ill)
　　　d.　*Who will John and meet Mary? (Cf. John and **who** will meet Mary?)
　　　e.　*I filed Bill's articles without reading. (cf. Which articles did you file without reading?)
　　　(see any linguistics text for countless more examples).

The (PSY) hypothesis enjoins us to ask: *what could possibly explain native speakers' rejection of such examples?* It is unlikely in the extreme that they were ever explicitly taught conventional rules about such cases, in the way they might have been taught not to split infinitives or swear in church. Indeed, they almost certainly have never produced or heard such strings with the indicated interpretations, precisely because they are in some peculiar way "unacceptable." This absence of experienced examples is, of course, insignificant in itself. There are, after all, an infinity of sentences that a speaker will never hear because they are far too long, or their meaning is bizarre, unclear, or contradictory (*Colourless green ideas sleep furiously / Stones drink procrastination*). What is interesting about the WhyNots in (1) is that the *thoughts* that one could guess might be intended by them are perfectly fine and simple; it is only their expression via the indicated sentential means that is somehow ruled out.

Other evidence points in the same direction, such as sensitivity to abstract grammatical structure; the speed, stability, and universality of acquisition; and its independence of general intelligence, memory, and computational ability.[8] What is to be systematically explained is a certain peculiar species of human cognition, not anything about our environment, social, conventional, or otherwise, or our general problem-solving abilities. Just *which* language an individual speaker will acquire depends upon comparatively contingent circumstances, specifically, which lexical items are learned, and how specific parameters are set, such as whether a language is SVO or SOV (i.e., whether or not a verb precedes its direct object). What's innate are the conditions that determine the kind of language that can be acquired in the sense of not being fixed by the data to which the language-acquiring child is exposed.

2.3. Devitt's Alternative

In the course of now more than thirty years of many articles and three books,[9] Devitt emphatically rejects the core claim of (PSY) that the explanatory scope of linguistics flows from its positing of complex internal structure to the mind/brain. Instead, he argues for:

> (LR) Linguistics has something worthwhile to study apart from the psychological reality of speakers: it can study a linguistic reality. This reality is in fact being studied by linguists in grammar construction. The study of this linguistic reality has a certain priority over the study of psychological reality. A grammar is about linguistic reality not the language faculty. Linguistics is not part of psychology. (Devitt, 2006a:40)

Indeed:

> A grammar is a theory of the nature of the expressions that constitute a language, not of the psychological reality of that language in its competent speakers. (Devitt, 2008a:205)[10]

Devitt is not committed to the staunch anti-mentalism of earlier behaviourists such as Skinner or Quine. He readily acknowledges that the nature of language

---

[8] We are very briefly summarizing a wealth of argument here. For more detail, see Lasnik et al. (2005); Collins (2008a); Smith and Allott (2016:ch 2); and Rey (2020b:ch 1).

[9] See Devitt (2003, 2006a, 2006b, 2008a, 2008b), as well as a similar, earlier discussion in Devitt and Sterelny (1987/99:chs 8–9).

[10] Devitt (2006a) provides a number of arguments for (LR) that we won't consider here, regarding competence and its objects, structural vs. processing rules, between the respecting of structure rules and the inclusion of them among processing rules (see Collins, 2020, and Rey, 2020b:§6.3, for objections, and Devitt, 2020:372–381 for some replies). They are independent of the common-sense conventionalism that is all that concerns us here.

mostly supervenes upon the minds of speaker/hearers, and so, as mentioned above, he differs from Katz (1981), too, in rejecting a Platonist realism. The realism on offer only considers language to be *theoretically* distinct from any physical or mental states, not *metaphysically* independent. In this sense, linguistics, according to Devitt, treats language as a *sui generis* kind of social, conventional activity, that neither psychology, much less biology or physics alone could explain. Of course, as a materialist, Devitt agrees that linguistics in some way supervenes on these other domains: but lots of domains supervene on other domains without the claims of one being eliminable in favour of those of the other. For Devitt, the psychologizing of linguistics is a kind of philosophical error, a conflation of a supervenience base with an apt domain for linguistic explanation.

Nor does Devitt have a quarrel with any of the specific principles of grammar that linguists propose; he simply objects to their regarding their theories as psychological theories rather than as theories of "linguistic reality" per (LR). This seems to be partly due to his insisting upon a common-sense conception about the reality of standard linguistic entities ("SLEs," such as words, phrases, sentences, phonemes, and/or phonological properties) and the conventions governing them:

> Symbols are *social* entities . . . . So they are like the unemployed, money, smokers and the like in having their properties in virtue of environmental, psychological, and social facts. (2006b:583)

One might think that here Devitt only has Saussurean "arbitrariness" in mind, that the relation between signifier (morpheme) and signified (meaning) is generally not underwritten by anything more than contingent association. But no; surprisingly, Devitt includes syntax:

> Meaning is constituted by conventional word meanings and *a syntax that is conventional to a considerable extent* . . . . (Devitt, 2006a:182; emphasis added)

Indeed, in an astonishingly sweeping characterization of linguistics, Devitt claims that:

> The study of the (largely) conventional meanings of actual linguistic entities, meanings constituted by a (partly) conventional syntax and conventional word meanings, is the concern of linguistic theory. *Our theoretical interest in language is in explaining the nature of these conventional meanings that enable language to play such an important role in our lives.*
> (Devitt, 2006a:189; emphasis added; see also p. 182)

These are pretty grand claims about linguistics and the interests of linguists. Again, they are not advertisements for an alternative set of grammatical principles, nor even a denial of some of their innate determinants. Devitt is only concerned to deny (PSY)'s commitment to those innate determinants being the proper focus of linguistic theory. As against (PSY), he wants to insist on a non-psychological focus on the social and conventional facts about language that, at least as regards syntax, generative linguists have regarded as marginal and comparatively fortuitous, for the reasons sketched above. What countervailing reasons does Devitt provide?

It's hard to find a definitive argument for this position, other than the short claim we quoted earlier:[11]

the syntactic differences between public languages *show* that much syntax is not innate. (2006a:181; emphasis ours)

But mere surface differences "show" no such thing, any more than the differences between people's faces show that much of their structure is not innate. The locus of explanatory action is what decides the issue, and generative linguists have proposed a serious theory that the action in the case of syntax (as in the case of faces) lies overwhelmingly in innate structure.[12]

Perhaps Devitt has a general, alternative conventionalist theory. But here too it is difficult to find anything that could begin to rival a psychologically based generative one in any detail. Devitt nowhere discusses the many phenomena, semantic and syntactic, that Chomskyan theories aim to explain. At best he at one point provides a sketch of how he thinks conventions could have evolved regarding inaudible elements, such as PRO:[13]

Consider the string "Bob tried to swim." The idea is, roughly, that each word in the string has a syntactic property by convention (e.g., "Bob" is a noun). Put the

---

[11] It might appear that he provides arguments when he claims that "conventional meaning is important in at least four ways" (2006a:181): acquisition, borrowed reference, guide to thoughts and explaining behaviour, and interpersonally shared meanings (2006a:182–184). But (i) the latter three might, at best, serve as arguments for conventionalism about *meanings*, especially of individual words, not of *syntax*; and (ii) Devitt doesn't begin to establish that convention is essential to explaining these phenomena, many of which could be explained in terms of shared features of I-languages.

[12] We suspect Devitt is supposing that, on the "Principles and Parameters" model that has been influential in generative grammar since the 1970s, conventional variation causes variation in the languages children acquire. This is not an argument *for* a conventional syntax, however, because parameter setting does not entail conventions, even if one supposes that parameters are in fact set by conventions. As it is, how parameters are set is a complex empirical issue. Models range from mere "triggering" accounts to various forms of entrainment, where the setting of one parameter depends upon the setting of another (see Yang, 2002; Roberts and Holmberg, 2010). Moreover, language is acquired without any sense of convention in the case of creolization, where children exposed to adult pidgins that are not "natural" are forced to ignore many regularities and settle on a natural grammar somehow nearest the mélange they hear. In general, that a linguistic property might hold because of a convention appears to play no explanatory role, i.e. parameters are sensitive to variation, not to *why* there is variation.

[13] PRO is a hypothesized covert subject of infinitival and gerundive phrases that enters into complex systematic syntactic and semantic relations with overt items. For example, in "Bob tried to persuade himself," 'PRO' is both controlled by 'Bob' and acts as the antecedent of 'himself'.

words with those syntactic properties together in that order and the whole has certain further syntactic properties largely by convention; these further properties "emerge" by convention from the combination. The most familiar of these properties is that the string is a sentence. A more striking discovery is that it has a "PRO" after the main [finite] verb even though PRO has no acoustic realization. There is no mystery here.   (Devitt, 2008a:217–218)

But it's hard to believe he thinks this is a serious explanation. Even if we pardon its under-specification, the fundamental problem with it is that PRO is simply not part of the heard string, but a position in an unpronounced hierarchical structure posited to explain how speakers understand the string, such as why the position *must* be interpreted, why it *can't* be interpreted as referring to a salient individual other than Bob, and why it is part of the subordinate phrase, as opposed to being an object of *try*. A convention is essentially *optional*, but these features aren't. The more one focuses on the surprising ineluctability, abstractness, and conscious inaccessibility of syntactic structures, the relevant relations defined by them, and the presence of constrained inaudible elements such as PRO, the claim that children just "put the words with those syntactic properties together in that order and . . . certain further syntactic properties . . . 'emerge' by convention" simply ignores all the intricate phenomena that have been the focus of syntactic theory for the past sixty years (would that the mysteries were so easily resolved![14]).

For lack of any serious argument or alternative theory of these standard linguistic phenomena, it's extremely hard to see how Devitt is relying on anything more than Lewis's common-sense "platitude" that we quoted at the start. Indeed, in the same passage, replying to Collins's (2008b) specific challenge about how conventions could in general account for the complexities of syntactic phenomena, Devitt (2008a) replies:

I don't know. But I don't need to know to sustain linguistic realism. . . . I have shown how it is possible for conventions to yield unvoiced elements [such as PRO]. I have indicated in a general way, referring to David Lewis (1969), how linguistic conventions, like other conventions (that are not stipulated), arise from regularities together with some sort of "mutual understanding." . . .

And he goes on to cite the passage from Lewis we quoted at the start:

---

[14] Cf. a lovely comparison Louise Antony (2002) made in an analogous context to Monty Python's explanation of "How to play the flute":

(Picking up a flute.) Well here we are. You blow there and you move your fingers up and down here. (See https://www.youtube.com/watch?v=tNfGyIW7aHM)

In response to Collins (2008b), Devitt (2008b: 253) does retreat to agnosticism about whether the rules on PRO are conventional or innate. He doesn't say what he thinks about all the other rules.

> Lewis begins his book by claiming that it is a "platitude that language is ruled by convention" (1969:1). This is surely right. (Devitt, 2008a:218)

Note that, quite apart from its disregard of the complexities of syntax, Devitt's work contains no discussions of phonology and doesn't engage in most of the semantic issues that typically occupy linguists (e.g., NPIs, conditionals, (a)telic verbs, quantifiers, adverbs, compositionality). To be sure, Devitt has had often perceptive and important things to say about *reference*, but, what with its involvement with the external world, that seems to be a marginal issue for many *linguists* (see, e.g., Fromkin, 2001:373; and §3.2 below). So it's puzzling that Devitt is prepared to second-guess linguists about the nature of their task. Although Devitt would vehemently protest this charge, it is hard not to regard his proclamations as mere armchair, virtually *a priori* "common-sense" speculations that he (2010:276–277) otherwise often reasonably deplores. One is reminded of a young A. J. Ayer telling chemists that their theories are really about sense data, not the molecular structures they take themselves to be studying.[15]

Interestingly, in his recent (2020) replies to critics, Devitt actually does acknowledge that it is virtually impossible to imagine a conventional, non-psychological explanation of WhyNots, such as those in (1) above, but he curiously adds:

> And so it is, because the phenomena are psychological! But the issue is whether *grammars* directly explain them. I would argue, along the lines of [(LR)] that grammars as they stand do not directly explain them, although their accounts of the syntactic structure of linguistic entities contribute to the explanation.
>
> (Devitt, 2020:379)

even adding in a footnote: "I grant the Chomskian view that the language has some of its syntactic properties, including perhaps the WhyNots?, as a result not of convention, but of innate constraints." (Devitt, 2020:379 fn11). The issue now seems strangely verbal. If, as research consistently shows, *the vast majority* of rules and constraints on grammar are indeed due to innate psychological constraints and not convention—which, moreover, seems powerless to explain them—then that's surely a reason to think that grammar *is* largely a matter of psychology and not convention! Grammar is no more conventional than visual illusions are. And

---

[15] The analogy is not far-fetched. Ayer, like Russell (1912) and many other philosophers of the period, thought that sense data provided the ultimate, neutral evidence for anything one says about the world, just as Devitt thinks tokens of natural language sentences do for linguistics. More on this in §2.4. We should stress that we raise these objections to Devitt fully aware of the very many passages in which he claims to be a champion of a "naturalistic" approach to philosophy that eschews the armchair for, so to speak, the empirically informed laboratory, and which he would certainly appear to be pursuing in much of his work. We are only questioning the extent to which he appears nevertheless to be *also* implicitly relying in his treatment of language on a traditional armchair or common-sense methodology, despite his best naturalistic intentions.

if those constraints are what linguists regard as the "grammar" they are studying, on what basis can Devitt second-guess them? Lewis's platitude? The ordinary use of the word? Perhaps there is some further argument that we've missed. As things stand, the answer is completely unclear.

Devitt further insists upon common sense playing a crucial role in linguistics along the lines he takes it to play in science generally:

> One doubt [about my characterization of the linguist's task] is about how the domain of study is to be determined: how do we select the tokens to be studied from all the other behavioral outputs of speakers? And the answer is: in the way science usually determines domains. That is, *guided by folk linguistics, we start with the intuitive idea of the domain of grammatical tokens to be studied.*
>
> (Devitt, 2006a:27; emphasis ours)

Indeed:

> These actual and idealized outputs, governed by a system of rules and fitting into a structure, *are* **what we would normally call a language**. Indeed, wherever there is a linguistic competence there *has* to be such a language, for the language is what the competence produces. (Devitt, 2006a:31; italics original; bold emphasis ours)

What warrants such a claim, whether for linguistics or any other science? Physicists surely don't think they should start with folk theories of teleology, impetus, or earth, air, fire, and water; or biologists with the biology of the Bible. It's hard to see why scientists should be in the least obliged to pay *any* heed to folk theories of their domain even at the start of their inquiries. Even if, per Quine and Ullian (1978:43–53) to whom Devitt appeals, common sense deserves a default credence via conservatism, surely it must be assessed on a case by case basis. Our present point is simply that the credence is very low in the case of linguistics, just as it is in other areas of science, largely because common sense and what "we would normally call a language" don't begin to speak to the central phenomena that occupy linguists, such as the WhyNots, general constraints on the architecture of languages, and the facts of universality and acquisition. In any case, all that scientists need do is to find phenomena that seem amenable to serious explanation. How those phenomena are related to ordinary thought is as may be, and need be of no concern to them.

2.4. Phonology

As we've already quoted, Devitt regards SLEs as "*social* entities…the unemployed, money, smokers and the like" (2006b: 283). Specifically, Devitt takes for granted the existence of "tokens" among the "behavioral outputs of speakers" that are the putative concern of linguistics. This is, however, seriously tendentious. To be sure, this was the view of behaviourists such as Bloomfield (1933); Skinner (1957); and Quine (1960/2013). We assume Devitt doesn't want to defend these long-discredited views. In the first place, it has become a common-place in phonology that the acoustic stream is not remotely *segmented* into the words and phrases that speakers take themselves to hear and that's essential to their syntax, so it's unclear how any such "tokens" of speech could actually be systematically identified (see, e.g., Liberman, 1996).[16] Indeed, the task of many linguists and psychologists has become to explain how speakers *understand* the noises they produce and encounter *as language*, a task for which they should surely find evidence wherever they can find it—what is ordinarily taken to be "speech," and "tokens," but also intuitions, paraphrase, puzzlement, pupillary dilation, brain scans, and so forth.

Indeed, Devitt's appeal to "tokens" betrays not only his behavioural, but also his *extensionalist* bias, inherited from the same behaviourists.[17] On this view, the object of inquiry is *the set of expressions* of a spoken language. Chomsky quite reasonably thinks this is a very dubious notion as soon as one departs from the stipulative definitions of formal sciences, where what counts as 'well-formed' can be decided in advance of any explanation:

> The class of expressions generated by the (I-)language should not be confused with a category of well-formed sentences, a notion that has no known sense in the theory of language, though informal exposition has sometimes obscured the point, leading to much confusion and wasted effort. (Chomsky, 2000:78)

Just think of the staggering difficulty of any would-be specification of the set of well-formed English expressions according to what might be supposed by some or other convention of making sense of them. One would need to separate the oral from the written, the ungrammatical from the computationally difficult (e.g., centre embeddings; the prose of Henry James), and then sort out idiolects, errors, diary shorthand, twitter-speak, poems, songs, archaic prayers, etc. In short, our behavioural linguistic output is due to a mass of highly variable and contingent factors, which have no relevance to the basic competence of mapping meaning to

[16] Devitt (2006a:26–27) appears to accept standard critiques of Bloomfeldean linguistics, and to reject brute physicalistic characterizations of speech tokens. However, he quickly endorses in their stead "high-level" relational characterizations (2006:27), presumably grounded in speaker/hearer's social-behavioural dispositions (see Devitt, 2006a:186, 2006b:583, 598ff, 2008a: 221), which, given the wide variability in speech production and perception, from regional accents to drunks and auctioneers, modern linguists would find no more plausible (see Rey, 2020b:§9.3, for discussion).

[17] This actually is more a common positivistic "philosophical sense" that was influential only between *c.*1930 and 1960.

structure that humans seem to share as a species property. In any case, the very idea of sorting out what counts as a linguistic token amidst such complexity is qualitatively distinct from the utter triviality of specifying the set of wffs for, say, first-order logic.

Indeed, in general, generative linguists are simply not interested in the strings that speaker-hearers might happen to produce or consume, but in how they *understand* or *represent* them,[18] and how such interpretations relate to each other. The ultimate task is to sort between different hypotheses about what is syntactically, semantically, or pragmatically (un)acceptable, given hypotheses about the underlying systems that sub-serve these capacities. Thus, that informants might find a string ambiguous or unacceptable is a datum, but it is a theoretical matter to explain the response. Their responses might be due to semantics, syntax, speech pragmatics, or merely a matter of style, social prohibitions, or perhaps computational complexity (as in the case of centre embeddings). It is not obvious, prior to any theory, what the answer will be, and the ultimate answer will depend upon the integration of linguistics into the rest of cognitive science.

In short, it is simply not true that the data to be explained by a grammar could be determined entirely externally, without substantive internalist theories. Pace Quine (1970a, 1970b), *we don't determine the relevant intensions from a predetermined extension, but, rather, the extension from a theory of the intensions and how the system that embodies them interacts with other mental states!*

3. Semantics and Common-Sense Metaphysics

Unlike the issues of syntax and phonology, issues in semantics have been at the forefront of much philosophy since the work of Frege and Russell. Although complex semantic issues arise for all expressions in natural language (see, e.g., Fromkin, 2001:part III), we shall be concerned here only with the case of nouns (and/or noun phrases; we won't distinguish) that have been the focus of that work, again, taking Devitt's work to be representative.

Not only, per the previous section, does common sense seem to be mistaken about the external existence of nouns, but at least common philosophical sense seems to have an over-simple view of the relation of these nouns to items in the world that they take to "pick out," "denote," or "refer to" (cf. (R) above). It seems

---

[18] Devitt (2020:379) oddly thinks that the two present authors have "very different" views about linguistics in this regard. However, the only tiny difference is that Rey (2020a, 2020b) uses "represent(ation)" where Collins (2020) uses "interpret(ation)." Collins just thought the latter was slightly less committal with regard to disputes about the former; otherwise we regard the terms as virtually interchangeable (cf. Collins and Rey, 2021).

as much a truism that "water" refers to water as that tokens of the word "water" are produced in the air as we speak. Chomsky challenges both assumptions:

> As far as is known, it is no more reasonable to seek something-in-the-world that is picked out by the word 'river' or 'tree' or 'water' or 'Boston' than to seek some collection of motions of molecules that is picked out by the first syllable or final consonant of the word 'Boston'. With sufficient heroism, one could defend such theses, but they seem to make no sense at all. Each such usage of the words may well pick out, in some sense, specific motions of molecules and things-in-the-world (the world as it is, or is conceived to be); but that is a different and entirely irrelevant matter.   (Chomsky, 1996:79)

In this section we shall give substance to the suggestion here that what typical nouns pick out cannot be plausibly placed in "reality." In putting "metaphysics first," of course, Devitt does not think that semantics is the right method for doing metaphysics. Still, as part of his general commitment to at least the "posits" of common sense, he would seem to be assuming that we can, by and large, read off much of what exists from ordinary talk whose semantics is his concern, and it is the ontology of ordinary talk that we think he and other philosophers are not entitled to take for granted. Like the relation of phonological representations to the complex noises people make when they speak, the relation of the words they take themselves to utter to actual phenomena in the world is in general far more complex and fortuitous—more dependent on luck—than philosophers like Devitt have seemed to suppose.

3.1. Extentionalism/Externalism

Reflecting on the point of semantics, Devitt (1996) writes:

> What significant purposes—explanatory, practical, or whatever—served by the ascription of meanings...? Doubtless there are several such purposes, but I shall focus on two: first, to **explain and predict the behavior of the subject**, which I shall abbreviate "to explain behavior"; and the second, to use thoughts and utterances of others as **guides to reality largely external to the subject**.
> (1996:57–68; c.p., pp. 63, 65, 70–71, 136–137, 140; bold emphasis ours;
> see also his 2006:29, 58, 126–127)

And he provides as examples, explanations of "why granny board[ed] the bus" (1996:58, 2006a:126), in terms of her saying she needs a drink (2006a:127).

Indeed, it is striking that Devitt, like too many philosophers of mind and language, invariably relies on common-sense examples of *singular events*, e.g. someone saying it's raining, (2006a:134); someone saying "He is in on fire" (2006a:128).[19] It is crucial in the context of distinguishing laws from luck to stress that science isn't generally interested in the explanation of singular events except insofar as they reveal *general* laws that we have claimed are its real goal. As in the case of grammar and phonology, generative linguists expect that what lawful explanations there are will concern the stable facts about internal human mental structure, not the complex mass of fortuitous relations speakers may or may not bear to the world around them.

3.2. Causal/Externalist Theories of Reference

An important and highly influential suggestion about reference emerged from the work of Saul Kripke (1972/82) and Hilary Putnam (1975), who presented a plethora of examples that challenged traditional "description" theories of reference (whereby the reference of a term was determined by the descriptions associated with it) and stressed instead the frequent role of causal aetiologies. This gave rise to a variety of "externalist" proposals about meaning that have dominated analytic philosophy for the last fifty years (see, e.g., Burge, 1979; Dretske, 1981; Fodor, 1990). Again, we shall treat Devitt's view as representative: much of what we will say about it will fairly clearly apply to the others.[20]

Although both Kripke (1972/80:93–97) and Putnam (1983:xvii) emphatically denied they were presenting a "*theory* of reference," Devitt (1981) and Devitt and Sterelny (1987/99:ch 4) nevertheless present it as a "theory"—indeed, not only about the reference of names and kind terms, but about their "sense" and speaker "competence" with them as well (p. 89)! Although the view does capture a great many intuitions about cases, they (1987/99:73) do acknowledge quite a number of serious problems confronting it as a full theory (see their §§4 and 5).

The problem we want to focus on is one that (so far as we have read) they don't consider, and which we regard as more fundamental: *why think that expressions in natural language generally stand in systematic causal relations to **any** stable or coherent "referent"*? To be sure, some common-sense cases suggest they do. Familiar uses of "Aristotle" are no doubt historically linked to the naming of the man in ancient Greece, as are uses of "France" to the naming of certain (varying?) regions in Europe, and "tigers" to a certain sort of feline, and this may indeed be

---

[19] There are occasional exceptions. For example, Devitt (2006:131) briefly discusses some of the evidence of the cognitive abilities of animals and children, but with no discussion there or elsewhere of how this data constrains a theory of language or content. For the irrelevance to generative grammar of Devitt's (1996:§§2.3–2.8) discussion of the "language of the bees" see Rey (2020b:§6.3.2).

[20] It is worth noting that Chomsky (1975:18) expresses some sympathy with Putnam's (1975) discussion, but only as it concerns terms used in natural science, not as a theory of the semantics of natural language.

important to many uses of the terms. But such cases may not be as typical of nouns as Devitt's focus upon them might seem to suggest. At any rate, careful linguistic examination of the behaviour of a larger variety of nouns in natural language seems to resist such an account.

The status and role of common sense in semantic theory is complex and we can't here arrive at final conclusions. All we hope to make clear is

(i) that semantic phenomena themselves appear neither to entail nor to presuppose anything resembling a commonsensical ontology of middle-sized dry goods or even the kind of "artefacts" philosophers conjure up on behalf of the folk;

and

(ii) that semantic theory has all too often been construed as being in the business of delivering a "sensible ontology" (Kennedy and Stanley, 2009);[21] to the contrary, nothing goes wrong in semantic theory if we construe it in a wholly structuralist or internalist manner, whether or not the ontology ultimately makes any sense according to non-linguistic criteria.

In short, we suggest that semantic theory should not be encumbered by a common-sense metaphysics that, we shall now proceed to argue, may well not be well-defined or even coherent.

3.3. "Defective" Phenomena

Nouns are standardly taken to refer to entities of various sorts and their properties (including relations). Sentences containing nouns with such referential properties are taken to specify ways the world might be, as composed of such entities and properties in a way that makes the sentence true or false. If all that were so, then a correct semantic theory would precisely tell us what the world is like, so long as the utterances whose semantics the theory characterizes were true.

A significant cloud on the horizon, however, is that lots of expressions (simple and complex) are what we may call "referentially defective":

(RD)   An expression e is referentially defective in a construction C iff
    (i) e is a proper constituent under a 'correct' analysis of C;
    (ii) utterances of C are often unproblematically regarded as true;
    (iii) e has no coherent referent by whatever ontological standards otherwise prevail, especially common sense.

---

[21] Note that this construal of semantics is not shared by Devitt; one of the points of his maxim, "Metaphysics first," is emphatically to reject such a view (see his 2010). But his rejection of (ii) here is compatible with his acceptance of (i).

We shall detail two classes of cases that signal such apparent defectiveness: (i) what we call the "quotidian queer," and (ii) polysemy and co-predication problems. We'll see that the second are so widespread as to support the thought that, in fact, defectiveness is really the norm, so that semantic phenomena ought really not be conceived of in terms of a predetermined, "Metaphysics first" ontology, whether metaphysical, scientific, or even "commonsensical," about which language is supposed to be "guiding us." Rather, it should be approached as a specific scientific project of explaining human linguistic competence, along the lines of (PSY). How it connects to an independently specifiable external world is a question that linguistics alone is not in a position to answer, except perhaps to point to the difficulties of doing so, which the following phenomena begin to reveal.[22]

(i) The quotidian queer.

Many expressions in natural language have no readily intelligible referents, even upon sustained reflection. We provide a wide range of examples to indicate the serious generality of the point, i.e. that these aren't "isolated" cases (we underline the problematic expression):[23]

(2) a. The sky is blue.
     b. The double rainbows are spectacular!
     c. The average American has 2.3 children and drives a Ford.
     d. Her beauty shared by her sister caused him to turn his head.
     e. The wave spread across the lake and crashed on the opposite shore.
     f. Three flaws mar the argument
     g. There's a hole in the dress
     h. My shadow is longer than yours.
     i. Sutherland's voice is so strong; listen to the purity of it in the recording of it I made before she lost it. (Dennett, 1969:9)
     j. The chess club left the meeting room in a mess.
     k. There are many things that don't exist, e.g. Zeus, Santa Claus, the largest prime.

---

[22] A view that's been very much in the air for the last fifty years is that the success of humans as a species depends upon their beliefs on the whole being true, their words referring to real phenomena; indeed, something like this is sometimes thought to be necessary just in order for their thoughts to have any content. This is not the place to reply to the many different versions of these views. Suffice it to say that there are many ways even intelligent animals could survive with contentful thoughts by having enough beliefs whose contents were "true enough," their words referring to real things "well enough." Thought and language needn't optimize, but merely satisfice (see, e.g., Cherniak, 1986, and Stich, 1990).

[23] Fiction, of course, provides a much-discussed case of referential defectiveness. Since fiction is a problem for everyone, however, we shall focus on phenomena much less discussed. We think, however, that fiction cuts in our favour insofar as the positing of various conjured referents for fictional expressions proves ultimately to be inadequate (see Collins, 2021).

   l.   He felt <u>pride in his breast</u>.
   m.   He had <u>a pain in his tooth</u> as a result of a cavity in it.

Note these are all the sorts of sentences that might be commonly uttered and often regarded unproblematically as true, and we are not proposing that, as ordinary talk, they shouldn't be. Some of these examples have attracted philosophical attention,[24] but what remains wholly unclear is whether any philosophical nuance is reflected in the semantics the competent user draws upon in understanding the sentences. *Are speakers really committed to there being serious, actual entities picked out by the underlined noun phrases?* We very much doubt that in most of these cases many people on a moment's reflection would seriously think so. And, needless to say, the existence of systematic causal links between the acoustic blasts occasioned by utterances of the nouns and their supposed referents is, at best, extremely dubious.[25]

   Consider (2a). What space does the sky occupy? Well, the atmosphere gives out in outer space, but then we see stars "in the night sky" that are light-years away. One's head is not in the sky, but that is only relative to one's surroundings; if you are on top of a mountain or a skyscraper, one might be in the sky along with clouds, while the sky is still above one, as one would say. 'The sky' appears to be usable as a kind of indexical, but we can simultaneously understand it generically, as in *The sky is mostly cloudy in winter, but clear at the moment.* Suppose some enterprising metaphysician could offer a sky ontology that resolves such quandaries with, e.g., fancy mereological and/or set theoretic constructions based on the scattering of light (and we know ones who try!). Would there be any reason at all to suppose it might correspond to our apparently confused notion? What's striking is precisely the fact that our notion *is* likely confused. Despite this fact, surely we share *some* common semantic notion, along with our children who know nothing about our atmosphere and the scattering of sunlight.

   Or consider (2e): it seems a perfectly correct locution until one remembers that waves on a lake are actually not the portions of water that, e.g., might crash on a shore, but rather a form of energy that moves through the water, causing portions

---

[24] See, for example, Lewis and Lewis (1970) and Casati and Varzi (1994) on holes; and Sorensen (2011) on shadows; Dennett (1969) on voices; Margaret Gilbert (1989) on clubs; and the innumerable discussions since Plato of "properties" (like the shared beauty) and "tropes" (like her beauty that turned his head), as well as of the problems of non-existents, such as Zeus and Santa (why is (2k) not heard as a contradiction?!). Much of the present point can be credited to Wittgenstein (1953/2016:§§244–316, 1981:§§484–504), who discusses the examples of "pain" and "pride," and deplores philosopher's presumption of a uniform relation of "reference." Chomsky (2000:127, 132, 2003:295) has cited Wittgenstein as an influence on him regarding this issue (even if Wittgenstein would likely have resisted many of Chomsky's positive theoretical proposals).

[25] With the possible exception of the last two, it also seems dubious that there's any "nearest natural kind" of thing that ordinary usages are "getting at," as is arguably the case for chemical, biological, and disease terms, along lines of Putnam (1962/75, 1975).

of water to crash on a shore. "The wave" we take ourselves to see is a subtle perceptual illusion.

Constructions of the form 'the average N' have occasioned a fair amount of philosophical and semantic discussion. The intent of many constructions is clear. So, (2c) seems to mean that the number of (relevant) children divided by the number of (relevant) Americans is 2.3. In other words, we are here relieved of entertaining the existence of the average American in addition to the actual Americans, because the analysis does away with any corresponding entity for "the average American" (Kennedy and Stanley, 2009). Such an analysis, however, is more a way of understanding what makes a particular construction true, rather than a general account of what renders the phrase non-defective. At any rate, the analysis doesn't fit other cases:

(3)   a. The average American drives a Ford
      b. The average American drives a Ford and has 2.3 children
      c. The average American neglects his 2.3 children
      d. Joe Sixpack has 2.3 children

In somewhat different ways, these constructions entail that we treat "the average American" as a genuine referring expression, albeit a defective one (see Collins, 2017a). Again, our general moral is that, even if some kind of semantic and metaphysical coherence can be given to this mess (and it's by no means clear that this is possible, or even to be desired), there is no reason to expect it to be aligned with common sense, and still less for it to forge a marriage between semantics and common sense. What's striking is that the quandaries only occur upon reflection; the bare semantic competence of speakers seems not to require them even to notice any problem, much less resolve it.

The general moral of the referentially defective cases is that we readily talk of things about which we have, on reflection, no coherent conception (we urge the reader to reflect in a similar fashion on the other cases that we haven't space to discuss). The entities are commonsensical in the minimal sense of being part of unscientific thought and talk, but they support no account of what they might be as real denizens of the world as described by an objective science. A more rigorous metaphysics might be forthcoming, but metaphysics cannot tell us what our words mean, as if it might turn out to be a *semantic* error to use a proper name to talk about Joe Sixpack.[26]

---

[26] There are actually *two* issues raised by the quotidian queer, one about "word" meaning, but another about what on a particular occasion of use a speaker even *intends to refer* to. We suspect that the latter intention is too often likely also to be understood by many semanticists in an external, extensionalist way. We doubt, however, that, in most conversations, speakers are at all clear about exactly *what* they take such "things" as, e.g., the sky, rainbows, or non-existent entities to be, beyond the quite modest demands of a conversation, and likely use "refer" not in the extensional way of a logician,

(ii) Polysemy and co-predication problems.

The expressions so far considered form fairly restricted or *ad hoc* categories whose putative referents are problematic upon reflection. It can be shown, however, that more or less any nominal is referentially defective in the sense that, while one may use it to speak truthfully, it may have categorically mismatched predicates or be the antecedent of a pronoun that does. The lead feature here is polysemy, where an expression has multiple related senses that can be simultaneously or selectively expressed relative to different predicates, either conjoined or anaphorically linked. This is what is now commonly referred to as the problem of co-predication:

(C) P is a co-predicative construction[27] iff P is acceptable and features an argument or an anaphoric relation to the argument that is modified by or predicated of categorically mismatched properties as expressed by two or more predicates.

Just what it is to be categorically mismatched is a famously difficult philosophical question, which we'll sidestep simply by letting the notion be exemplified by cases. It bears emphasis that the argument of a co-predicative construction can be pronominal, but the phenomenon is most clearly in view with polysemy. So, consider:

(5) a. Lunch was delicious, but lasted hours
   b. The bank was vandalized after calling in Bob's debt
   c. The book is fascinating despite its small print

In (5a), lunch appears to be construed as referring to both foodstuff (*qua* delicious) and an event (*qua* lasting hours). In (5b), *bank* appears to be construed as referring to both a building (*qua* vandalized) and as an institution (*qua* calling in a debt). Note that this is quite unlike the homophony or ambiguity of *bank* as financial institution and a *bank* as a riverside (where "#" indicates semantic anomaly):

(6) #The bank gave him interest on his savings, but was eroded by the river.

Unlike (6), (5b) could be effortlessly understood. Similarly, (5c) seems fine, even though *book* appears to be construed as both referring to a body of information

---

but merely as a way of indicating what they are "talking or thinking about" in the ordinary sense that need not entail any actual existence (as when they might claim they are "referring/talking about" the sky, Joe Sixpack, or Santa Claus).

[27] The term "co-predication" has come to be used for just the cases that raise problems. There are, of course, normal cases of co-predication that don't raise any concerns.

(*qua* fascinating) and as referring to a concrete particular (*qua* having small print). Use of anaphora can readily extend the construals beyond two:

(7)   London tends to vote conservatively, despite its being the largest urban area in the UK. But its cost of living is driving out the poorer residences.

London is here construed as referring to a population, an area, and a social/economic entity.

As Chomsky (2000) writes:

In general, a word, even of the simplest kind, does not pick out an entity of the world, or of our "belief space". Conventional assumptions about these matters seem to me to be very dubious. (p. 17)

The thought here has three parts. (i) The world does not contain entities with the apparently conflicting properties, such as a thing that is both a population and an area; (ii) nor do we take there to be such entities as part of our general conceptual or practical engagement with the world; and (iii) the semantic properties of the relevant nominals and their host constructions do not entail or presuppose any such entities. Indeed, it's by no means clear that in using these defective terms speakers are in any serious way even *intending* to refer (as opposed to merely "loosely talking about") such entities. Nonetheless, we can say true things with co-predications like those of (5) (see Pietroski, 2003, 2005, 2018; Collins, 2009, 2011, 2017b; and Azzouni, 2010). Within the space available, rather than rehearse the extant lengthy discussions, we'll briefly respond to some general objections.

(a)   *Broadening ontological horizons.*

A potential move would be to deny the claim that either the world or "belief space" lacks the relevant ontology. One might think, 'Look, books just are material things with informational content; cities (*mutatis mutandis*, countries, continents, etc.) just are geographical areas with populations and legal and legislative structures'. The thought might be followed by the qualification that 'of course, such things are not objects of science; they are a kind of cognitive artefact, but are no worse for that as referents of our expressions' (cf., Ludlow, 2003; Thomasson, 2007). The move is both false and otiose.

On the first count, it is simply a pun to think London is a thing that is happy, mostly burnt down in 1666, and Labour-run. Imagine playing a 'Who am I?' game and pretending to be "London." Both the difficulty of combining the properties for the identification of the thing, and the sense of being misled in the reveal, shows that we do not sanction the would-be ontology, either as what the word means or as a possible entity. Further, there is no stable or robust relation between the properties. For example, London as a population doesn't have to be located in a definite area (one can vote for a London mayor without being *in* London), and London might be destroyed and rebuilt elsewhere with, of course, an entirely different population.

Regardless of the semantic and cognitive issues, it is not even straightforward to get the ontology right. For example, one might think in a simple-minded metaphysical spirit that a book is a concrete particular with content in some medium (park the issue of types). Such a putative unity, of course, does not explain polysemy or co-predication, where we can selectively pick out aspects of such a would-be entity at the expense of others (in saying *War and Peace* is moving, one need have no particular in mind at all).

Still, we might be content to think books are at least out there in the world to be univocal referents, with different predicates picking up on their different properties (a table might be said to be green even if only its surface is). The characterization of the ontology of books, however, is not so innocent. There are e-books, whose ontological status, *qua* software, as concrete particulars remains moot. There are books with no content, such as Sheridan Simove's *What Every Man Thinks about Apart from Sex*, and there are books we may speak of that don't exist without merely being intensional (*The Book I Shall Never Write Is My Autobiography*). The point here is not that the simple-minded metaphysics leads us astray, signalling the need for a better ontology; rather, we simply don't think twice of extending "book" to cover *outré* cases in the absence of sorting out the metaphysics, which indicates that the semantics of "book" is not referentially univocal in the first place, even if the *outré* cases are not in consideration. Nothing in metaphysics prevents our conjuring up any "objects" we want, but the resulting ontology is not a contribution to understanding how people ordinarily think and talk.

On the second count, the move fails to explain the semantic phenomena. Suppose there is a relevant complex object, however constituted. Polysemy, in distinction to ambiguity, supports the one occurrence of an item *simultaneously* expressing or supporting two or more construals, as the cases above demonstrate. A complex object would provide a putative referent. A construal, however, is also relative to a predicate selecting or being co-construed with an interpretation of the nominal. Call this the *selective feature of polysemy*. Whether a particular construal is active or not simply depends upon which predicates modify or have the relevant item as an argument. Thus, matters of polysemy can often be settled internal to the language, with no recourse to extra-linguistic matters. In other words, we precisely do not want a relevantly complex object as a referent of *London, book*, etc., for what we are referring to by the nominal depends upon how the nominal is modified or the kind of verb of which it is an argument. If one says the book is interesting, one need not be referring to any concrete particular at all, for there need not be any, just as to refer to the school as happy does not require a building, which might have burnt down or never existed (the school might be on-line). One might think that a complex object is required in order for its component parts to be selected. This is false for the same reason. A school might or might not have a building, just as a book might or might not have pages, but 'book' and 'school' can be used either way. So, we precisely don't want a complex object with all possible properties.

(b) *Just ambiguity.*

In light of the kind of examples discussed throughout the chapter so far, King (2018:779–780) argues that the defective expressions here are simply displaying ambiguity. But, as example (6) above shows, ambiguity precisely does *not* admit co-predication across anaphora, conjunction, or modification, which is the very phenomenon at issue: how can a non-ambiguous nominal be understood to have a univocal external semantic value when it expresses different senses, simultaneously or selectively, that support categorically mismatched predicates? King's answer is that "strictly speaking" no such nominal can have such a semantic value, which is true enough, but then the position King defends is false.

What King does offer, it appears, is the idea that different senses of the nominal can be triggered by distinct pronouns (in the anaphoric case). The problem here is twofold. First, even if acceptable, non-anaphoric co-predication is unaccommodated, for in such cases one does not have two or more tokens to pick up divergent meanings; one just has the single nominal. Secondly, it is not clear what the position is supposed to be anyway. It appears as if co-predication is to be rendered as a form of context sensitivity. This is, in effect, then, a third option.

(c) *Context sensitivity.*

Liebesman and Magidor (2017; "L&M") claim that:

> there are different ways to be a book. This puts "book" perfectly on a par with other predicates and the property of being a book perfectly on a par with other properties. (2017:143)

> The basic thought is that an object can inherit properties, whereby, say, a physical object can inherit the properties of an informational object, and vice versa. Thus, "[i]nformational books are distinct from physical books, but there are many properties that both can instantiate" (2017:137). What licenses the inheritance is context:

> Physical books, on our view, can be both red and informative ... context determines that "books" designates physical books, and these are informative in virtue of the information they express. (2017:149–150)

Much could be said here, but we shall just raise just two general problems.

First, contextual restriction works by selecting an extension based on the lexical set, normally some proper subset, from, say, books as such to books of a particular sort (e.g., scholarly: "Professor Bloggs wrote a book"—but not a travel guide); it does not operate by picking out specifications of the lexical set as a whole. This is clear enough where the polysemous item is a proper name, such as *London* or *Germany*. There is, trivially, no contextual *restriction* of the singleton set here across different uses, but a selection of different aspects of the one understood thing: London, Germany, etc.

The same holds when the extension is plural. Take *book*. In no clear sense is one restricting the set of books by referring to the informational ones or the physical ones. In picking out the informational books, say, a speaker is not thinking about books as such, as realized by some subset, such as the books on the table as opposed to every book, but is thinking about books as such in one specific way rather than another specific way. Whatever mechanism one thinks is operative that allows speakers to flip between polysemous senses, it looks to be quite unlike contextual restriction.

Secondly, L&M's context-sensitive conception of nominals faces a dilemma. Officially, we are supposed to think of *book*, say, as variably taking different values depending upon context. Yet, one may ask, what stops *book* from picking out a banana or the number 2, context willing, much as "it" may? Presumably, it is the same reason why "I" picks out the speaker, "now" picks out the present time, and so and so forth; viz., the lexical items have an invariant "character" (Kaplan, 1989).

Here we have a dilemma for L&M. On the one horn, they need to posit a character for *book* and every other polysemous item, the purpose of which is to preserve the univocity of the item and preclude it from being an indefinite dietetic. Yet the moral of polysemy is just that no such character is forthcoming; or, at any rate, no-one really has much of a clue how to specify such a character for *any* open class lexical item. The other horn is to renounce character-based univocity. Without further ado, however, this is to render every nominal as some kind of disguised indefinite pronoun. Whether one calls the relevant property 'character' or not is by the by. The crucial point is simply that there *are* lexical invariances that constrain what words can be used to refer to, hence it is that polysemy is not open-ended, even if the informational routes by which a hearer can arrive at one understanding rather than another are open-ended.

3.4. The Status of Truth-Conditional Semantics

Given our considerations in support of the ubiquity and insuperability of referentially defective phenomena, it might seem that we are ruining a nice combination of ideas: truth-conditional semantics, a simple model of communication, and a metaphysics of the ordinary. Such foreboding certainly animates many of those who seek to ameliorate the threat of referential defectives. We here don't want to judge the ultimate fate of truth-conditional semantics, and there are serious theorists who think referential defectiveness (*inter alia*) militates for an alternative conception of semantics to a greater or lesser extent.[28]

We think, however, that traditional semantics really carries *no* commitments either to commonsensical entities or to artefactual exotica posited by philosophers. In essence, semantic theory targets structural phenomena and accounts for them by detailing how lexical kinds are interpreted in composed structures that map onto independently specified syntactic structure (Azzouni, 2010; Glanzberg, 2014; Collins, 2017b, 2020). As, again, we think Devitt would be the first to agree, it is not the business of semantics to tell us what *books* actually are, or even what we think they are; nor will it mark the fact that Donald Duck is a fiction whereas Donald Trump isn't.

For example, on this view, a semantic theory might include the following clauses (somewhat simplified):

(7) a. $[[[_N \text{London}]]] = \text{London}'$
     b. $[[[_{ADJ} \text{happy}]]] = \lambda x.\text{happy}'(x)$
     c. $[[[_{ADJ} \text{expensive}]]] = \lambda x.\text{expensive}'(x)$

The two predications come out as expected (ignoring tense):

(8) a. $[[[_{TP} [_N \text{London}][_{T'} \text{ is } [_{ADJ} \text{happy}]]]]] = T$ iff $\lambda x.\text{happy}'(x)(\text{London}')$
     b. $[[[_{TP} [_N \text{London}][_{T'} \text{ is } [_{ADJ} \text{expensive}]]]]] = T$ iff $\lambda x.\text{expensive}'(x)$ (London')

Two things should be noted here. First, while the statements specify the meanings of the expressions on the left, they do so without analysing the concepts the words express, but merely register their compositional features (e.g., that "expensive" is a 1-place predicate). Such a theory proves to be genuinely enlightening when it is unclear just what the compositional features of an expression are, such as with quantifiers. If such revelations count as analysis, though, it is purely structural or compositional. Secondly, the expressions on the right are simply our metalinguistic way of talking about whatever the expressions of the language contribute to the truth conditions of their potential host sentences. So, "$\lambda x. Fx$" just means "the property of being F" without any kind of analysis.

---

[28] For discussions of defectives, see Higginbotham (1989), Carlson and Pelleitier (2002), Ludlow (2003), Stanley (2007), Kennedy and Stanley (2009), Borg (2009), King (2018), Vicente (2018); of non-truth-conditional semantics, Jackendoff (1990), Pustejovsky (1995), Asher (2011), and Pietroski (2018).

So much tells us *something*: the adjectives are 1-place, the nominal is 0-place, the former can take the latter as an argument, with the result being true iff London is happy/expensive. What we are not told is what the world must be like such that either is true, for the difference between them is unmarked. Whatever the world must be like, it will be accurately described as London being happy or expensive, but of a granularity to elide the difference between a population and a lifestyle or the value of a property. Similar reasoning applies across the board, whatever the species of defectiveness.

That such a semantics tells us virtually nothing about the world and its furniture is reason enough to seek an explanation of how a nominal like *London* is polysemous, and how its senses can be simultaneously or selectively triggered by different predicates, and so differentially contribute to the truth of different constructions. What is uncalled for, at least as far as semantics goes, is any greater ambition to have semantics either do metaphysics or even reflect it. Semantics appears to deliver up a univocal *London* and *book*, and the rest only because it tells us so little of how the world makes truths true, resting content with structural invariances. It is a mistake to confuse the indifference of semantics to worldly detail with a simplified view of the world that answers to it.

3.5. Conclusion

We hope enough has been said to indicate that the view on offer is not remotely a proposal to in some unimagined way *reform* natural language. The concern here is in distinguishing the scientifically tractable issues of the I-language from the less tractable issues of its ordinary use, which we're happy (as someone once said) to leave entirely as it is. On the proposed view, the best the I-language can provide are either merely the syntactic forms for a truth-conditional semantics, or instructions to the conceptual system of how to construct forms to produce utterances with substantive truth-conditions appropriate to the specific conditions of the speech occasion. These latter conditions are not systematically provided by a theory of the I-language, but by a discussion of the variety of purposes and contexts in which speech is produced.[29] Although the principles of the I-language responsible for the forms may be law-like, this is unlikely to be true of these purposes and contexts. These latter are the results of massive interaction effects between the speaker's beliefs, intentions, creative imagination, and other vicissitudes of the world, and so are likely to be largely a matter of luck.

---

[29] We regard the use of language in science being a rather special context, one in which speakers generally at least aspire to a characterization of the world independently of varying human interests and contexts, an aspiration that is generally quite far from the concerns of ordinary talk.

4. How Not to Be an Idealist

Having criticized Devitt for his reliance on common sense, we will end by seconding his admirable resistance to the lure of a general idealism, which is liable to seduce the unwary.

One of the main motives for idealism (or "constructivism" as it is more recently called) is a recognition of the sometimes surprising degree to which our conceptions of the world owe at least as much to us as to the world, a fact that linguistics makes particularly vivid. Kant (1787/1968) argued that our concepts could only coherently categorize determinate objects within the "phenomenal" realm of experience, and that consequently we couldn't know the "noumena" as would-be determinate objects independent of experience although we could think of them. Yet if, as Chomsky would recommend, we give up the empiricist premise about our concepts being restricted to experience, then (in terms of the "cookie-cutter" metaphor often misleadingly used to characterize the view) even if our concepts are cutters of our own invention, still the cookies they cut out may well exist before and after we (conceptually) cut them. Sometimes we may even be fortunate enough in our cutter concepts to "carve nature at its joints," joints that were there all along, never needing the services of the cutter.

Despite his general dismissal of empiricism, Chomsky (1996) nevertheless writes:

> There need be no objects in the world that correspond to what we talk about, even in the simplest cases, nor does anyone believe there are. (Chomsky, 1996:22)

And he and Robert Berwick (2016) write:

> The symbols of human language and thought...do not pick out mind-independent objects or events in the world.... What we understand to be a river, a person, a tree, and water and so on, consistently turns out to be a creation of what the seventeenth century investigators called the "human cognoscitive powers," which provide us with a rich means to refer to the outside world from intricate perspectives. (Chomsky and Berwick, 2016:39)

These remarks echo the points we have made above concerning semantics. Still, they seem to go further and propose a more thorough-going constructivism or idealism. But there is no need to pursue such a course. Nothing about the appropriate narrowness of the explanatory ambitions of semantics should lead one to think that rivers or trees are "creations" or do not exist "mind-independent[ly]." In other words, while our cognoscitive or semantic powers are conditions for us to refer at all, and do not entail or presuppose a univocal entity for each word type, nothing is "created" that substitutes for an external entity.

At any rate, Chomsky's point in the above passages is not really to deny a realism about serious scientific posits. He would likely entirely agree with Devitt's (1984/97) defence of a *scientific* realism, and with his invoking of the simple Moorean point that we generally have more reason to believe in the existence of an independent external world than we do in the premises of the idealist who denies it.[30]

Indeed, our norms of truth, objectivity, and evidence both guide us away from representational parochialism (you have your world; I have mine) and, more fundamentally, allow us to ask the very question of the entanglement of referential means with our intended referential ends. We can also seek to disentangle them, which is precisely an aspect of the scientific endeavour: to see the world in an invariant way, not from this or that perspective. In this light, there is an innocent constructivism, by which science is *our* business of trying to get the world right, as best we can with meagre means. Yet sometimes we succeed.[31]

One might wonder whether any common-sense entities, such as trees, tables, and chairs, could ever be regarded as real, given that, e.g., tables *qua* tables don't enter into any serious science.[32] One of us (Rey, 2020b:§9.2) has argued that there are two conditions under which it's reasonable to take a common-sense expression realistically: (i) if there's enough *stability* in its extensional usage across people and time; and (ii) if all the *central properties* connected to the usage of the term can be *preserved* under the assumption that it applies to something that can be delineated by a serious explanatory science. Skies, rainbows, fates, and average Americans, as well as (per §2.4) SLEs are either unstable and/or have features that aren't satisfied by anything in the physical world. By contrast, tables and chairs seem to satisfy both these conditions: tables, say, are just hunks of matter occupying a certain space-time position that, *modulo* vague boundaries, are stably picked out by the relevant uses of "table" upon an occasion of utterance. Thus, in rejecting Devitt's presumption that "most" common-sense objects exist, we see no reason to claim that *none* of them do.

---

[30] Thus, Chomsky (1995b:1, 24, 2000:53) does seem prepared to be completely realist about the referents of concepts not involving human interests, notably the concepts of "naturalistic theory, which seeks to set such factors [as human interests and unreflective thought] to one side" (2000:22). Indeed: "We construct explanatory theories as best we can, taking as real whatever is postulated in the best theories we can devise (because there is no other notion of 'real')" (Chomsky, 1995b:35).

[31] Devitt and Sterelny (1987/99:ch 13) point out that linguistics has been a source of anti-realism since the influential work of Saussure (1914/77). Indeed, the Chomksyan linguist, Ray Jackendoff (2006) has often championed a general anti-realism. For other passages of Chomsky's that seem to support a more constructivist attitude, see Chomsky (2000:181); Chomsky and Berwick (2011:39); Chomsky and McGilvray (2012:125); and Chomsky (2016:4). In his study of Chomsky, McGilvray (1999:5–6) explicitly construes Chomsky as a "constructivist" about everything! For passages that, however, seem to express at least a scientific realism, see Chomsky (1995:1, 24, 35, and 2000:22, 134, 153). Rey (2020b:§§9.1 and 10.4) tries to sort out Chomsky's views in this regard.

[32] This is in reply to Devitt's (2020:fn12) worries that a denial of SLEs would bring with it a denial of everything, a worry that overlooked the crucial fn 7 of Rey (2020a), much of which the present paragraph repeats.

We think this last claim is enough to capture what is important in Devitt's general realism. We simply demur over his commitment to "most" common-sense entities, as well as about what appears to be his reliance on common-sense conceptions of language and its conventionality that are not supported by serious linguistic inquiry in search of laws.[33]

References

Antony, L. (2002), "How to Play the Flute: A Commentary on Dreyfus's 'Intelligence without Representation'," *Phenomenology and the Cognitive Sciences* 1 (4): 395–401.

Asher, N. (2011), *Lexical Meaning in Context: A Web of Words.* Cambridge: Cambridge University Press.

Azzouni, J. (2010), *Talking About Nothing: Numbers, Hallucinations, and Fictions.* Oxford: Oxford University Press.

Bloomfield, L. (1933), *Language,* New York: Henry Holt.

Borg, E. (2009), "Must a Semantic Minimalist be a Semantic Internalist?" *Aristotelian Society Supplementary Volume* 83: 31–51.

Burge, T. (1979), "Individualism and the Mental," *Midwest Studies in Philosophy* 4 (1): 73–121.

Carlson, G. and F. J. Pelletier (2002), "The Average American Has 2.3 Children," *Journal of Semantics* 19: 73–104.

Casati, R. and Varzi, A. (1994), *Holes and Other Superficialities.* Cambridge: MIT Press.

Cherniak, C. (1986), *Minimal Rationality.* Cambridge: MIT Press.

Chomsky, N. (1957), *Syntactic Structures.* The Hague: Mouton.

Chomsky, N. (1965), *Aspects of the Theory of Syntax.* Cambridge MA: MIT Press.

Chomsky, N. (1975), *Reflections on Language.* New York: Pantheon Books.

Chomsky, N. (1980), *Rules and Representations.* Oxford: Blackwell.

Chomsky, N. (1981), *Lectures on Government and Binding.* Dordrecht: Foris.

Chomsky, N. (1995a), *The Minimalist Program.* Cambridge, MA: MIT Press.

Chomsky, N. (1995b), "Language and Nature," *Mind* 104 (413): 1–61.

Chomsky, N. (1996), *Powers and Prospects.* Boston: South End Press.

Chomsky, N. (2000), *New Horizons in the Study of Language.* Cambridge: Cambridge University Press.

Chomsky, N. (2003), "Replies," in L. Antony and N. Hornstein (eds.), *Chomsky and His Critics.* Oxford: Blackwell.

---

[33] We are indebted to Devitt for comments on earlier drafts. Although he emphatically rejects our claim that his views about language rest largely on common sense, we stand by the evidence we provide for it.

Chomsky, N. (2016), *What Kind of Creatures Are We?* New York: Columbia University Press.

Chomsky, N. and Berwick, R. (2016), *Why Only Us: Language and Evolution.* Cambridge: MIT Press.

Chomsky, N. and McGilvray, J. (2012), *The Science of Language: Interviews with James McGilvray.* Cambridge: Cambridge University Press.

Collins, J. (2008a), *Chomsky: A Guide for the Perplexed.* London: Conintuum.

Collins, J. (2008b), "A Note on Conventions and Unvoiced Syntax," *Croatian Journal of Philosophy* 7: 241–7.

Collins, J. (2009), "The Perils of Content," *Croatian Journal of Philosophy,* 9: 259–89.

Collins, J. (2011), *The Unity of Linguistic Meaning.* Oxford: Oxford University Press.

Collins, J. (2017a), "The Semantics and Ontology of 'The average American'," *Journal of Semantics* 34 (3): 373–405.

Collins, J. (2017b), "The Copredication Argument," *Inquiry* 60: 675–702.

Collins, J. (2020), "Invariance as the Mark of the Psychological reality of Language." in A. Bianchi (ed.), *Language and Reality from a Naturalistic Perspective.* Dordrecht: Springer, pp. 7–44.

Collins, J. (2021), "The Diversity of Fiction and Copredication: An Accommodation Problem." *Erkenntnis* 86 (5): 1197–23.

Collins, J. and Rey, G. (2021), "Chomsky and Intentionality," in N. Allott, T. Lohndal, and G. Rey (eds.), *A Companion to Chomsky.* Hoboken, NJ: Wiley-Blackwell, pp. 488–502.

Dennett, D. (1969), *Content and Consciousness.* London: Routledge.

Devitt, M. (1984/97), *Realism and Truth.* Princeton, NJ: Princeton University Press.

Devitt, M. (1996), *Coming to Our Senses.* Cambridge: Cambridge University Press.

Devitt, M. (2003), "Linguistics Is Not Psychology," in A. Barber (ed.), *Epistemology of Language* Oxford: Oxford University Press, pp. 107–39.

Devitt, M. (2006a), *Ignorance of Language.* Oxford: Clarendon Press.

Devitt, M. (2006b), "Defending Ignorance of Language: Responses to the Dubrovnik Papers," *Croatian Journal of Philosophy* VI (18): 571–609.

Devitt, M. (2008a), "Explanation and Reality in Linguistics," *Croatian Journal of Philosophy* VIII (23): 203–31.

Devitt, M. (2008b), "A Response to Collins' Note on Conventions and Unvoiced Syntax," *Croatian Journal of Philosophy* VIII (23): 249–55.

Devitt, M. (2010), *Putting Metaphysics First.* Oxford: Oxford University Press.

Devitt, M. (2020), "Stirring the Possum: Responses to the Bianchi Papers," in A. Bianchi (ed.), *Language and Reality from a Naturalistic Perspective: Themes From Michael Devitt.* Cham: Springer, pp. 371–455.

Devitt, M. (2021), *Overlooking Conventions: The Trouble with Linguistic Pragmatism.* Cham: Springer.

Devitt, M. and Sterelny, K. (1987/99), *Language and Reality*, 2nd edn. Cambridge, MA: MIT Press.

Dretske, F. (1981), *Knowledge and the Flow of Information*. Cambridge. MA: MIT Press.

Fodor, J. A. (1990), *A Theory of Content and Other Essays*. Cambridge, MA: MIT Press.

Gilbert, M. (1989), *On Social Facts*. London, New York: Routledge.

Glanzberg, M. (2014), "Explanation and Partiality in Semantic Theory," in A. Burgess and B. Sherman (eds.), *Metasemantics: New Essays on the Foundations of Meaning*. Oxford: Oxford University Press, pp. 259–92.

Higginbotham, J. (1989), "Knowledge of Reference," in A. George (ed.), *Reflections on Chomsky*. Oxford: Blackwell, pp. 153–74.

Jackendoff, R. (1990), *Semantic Structures*. Cambridge, MA: MIT Press.

Jackendoff, R. (2006), "Locating Meaning in the Mind (Where it Belongs) (Excerpt from Foundations of Language)," in R. Stainton (ed.), *Contemporary Debates in Cognitive Science*. Malden, MA: Blackwell, pp. 219–36.

Kaplan, D. (1989), "Demonstratives: An Essay on the Semantics, Logic, Metaphysics and Epistemology of Demonstratives and Other Indexicals." In J. Almog, J. Perry, and H. Wettstein (eds.), *Themes from Kaplan*, pp. 481–563.

Katz, J. (1981), *Language and Other Abstract Objects*, Totowa, NJ: Rowman and Littlefield.

Kennedy, C. and J. Stanley (2009), "On 'Average'," *Mind* 118: 583–646.

King, J. (2018), "W(h)ither Semantics!(?)," *Noûs* 52 (4): 772–95.

Kripke, S. (1972/1982), *Naming and Necessity*. Cambridge, MA: Harvard University Press.

Lasnik, H. and Uriagereka, J. with Boeckx, C. (2005), *A Course in Minimalist Syntax*. Oxford: Blackwell.

Lewis, D. (1969), *Convention: a Philosophical Study*. Cambridge, MA: Harvard University Press.

Lewis, D. and Lewis, S. (1970), "Holes," *Australasian Journal of Philosophy* 48 (2): 206–12.

Liebesman, D. and Magidor, O. (2017), "Copredication and Property Inheritance," *Philosophical Issues* 27 (1):131–66.

Ludlow, P. (2003), "Referential Semantics for I-languages?," in L. M. Antony and N. Hornstein (eds.), *Chomsky and His Critics*. Oxford: Blackwell, pp. 140–61.

McGilvray, J. (1999), *Chomsky: Language, Mind and Politics*, 1st edn. Cambridge: Cambridge University Press.

Moore, G. E. (1925/59), "A Defence of Common Sense," in T. Baldwin (ed.), *G.E. Moore: Selected Writings*. London: Routledge, pp. 106–33.

Pietroski, P. (2003), "The Character of Natural Language Semantics," in Alex Barber (eds.), *Epistemology of Language*. Oxford: Oxford University Press, pp. 217–56.

Pietroski, P. (2005), "Meaning before Truth," in G. Preyer and G. Peters (eds.), *Contextualism in Philosophy*. Oxford: Oxford University Press.

Pietroski, P. (2010), "Concepts, Meanings, and Truth: First Nature, Second Nature, and Hard Work," *Mind & Language* 25: 247–78.

Pietroski, P. (2018), *Conjoining Meanings: Semantics without Truth Values*. Oxford: Oxford University Press.

Pustejovsky, J. (1995), *The Generative Lexicon*. Cambridge, MA: MIT Press.

Putnam, H. (1962/75), "Dreaming and Depth Grammar," *Philosophical Papers: Mathematics, Matter and Method (1975)*, vol. 2. Cambridge: Cambridge University Press, pp. 304–24.

Putnam, H. (1975), "The Meaning of 'Meaning'," *Philosophical Papers: Mathematics, Matter and Method (1975)*, vol. 2. Cambridge: Cambridge University Press, pp. 215–71.

Putnam, H. (1983), Collected Papers, vol 3, Cambridge: Cambridge University Press.

Quine, W. (1960/2013), Word and Object, 2nd edn, ed. Dagfinn Føllesdal, Cambridge, MA: MIT Press.

Quine, W. (1970a), "Methodological Reflections on Linguistic Theory," *Synthese*, 21 (3–4): 386–98.

Quine, W. (1970b), "Philosophical Progress in Language Theory," *Metaphilosophy* 1 (1): 2–19.

Quine, W. and Ullian, J. (1978), *The Web of Belief*, New York: McGraw Hill.

Rey, G. (2020a), "Explanation First! The Priority of Scientific over 'Commonsense' Metaphysics," in A. Bianchi (ed.), *Language and Reality from a Naturalistic Perspective: Themes From Michael Devitt*. Cham: Springer.

Rey, G. (2020b), *Representation of Language: Philosophical Issues in a Chomskyan Linguistics*. Oxford: Oxford University Press.

Roberts, I. and Holmberg, A. (2010), "Introduction: Parameters in Minimalist Theory," in T. Biberauer, A. Holmberg, I. Roberts, and M. Sheehan (eds.), *Parametric Variation Null Subjects in Minimalist Theory*, Cambridge University Press, pp. 1–57.

Russell, B. (1912), *Problems of Philosophy*. New York: Henry Holt.

de Saussure, F. (1914/77), *Cours de linguistique générale*, ed. C. Bally and A. Sechehaye, with the collaboration of A. Riedlinger. Lausanne, Paris: Payot; trans. W. Baskin (1977), *Course in General Linguistics*. Glasgow: Fontana/Collins.

Skinner, B. (1957), Verbal Behavior, Acton, MA: Copley Publishing Group.

Smith, N. and Allott, N. (2016), *Chomsky—Ideas and Ideals*, 3rd edn. Cambridge: Cambridge University Press.

Soames, S. (1984), "Linguistics and Psychology," *Linguistics and Philosophy* 7: 155–79.

Sorensen, R. (2008), *Seeing Dark Things: The Philosophy of Shadows*. Oxford: Oxford University Press.

Stanley, J. (2007), "Introduction." *Language in Context: Selected Essays*. Oxford: Oxford University Press.

Stich, S. (1990), *The Fragmentation of Reason*. Cambridge, MA: MIT Press.

Thomasson, A. L. (2007), *Ordinary Objects*. Oxford: Oxford University Press.

Vicente, A. (2018), "Polysemy and Word Meaning: An Account of Lexical Meaning for Different Kinds of Content Words," *Philosophical Studies* 175 (4): 947–68.

Wittgenstein, L. (1953/2016), *Philosophical Investigations*, 4th rev edn, ed. and trans. G. E. M. Anscombe, P. M. S. Hacker, and J. Schulte. Chichester: John Wiley and Sons Ltd.

Wittgenstein, L. (1981), *Zettel*, ed. G. E. M. Anscombe and G. H. von Wright. Oxford: Blackwell.

Yang, C. (2002), *Knowledge and Learning in Natural Language*. Oxford: Oxford University Press.

6

Linguistic Luck

A Response to Rey and Collins

Michael Devitt

1. Introduction

Expressions of thought by members of a linguistic community are typically, to some extent, governed by the rules and principles (briefly, rules) of a shared language. Georges Rey and John Collins ("RC"), in "Laws and Luck in Language: Problems with Devitt's Conventional, Common-Sense Linguistics" (Chapter 5, this volume), helpfully describe "a matter of 'luck'" as something "accidental relative to a certain principled system" (p. 88). So, relative to the system of rules that constitute a language, an expression of thought that is not governed by the rules is a matter of linguistic "luck": the linguistic rules are luck-reducing mechanisms. I am mainly concerned with the extent of that luck: To what extent are the semantic and syntactic properties of the linguistic tokens in expressions of thought, in utterances, not governed by the rules of the language and hence "lucky"? I am also concerned with the source of those rules. Are they innate or learned? Insofar as they are learned, they are accidental relative to innate human nature; they are a matter of luck. And insofar as the rules are thus lucky, so too are the expressions governed by them. So the concern is with two distinct sorts of linguistic luck: linguistic tokens that are accidental relative to linguistic rules are "*r*-lucky"; and linguistic rules, hence expressions governed by them that are accidental relative to human nature are "*i*-lucky."

Having addressed these questions in §I, I will consider RC's critique in §II. I will respond first to their discussion of my views of language and linguistics, the views that underlie my theses about linguistic luck. I will then respond to their egregious misrepresentation of my methodology, a misrepresentation that they use to discredit my views and promote their own.[1]

---

[1] RC's misrepresentation builds on Rey's earlier one (2020a), to which I have responded (2020: 428–32). I gave RC detailed comments on three prior drafts of their chapter, but the misrepresentation continued with little abatement. So I asked the editors of this volume, Abrol Fairweather and Carlos Montemayor, for the opportunity to reply. I am grateful to them for giving it to me.

Michael Devitt, *Linguistic Luck: A Response to Rey and Collins* In: *Linguistic Luck: Safeguards and Threats to Linguistic Communication*. Edited by: Abrol Fairweather and Carlos Montemayor, Oxford University Press.
© Oxford University Press 2023. DOI: 10.1093/oso/9780192845450.003.0006

I. Linguistic Luck

2. *R*-Luck and the Semantics-Pragmatics Distinction

Perhaps the most exciting development in recent philosophy of language has been the debate surrounding a group of philosophers and linguists who emphasize the "pragmatic" features of language over those of traditional "truth-conditional semantics." The group, roughly identified as "linguistic pragmatists" and/or "linguistic contextualists," emphasizes the extent to which the content (meaning)[2] conveyed by a sentence varies in the context of an utterance. They argue that this content, the utterance's "message," is seldom, perhaps never, constituted solely by a traditional semantic "what is said"; rather, there is "semantic underdetermination"; many think that we need to move to "truth-conditional pragmatics." The group's seminal work is Dan Sperber and Deidre Wilson's *Relevance* (1995). Major contributors to the debate include Kent Bach (1994, 1995, 2001); Robyn Carston (2002, 2004); François Récanati (2004, 2010); and Stephen Neale (2004, 2007, 2016).

Linguistic pragmatism clearly bears on the issue of *r*-luck. To the extent that a token's message is constituted pragmatically in context it is *r*-lucky. So if the pragmatists are right there is a lot more *r*-luck around than has customarily been thought. In a series of works, culminating in the recent book, *Overlooking Conventions: The Trouble with Linguistic Pragmatism* (2021b), I have argued that they are not right. So these works can be considered "essays in anti-luck semantics."

It is taken for granted by almost all that "what is said" involves disambiguation and reference determination in context as well as the conventional meanings of the language employed, as well as what is strictly encoded. The controversy is over whether there is anything else that is determined in context and goes into the truth-conditional message, perhaps into "what is said." And over whether the constitution of any such context-determined extra is "semantic" or "pragmatic." Pragmatists think there is a lot extra and that it is "pragmatic." This yields their theses of semantic underdetermination and truth-conditional pragmatics.

Linguistic pragmatists are led to their theses by a range of interesting phenomena. Consider the following utterances:

(1) I've had breakfast.
(2) You are not going to die.
(3) It's raining.
(4) Everybody went to Paris.

---

[2] I use 'content' and 'meaning' fairly interchangeably.

(5)   The table is covered with books.
(6)   John is a lion.
(7)   The party was fun until the suits arrived.
(8)   The road was covered with rabbit.

Taken literally, (1) seems to say that the speaker has had breakfast sometime in the past and yet, in context, it likely means that she has had breakfast this morning. Similarly, (2) seems to attribute immortality to the addressee but, in context, will mean something like that he will not die from that minor cut. Although (3) does not say so explicitly it surely means that it is raining in a certain location. (4) seems to say that every existing person went to Paris and yet the message it surely conveys is that everyone in a certain group went to Paris. According to the standard Russellian quantificational account, (5) makes the absurd claim that there is one and only one table and it is covered with books. Yet it is surely being used to say that a certain table is so covered. (6) says that John is a charismatic feline but means that he is courageous. What ruined the party according to (7) was not really the suits but the business executives wearing them. And what covered the road according to (8) was the remains of rabbits. Examples like these are taken to show that a deal of "pragmatic" enrichment is needed to get from what is "semantically" determined to the message, perhaps to "what is said."

My view of the semantics-pragmatics distinction (2013a) starts with an idea about languages, an idea that is rejected by Chomskians, as we shall discuss in §II. My idea is that languages are representational systems that scientists attribute to species such as bees, prairie dogs, and humans to explain their communicative behaviors. We then have a powerful theoretical interest in distinguishing two sorts of properties of any particular utterance: (a) the representational properties that it has simply in virtue of being a token-expression in a language, that it has simply as a result of the organism's exploitation of that language; (b) any other properties that may constitute the organism's message. I call the (a) properties part of "what is said," and "semantic"; and the (b) ones—for example, certain "modulations" and Gricean "implicatures"—part of "what is meant but not said," and "pragmatic." "Semantics" is the study of semantic properties, "pragmatics," pragmatic ones.[3] This theoretical basis then provides an argument for the view that what is said is constituted by properties arising from three sources: (i) from (largely)[4] conventional linguistic rules in the speaker's language, rules that determine what is *encoded* in the language; (ii) from disambiguations, where more than one rule

---

[3] "Pragmatics" is also used for "the theory of interpretation," the study of the *processes* of interpreting utterances. So the term is ambiguous (Devitt, 2013a: 103–5).
[4] I say "largely" because I accept the Chomskian view that some syntax is innate (§3). Chomskians may think the qualification inadequate, as we shall see (§6).

governs an expression in the language; (iii) from "saturations," for example, the reference fixing of indexicals (and tenses), deictic demonstratives, and pronouns.

This is a fairly traditional semantics-pragmatics distinction for which I claim to have given a theoretical, not just intuitive, basis.

The key thing about semantic properties is that they are (largely) conventional: conventions *create* linguistic meanings. But, what is a linguistic convention? It is a convention of using a certain physical form to express a certain part of a thought/ message, a concept. Putting this in Gricean terms, it is a convention of using that form with a certain "speaker meaning."

How do we *tell* when there is such a convention? We should not follow the custom of simply relying on our intuitions. Rather, we should look for evidence mainly from regularities in behavior (2013a). Is this physical form regularly used to express a certain concept, used with a certain speaker meaning? If so, it is likely, though not certain of course, that this regularity is *best explained* by supposing that there is a convention of so using the form. In principle, evidence could be found also in mental processes but in fact, I have argued (2021a: 147–55), we lack any such evidence.

What precisely is the pragmatist challenge to the semantic tradition from the perspective I have summarized? It is helpful to answer this in terms of a three-way distinction among the possible "meaning" properties of an utterance: (A) an encoded conventional meaning; (B) a what-is-said, arising from encoding, disam- biguation, saturation; (C) a pragmatic modification, perhaps a modulated what-is- said, an implicature, or whatever. (A) and (B) meanings are semantic properties; (C) are at least partly pragmatic. We should all accept—and I assume the tradition did—that there are novel uses of language, "spur of the moment" uses "on the fly," that yield pragmatic meanings. Thus there can be implicatures like Grice's famous reference letter (1989: 33). And spontaneous ellipses are surely common, requir- ing what-is-said to be pragmatically enriched or impoverished to get the precise message. Such novel uses are, of course, r-lucky. Now one might argue that novel uses of these sorts are more widespread than has been traditionally thought. That is an empirical issue that does not seem theoretically interesting because, however widespread these phenomena, they *obviously* must be explained pragmatically. The interesting pragmatist challenge to the tradition is posed by *the expressions— like those in (1) to (8) above—that motivated linguistic pragmatism*, for these expressions have regular uses that are alleged to be pragmatic; for example, regular saturations of quantifiers with domain restriction, of weather reports with refer- ence to a location, of definite descriptions with reference to a particular object in mind; and, turning to polysemy, regular uses of 'foot' to refer to the bottom of a mountain, of 'suit' to refer to business executives, of 'rabbit' to refer not only to rabbits but also to rabbit stuff. This interesting challenge is to the view that the truth-conditional meaning communicated in such regular uses is typically constituted only by my semantic what-is-said, arising from (i) conventional encodings, (ii) disambiguations, and (iii) saturations. The challenge is to the view that, absent novel spur-of-the-moment modulations and implicatures, the message of an utterance is typically that what-is-said. In challenging that view, pragmatism claims that, even setting aside the novel, the message, the meaning communicated, is seldom, perhaps never, constituted solely by that what-is-said; pragmatic modifications of some sort always, or almost always, play a role; there is always, or almost always, some r-luck.

In response to this challenge, I have argued, particularly in *Overlooking Conventions* (2021b), that almost all of the striking phenomena that pragmatists have emphasized exemplify properties of sorts (i) to (iii). There are more of such properties than we have previously acknowledged: much more of the content of messages should be put into the convention-governed what-is-said—into semantics—than has been customary; conventions have been overlooked. Contrary to what the pragmatists claim, there is no extensive semantic underdetermination. The new theoretical framework of truth-conditional pragmatics is a mistake. The striking phenomena should be accommodated within a traditional framework. Here is a summary of my case for this.

The challenge arises from the many examples of context relativity, like (1) to (8), produced by pragmatists. In arguing for my semantic rather than a pragmatic approach, I divide these examples into three groups. One group is of examples like (1) to (4) exemplifying "saturation" in context. Another is of examples like (6) to (8) exemplifying polysemous ambiguity. Finally, there are examples of "referentially" used definite descriptions, like in (5), "The table is covered with books," which exemplify *both*: they need to be saturated in context by a particular object in mind; and they have another meaning, the quantificational meaning described by Russell, that yields "attributive" uses.[5]

To meet the pragmatists' challenge I need to show that semantic explanations of these examples are "the best." My strategy is to show, first, that a semantic explanation is good and, second, that it is much better than its pragmatic rival.

I start showing that semantic explanations are good by considering referentially used definite descriptions. For, my discussion of them (1981, 1997, 2004, 2007a, 2007b) is a paradigm of the semantic approach I urge to the pragmatists' examples. I argue that these uses exemplify a non-Russellian referential meaning. So definite descriptions are ambiguous.

Many treat these referential uses pragmatically in a Gricean way as involving, for example, conversational implicatures (Kripke 1979; Neale 1990; Bach 1994). Others treat them pragmatically in a Relevance-Theoretic way where both referential and attributive uses involve other sorts of pragmatic modifications (Recanati 1989; Bezuidenhout 1997; Powell 2010). A pragmatic response to

---

[5] See Donnellan (1966) for the referential/attributive distinction.

referential uses was encouraged by the indubitable fact that we seem to be able to give a pragmatic explanation of the referential use of *any* quantifier. Neale has a nice example with 'everyone': Jones says despondently, "Well, everyone taking my seminar turned up" (to Jones' party), in circumstances in which the hearer can use Grice's Cooperative Principle, and the common knowledge that Smith is the only person in Jones' seminar, to derive the message that only Smith attended. As Neale says: "The possibility of such a scenario, would not lead us to complicate the semantics of 'every' with an ambiguity" (1990: 88). Nor, Neale is suggesting, should the possibility of referential uses of 'the *F*' lead us to complicate the semantics of it with an ambiguity (pp. 87–8).

I responded to this nice point with what Neale later called "The Argument from Convention."[6]

> The basis for [the semantic explanation] is not simply that we can use a definite referentially, it is that we *regularly* do so. When a person has a singular thought, a thought with a particular *F* object in mind, there is a regularity of her using 'the *F*' to express that thought.... This regularity is strong evidence that there is a *convention* of using 'the *F*' to express a thought about a particular *F*, that this is a *standard* use. This convention is semantic, as semantic as the one for an attributive use. In each case, there is a convention of using 'the *F*' to express a thought with a certain sort of meaning/content.
>
> 'Every' and other quantifiers are different. There is no convention of using them to convey a thought about a particular object in mind. With special stage setting they certainly can be used for that purpose, as Neale illustrates. But then Grice shows us that with enough stage setting almost any expression can be used to convey almost any thought.   (2004: 283)

The idea is that there is a convention for 'the *F*', but not for 'every', that demands saturation by the particular object in mind; the saturation is semantic. So 'the *F*' is ambiguous, having both a quantificational meaning that yields attributive definites and a referential meaning that yields referential definites. And the referential use is not *r*-lucky.

I argue in the same way that other pragmatist examples of expressions being saturated in context should be treated semantically. Each such utterance, like referentially used descriptions, has an implicit slot to be filled; each requires saturation by an implicit reference to something the speaker has in mind:

(1)   I've had breakfast. [Implicit reference to a period]
(2)   You are not going to die. [Implicit reference to a potential cause of death]

---

[6] See also Reimer (1998).

(3) It's raining. [Implicit reference to a location]
(4) Everybody went to Paris. [Implicit reference to a domain][7]

Note that, in each case, the implicit reference, can be made explicit: "I have had breakfast this morning"; "You are not going to die from that minor cut"; "It is raining in New York"; "Everyone at the conference went to Paris." Note also that there are indefinitely many possible saturations for the sentences in utterances (1) to (4), just as there are for referential definites or demonstratives. We know from informal observation that each of (1) to (4) exemplify a *regularity* of saturating expressions of a certain form to convey a message. Indeed, pragmatists don't just note these regularities they emphasize them. These regularities can be plausibly explained by supposing that there are linguistic rules for these expressions, brought about by conventions, that demand saturation in context. So they are not *r*-lucky.

The same line of argument works for many other expressions; for example, 'eat', 'dance', 'sing'. And a similar one works for many others including 'ready' and genitives like 'Peter's bat'.

Turn now to polysemy and examples like the following:

(6) John is a lion.
(7) The party was fun until the suits arrived.
(8) The road was covered with rabbit.

I argue that such utterances should be explained as examples of semantic polysemy that are disambiguated in context. 'Lion' in (6) is an example of metaphor-based polysemy; 'foot' and 'warm' are among countless others. 'Suits' in (7) is an example of metonymy-based polysemy; 'glass', denominal verbs like 'to google', and compound nouns like 'language teacher', are among countless others. 'Rabbit' in (8) is an example of "regular" ("systematic") polysemy: any count noun for an organism yields a mass noun for the stuff of which it is made. There are countless other regular polysemies; for example, a word for the producer of some item yields a word for the item produced (or vice versa), as with 'Honda' and 'newspaper'. All of these polysemous words are regularly used with more than one meaning. The case for treating them semantically is that these regularities are well-explained as conventions. Once again, no *r*-luck.

The second step in meeting the pragmatists' challenge is to show that these good semantic explanations are better than pragmatic ones. We can then conclude that the semantic explanations are "the best."

---

[7] I tell a similar story about many sub-sentential utterances (2018).

The general problem for pragmatic explanations stems from "the psychological-reality requirement" (2007a: 12–16). Consider any pragmatic explanation of the speaker meaning (message) conveyed by an utterance's sentence. The explanation involves a derivation of that meaning from the sentence's conventional meaning in the context. A paradigm example is the derivation of a Gricean implicature. Now, it is not enough for a pragmatic explanation to be good that there *is* a pragmatic derivation, discoverable by a linguist, of the speaker meaning from the conventional one. For, there is always such a derivation with a "dead metaphor." The metaphorical meaning of a word is derived from its conventional meaning. Over time, a metaphorical meaning often becomes regularized and conventional: the metaphor "dies." Yet a derivation of what is now a new conventional meaning from the old conventional meaning will still be available.[8] For the pragmatic explanation to be good, its derivation must have an appropriately active place in the cognitive lives of speakers and hearers: in brief, the hearer must go through the derivation and the speaker must make the utterance on the assumption that the hearer will go through the derivation. *That's the psychological-reality requirement.* And it may be met easily with a *novel* use, like Jones', "Well, everyone taking my seminar turned up," because speaker and hearer may be *conscious* of the derivation. But there is unlikely to be any such awareness with the likes of (1) to (8). So, if the derivations are present at all, they must be *subconscious.* A pragmatic explanation then faces two powerful objections (Devitt 2021a: 138–40).

Occamist Objection: The pragmatic explanation has heavy psychological commitments that we have no reason to suppose can be met. I have argued (2021a: 147–55) that though psycholinguistics has discovered many interesting facts about language processing, they have not produced any evidence of the subconscious processes that pragmatism requires. One might reasonably respond that, despite years of impressive work, we know quite little about how we process language *in general.* Still we do know that there *must be* the largely subconscious convention-exploiting processes of saturation and disambiguation in speakers and hearers, even if we do not know the details. For, those are standard processes of language use. So we already know that there must be the sort of processes required by the semantic explanation, the rival of the pragmatic one. This is a crucial part of the background knowledge that is so important in assessing which is the better explanation of the phenomena in question. The semantic explanation is committed to mechanisms that we already know exist, even though we are short on the details. The pragmatic explanation is committed to subconscious processes for which we need independent evidence before we should suppose that they exist at all. There is no such evidence and so we should prefer the semantic explanation.

---

[8] I have used this consideration against Modified Occam's Razor, as normally construed (2013b: 297–300).

Developmental Objection: Not only should we prefer the semantic to the pragmatic on Occamist grounds, if we lack evidence of the existence of the required new psychological processes, there is a good reason to suppose, *a priori*, that these processes do *not* exist. Consider an expression that does not have a certain meaning conventionally in a language but that comes to be regularly used with that meaning in successful communications by speakers of that language. That success tends to lead to the expression having that meaning by convention, thus building the language. So, why would the regular saturation of the expressions in (1) to (5), and the regular use of the polysemes in (5) to (8), not have had that same happy result? A convention eliminates the need for the demanding mind-reading processes in speakers and hearers that a pragmatic explanation requires. This is how having a language aids communication. Why would we have denied ourselves the benefit of conventionalization with the expressions in (1) to (8)?

In sum, the semantic explanations of the likes of (1) to (8) are good. In contrast, the pragmatic explanations posit subconscious processes that we have no independent reason to suppose exist: the Occamist Objection. Worse, our background knowledge makes it unlikely that those processes do exist: the Developmental Objection. The semantic explanation is "the best." There is much less *r*-luck than pragmatists imply. Novel uses of language aside, utterances are typically *r*-unlucky.

3. *I*-Luck and Universal Grammar

What about *i*-luck? Are linguistic rules innate or learned? Insofar as they are learned they are *i*-lucky; hence the expressions governed by them are *i*-lucky. Chomsky has famously argued that some fundamental rules of syntax, the rules of Universal Grammar (UG), are innately determined. So it is not *i*-luck that our language does not contain expressions that offend these rules. Thus, to take one of RC's examples (p. 95), it is not *i*-luck that "Who will John and meet Mary?" is not in our language although "John and **who** will meet Mary?" is: the absence of the former is not accidental but ruled out by innate constraints. I *emphasize* that I accept this innateness, because one might get the impression from RC's Chapter 5 (this volume), and particularly from Rey's important recent book (2020b), that I do not really.[9] My acceptance is clear in the conclusion of the relevant chapter in *Ignorance of Language*:

---

[9] Rey states: "[Devitt] does allow that *some* features may be innate (2006a: 13,103), but this seems mostly lip-service, since, so far as I can find, he never provides any serious examples.... His claim does suggest that he does not take the oddities of UG rules to seriously tell against his conventionalist conception. To the contrary, Devitt sometimes seems actually to think that conventional rules would

I think that the [arguments from the universality of UG-rules, from the poverty of stimulus, from language creation, and from the continuity hypothesis], taken jointly, present a persuasive case for [the interesting thesis that] humans are innately predisposed to learn languages that conform to the UG-rules; the initial state respects the UG-rules.[10]   (2006a: 271)

This thesis raises the question: *In virtue of what* does the initial state "respect" the UG-rules? I took Chomsky to embrace the "even more interesting" thesis:

The initial state respects the UG-rules *because it embodies the UG-rules*. Not merely do we inherit some language-constraining rules that makes us respect the UG-rules, which is all that [the above thesis] requires, we inherit the UG-rules themselves.   (2006a: 246)

I'm dubious, but still argue:

If we assume [that] a person thinks in a Mentalese governed by structure rules that are similar to those of her language [then] we have good reason to suppose that something close to [the even more interesting thesis] will explain that respect and hence be part of a persuasive future explanation of language acquisition; we have good reason to suppose that the UG-rules are, for the most part, innate structure rules of thought.   (2006a: 271)

I point out that:

neither of these theses entail that speakers have innate representations of linguistic rules or innate propositional knowledge—knowledge-that—about them: the innate rules might be simply embodied and any innate knowledge might be simply knowledge-how…. As a result, these theses alone do not entail the existence of any innate *concepts* and so do not seem to bear on the traditional debate over innate ideas.   (pp. 246–7)

suffice *instead* of innate ones. As we noted from the start, a major challenge to a conventionalist view is to explain, *inter alia*, the WhyNots" (2020b: 206).

Rey does not mention my argument (2006a: 248–51) that leads to the unequivocal conclusion quoted in the text. This argument is surely not "lip-service." And the fact that its conclusion is *inconsistent with* treating "the oddities of UG rules" as conventional shows that I take those oddities "to seriously tell against" their being conventional! And it is baffling that he finds "baffling" (2020b: 210) my recent footnote about his (neatly named) WhyNots, which reads: 'To avoid misunderstanding, perhaps I should emphasize that I grant the Chomskian view that the language has some of its syntactic properties, including perhaps the WhyNots, as a result not of convention but of innate constraints on the sorts of language that humans can learn "naturally"' (2006a: 244–72, 2020: 379, n. 11)

Rey seems to take this as a change of heart, but it has always been my view, as is obvious from the cited discussion in *Ignorance*.

[10]   But see Scholz and Pullum (2006) for some skepticism.

In any case, I found no basis for this "very exciting" thesis that linguistic rules are indeed innately represented and propositionally known, no basis for the thesis that UG itself, the *theory* of those rules, is innately known (p. 272).

I turn now to the critique of my linguistic views by Rey and Collins (RC).

II. Response to Rey and Collins

4. The Linguistic Conception

As can be seen, I agree with RC that language is, to an interesting degree, *i*-unlucky. But I think that the linguistic expressions in utterances are governed by rules that are mostly not innately determined and so those expressions are *r*-unlucky, something that RC do not seem to contemplate. My stance on linguistic *r*-luck reflects a view of language and linguistics that RC emphatically reject. Our most serious disagreement is over *what grammars are about*: I oppose the Chomskian "psychological conception" and urge the "linguistic conception." So, RC rightly introduce the linguistic conception in their §2.3 as "Devitt's Alternative" view of "the explanatory scope of linguistics" (p. 96). But, it needs to be emphasized, my alternative view of this scope is *not* "conventionalism," which is the second part of RC's mantra, "common-sense conventionalism," that begins in their title and dominates their discussion of my views in what follows. We may have a disagreement over the role of conventions in the explanation of language but, we shall see in §5, this is not of much significance generally and is *totally irrelevant* to my alternative view of "the explanatory scope of linguistics." Unfortunately, RC conflate the serious disagreement with the irrelevant one throughout their discussion of my views, thoroughly muddying the waters.

I shall discuss the linguistic conception and identify the conflation in this section. I shall discuss my alleged "conventionalism" in the next. In §6, I shall address their baseless charge, exemplified in the first part of the mantra, that my methodology is one of relying on common sense.

As RC note, according to the linguistic conception, which they call "(LR)," a grammar is about a non-psychological realm of linguistic expressions, physical entities forming symbolic or representational systems. In contrast, the received Chomskian psychological conception is that a grammar is about a speaker's linguistic competence and hence about mental states. RC dismiss the linguistic conception, but without any attention to the argument for it, a matter to which I will return. Here is a very brief summary of the argument.[11]

---

[11] The argument was first presented in Devitt (2003), which formed the basis for Devitt (2006a: ch 2). Later presentations and developments are in Devitt (2006b: 574–87, 2008a,b, 2013c). Devitt and Sterelny (1989) is an earlier version of the argument, but contains many errors.

The argument starts with three general distinctions. The distinctions are, first, between the theory of a competence and the theory of its outputs or inputs; second, between the structure rules governing the outputs and the processing rules governing the exercise of the competence; third, between the "respecting" of structure rules by processing rules and the inclusion of structure rules among processing rules. ("Respecting" is a technical term here: processing rules and competence "respect" the structure rules in that they are apt to produce outputs governed by those structure rules; analogously, apt to process inputs.)

The argument continues: these general distinctions apply to humans and their languages. To take my favorite example, just as the theory of the representational system that is the bee's "waggle dance" is one thing, the theory of the bee's competence to produce the dance, another, so also is the theory of the representational system that is a human language one thing, the theory of the speaker's competence to produce it another. Karl von Frisch proposed a theory of the structure rules of the representational system that is the bee's dance. We need an analogous theory that explains the nature of the representational system that is a human language. That theory will surely be even more interesting than the one that got von Frisch a Nobel Prize.

Why is a theory of the nature of that representational system so interesting? We posit the system to explain behavior, particularly communicative behavior: a noise (or inscription) is produced *because* it has certain linguistic properties, including syntactic ones, and it is *because* it has these properties, and hence is a linguistic expression (symbol), that an audience responds to that behavior as it does. The linguistic properties of symbols explain their striking causal roles in our lives, roles that we may hope to capture in laws. I shall return to the causal role of symbols in §5.

What do such theories tell us about competence? Not much. Simply on the strength of von Frisch's theory we know this minimal proposition about any competent bee: that there is something-we-know-not-what within the bee that respects the structure rules that von Frisch discovered. But the theory does not tell us *what* there is in the bee that does this job. Indeed, last I heard, we know very little about that. Similarly, a theory of the structure rules of our language tells us that there is something-we-know-not-what within any competent speaker that respects the structure rules it describes. This is the minimal position on psychological reality that I call "(M)" (2006a: 57). But the theory of the language provides nothing more about the mind than (M): it does not tell us *what* there is in the speaker that does the respecting. In particular, we don't know whether any of the theory's rules are embodied some way or other in the mind and so also part of the psychological reality that produces language. To move beyond the minimal claim and discover *the way in which* a speaker respects the grammar's rules, we need further psychological evidence of actual processing.

Finally, I argue that a grammar, produced by linguists, is the syntactic part of the theory we need of the representational system that is a human language:

> A grammar is a theory of the nature of the system that is a language, not of the psychological reality of that language in its competent speakers (beyond the minimal (M)).   (2008a: 206)

We have arrived at the linguistic conception (LR).

In support of the final move in the argument for (LR), consider some typical grammatical rules (principles):

> An anaphor must be bound by another expression in its governing category.
> A pronoun must not be bound by another expression in its governing category.
> Accusative case is assigned by a governing verb or preposition.
> A verb which fails to assign accusative case fails to theta-mark an external argument.

Such claims about anaphors, pronouns, verbs, prepositions, and the like are about *expressions*, symbols in a human language. These claims are not about mental states: they *do not mention* understanding or mental capacities. Building on this, with reference to Quine (1961), I offered the follow deductive argument for the above view of grammars:

(a) Any theory is a theory of x's iff it quantifies over x's and if the singular terms in applications of the theory refer to x's.

(b) A grammar quantifies over nouns, verbs, pronouns, prepositions, anaphors, and the like, and the singular terms in applications of a grammar refer to such items.[12]

(c) Nouns, verbs, pronouns, prepositions, anaphors, and the like are linguistic expressions/symbols (which are entities produced by minds but external to minds).

(d) So, a grammar is a theory of linguistic expressions/symbols. (Devitt 2020: 375–6)

The truth of the grammar of a language entails that its rules govern linguistic reality, giving a rich picture of this reality. In contrast, the truth of the grammar does not entail that its rules govern the psychological reality of speakers competent in the language, and it alone gives a relatively impoverished picture of that reality (just (M)).

---

[12] For a discussion of some examples in Liliane Haegeman's textbook (1994), see my (2008b: 250–1).

Grammatical rules *directly* explain the natures of expressions but this is not to say, of course, that they play no role in explaining cognitive phenomena:

> It is *because* the grammar gives a good explanation of the symbols that speakers produce that it can contribute to the explanation of the cognitive phenomena . . . . *English speakers construe English expressions as if they had certain properties because, as the grammar explains, the expressions really have those properties.*
>
> (2008a: 215)

The grammar would not be a complete theory of the language (even if finished): a grammar is a theory of the syntax of a language (broadly construed) and, it is common to think, needs to be supplemented by theories of the word-world connections that constitute word meanings. So, I think we need theories of reference. Rey notes this, and notes the doubts that Chomsky and others have "that we will ever get anything like a serious *theory* of the topic."[13] But then Rey continues:

> What Devitt needs to show in order for his focus on LR to even begin to compete with Chomsky's on psychology is that these mind/world relations are as remotely susceptible to theories as deep as those of I-languages seem to be.   (2020b: 201)

This is quite false. (a) The linguistic conception (LR) is about grammars and hence only concerned with syntax. (LR) claims that grammars are theories of the syntactic properties of external-to-the-mind symbols. That is true even if a "serious theory" of the reference of those symbols is beyond us. (b) More importantly, *as theories of the syntactic nature of symbols, grammars are as deep as one could want. In contrast, as theories of the mind, grammars are shallow;* see the minimal (M) above.

I have taken to concluding my presentations of my argument for the linguistic conception by

> emphasizing that the linguistic conception does *not* involve the absurd claim that psychological facts have nothing to do with linguistic facts. Some psychological facts *cause* linguistic facts (pp. 23–4), some *"respect"* them (p. 25), some *partly constitute* them (pp. 39–40, 132–3, 155–7), some *provide evidence* for them (pp. 32–4), and some make them *theoretically interesting* (pp. 30, 134–5). But psychological facts are not the *subject matter* of grammars. The dispute is not over whether linguistics relates to psychology but over the way it does.
>
> (2008a: 207; the cited passages are in Devitt 2006a)

---

[13] I sympathize with the doubts and come close to sharing them on bad days.

The linguistic conception provoked a deal of outrage in Chomskian circles.[14] Some responses by Rey and Collins stand out for the admirable amount of *argument* they contain. First, in a series of papers (2006a, 2006b, 2008), Rey challenged a key presupposition of the linguistic conception: that there really is an external-to-the-mind linguistic reality for grammars to explain; he challenged "linguistic realism." For, according to that conception, grammars explain the nature of that linguistic reality, and one can't explain what doesn't exist. Furthermore, it has to be the case that the *theoretical interest* of grammars comes primarily from such explanations. I reject Rey's anti-realism, of course (2006a: 184–9, 2006b: 597–604, 2008a: 221–9), but he did a service in arguing for something that is usually just taken for granted by Chomskians. Second, recently both Collins (2020) and Rey (2020a: 306–13), in a volume edited by Andrea Bianchi (2020), have tried to challenge the linguistic conception by offering "paraphrase responses." As Quine points out, a scientist can avoid the ontic commitments of a theory by proposing another one that paraphrases away that commitment while still serving the theoretical purpose well enough.[15] In my reply to Collins and Rey in the Bianchi volume, I noted that those wanting to mount this defense of the psychological conception in the face of my argument need to do three things:

> First, *they need to acknowledge* that grammars should not be taken literally but rather should be taken as standing in for a set of paraphrases that do not talk about expressions.... Second, *they should tell us what the paraphrases are* or, at least, tell us how they are to be generated from what grammars actually say. Third, *they should give examples of how this paraphrased grammar directly explains cognitive phenomena.* (2020: 377)

Admirably, Collins and Rey have attempted to meet these requirements, Collins, at great length.[16] I gave detailed criticisms of these attempts, including:

> *The rewriting adds no explanatory power.* And the rewriting is pointless if the grammar is indeed a more or less true account of linguistic reality, as the linguistic conception claims. (2020: 379–80)

I concluded with this ringing reaffirmation of the linguistic conception:

---

[14] Collins (2006, 2007, 2008a, 2008b, 2020); Rey (2006a, 2006b, 2008, 2020a, 2020b); Smith (2006); Antony (2008); Pietroski (2008); Slezak (2009); Longworth (2009); Ludlow (2009).

[15] In his book, Rey oddly accuses me of having "carelessly neglected" this "crucial caveat in Quine's discussion of these issues" (2020b: 209). Yet I introduce my long discussion of "The Paraphrase Response" with the remark that it would be "a bit flatfooted" to overlook it (2020: 377).

[16] And Rey describes well how what Chomskians *actually say* in presenting grammars poses an ontological problem for them (2020b: 213–16).

There are, external to the mind, entities playing causal roles in virtue of their linguistic properties. Grammars are approximately true theories of some of those properties, the syntactic ones.   (2020: 380)

So one would think that if Rey and Collins wanted to continue challenging the linguistic conception, "Devitt's Alternative," they would focus on this Bianchi exchange on that very subject. Yet that exchange goes virtually undiscussed in their present chapter.[17] What is going on? The aforementioned conflation is central to the answer, as we shall now see.

1. Although RC do not discuss the Bianchi exchange they do mention it. They attach a footnote (p. 96) to the quote from Devitt (2008a: 205) that they use to introduce the linguistic conception (LR). The footnote acknowledges that "Devitt (2006a) provides a number of arguments for (LR)" but then say astonishingly that they "won't consider [those arguments] here," citing the Bianchi exchange (p. 96 n. 10). *Why not consider arguments for the topic under discussion?!* RC explain: those arguments "are independent of the common-sense conventionalism that is all that concerns us here." But if (LR) is independent of what concerns them, why is it introduced as "Devitt's Alternative" to the Chomskian view of linguistics? And, *as a matter of fact*, it *is* my alternative and the alleged "common-sense conventionalism" of their mantra is *not*, as we shall see.

Set aside the "common-sense" part of the mantra until §6. We see here the first clear sign of the conflation that bedevils RC's critique, the conflation of the linguistic conception of grammars with my alleged "conventionalism," the other part of the mantra. More signs of the conflation are to come.

The conflation matters because my view of the role of conventions is *irrelevant* to the linguistic conception. This was apparent from the start given the place of the bee's dance in my argument for the linguistic conception: for, as I noted, "the bee's competence to dance is surely innate" (2006a: 39). I later added the example of prairie dogs in bringing home just how irrelevant it is to the linguistic conception whether linguistic rules are innate or conventional:

The rules of the prairie dog's language seem to be partly learned and, perhaps we should say, "conventional": its alarm calls vary a bit from colony to colony; and when an experimenter used a plywood model to simulate a new sort of predator, the prairie dogs introduced a new call (Slobodchikoff 2002). In any case, whether a language used to communicate information is innate or conventional, we have a powerful theoretical interest in that language and its rules. Serious scientists

---

[17] The exception is in footnote 18, p. 103 where they rightly object to my claim (2020: 379) that their paraphrases of grammatical claims are "very different." But this minor matter is quite incidental to the linguistic conception.

work to discover the natures of the symbols in these representational systems, to
discover their *meanings*.   (2013a: 95–6)

That the rules of human languages "differ from those of the bees in being
conventional not innate . . . is beside the point" (p. 99).

Contrast this with Rey's claim that Chomskians:

offer a substantial theory that the innate properties are *the main and fundamental properties of grammar*, . . . those properties arguably *constitute* what a
grammar *is*! This is precisely why they regard grammar as part of human
psychology.   (2020b: 210)

Even if *all* the properties that a grammar attributes to a language were innate that
would not make the grammar "part of human psychology." The grammar is about
the syntactic properties of the expressions of a language whatever the cause of
their having those properties.

2. RC follow the quote that introduces the linguistic conception with an
account that nicely identifies some views that are *not* part of the conception.
They conclude:

Nor does Devitt have any quarrel with any of the specific principles of grammar
that linguists propose. Rather he simply objects to their regarding their
theories as psychological theories rather than as theories of "linguistic reality"
per (LR).   (p. 97)

All well and good. But then, remarkably, RC go on:

This seems to be partly due to his insisting upon a common-sense conception
about the reality of standard linguistic entities ("SLEs," such as words, phrases,
sentences, phonemes, and/or phonological properties) and the conventions
governing them.   (p. 97)

RC follow this by quoting my claim that "symbols [SLEs] are social entities"
(2006b: 583).

Let us take stock. RC are speculating that my reason for the linguistic conception (LR) lies in my view that SLEs are conventional. Yet my reason *obviously does
not*: the conception would apply even if our language were entirely innate; see
above. More importantly, *why the uncharitable speculation? Why not just look to
my actual arguments to find my reason?* (I will return to this point in §6.) RC are
very familiar with these arguments, having responded to them at length in print.
Yet, as noted a page back, these are the very arguments that they set aside as

"independent of the common-sense conventionalism that is all that concerns us here." Well, the arguments are obviously *not* independent of the *linguistic conception* and we have already seen ample evidence that this conception *does* concern them. And so it should, if they are concerned to rebut "Devitt's Alternative" view of "the explanatory scope of linguistics." For, whereas Chomskians think that linguistics' scope "flows from its positing of complex internal structure to the mind/brain" (p. 96), my alternative view is that much of its scope "flows from" a grammar's explanation of the syntactic natures of external-to-the-mind symbols in a linguistic system. *That* is my real alternative. And it is the linguistic conception. RC are conflating it with "conventionalism."

3. RC note that I am not urging "an alternative set of grammatical principles" nor denying "some of their innate determinants." "Devitt is only concerned to deny...commitment to those innate determinants being the proper focus of linguistic theory" (p. 98).[18] RC continue: Devitt "wants to insist on a non-psychological focus on *the social and conventional facts about language*" (p. 98; emphasis added). But this is *not* what the linguistic conception insists on. It insists that the focus of grammars is on *facts about linguistic expressions*, whether those facts are caused by conventions or not. RC have welded the view that these facts are conventional into the linguistic conception: the conflation again.

4. The conflation is very evident in RC's discussion that follows, particularly in this:

It's hard to find a definitive argument [in Devitt's writing] other than...the syntactic differences between public languages *show* that much syntax is not innate (2006a:180; emphasis ours)   (p. 98)

But this quote is part of an argument for my alleged "conventionalism" not an argument for the linguistic conception. Yet it is that conception, not "conventionalism," that is "Devitt's Alternative," which is what §2.3 is supposed to be about. And finding an argument for that conception doesn't require any scouring: they can just look at the arguments that they decided not to consider!

---

[18] I may sometimes have written loosely as if making such a denial about "linguistic theory"— "hyperbolic moments"?—but all I ever meant to deny was that those innate determinants are the focus of *grammars*; thus, the title of the relevant chapter of *Ignorance* is "A Grammar is a Theory of Linguistic Reality" (2006a: ch. 2). *Linguistic theory* is a big tent that covers more than grammars. I certainly think that UG, which obviously is concerned with the innate determinants, is *a*, though not *the*, "proper focus of linguistic theory."

Relatedly, consider this: "Devitt's main error is to claim that Chomsky is somehow mistaken in having the internal, psychological interest he pursues" (Rey 2020b: 197). But I do not belittle an interest in UG and the psychology of language. Indeed, almost all of *Ignorance* is about that psychology. I think, however, that there is something else of theoretical interest, which grammars help to explain, external-to-the-mind languages. RC's "main error" is to deny this interest. So, the belittling seems to be on the other foot.

(And, I might add, finding an argument for my alleged "conventionalism" is not hard either; see §5 below.)

In conclusion, there is nothing in RC's discussion of the positions they conflate that counts against the considerations leading to my ringing affirmation of the linguistic conception (§4). And the linguistic conception is the real "Devitt's Alternative."

I turn now to the other side of the conflation, my alleged "conventionalism."

5. The Role of Linguistic Conventions

What exactly is the "conventionalism" that RC object to? I have already indicated my view that their disagreement with me over the role of conventions in the explanation of language is not of much significance generally and is *totally irrelevant* to my alternative view of "the explanatory scope of linguistics." Here's why.

I start with something that we surely agree on: grammatical rules are not entirely innate. Innate principles of UG are thought to demand the settings of parametric values that yield the grammatical rules of a particular language. As RC put it:

> Just *which* language an individual speaker will acquire depends upon comparatively contingent circumstances, specifically, which lexical items are learned, and how specific parameters are set, such as whether a language is SVO or SOV. (p. 96)

Let us set aside lexical items and consider only the acquisition/learning of syntax. To the extent that the grammatical rules of that speaker's language are constituted by those contingent parameter settings, the rules are not innate but *i*-lucky. My explanation of parameter setting appeals to conventions:

> Very occasionally an idiolect's parameter settings may be eccentric but almost always they will be conventional. Thus most people in the USA participate in parameter-setting conventions that lead them to speak an SVO language; most people in Japan participate in parameter-setting conventions that lead them to speak an SOV language. (2006a: 181)

This is where conventions get into my story of syntax: the members of a speech community have idiolects with the same grammatical rules partly because they acquire/learn the conventional parameter settings in that community.

RC object to my talk of conventions. Set that objection aside for a moment. There seems to be another. With parameter setting in mind, I went on to describe the syntax of a language as "largely" conventional (p. 181). I have often used such descriptions. RC (p. 91) quote an example (from Devitt 2020: 425) and add emphasis to its "largely." This suggests that RC may object to the view that syntax is "largely" non-innate, independently of their objection to the non-innate part being called "conventional." And, consider this: "*the vast majority* of rules and constraints on grammar are indeed due to innate psychological constraints and not convention" (p. 100). So, why do I say "largely"? Because, although theorists disagree about the list of parameters, they agree that the list is quite long. This yields literally millions of alternative settings for a language. That amounts to an awful lot of non-innate determination of syntactic rules, whether properly called "conventional" or not.

But who knows how to count ways of determining syntax? I insist, and Chomskians surely agree, that *some* syntactic properties are not determined innately. Chomskians insist, and I agree, that *some* syntactic properties are determined innately. And we agree that it is theoretically interesting to discover which is which. Maybe "largely" is not the right quantifier to capture the proportion determined non-innately. Perhaps, it should be "a significant proportion." This does not seem to be a theoretically interesting issue.

There may be another disagreement. RC may think that, whatever the *quantity* of non-innate syntax, that syntax is altogether not of much theoretical interest. The "deep" theoretical action is with the innate syntax:

> (despite occasional hyperbolic moments, e.g. Chomsky, 1980:81–3, 1996:47–8) Chomsky is not committed to denying a role for convention in any conceivable descriptive or explanatory task; he simply thinks any such role will be far less significant than is commonly supposed, and certainly less than the role of innate constraints ... Chomsky claims the *laws* of linguistics are to be found in a nativist psychology, and regards social conventions as largely a matter of luck, and so not what linguistic theory targets. We take Devitt to be denying this.   (p. 91)

> generative linguists expect that what lawful explanations there are will concern the stable facts about internal human mental structure, not the complex mass of fortuitous relations speakers may or may not bear to the world around them.   (p. 105)

So the idea is that the innate features of language determination differ from the non-innate ones in being "deep explanatory," adverted to in "laws," and "stable." I wonder about this developmental point. The cause of a person developing a language with certain grammatical rules, like the cause of an organism developing any phenotypic property, is to be found partly in what is innate and partly in the environment. Here's an example of the role of the environment. The Himalayan Rabbit, a breed of the Common Rabbit, comes to have white fur when raised in moderate temperatures but black fur when raised in cold temperatures (Sawin 1932). Similarly, a human comes to speak English when raised in an English-speaking environment but Mandarin when raised in a Mandarin-speaking one. In both cases, the role of the environment seems law-like and stable. Should we say that it is less so than the role of what is innate? And not as deep? Perhaps so, but why? And what hangs on this? We still need the environment to explain the white fur and the English speaking.

But, whatever we say about these developmental issues, a much more important point needs to be made: *there is more to "the explanatory scope of linguistics" than developmental laws. Science studies natures as well as laws.* Thus, science discovered that water is H_2O, that genes are DNA molecules, and so on.[19] Why spend scientific energy discovering these natures? Because entities, like water and genes, play their causal roles, hence may feature in laws, in virtue of their natures. Similarly, the symbols of a language play their causal roles, hence may feature in laws, in virtue of their natures, as noted in §4. So it is appropriate to spend scientific energy discovering those natures. And that, on the linguistic conception, is precisely what grammars do: they discover grammatical rules that constitute the syntactic part of the natures of the symbols that play striking causal roles in our lives.[20] So, *insofar as "linguistic theory" consists in grammars, it "targets" all grammatical rules whether innate or acquired, without discrimination*; the developmental story provides evidence about these rules but it is not what *grammars* target.

In sum, haggling over the right quantifier to capture the proportion of non-innate syntax is not theoretically interesting. Even if innate syntax plays a deeper explanatory role than non-innate syntax in language development, they are equally explanatory of the nature of symbols. And explaining that nature is the task of grammars.

Finally, I turn to the feature of my "conventionalism" that RC seem to find particularly objectionable: my calling the non-innate syntax "conventional." David Lewis claims that "it is a platitude—something that only a philosopher would dream of denying—that there are conventions of language" (1983: 166). RC are clearly not amused. They must also disapprove of this from Jerry Fodor: "think of a natural language as a system of conventional vehicles for the expression of thoughts (a view to which I know of no serious objections)" (1981: 196). Lewis and Fodor seem pretty right to me. When it comes to syntax, these claims need a qualification, of course, but the rest of language, and there is a lot of it, is explained by conventions. Indeed, languages provide a paradigm of explanation

---

[19] RC state: "For brevity, we shall use 'laws' as a cover term for what good explanations ought to provide" (88 n. 1). Well, explanations of natures—like those of water, genes, and, I claim, linguistic symbols—can be "good," but RC's use of "laws" does not seem to cover them.

[20] Cf. "Whether or not E-languages...are a scientifically important focus of attention depends...on whether there are actually any stable laws and generalizations about E-languages themselves" (Rey 2020b: 219–20). E-languages are scientifically important because their symbols play causal roles in virtue of their semantic and syntactic properties.

by convention. I have argued for this at length elsewhere (2006a: 178–84, 2008a: 216–21, 2008b: 251–4, 2021b: ch. 5). I shall not repeat these arguments, but RC prompt two further points.

First, I have already quoted RC's concessive remark about the role of conventions: "Chomsky is not committed to denying that conventions play *any* role in language. He simply thinks they play far less a role than is commonly supposed" (p. 91).[21] And consider these remarks from Rey on his own:[22]

> Of course, some aspects of our speech may well be conventional … the fact that certain phonemes and not others are used to indicate single word meaning and grammatical structure. Many such facts may be due to people coordinating their speech with those of others.   (2020b: 94)

> Chomsky certainly has no particular reason to deny that the specific phonological forms that a speaker attaches to meanings and syntactic structures may sometimes be largely conventional.   (2020b: 220)

The message I take from such passages is that Chomskians may accept that there are non-innate aspects of syntax explained by conventions, but are rather grudging about the *quantity* of them. Now, on the received Chomskian view of language acquisition, the only possible explanatory role for conventions is in parameter settings. If the Chomskian view is that conventions set *all* these, then we agree. So the grudging tone would just reflect a rather uninteresting haggle over the appropriate quantifier; see above. If, on the other hand, the view is that only *some* of these settings are by convention, then we wonder how the *others* are set.

Second, we need to explain the *uniform* parameter settings within a speech community. How does it come about that most people in the USA set parameters that lead them to speak an SVO language, most people in Japan, an SOV language? What else but conventions could explain this? *This is the only theory in town to explain the uniformity.*[23] But is this too hasty? I have admitted that

---

[21] Of course, Chomsky does have his "hyperbolic moments," as RC nicely put it. Here are two: Chomsky claims that the "regularities in usage" needed for linguistic conventions "are few and scattered" (1996: 47; see also 1980: 81–3). Furthermore, such conventions as there are do not have "any interesting bearing on the theory of meaning or knowledge of language" (1996: 48). I have responded (2006a: 178–89).

[22] Collins on his own, in contrast, has not been concessive (2008a, 2008b). I have responded (2008b, 2021b: §5.3). It is also worth noting that, not long ago, Rey presupposed an extensive role for linguistic conventions in his ingenious argument for anti-realism about SLEs (2006b: 558–9, 2008: 188–211).

[23] RC complain: "Devitt doesn't begin to establish that convention is essential to explaining these phenomena, many of which could be explained in terms of shared features of I-languages" (98 n. 11). But "shared features" is obviously an empty explanation of the sharing! Conventions explain the sharing. RC later remark: "just how parameters are set is a complex empirical issue, models ranging from mere 'triggering' accounts, to various forms of entrainment, where the setting one parameter depends upon the setting of another" (98 n. 12). And it surely is a complex empirical issue. So too is the learning of many conventions. But how else can we explain the uniformity of much non-innate behavior but by appeal to conventions?

we don't have a complete and satisfactory theory of conventions to hand (2006a: 179–80, 2021b: §5.3). Perhaps our notion of convention cannot bear the explanatory burden here. We have been given no reason to believe that it cannot, but should it turn out that it cannot we will need some similar, but more "technical," social notion, X, to explain lots of uniform behavior, including uniform parameter settings. This would certainly require a modification of my view of language—my recent book (2021b) should have been called '*Overlooking* X'!—but nothing serious. In particular, the modification is totally irrelevant to "Devitt's Alternative" view of "the explanatory scope of linguistics." Discovering that non-innate syntax was to be explained by X and not by convention would *make no difference to the linguistic conception*.

I quoted RC's statement of Chomsky's position ending with: "We take Devitt to be denying this" (p. 91). Later RC claim that, in "many articles and three books," I "emphatically" reject a "core claim" (p. 96) of a complex doctrine, (PSY), that RC introduce as the "core psychological hypothesis" of generative linguistics (p. 94). Now, there are many parts to these Chomskian position statements. In light of our discussion, *the only significant part that I have ever emphatically denied is the psychological conception of grammars*, the view that a grammar is about a speaker's linguistic competence and hence about mental states. My linguistic conception is indeed diametrically opposed to that. On the linguistic conception, grammars "target" all the grammatical rules, whether innate or not, that constitute the syntactic part of the natures of symbols. It is in virtue of those natures that the symbols play their important causal roles. But beyond that denial, despite RC's "conventionalism" mantra, my view of the role of linguistic conventions does not deny much if anything of the Chomskian position (hyperbole aside), and nothing significant. *This mantra is a red herring.* (a) I do not deny RC's developmental claims about laws and explanatory depth, though I do wonder about them; they are beside my concerns. (b) I do not deny, of course, that there are innate aspects to syntax. (c) I do claim that all the non-innate aspects are explained by conventions. Does this deny a Chomskian position? If so, what precisely? I don't know of an alternative explanation, let alone a better one. But if Chomskians come up with an alternative, X, any argument over whether X is better is surely not of much significance to a view of language and linguistics.

6. Methodology

As noted, Collins and Rey have each argued long and hard in earlier works for the Chomskian psychological conception of grammars and against my linguistic conception. The present chapter represents a change of tactic, reflected in the "common-sense conventionalism" mantra. (Were they perhaps thinking, quite correctly in my view, that the old tactic of arguing the matter wasn't working?) We have just discussed one part of that change: conflate the linguistic conception with "conventionalism." The other part charges me with an awful methodology and uses this to discredit my position. Whereas their Chomskian position is based on science, my position is based on nothing but common sense and so should be dismissed. I shall now discuss this damaging charge.

RC sum up my alleged methodology as "reliance on common sense" (p. 117) This charge is not novel: Rey (2020a) has made it at length before, attributing to me a "commitment" to "Moorean Commonsense" (p. 307), and using this to discredit my views not only of linguistics but of much else: indeed, he wonders whether it is "a serious indictment of Devitt's work as a whole" (p. 324).

My actual methodology is dictated by my Quinean epistemological naturalism (1998, 2011). This yields my attitude to common sense, or "folk theory." I described this briefly in my response to Rey:

> Folk theory can be a helpful place to start in the absence of science. We then look to science to discover whether folk theory, so far as it goes, is right. And we look to science to go further, much further. Some past folk theories have turned out to be spectacularly wrong. Still, given that conservatism is among the theoretical virtues (Quine and Ullian 1970: 43–53),[24] being in accord with common sense is an advantage for a theory, though, of course, very far from a decisive one. My most explicit and detailed presentation of this attitude to folk theory and common sense is probably in *Language and Reality* (Devitt and Sterelny 1999: 286–7).[25]   (2020: 430)

After citing a lot of evidence that this is a methodology that I practice as well as preach, I continued:

> In the face of all this obvious and apparently overwhelming evidence that I am very far from a devotee of "Moorean commonsense"…what we need [from Rey] is evidence that I engage in *arguments resting on "Moorean commonsense."*   (p. 430)

I point out that Rey (2020a) produces no such evidence (pp. 430–2).

In light of this, if Rey, now joined by Collins, wishes to continue charging me with this common-sense methodology, we should expect him to produce evidence

---

[24] "[T]heoretical conservatism is the only sensible policy for theorists of limited powers, who are duly modest about what they could accomplish after a fresh start" (Lewis 1986: 134).

[25] Note that the view is not, as RC misreport, that scientists "should be…*obliged*" to pay heed to folk theories (p. 101; emphasis added). The view is rather that paying heed "can be a helpful place to start"; proto-science can lead to science.

that my arguments really do rest on common sense. RC imply that this is what they will do:[26]

> Devitt (2020: 429–32) protested, claiming no cases had been cited where he was in fact relying on common sense. In §2 below, we shall set out Devitt's general views about the role of common sense in metaphysics (§2.1), proceeding to indicate in detail how it seems to be the basis of his disagreements with current scientific linguistics.   (p. 91)

Now the promise to set out my "general views about the role of common sense" is vague. The promise that they need to make, *given their methodological charge*, is to show that I *rely on common sense in my arguments* in metaphysics. RC do not deliver on that promise. Rather, in §2, "Devitt's Common-Sense Linguistics," they try to convey an impression of giving evidence for their charge while in fact giving none that should be taken seriously. Let us consider §2.

In §2.1, RC base their description of my views of the role of common sense in metaphysics on the Moorean strategy that I use (1991, 2010) as *part of* my argument for realism about the external world (pp. 93–94). That strategy does indeed stress that realism about ordinary physical objects like stones, trees, and cats is the core of common sense. RC's discussion of the strategy is similar to Rey's earlier one (2020a: 301–3). In responding to Rey, I emphasized two points. First, the strategy "*involves no commitment to common sense.*" Second, the argument for that realism does not rest on this strategy but on "naturalism" (2020: 431). I expanded on this:

> "the Moorean response is not of course sufficient" (2010: 63). Indeed, how could it be? "Realism might be wrong: it is an overarching empirical hypothesis in science" (1991: 20). So, I follow up with a naturalistic argument for it (2010: 63–66; see also 1991: 73–82).   (p. 431)

I concluded that Rey had provided "no basis at all for attributing to me the methodology that [he] disparages with such relish" (p. 431).

Obviously, I made these two points to refute Rey's charge that my argument for realism relies on common sense. So, how do RC respond to the points? They may seem to be taking some account of them in remarking that "while Devitt endorses the Moorean stratagem, in his (2020: 430) he endorses a defense of common sense based more on Quine and Ullian (1970: 43–53)" (p. 94). But, we should note, though the naturalistic methodology I have described certainly

---

[26] RC mention Rey's defense (2020a) of his "maxim of 'Explanation first!,' against Devitt's (2010) maxim of 'Metaphysics first'" (p. 91) as if it were relevant to their methodological charge. It is not, for reasons to be found in my response (2020: 428): I agree with Rey's maxim and it is not in competition with mine. The maxims have different purposes.

implies the (unsurprising) view that science might endorse *some* common sense, the methodology is far from a blanket "defense of common sense." More importantly, if my realism argument exemplifies that naturalistic methodology, as I claim, then that argument is not what RC need: it's not an argument resting on common sense. RC make no attempt to show that my realism argument does not exemplify that naturalistic methodology.

Instead, RC make this revealing remark:

> We should also stress that, while Devitt endorses common sense both broadly and with particular respect to language, he doesn't always endorse these positions *because* they are common sense; he simply thinks that common sense happens to be correct across a range of cases. Our intent is to dispute this.   (p. 94)

So RC think that I endorse some common-sense views that I should not, including, of course, views about language (though not including, I gather, realism about the likes of stones, trees, and cats). Fair enough. So RC can argue against those endorsements, as indeed they used to. But their new tactic requires them to show that I *rely on* common sense in endorsing those views. As they nicely point out, endorsing a common-sense view is not the same as endorsing it *because* it is common sense. Their new tactic requires them to show that I do the latter, to show that I *rely on* common sense. In claiming that I don't "always" do so, they imply that they have shown that I sometimes do so. Indeed, the implication is that their very discussion of my realism argument has shown this. Later, they make it very clear that this is exactly what they think that they have accomplished:

> Still, as part of his general commitment to at least the "posits" of common sense, he would seem to be assuming that we can, by and large, read off much of what exists from ordinary talk.   (p. 104)

This is a breathtaking misrepresentation. Of course, we cannot "read off much of what exists," or much of anything at all, "from ordinary talk"; see the description of my "actual methodology," and citations, in the long quote (from Devitt 2020: 430) displayed two pages back.[27] For, to repeat, my realism argument exemplifies

---

[27] RC have an earlier note containing another serious misrepresentation of my argument for realism: they claim that the doctrine, (R), "Words refer to things in the world"

seems to us implicit in many passages of Devitt...especially in his defense of "most" common-sense posits (1984/97: 18, 23, 73), which we presume are what are referred to in common-sense talk. (p. 92 n. 5)

This careless note could hardly be further from the truth. Perhaps the most distinctive feature of *Realism and Truth* (1991, cited above as 1984/97) is that it *explicitly excludes* all semantic claims, hence excludes (R), from a defense of realism. Thus, Maxim 3, the book's most active maxim, reads as follows: "Settle the realism issue before any epistemic/semantic issue" (1991: 4). See also the maxim "Put Metaphysics First" mentioned in the previous note, which is also the name of a book (2010).

the naturalistic methodology that I espouse not the common-sense one that RC foist on me. Rather than attempting to show otherwise, RC are simply assuming otherwise.

So RC have not yet produced any evidence of my offering arguments that rest on common sense. This is important because their discussion of my view of linguistics, in "2.3 Devitt's Alternative," proceeds as if they had shown this: as if their discussion of my realism argument has made it plausible that my alleged reliance on common sense in metaphysics is "the basis of [Devitt's] disagreements with current scientific linguistics." Indeed, that is the point of their discussion of the realism argument.

So, let us return to RC's discussion of "Devitt's Alternative," this time looking critically at its claimed evidence that my linguistic views rely on common sense. I have already labeled one of these claims "uncharitable speculation" (§4) and that fits them all. RC produce no real evidence. But proving an absence is tricky and in danger of being tedious. I shall content myself with discussing the three passages where RC most clearly represent themselves as providing the needed evidence of my methodology.

These passages are of two sorts. In the first sort, RC *disparage* my actual argument that does not rest on common sense to speculate that my real reason does. In the second sort, RC *ignore* my actual argument that does not rest on common sense to speculate that my real reason does. I'll start with the first sort.

(1) RC make a claim of this sort in discussing my view of how conventions might explain unvoiced syntax: "At one point [Devitt] does provide a sketch of how he thinks conventions could have evolved regarding inaudible elements, such as PRO." After quoting the sketch, RC comment: "But it's hard to believe he thinks this is a serious explanation." RC go on to indicate why they have such a dim view of the explanation before concluding:

> For lack of any serious argument or alternative theory of these standard linguistic phenomena, it's extremely hard to see how Devitt is relying on anything more than Lewis's common-sense "platitude"   (p. 99)

But disparaging an argument that makes no mention of common sense, and that I give every sign of believing, is clearly not a good basis for claiming that I am really relying on common sense. Furthermore, their disparagement is mistaken as I have, in effect, argued in a response (2008b: 252–4) to a similar criticism from Collins alone (2008b: 244–5). This argument of mine provides further evidence that the explanation that RC disparage, not their claimed insight into my mind, is indeed the reason for my view of unvoiced syntax. RC do not mention this argument.

One further comment is called for. My sketch was of how PRO might be acquired conventionally, but I allowed that it might in fact be innate (2008b: 253). Suppose it is. Still, surely some unvoiced syntax is not innate. How is it to be explained? My discussion of PRO is a sketch of how any unvoiced syntax might be acquired conventionally. Given their disparagement of this, RC owe us an alternative. How do they explain the *uniform* acquisition of non-innate unvoiced syntax? What is their X (see §5 on "the only theory in town")? Or do RC claim that all unvoiced syntax is innate? Even that in, "Mary went to visit the zoo, John, the museum"? That would be a bold claim.

(2) In the second sort of claim, RC ignore rather than disparage an actual argument that does not rest on common sense to speculate that my real reason does. We have already come across an example of this sort in §4. After a nice account of what the linguistic conception (LR) opposes, RC offer this as the reason for my opposition:

> This seems to be partly due to his insisting upon a common-sense conception about the reality of standard linguistic entities ("SLEs," such as words, phrases, sentences, phonemes and/or phonological properties) and the conventions governing them... (p. 97)

This uncharitable speculation is manifestly false: my actual reasons for the linguistic conception are to be found in many places and are known only too well to RC because they used to argue against them. See §4 for further information and discussion.

A second claim of this sort follows another quote from my discussion of unvoiced syntax. RC comment on this discussion as follows:

> Note that, quite apart from its disregard to the complexities of syntax, Devitt's work contains no discussions of phonology and doesn't engage in most of the semantic issues that typically occupy linguists (e.g., NPIs, conditionals, (a)telic verbs, quantifiers, adverbs, compositionality).... So it's puzzling that Devitt is prepared to second-guess linguists about the nature of their task. Although Devitt would vehemently protest this charge, it is hard not to regard his proclamations as mere armchair, virtually *a priori* "common-sense" speculations that he (2010: 276–7) otherwise often reasonably deplores. (p. 100)

There is no puzzle about why I urge my allegedly "second-guessing" view of the grammatical task: simply look at my arguments for the linguistic conception, arguments that RC used to try to answer and are now carefully ignoring.

What about the criticism that I do not discuss various linguistic topics—phonemes, NPIs, and so on—topics that have yielded many interesting discoveries? I anticipated this sort of criticism in the "Preface" of *Ignorance of Language* and responded: "what needs to be asked is whether the discovery is relevant to the issue in question" (2006a: vii). The issue in question here is the linguistic conception of grammars. One key feature of the mentioned topics is very relevant to this issue, the feature that the topics are *all about linguistic expressions*. Thus, commenting on the grammatical claim, "An NPI must be *c*-commanded by a licensor," Rey rightly remarks: "An NPI would certainly appear to be a word..., tokens of which are uttered or appear in print on a page" (2020b: 213). Exactly. And, of course, I certainly discuss, indeed, emphasize this feature. So far as I know, no other feature of those topics is relevant to the linguistic conception. If RC think otherwise, they should demonstrate.

A word about the "second-guessing." There is no doubt that Chomskian philosophers of linguistics embrace the psychological conception of grammars (it's a price of survival). Perhaps most linguists working in the Chomskian tradition will say that they do too:[28] it is, after all, what they are told firmly in Syntax 101. But, as the argument for the linguistic conception shows, the psycho-logical conception is at odds with *what linguists actually do in constructing grammars*. For, the claims that fill grammar books, as Rey has just illustrated, are about linguistic expressions (SLEs) not about the mind. *Prima facie*, the scientific task that these linguists are actually performing, whatever they say about it, is the task of explaining the syntactic nature of expressions. If these linguists *really believe*, rather than *just say*, that grammars are about the mental, then they should have in mind a thorough-going rewrite of their grammar books. Is there any evidence that they do?[29] As I recently remarked:

> Given the centrality of the psychological conception to the promotion of Chomskian linguistics, it is striking that there has been so little sensitivity to [the need for paraphrase] in presentations of grammars. Sensitivity to the ontology of one's theory is a mark of good science.   (2020: 377–8)

In a note to the just-quoted passage from their chapter, RC acknowledge that I "would certainly appear to be pursuing" a "naturalistic" approach in much of my work. But they add: "We are only questioning the extent to which [Devitt] appears nevertheless to be *also* implicitly relying on a traditional armchair or common-sense methodology, despite his best naturalistic intentions" (p. 100 n. 15). But where is the *evidence* of this implicit reliance? What we have just discussed is the best RC have to offer. It is not evidence to be taken seriously. Given the arguments I actually provide for my views of language and linguistics, RC need much more to justify their methodological charge than what they claim to find "hard to see" and "hard not to regard" as they peer into my mind.

---

[28] But some eminent linguists certainly do not; see, e.g., Gazdar et al. 1985.

[29] One is reminded of the old debate over scientific realism. It was apparently once common for physicists, when asked, to assent to the sort of positivistic instrumentalism that they had been taught in undergraduate philosophy classes. Yet, as realists were fond of pointing out, the actual practice of those physicists showed that they were, deep down, realists not instrumentalists.

RC, like Rey alone, have not produced a single example of an argument of mine, let alone one on linguistics, that relies on common sense. How then should we explain their persistent baseless misrepresentation of my methodology? My hypothesis is that RC are driven by a sort of "transcendental argument": "The scientific case for the Chomskian psychological conception of grammars is so overwhelming that we know *a priori* that rejection of that conception must be based solely on appeals to common sense." We have a case of *just knowing* that the election was stolen.

7. Conclusion

§I of the chapter was concerned with two questions: To what extent are linguistic tokens in utterances accidental relative to linguistic rules and hence are "*r*-lucky." To what extent are linguistic rules, hence expressions governed by them, accidental relative to human nature and hence are "*i*-lucky."

Linguistic pragmatists (contextualists) have argued, in effect, that there is a lot more *r*-luck around than has customarily been thought. Using a range of striking examples, they argue that a token's message is never, or hardly ever, solely constituted in the traditional way of truth-conditional semantics. Rather, it is always, or almost always, constituted pragmatically in context. I presented a case, drawing on more detailed presentations elsewhere, that the pragmatists are not right about this (§2). So I am urging a sort of "anti-luck semantics."

Chomsky has argued, in effect, that there is a lot less *i*-luck than used to be thought. For, he thinks that some fundamental rules of syntax, the rules of UG, are innately determined. So they are *i*-unlucky. I agreed (§3).

In §II, I considered Rey and Collins' (RC's) critique (Chapter 5 of this volume) of my views of language and linguistics, views that underlie my theses about linguistic luck. They are particularly concerned to rebut my alternative view to the Chomskians' of "the explanatory scope of linguistics." That alternative is the "linguistic conception" of grammars according to which a grammar is about a non-psychological realm of linguistic expressions, physical entities forming a representational system. This contrasts with the received Chomskian psychological conception according to which a grammar is about a speaker's linguistic competence and hence about mental states.

Collins and Rey have each, independently, argued long and hard in earlier works for the psychological conception and against my linguistic one. The mantra of their present joint chapter, "common-sense conventionalism," represents a change of tactic. With one half of the mantra, RC conflate the linguistic conception with my alleged "conventionalism." "Conventionalism" is a red herring. Such disagreement as there may be over the role of conventions is not of much significance generally and is *totally irrelevant* to my alternative view of the scope of linguistics. RC's discussion does not even bear on my real alternative, the linguistic conception (§§4 and 5).

The other half of RC's mantra charges me with an awful methodology and uses this to discredit my position. Whereas their Chomskian position is based on science, my position is alleged to be based on nothing but common sense and so should be dismissed. This charge about my methodology is baseless. My actual methodology, both practiced and preached, stems from my Quinean epistemological naturalism. RC do not present a single argument from my work that shows otherwise. Rather, ignoring or disparaging my actual arguments, they claim, looking into my mind, to *just see* that the real reason for my views about language and linguistics is an appeal to common sense. This is not an adequate basis for their methodological charge, to put it delicately (§6).

In sum, RC's critique is a combination of red herring and egregious misrepresentation.[30]

References

Antony, Louise. 2008. "Meta-linguistics: Methodology and ontology in Devitt's ignorance of language. *Australasian Journal of Philosophy* 86: 643–56.

Bach, Kent. 1994. Conversational impliciture. *Mind and Language* 9: 124–62.

Bach, Kent. 1995. Standardization vs. conventionalization. *Linguistics and Philosophy*, 18: 677–86.

Bach, Kent. 2001. You don't say? *Synthese* 128: 15–44.

Bach, Kent. 2004. Descriptions: Points of reference. In Reimer and Bezuidenhout 2004, 189–229.

Bach, Kent. 2007a. Referentially used descriptions: A reply to Devitt. *European Journal of Analytic Philosophy* 3: 33–48.

Bach, Kent. 2007b. The main bone of contention. *European Journal of Analytic Philosophy* 3: 55–7.

Bezuidenhout, Anne. 1997. Pragmatics, semantic underdetermination, and the referential/attributive distinction. *Mind* 106: 375–410.

Bianchi, Claudia, ed. 2004. *The Semantic/Pragmatics Distinction*. Stanford: CSLI Publications.

Bianchi, Andrea, ed. 2020. *Language and Reality from a Naturalistic Perspective: Themes from Michael Devitt*, ed. Andrea Bianchi. Cham: Springer.

Carston, Robyn. 2002. *Thoughts and Utterances: The Pragmatics of Explicit Communication*. Oxford: Blackwell Publishing.

[30] Thanks to Andrea Bianchi and Dunja Jutronić for comments on a draft.

Carston, Robyn. 2004. Truth-conditional content and conversational implicature. In Bianchi 2004, 65–100.

Chomsky, Noam. 1980. *Rules and Representations*. New York: Columbia University Press.

Chomsky, Noam. 1996. *Powers and Prospects: Reflections on Human Nature and the Social Order*. Boston: South End Press.

Collins, John. 2006. Between a rock and a hard place: A dialogue on the philosophy and methodology of generative linguistics. *Croatian Journal of Philosophy* VI: 469–503.

Collins, John. 2007. Review of Devitt 2006a. *Mind* 116: 416–23.

Collins, John. 2008a. "Knowledge of language redux." *Croatian Journal of Philosophy* VIII: 3–43.

Collins, John. 2008b. "A note on conventions and unvoiced syntax." *Croatian Journal of Philosophy* VIII: 241–7.

Collins, John. 2020. Invariance as the mark of the psychological reality of language. In Bianchi 2020: 7–44.

Devitt, Michael. 1981. Donnellan's distinction. *Midwest Studies in Philosophy*, Volume VI: *The Foundations of Analytic Philosophy*, ed. Peter A. French, Theodore E. Uehling Jr., and Howard K. Wettstein, 511–24. Minneapolis: University of Minnesota Press.

Devitt, Michael. 1991. *Realism and Truth*. 2nd edn. 1st edn 1984. Oxford: Basil Blackwell. (Reprint of 2nd edn with new "Afterword." Princeton: Princeton University Press: 1997.)

Devitt, Michael. 1996. *Coming to Our Senses: A Naturalistic Program for Semantic Localism*. Cambridge: Cambridge University Press.

Devitt, Michael. 1997. Meanings and psychology: A response to Mark Richard. *Nous* 31: 115–31.

Devitt, Michael. 1998. Naturalism and the a priori. *Philosophical Studies* 92: 45–65. (Reprinted in Devitt 2010a.)

Devitt, Michael. 2003. Linguistics is not psychology, *Epistemology of Language*, ed. Alex Barber, 107–39. Oxford: Oxford University Press.

Devitt, Michael. 2004. The case for referential descriptions. In Reimer and Bezuidenhout 2004: 280–305.

Devitt, Michael. 2006a. *Ignorance of Language*. Oxford: Clarendon Press.

Devitt, Michael. 2006b. Defending ignorance of language: Responses to the Dubrovnik papers. *Croatian Journal of Philosophy* 6: 571–606.

Devitt, Michael. 2007a. Referential descriptions and conversational implicatures. *European Journal of Analytic Philosophy* 3: 7–32.

Devitt, Michael. 2007b. Referential descriptions: A note on Bach. *European Journal of Analytic Philosophy* 3: 49–53.

Devitt, Michael. 2008a."Explanation and reality in linguistics. *Croatian Journal of Philosophy* 8: 203–31.

Devitt, Michael. 2008b. A response to Collins' note on conventions and unvoiced syntax. *Croatian Journal of Philosophy* VIII: 249–55.

Devitt, Michael. 2008c. Methodology in the philosophy of linguistics. *Australasian Journal of Philosophy* 86: 671–78.

Devitt, Michael. 2009. Psychological conception, psychological reality. *Croatian Journal of Philosophy* IX: 35–44.

Devitt, Michael. 2010. *Putting Metaphysics First: Essays on Metaphysics and Epistemology*. Oxford: Oxford University Press.

Devitt, Michael. 2011. No place for the a priori, *What Place for the A Priori?*, ed. Michael J. Shaffer and Michael L. Veber, 9–32. Chicago and La Salle: Open Court Publishing Company. (Reprinted in Devitt 2010a.)

Devitt, Michael. 2013a. What makes a property 'semantic'?, *Perspectives on Pragmatics and Philosophy*, ed. A. Capone, F. Lo Piparo, and M. Carapezza, 87–112. Cham: Springer.

Devitt, Michael. 2013b. Three methodological flaws of linguistic pragmatism, *What is Said and What is Not: The Semantics/Pragmatics Interface*, ed. Carlo Penco and Filippo Domaneschi, 285–300. Stanford: CSLI Publications.

Devitt, Michael. 2013c. The linguistic conception' of grammars. *Filozofia Nauki* XXI: 5–14.

Devitt, Michael. 2018. Sub-sententials: Pragmatics or semantics?, *Further Advances in Pragmatics and Philosophy*, Part 1: *From Theory to Practice*, ed. A. Capone, M. Carapezza, and F. Lo Piparo, 45–64. Cham: Springer.

Devitt, Michael. 2020. Stirring the possum: Responses to the Bianchi papers. In Bianchi 2020: 371–455.

Devitt, Michael. 2021a. "Semantic polysemy and psycholinguistics. *Mind and Language* 36: 134–57. doi.org/10.1111/mila.12327

Devitt, Michael. 2021b. *Overlooking Conventions: The Trouble with Linguistic Pragmatism*. Cham: Springer.

Devitt, Michael and Kim Sterelny. 1989. "Linguistics: What's wrong with 'the right view', *Philosophical Perspectives*, 3: *Philosophy of Mind and Action Theory*, ed. James E. Tomberlin, 497–531. Atascadero: Ridgeview Publishing Company.

Devitt, Michael and Kim Sterelny. 1999. *Language and Reality: An Introduction to the Philosophy of Language*, 2nd edn. Cambridge, MA: MIT Press. (1st edn. 1987.)

Donnellan, Keith S. 1966. Reference and definite descriptions. *Philosophical Review* 75: 281–304.

Fodor, Jerry A. 1981. *Representations: Philosophical Essays on the Foundations of Cognitive Science*. Cambridge, MA: Bradford Books/MIT Press.

Gazdar, Gerald, Ewan Klein, Geoffrey Pullum, and Ivan Sag. 1985. *Generalized Phrase Structure Grammar*. Oxford: Basil Blackwell.

Grice, Paul. 1989. *Studies in the Way of Words*. Cambridge, MA: Harvard University Press.

Haegeman, Liliane. 1994. *Introduction to Government and Binding Theory*, 2nd edn. Oxford: Blackwell Publishers. (1st edn 1991.)

Kripke, Saul A. 1979. Speaker's reference and semantic reference, *Contemporary Perspectives in the Philosophy of Language*, ed. Peter A. French, Theodore E. Uehling Jr., and Howard K. Wettstein, 627. Minneapolis: University of Minnesota Press.

Lewis, David K. 1961. *From a Logical Point of View*, 2nd edn. Cambridge, MA: Harvard University Press. (1st edn, 1953.)

Lewis, David K. 1983. *Philosophical Papers*, vol. 1. New York: Oxford University Press.

Lewis, David K. 1986. *On the Plurality of Worlds*. Oxford: B. Blackwell.

Lewis, David K. 1990. *Descriptions*. Cambridge, MA: MIT Press.

Lewis, David K. 2004. This, that, and the other. In Reimer and Bezuidenhout 2004: 68–182.

Lewis, David K. 2007. On location, *Situating Semantics: Essays on the Philosophy of John Perry*, ed. Michael O'Rourke and Corey Washington, 251–393. Cambridge, MA: MIT Press.

Lewis, David K. 2016. Silent reference, *Meanings and Other Things: Essays in Honor of Stephen Schiffer*, ed. Gary Ostertag, 229–344. Oxford: Oxford University Press.

Lewis, David K. and J. S. Ullian. 1970. *The Web of Belief*. New York: Random House.

Longworth, Guy. 2009. Ignorance of linguistics. *Croatian Journal of Philosophy* IX: 21–34.

Ludlow, Peter. 2009. Review of Devitt 2006a. *Philosophical Review* 118: 393–402.

Neale, Stephen. 1990. *Descriptions*. Cambridge, MA: MIT Press.

Neale, Stephen. 2004. This, that, and the other. In Reimer and Bezuidenhout 2004, 68–182.

Neale, Stephen. 2007. On location. In *Situating Semantics: Essays on the Philosophy of John Perry*, ed. Michael O'Rourke and Corey Washington, 251–393. Cambridge, MA: MIT Press.

Neale, Stephen. 2016. Silent reference. In *Meanings and Other Things: Essays in Honor of Stephen Schiffer*, ed. Gary Ostertag, 229–344. Oxford: Oxford University Press.

Pietroski, Paul. 2008. Think of the children. *Australasian Journal of Philosophy* 86: 657–9.

Powell, George. 2010. *Language, Thought and Reference*. London: Palgrave Macmillan.

Recanati, François. 1989. Referential/attributive: A contextualist proposal. *Philosophical Studies* 56: 217–49.

Recanati, François. 2004. *Literal Meaning*. Cambridge: Cambridge University Press.

Recanati, François. 2010. *Truth-Conditional Pragmatics*. Oxford: Clarendon Press.

Reimer, Marga. 1998. Donnellan's distinction/Kripke's test. *Analysis* 58: 89–100.

Reimer, Marga and Anne Bezuidenhout eds. 2004. *Descriptions and Beyond*. Oxford: Clarendon Press.

Rey, Georges. 2006a. The intentional inexistence of language—But not cars, *Contemporary Debates in Cognitive Science*, ed. R. Stainton, 237–55. Oxford: Blackwell Publishers.

Rey, Georges. 2006b. Conventions, intuitions and linguistic inexistents: A reply to Devitt. *Croatian Journal of Philosophy* VI: 549–69.

Rey, Georges. 2008. In defense of Folieism: Replies to critics. *Croatian Journal of Philosophy* VIII: 177–202.

Rey, Georges. 2020a. Explanation first! The priority of scientific over Commonsense' metaphysics. In Bianchi 2020: 299–327.

Rey, Georges. 2020b. *Representation of Language: Foundational Issues in a Chomskyan Linguistics*. Oxford: Oxford University Press.

Sawin, P. B. (1932). Hereditary variation of the chin-chilla rabbit: In coat and eye color. *Journal of Heredity* 23: 39–46.

Scholz, Barbara and Geoffrey Pullum. 2006. Irrational nativist exuberance, *Contemporary Debates in Cognitive Science*, ed. R. Stainton. Oxford: Blackwell Publishers.

Slezak, Peter. 2009. Linguistic explanation and 'psychological reality'. *Croatian Journal of Philosophy* IX: 3–20.

Slobodchikoff, C. N. 2002. Cognition and communication in prairie dogs, *The Cognitive Animal: Empirical and Theoretical Perspectives on Animal Cognition*, ed. Marc Bekoff, Colin Allen, and Gordon M. Burchardt, 257–64. Cambridge MA: MIT Press.

Smith, Barry C. 2006. Why we still need knowledge of language. *Croatian Journal of Philosophy* VI: 431–56.

Sperber, Dan, and Deirdre Wilson. 1995. *Relevance: Communication and Cognition*, 2nd edn. Oxford: Blackwell Publishers. (1st edn 1986.)

Quine, W. V., and J. S. Ullian. 1970. *The Web of Belief*. New York: Random House.

7

Epistemicism without Metalinguistic Safety

Justin Khoo

Terry has volunteered to be zapped by the Shrink Ray 3000, a device that causes the target to shrink in height quickly and continuously over one minute. We type in the setting that causes a rate of diminishment of one-quarter inch per second. Terry's height at t_0, just before he is zapped, is 6'7", which is sufficient for him to be tall (for an average American 30 year old man). After sixty seconds of zapping, at t_{60}, his height is 5'4", which is sufficient for him to be not tall (for an average American 30 year old man). So, at some point in the process, he went from being tall to being not tall—but when?

Here are two answers to this question. The supervaluational answer says that there is some time t_i which was the last moment at which Terry was tall, but that for each time t_i, it is not the case that it was the last moment at which Terry was tall. The fact that this sounds like a contradiction has motivated an alternative, epistemicist answer, which agrees that there is some time t_i which was the last moment at which Terry was tall, but holds merely that we do not, and cannot, know which moment that is.

The epistemicist thus differs from the supervaluationist in holding that not only is there a last moment at which Terry was tall, but that someone who says, at each moment, *this is the last moment at which Terry is tall*, would at some point say something true. Let t_n be that moment, and H_{t_n} be Terry's height in inches at that moment. The epistemicist is committed to accepting that:

(1)   Someone is tall iff their height is H_{t_n} inches or greater.

Furthermore, there seems to be nothing more to being tall than having a height greater than or equal to H_{t_n}; as Williamson puts it, the vague strongly supervenes on the precise (see Williamson 1994: 202). Given this assumption, not only is (1) true, it is necessarily true—it states the exact conditions under which anyone is, or would be, tall.

So, the epistemicist is committed not just to unknowable contingencies, but also to a striking number of unknowable necessities. Thus, crucial to assessing the outlook of the epistemicist strategy is evaluating her prospects of making sense of

Justin Khoo, *Epistemicism without Metalinguistic Safety* In: *Linguistic Luck: Safeguards and Threats to Linguistic Communication*. Edited by: Abrol Fairweather and Carlos Montemayor, Oxford University Press.
© Oxford University Press 2023. DOI: 10.1093/oso/9780192845450.003.0007

these unknowable necessary truths. And, while it is correct that unknown necessities are a fact of life (as Kripke and others have helped us see clearly), it is not enough for the epistemicist to simply claim companions in guilt with our ignorance of mathematical truths (for example), for it is not obvious that the kinds of strategies for explaining unknown necessities in those domains will work equally well to explain our ignorance about the cutoffs of vague predicates.

To see why, notice that a common strategy for capturing ignorance about mathematical truths appeals to impossible worlds where (for instance) certain necessary truths fail to hold. However, such a strategy will struggle to predict that someone ignorant of the precise height cutoff for tallness can believe that tallness facts strongly supervene on precise height facts.

To see why, suppose you know that Jones's height is between H_{tn} and $H_{tn} + .01$ inches. Still, plausibly, you don't know that Jones is tall, because his height is too close to the cutoff.

Therefore, worlds in your belief state will include:

- w_1: Jones's height is H_{tn} inches and he is tall.
- w_2: Jones's height is H_{tn} inches and he is not tall.

Given the necessity of (1), w_2 is an impossible world. But this pair of worlds together violate the principle that tallness facts strongly supervene on height facts, but since both are among your belief worlds, you don't believe that tallness facts strongly supervene on precise height facts. For an epistemicist who wants to maintain both ignorance about cutoffs as well as believe her theory (which includes the strong supervenience of the vague on the precise), this is an unwelcome result.

As a matter of fact, the most prominent defender of epistemicism, Timothy Williamson, does not explain the unknowability of the cutoff thresholds of vague predicates by appealing to impossible worlds. Rather, he appeals to an extension of the safety condition of knowledge, which he calls *metalinguistic safety*. Whereas the safety condition says that what distinguishes knowledge from merely true belief is that the believer isn't lucky—couldn't easily have been wrong—metalinguistic safety says that knowledge that p requires that the believer be free of metalinguistic luck—that is, that the sentence she uses to express her belief that p couldn't easily have meant something false. Although (1) in fact expresses a necessary truth (we're supposing), we are metalinguistically lucky in expressing a necessary truth with it, since it could have easily expressed a necessary falsehood even though we still endorsed it; this is why we do not know (1).

In this chapter, I argue against metalinguistic safety as a necessary condition on knowledge. This puts pressure on epistemicists to find some other way to explain our ignorance of the cutoffs of vague predicates. However, I argue that there is a way out: the epistemicist can deny that the vague strongly supervenes on the precise. I articulate an alternative version of epistemicism that appeals to diagonalized contents that combine metalinguistic and first order material. The primary advantage of diagonalized epistemicism is that it requires only regular (non-metalinguistic) safety to account for our ignorance of cutoffs, and I argue that the cost of denying strong supervenience of the vague on the precise is one worth paying for. However, in a twist, I argue that even diagonalized epistemicism is false. It is not a matter of luck (epistemic or linguistic) that we do not know claims like (1), since such claims express no facts to be known (or not) at all.

1. Metalinguistic Safety

Williamson's strategy for explaining our ignorance of the cutoffs of vague predicates involves two independent commitments: (i) a commitment to the semantic plasticity of vague predicates, and (ii) a commitment to metalinguistic safety as a necessary condition of knowledge.

An expression *t* is semantically plastic iff slight changes in its use lead to slight changes in its meaning. Williamson contends that vague predicates are semantically plastic in this sense:

> For any difference in meaning, there is a difference in use ... A slight shift along one axis of measurement in all our dispositions to use 'thin' would slightly shift the meaning and extension of 'thin'. On the epistemic view, the boundary of 'thin' is sharp but unstable.   (Williamson 1994: 231)

Thus, suppose that Jones is exactly *n* inches tall. There will be a nearby world in which Jones is also exactly *n* inches tall but in which the usage facts of *tall* differ slightly, leading to the cutoff for *tall* to be slightly different, such that Jones is just barely over the actual cutoff for *tall* but not over the cutoff for *tall* at these nearby worlds. The sentence *Jones is tall* is thus actually true but very easily could have expressed a false proposition. It follows that, if I accept the sentence *Jones is tall*, there is a very real sense in which I am linguistically lucky—the words just happened to express a truth for me, but they very well might not have (and I would have continued to accept the sentence).

This kind of linguistic luck is largely uncontroversial. What I will challenge as controversial is Williamson's claim that my being linguistically lucky with the sentence "Jones is tall" also undermines my knowledge that Jones is tall:

> On the epistemic view, an utterance of a vague sentence such as 'n grains make a heap' may express a necessary truth in a borderline case. A speaker who made such an assertion would not be expressing knowledge that n grains make a heap, for he might easily have used those words even if their overall use had been

slightly different, so that they expressed a necessary falsehood. His utterance u does not manifest a disposition to be reliably right.   (Williamson 1994: 235)

This suggests the following:

Metalinguistic Safety (First Pass)
X's utterance of sentence S expresses knowledge that p only if it couldn't have easily been the case that X uttered S and it meant something false.

This principle, together with the semantic plasticity of vague expressions, predicts that when Jones is just barely over the cutoff for *tall*, an utterance of a sentence like *Jones is tall* would not express knowledge. Similarly, supposing the cutoff for *tall* is being n inches tall. Then, still, an utterance of the sentence:

(2)   Someone is tall iff their height is n inches or greater.

would not express knowledge, since this sentence very easily could have expressed a proposition that was false (say, at a world where the cutoff for "tall" is $n + .01$ inches).

1.1. Refining

An immediate problem with Metalinguistic Safety (First Pass) is that it says only when *utterances* of sentences *express* knowledge, but we are also interested in when some individual knows some proposition, whether or not they utter any sentence that expresses it. Take Smith, who has formed the belief that Jones is tall by measuring him and finding his height to be n inches, yet hasn't uttered any sentences. The epistemicist should still want to predict that Smith doesn't know Jones is tall even though his belief is true and Smith knows that Jones is n inches tall.

Anticipating this kind of thought, Williamson suggests that what goes for sentences goes for concepts too, remarking:

> The vagueness of an expression consists in the semantic differences between it and other possible expressions that would be indiscriminable by those who understood them. Similarly, the vagueness of a concept consists in the differences between it and other possible concepts that would be indiscriminable by those who grasped them.   (Williamson 1994: 237)

> You have no way of making your use of a concept on a particular occasion perfectly sensitive to your overall pattern of use, for you have no way of surveying that pattern in all its details. Since the content of the concept depends on the overall pattern, you have no way of making your use of a concept on a particular

occasion perfectly sensitive to its content. Even if you did know all the details of the pattern (which you could not), you would still be ignorant of the manner in which they determined the content of the concept.   (Williamson 1994: 231–2)

In fact, it's not easy to reconcile these two thoughts. The first remark suggests that what's indiscriminable is not the relation of a vague expression to its concept, but rather various distinct concepts themselves. However, the second remark suggests that what's indiscriminable is what content a particular concept (expressed by some vague expression) has. I am not sure which view Williamson ultimately has in mind, but I will opt to flesh out the second view here (I suspect similar remarks will apply to the first).

Here is a way to make Williamson's second suggestion more precise. Suppose that an agent's occurrent beliefs are grounded in mental representations that play some role in their cognitive economy, and say that the relation an agent bears to such mental representations is the belief* relation. Suppose also that mental representations have as their meanings propositions (something like this view is endorsed by Fodor 1981, 1987). Thus,

X believes that p iff there is a mental representation S such that X believes* S and S means that p.

When X believes that p, call the corresponding mental representation S that X believes*, and which means that p, the *mental representative* of X's belief. Then, we can reformulate metalinguistic safety as follows:

Metalinguistic Safety (Second Pass)
X knows that p only if X truly believes that p and the mental representative of X's belief that p could not have easily meant something false and still been believed* by X.

Supposing that the mental representatives of beliefs involving vague predicates are similarly semantically plastic—such that at nearby worlds, slightly different applications of the mental representatives lead to them having slightly different meanings—and we again predict the result we wanted, without appeal anywhere to utterances of sentences: Smith doesn't know that Jones is tall (even though he truly believes this) and we don't know that someone is tall iff their height is n inches or greater even though we truly believe it.

1.2. Problems

Nonetheless, there is a further problem facing this approach, which stems from the fact that we often have multiple mental representatives underlying the same belief. Take the proposition that Jones is tall. The epistemicist endorsing the supervenience of the vague on the precise must hold that this proposition has the same truth conditions as the proposition that Jones is at least n inches tall (where n is the actual cutoff for tallness). It is no part of the epistemicist's view that we cannot come to know that Jones is at least n inches tall—this is something we can come to know by measuring him for instance. Suppose Smith does come to know this in this way. Then, there is some mental representative underlying this belief, call it S_1, such that:

(3)   a. Smith truly believes* S_1, and
     b. It couldn't easily have been the case that S_1 meant something false and Smith believes* S_1.

However, in order for Smith not to thereby know that Jones is tall, it must then be the case that there is some distinct mental representative underlying this belief, call it S_2, such that:

(4)   a. Smith truly believes* S_2, and
     b. It could easily have been the case that S_2 meant something false and Smith believes* S_2.

But the problem is that what Smith believes is the same in both cases. Thus, there is no single mental representative underlying Smith's belief, and this causes trouble for Metalinguistic Safety (Second Pass), which presupposes each belief has a unique mental representative. Thus, the view predicts that the claim that Smith knows that p is either undefined or false (depending on their view of uniqueness failures of definite descriptions).

In response, we might modify Metalinguistic Safety (Second Pass) to existentially quantify over mental representatives:

Metalinguistic Safety (Third Pass) X knows that p only if X truly believes that p and *there is some* mental representative of X's belief that p could not have easily meant something false and still been believed* by X.

However, this yields the result that Smith knows Jones is tall. Alternatively, we might universally quantify over mental representatives:

Metalinguistic Safety (Fourth Pass)
X knows that p only if X truly believes that p and *every* mental representative of X's belief that p could not have easily meant something false and still been believed* by X.

But this yields the result that Smith doesn't know that Jones is at least n inches tall.

Another possibility is to relativize knowledge to a mental representative:[1]

Metalinguistic Safety (Fifth Pass)

X knows that p relative to mental representative M only if X truly believes that p and M could not have easily meant something false and still been believed* by X.

It is unclear to me whether knowledge relative to a mental representative bears enough similarities to our ordinary notion of knowledge to warrant serious consideration as an account of the latter. However, let's suppose I'm wrong about this. Nonetheless, it still seems wrong that knowing that p depends on some metalinguistic facts about the representational vehicle M through which we believe that p, such that the semantic plasticity of M could undermine your knowledge of beliefs you have via M.

We can assess Metalinguistic Safety (Fifth Pass) by exploring whether other expressions are semantically plastic in ways not tracked by our dispositions to apply them, and, if so, whether that undermines knowing via beliefs got through mental representatives involving those expressions. For instance, Burge (1979) proposes that the meaning of *arthritis* for a speaker S may depend on the dispositions of his broader social community. Consider the following inversion of Burge's classic case. Given the actual community dispositions, *arthritis* means an inflammation of the joints. Suppose Smith picked up on the use of the term from unreliable sources—suppose he got it from Dr. Jones, who always mixes up medical terminology for joints and muscles. In the actual case, Dr. Jones got it right—applying *arthritis* to inflammation of the joints—and so Smith's usage is correct. Smith feels inflammation in his right knee and thus on that basis comes to believe (and know, it seems) that:

(5)   I (Smith) have arthritis in my right knee.

But the broader community might have used *arthritis* differently, so that it applied not to inflammation of the joints but rather to muscle inflammation. At some such nearby possibilities, when Dr. Jones meets with Smith, he uses *arthritis* correctly (at that world) to talk about muscle inflammation. But at other such nearby possibilities, when Dr. Jones meets with Smith, he uses *arthritis* incorrectly (at that world), applying it to joint inflammation only (remember, he tends to mix up medical terminology for joints and muscles):

---

[1] Even another is to distinguish propositions by mental representatives; I'll set this one aside for now.

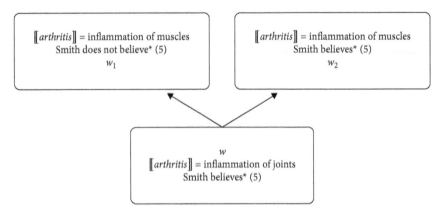

Figure 1

Focus on the latter kind of world, w_2. At that world, Smith's dispositions to use *arthritis* are incorrect (given what it means). As such, since Smith continues to have inflammation in his knee joint at w_2, he continues to believe* the mental representative of his belief that he has arthritis in his right knee. And at w_2, this mental representative expresses a false proposition—the proposition that Smith has muscle inflammation in his right knee. Thus, by Metalinguistic Safety (Fifth Pass), Smith does not know (at w) that he has arthritis in his right knee.

But that result seems wrong. Whether Smith knows that he has arthritis in his right knee doesn't depend on whether the word *arthritis* (or the corresponding mental representative word) could have easily meant something different in a way not tracked by Smith.[2] Knowledge concerns the content of the belief, not the vehicle for it.

This case was designed to mimic a standard fake barn case, which the usual safety condition on knowledge aims to make sense of. In the fake barn case, Smith is driving through an area with nine fake barns and one real barn. Not recognizing the difference between the fake and real barns, he sets his sights on the one real barn and on that basis comes to believe that there is a barn in the field. Smith does not know there is a barn in the field because he very easily could have believed falsely that there was a barn in the field (by, say, forming the belief by looking at a fake barn). The metalinguistic case substitutes possible alternative meanings for *arthritis* in place of fake barns, but the structure of the cases seems otherwise analogous.

Here is a second example, due to Kearns & Magidor (2008).

> Smith is again in fake barn country and again sets his sights on the one real barn in the vicinity. He walks up to it and inspects it thoroughly from all sides, and concludes, pointing to it, "That is a barn."

[2] A similar case is discussed in Bacon (2018: 81–8).

I think it is incredibly plausible to think that, in such a case, Smith knows that this thing is a barn. His vision is good, he is paying close attention, has seen it from all angles, and thus he has a true justified *de re* belief of this thing that it is a barn— had it not been a barn, he would have not believed it to be one.

However, given metalinguistic safety, Smith does not know that this is a barn, since his mental representative could have easily expressed a false proposition. These cases together put a lot of pressure on metalinguistic safety. The lesson I think we should draw is that the semantic properties of the mental representations underlying our beliefs simply do not matter to knowledge: metalinguistic safety is wrong.[3]

2. Supervenience, Weak and Strong

Let's switch gears to an alternative explanation of the lack of knowledge of borderline cases of vague predicates. If the vague doesn't supervene on the precise, then two possible things could be precisely alike but not vaguely alike, and thus we could know how they are in their precise respects without knowing how they are in their vague respects. Williamson denies this, holding instead that the vague strongly supervenes on the precise:

> If two possible situations are identical in all precisely specified respects, then they are identical in all vaguely specified respects too. For example, if x and y have exactly the same physical measurements, then x is thin if and only if y is thin. (Williamson 1994: 202)

We can formulate this principle as follows:

Strong Supervenience: Necessarily, for any vague property F there is some precise property G such that necessarily, something is F iff it is G.

This says that at every world, every vague property has some precise correlate such that necessarily, the two are co-instantiated. However, by ruling out the possibility of a possibly differing from b in its vague respects but not its precise respects, commitment to strong supervenience forces the epistemicist to explain our ignorance of the vague either metalinguistically or hyperintensionally.

However, notice that we can still capture a sense in which the vague supervenes on the precise without running into this problem. Contrast Strong Supervenience with Weak Supervenience:

[3] For additional arguments against metalinguistic safety, see: Mahtani (2004); Caie (2012); Sennet (2012).

Weak Supervenience: Necessarily, for any vague property F there is some precise property G such that something is F iff it is G.

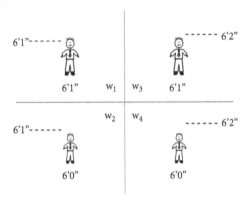

Figure 2

This says that at every world, every vague property has some precise correlate such that the two are co-instantiated. The difference with Strong Supervenience is that the requirement on co-instantiation is world-bound—thus, which precise property is the supervenience base for some vague property may vary from world to world. Notice, then, that ignorance about which precise G makes something F is ordinary first order factual ignorance, and it could account for our ignorance about the cutoff of vague predicates. This is so, even though at any world, there can be no difference in an object's vague properties without a difference in its precise properties—that is, throughout the class of worlds that agree on the precise supervenience base for some vague property, varying the object's vague properties requires varying their precise properties (in other words: you can never find two actual people who share the same height but differ in whether they are tall). Just as worlds can vary in their distribution of precise properties, they can differ in their supervenience base of the vague. Here's a graphic to illustrate the difference:

At w_1 and w_2, the cutoff for tallness is 6'1", while at w_3 and w_4 the cutoff for tallness is 6'2". Meanwhile, Jones's height is 6'1" at w_1 and w_3, while his height is 6'0" at w_2 and w_4. These worlds illustrate the dual aspect of our ignorance of vague properties: we are ignorant both about the precise—Jones's precise height—as well as the vague—whether Jones is tall. Furthermore, learning Jones's precise height is not sufficient for learning whether Jones is tall. Learning that, say, Jones is 6'1" would allow us to rule out worlds w_2 and w_4, but we still wouldn't know whether Jones is tall, since we wouldn't know whether being 6'1" is sufficient for being tall.

Finally, if we were to come (somehow) to believe that Jones is 6'1" and that he is tall, we would believe ourselves to be in a world like w_1. But we still wouldn't know that Jones is tall, since our belief isn't safe—there is still a nearby possible world where we believe that Jones is tall, and Jones is 6'1", but the cutoff for being tall is a bit higher, say being 6'2" (a world like w_3 fits the bill).

The extension of a vague predicate like *tall* depends on two factors: the precise height facts, and a minimum cutoff. For the Williamsonian epistemicist, the language fixes the minimum cutoff, and thus the content of *tall* can be specified by a unique precise property of heights. At worlds where the language fixes a different cutoff, the content of *tall* will be a distinct precise property of heights. By contrast, on our alternative version of epistemicism, the content of tall incorporates the minimum cutoff, and thus does not vary across worlds with different cutoffs.[4]

Looking back to Figure 2 above, suppose for a moment that w_1 is the actual world. Then, according to the Williamsonian epistemicist,

(6)   Jones is tall.
(7)   Anyone at least 6'1" is tall.
(8)   It is necessarily true that anyone at least 6'1" is tall.

By contrast, according to our alternative view, (6) and (7) are true, but (8) is false: it is a contingent fact that anyone at least 6'1" is tall.

3. Diagonalizing

So far, we've followed Williamson in assuming, plausibly, that it is not essential to a language that its meaningful parts have the meanings they do have—they might have meant different things had the facts relevant to their metasemantics been different. Thus, we can define a possibly partial interpretation function ⟦ ⟧ that assigns a propositional content to a sentence relative to a possible world. So,

$\llbracket A \rrbracket_w$ = the content of A at w.

Given our assumption that propositional contents can be modeled as sets of possible worlds, we have that:

$\llbracket A \rrbracket_w(w')$ = 1 (true) iff the content of A at w is true at w'.

For terminology, we'll say that the world that determines the expression's content is the **determining** world, while the world we evaluate the resulting

---

[4] I count Barker (2002, 2013) among epistemicists who endorse this latter kind of epistemicism, although I'm not sure Barker would agree with my interpretation of his view. See also MacFarlane (2020) for a characterization of diagonalized epistemicism that matches the version I describe here.

content relative to is the **evaluation** world. So, above, w is the determining world and w' the evaluation world. Next, we'll suppose for illustration that vague predicates like *tall* have a covert variable s whose value is fixed by the determining world:

$[\![$ *Jones is tall$_s$* $]\!]_w(w') = 1$ iff Jones's height is at least $[\![s]\!]_w$ at w'.

With this notation in hand, we can state Williamsonian epistemicism and our alternative. Let α be the actual world. Then:

Williamsonian Epistemicism
The content of *Jones is tall* at α is $\{w: [\![$ *Jones is tall$_s$* $]\!]_\alpha(w) = 1\}$. (In other words, the set of worlds where Jones's height meets the actual standards of tallness.)

Our alternative, Diagonalized Epistemicism, can be stated as follows:

Diagonalized Epistemicism
The content of *Jones is tall* at α is $\{w: [\![$ *Jones is tall$_s$* $]\!]_w(w) = 1\}$. (In other words, the set of worlds w where Jones's height at w meets the standards of tallness at w.)

What looks like an incredibly small difference here in fact makes *all* the difference for avoiding the challenges put forward in §1. To see this, let's first see why these views agree about (6) and (7) but disagree about (8).

Recall: Jones is actually 6'1" and 6'1" is the minimum height to count as tall. Thus, both views predict *Jones is tall* is true and that *Anyone who is at least 6'1" is tall* is true. This is unsurprising, since both views hold that Jones is tall is true at α iff Jones's height at α meets the standards of tallness at α.

Things change when the content of *Anyone who is at least 6'1" is tall* is embedded. According to Williamsonian epistemicism, the determining world plays no role after fixing the content of *Anyone who is at least 6'1" is tall*. Once fixed by the actual world, the content is $\{w: [\![$ *Anyone who is at least 6'1" is tall$_s$* $]\!]_\alpha(w) = 1\}$. Then, when embedded under a modal operator like "Necessarily" we have:

$[\![$ *Necessarily, anyone who is at least 6'1" is tall$_s$* $]\!]_\alpha(\alpha) = 1$ iff

at all worlds w: $[\![$ *Anyone who is at least 6'1" is tall$_s$* $]\!]_\alpha(w) = 1$ iff

at all worlds w: Anyone whose height is at least 6'1" at w has a height of at least $[\![s]\!]_\alpha$ at w iff

at all worlds w: Anyone whose height is at least 6'1" at w has a height of at least 6'1" at w

And thus we predict that (8) is true.

(8)   It is necessarily true that anyone at least 6'1" is tall.

By contrast, according to diagonalized epistemicism, the determining world shifts alongside the evaluation world when determining the content of *Anyone who is at least 6'1" is tall*. Thus,

$[\![$*Necessarily, anyone who is at least 6'1" is tall$_s$* $]\!]_\alpha(\alpha) = 1$ iff

at all worlds w: $[\![$*Anyone who is at least 6'1" is tall$_s$* $]\!]_w(w) = 1$ iff

at all worlds w: Anyone whose height is at least 6'1" at w has a height of at least $[\![s]\!]_w$ at w iff

The derivation ends here, since $[\![s]\!]_w$ depends on the world w that has been shifted by the modal operator. Since this condition won't hold for all worlds, we predict that (8) is false.

We can also see now why Williamsonian epistemicism entails Strong Supervenience, whereas diagonalized epistemicism only entails Weak Supervenience:

Strong Supervenience: Necessarily, for any vague property F there is some precise property G such that necessarily, something is F iff it is G.

Weak Supervenience: Necessarily, for any vague property F there is some precise property G such that something is F iff it is G.

Our candidate vague property is tallness. Recall the model from above:

Let's suppose w_1 is the world of utterance. Then, we can calculate the truth values of the contents of *Jones is tall* at each of these worlds, given Williamson epistemicism and diagonalized epistemicism. Recall the difference in their predicted contents:

Williamson Epistemicism: {w: $[\![$*Jones is tall$_s$* $]\!]_{w_1}(w) = 1$}
Diagonalized Epistemicism: {w: $[\![$*Jones is tall$_s$* $]\!]_w(w) = 1$}

For the Williamsonian Epistemicist, the precise property necessarily co-extensive with *tall$_s$* as uttered in w_1 is being at least 6'1" tall. And so, two possible individuals (Jones at w_1 and Jones at w_2, for instance) can differ in whether they are tall only if they differ in their heights. By contrast, for the diagonalized epistemicist, there is no precise property that is necessarily co-extensive with *tall$_s$* uttered in w_1. And, thus, there can be two possible individuals (Jones at w_1 and Jones at w_3) who differ in whether they are tall but do not differ in their heights; thus, the view predicts violations of Strong Supervenience. However, the diagonalized epistemicist still predicts that at any world, no two individuals can differ in whether they are tall without differing in their height at that world—this is because the cutoff for tallness is a property of the world. Thus, the view predicts Weak Supervenience.

4. Motivating Diagonalized Epistemicism

Suppose you are already a committed epistemicist—that is, you think that vague predicates have precise but unknowable cutoffs—but you don't want to endorse metalinguistic safety as the explanation for our ignorance of such cutoffs. Then, you have a reason to be a Diagonalized Epistemicist. Your ignorance of the cutoffs of vague predicates is just ordinary factual ignorance that can be predicted by the standard safety condition on knowledge.

Here's another argument in favor of diagonalized epistemicism over Williamsonian epistemicism. The argument draws on Stalnaker's theory of communication (see Stalnaker 1978, 1999, 2002). For Stalnaker, to assert a proposition p is to propose making p jointly believed (or taken for granted, for the purposes of the conversation). We do this by uttering a sentence S with the requisite assertoric intentions in the right context (where we can reasonably believe to be taken seriously). If all goes well, that sentence expresses a unique proposition p, which is recognized by our interlocutors to be the proposition we are proposing to be jointly accepted. If we are in fact sincere and they trust us, then the proposition will become jointly accepted between us.

However, when an utterance of S occurs in a context in which there is joint ignorance about what S's propositional content is, it will be unclear to hearers just what belief they should adopt. Suppose Jones utters S to Smith, but Smith doesn't know whether S means p or S means q. Then, Smith won't know whether Jones has proposed that they jointly believe p or jointly believe q, and hence Jones's assertion will be infelicitous.[5] This is borne out in some cases:

(9) a. *Doctor to patient*: You are suffering from acute myositis of the extensor retinaculum and require an arthroscopic myectomy to fully recover.
 b. *Patient*: What??

Williamsonian epistemicism predicts, for this reason, that some assertions should warrant such a response.[6] Consider the following context:

Alice is a fifth grade basketball coach, and her friend Beth is a college basketball coach. Beth never spends time around fifth graders, so she has no idea how tall

---

[5] This reasoning motivates Stalnaker's Uniformity constraint (Stalnaker 1978: 325):

Uniformity: Utterance U expresses the same proposition at every world compatible with what is mutually presupposed in the context.

[6] Of course, they need not warrant such a response. For instance, when the possible propositional contents p and q are equivalent given what's commonly believed, the hearer can recognize without harm to the speaker's intentions that the belief proposed is $p \cap q$. The cases we are considering here are not of this kind.

they are on average. The two are discussing a student, Cathy, and whether she would be a good fit on Alice's team of fifth graders. Beth knows Cathy's on-court stats, but not her height or whether she is taller on average than other fifth graders, whereas Alice knows the latter but not the former. Finally, let's suppose they know these facts about each other.

For simplicity, we'll suppose that for all Beth knows, every combination of the following are possible:

- For each n: 4'0" $\leq n \leq$ 7'0": Cathy is n feet tall.
- For each i: 5'0" $\leq i \leq$ 6'5": A fifth grade basketball player must be at least i feet tall to be tall.

Now, suppose Alice tells Beth:

(10)   Cathy is tall.

Williamsonian epistemicism predicts that Beth should regard Alice's claim with the same confusion as the patient responding to the doctor above. Beth has no idea what proposition Alice has expressed, and thus no idea what proposition has been proposed for her to believe.[7]

However, that is not how Beth should respond to Alice's claim. Remember, Beth knows that Alice is better positioned than she is to know what the standards of being tall for a fifth grade basketball player are. Thus, it seems much more plausible that Beth would respond by accepting Alice's assertion and thus rule out possibilities in which Cathy's height is below the minimum standards for what it takes to be tall for a fifth grade basketball player. In other words, she rules out any possibility in which:

Cathy is n feet tall and a fifth grade basketball player must be at least i feet tall to be tall and $n < i$.

This is not predicted by Williamsonian epistemicism, but it is predicted by diagonalized epistemicism (see also Barker 2002, MacFarlane 2020 for similar arguments). Count one more for diagonalized epistemicism.

---

[7] This case presents a different challenge to Williamsonian epistemicism than the arthritis case from §1.2. In the arthritis case, the agent doesn't know that they have arthritis in their knee because the mental representative of that belief could have meant something (they know) it does not. In this case, Beth doesn't know what claim Alice has made, and thus doesn't know how to update her beliefs.

5. Against Epistemicism

I've argued so far that, if you are an epistemicist about vagueness, you should be a diagonalized epistemicist. But, alas, now we come to the rub: I think you shouldn't be an epistemicist about vagueness. Let's start with a case that might, at first sight, be taken to be friendly to the epistemicist (adapted from Schiffer 2000: 223–4).[8] Remember Terry, who is 6'7" and is clearly tall, and who is about to be zapped by the Shrink Ray 3000 (and thus be shrunk by a quarter inch per second for one minute). Since Terry is clearly tall at t_0, we can suppose the following:

At t_0,
i. You are certain that Terry is tall.
ii. It would be correct to assert that Terry is tall.

After twenty-eight seconds in the shrink ray (at t_{28}), when Terry is now 6'0" and, we may suppose, clearly a borderline case of being tall, it seems that:

At t_{28},
iii. You are not certain that Terry is tall.
iv. It would not be correct to assert that Terry is tall.

Between t_0 and t_{28}, what happens? According to Schiffer, you slowly lose confidence that Terry is tall, and, if asked whether Terry is tall, should respond with qualifications ("Well, he kind of is."). Nicholas Smith concurs, noting that, as Terry shrinks, you would become "less and less sure" that Terry is tall, and "more and more sure" that he isn't (see Smith 2010: 3).

Are these claims correct? Is it correct to be less and less sure that Terry is tall as he shrinks? Diagonalized epistemicism says yes: as Terry shrinks, since you aren't sure what the standards for tallness are, whether his height meets the standards of tallness becomes less and less likely. However, I think your subjective probability that Terry is tall does not decrease as he shrinks. Rather, I will argue that, as he shrinks, it eventually ceases to be the case that you ought to be certain that Terry is tall. But this is not because you ought to be less than certain that Terry is tall; rather, it is because there is no n: $0 < n < 1$ such that it is determinate that you think it is n-likely that Terry is tall.

To see why, consider a variant case. Suppose you are told to estimate the probability that the ball drawn from (and then put back into) a jar was striped. At first, you're told by a reliable source that the ball was selected from Jar 0, which you can see contains only striped balls. In that case, the following seem correct:

---

[8] See also Smith (2009, 2010).

At J_0,

i. You are certain that the ball was striped.

ii. It would be correct to assert that the ball was striped.

But now suppose you're told that, actually it was chosen from (and put back into) Jar 1, which you can see contains all striped balls except for one. In that case, it seems that:

At J_1,

i. You are not certain that the ball was striped.

ii. It would not be correct to assert that the ball was striped.

The reason it would not be correct to assert that the ball was striped is that there is a salient possibility that you can't rule out—namely that the ball drawn was the one non-striped ball.

Suppose this process is iterated so that at each stage you're told, actually, it was chosen from Jar n, where you can see that the proportion of striped to non-striped balls is lower than the previous stage (we might imagine your memory is wiped so you may continue to believe your information source is reliable). Here, I think it is clear that over the course of this operation, your subjective probability that the ball was striped should decrease overall (whether it will decrease monotonically will depend on your eyesight and ability to estimate proportions of striped/non-striped balls), and it would remain incorrect to assert that the ball was striped. By the point at which there is a close to even ratio of striped to non-striped balls in the jar, you should think it around .5 likely that the ball was striped. These judgments are quite clear.

Compare these probability judgments with those in Terry's case. At t_0, Terry is 6'0"—a clear borderline case of being tall (we've supposed). We've agreed that you shouldn't be certain that he's tall, nor certain that he's not tall. Suppose we pause the shrink ray at this point and I ask you how likely it is that Terry is tall. Here, while the (A) response sounds odd, the (B) and (C) responses are perfectly acceptable:

(A) #He's (about) as likely tall as not.

(B) What do you mean? He's only kind of tall.

(C) Well, I'm not certain he's tall.

The infelicity of (A), especially when compared to the acceptability of (B) and (C), suggests that you should not think Terry is around .5 likely tall. However, the acceptability of (C) confirms the initial Schiffer/Smith intuition that:[9]

---

[9] This principle, and the one following, provide constitutive connections between credences in indeterminacy with determinate/indeterminate credences. An alternative conclusion to draw is that what's motivated here are principles about what credence you ought to have, given certain credences in indeterminacies. I will set aside the distinction between these types of principles here.

Indeterminacy undermines certainty: If you are certain that it is indeterminate whether S is F, then it is determinate that you are not certain that S is F, nor certain that S is not F.

But the combination of (A) and (B) reveals something further. Given that it is indeterminate that S is F iff S is only kind of F, we can motivate the following principle:[10]

Indeterminacy undermines (determinate) probability: If you are certain that it is indeterminate whether S is F, then for any n: $0 < n < 1$, it is indeterminate whether you think S is n-likely F.

One argument for this conclusion is that strings of the following form are infelicitous:

(11) S is only kind of F, and in fact S is n-likely F.
    a. #John is only kind of a jerk, and in fact he's likely / not likely a jerk.
    b. #That table is only kind of flat, and in fact it's likely / as likely as not flat.

This infelicity mirrors the infelicity exhibited by:

(12) S is only kind of F, and in fact S is/isn't F.
    a. #John is only kind of a jerk, and in fact he is/isn't a jerk.
    b. #That table is only kind of flat, and in fact it is/isn't flat.
    c. #Terry is only kind of tall, and in fact he is/isn't tall.

Just as the sentences in (12) are infelicitous because one ought not assert that p if one is sure that it is indeterminate whether p, so it is that one ought not assert that it is n-likely that p when one is sure that it is indeterminate whether it is n-likely that p. Thus, given Indeterminacy Undermines (Determinate) Probability, we explain why the sentences in (11) are infelicitous too. And thus, contra Schiffer and Smith, as Terry shrinks, it would not be correct to be less and less sure that he is tall. Nonetheless, this view can explain what might have motivated the Schiffer/Smith intuition: given Indeterminacy Undermines Certainty, you are not certain that Terry is tall when you're sure he's only kind of tall.

Unfortunately, epistemicism does not predict Indeterminacy Undermines (Determinate) Probability. Instead, the diagonalized epistemicist predicts that when you are certain that it is indeterminate whether S is F, there will be some

---

[10] The shift to the "kind of" locution is to avoid complications arising from the fact that "indeterminate" isn't obviously a term of ordinary English, and hence one that we can rely on pre-theoretical intuitions about.

n: $0 < n < 1$ such that, determinately, you think S is n-likely F.[11] Take Terry's case at t_{28}, where you know he is 6'0" but (let's say) are uncertain whether being 6'0" is sufficient to be tall. Idealizing, let's suppose you're uncertain between two possible cutoffs for tall: 6'0" and 6'1". Then, the diagonal of Terry is tall is:

$$\{w: [\![\textit{Terry is tall}_s]\!]_w(w) = 1\}$$

and this proposition will be true at w_1, where the cutoff is 6'0" and Terry is 6'0", and false at w_2, where the cutoff is 6'1" and Terry is 6'0". Since these are the only epistemically possible worlds (again, we are idealizing, so these will be classes of worlds), your probability in the diagonal of Terry is tall will be .5, and there is nothing indeterminate about this—contra Indeterminacy Undermines (Determinate) Probability.

That is why I am not an epistemicist.[12]

Conclusion

I started with an objection to epistemicism: according to the view, why is it that we cannot know the precise cutoffs of vague predicates? I argued against the standard, Williamsonian, answer, that appeals to metalinguistic safety. In its place, I suggested that epistemicists should be diagonalized epistemicists. But, then I argued against diagonalized epistemicism. Thus, ultimately, I think the best version of epistemicism fails—we should not be epistemicists about the vague.[13]

References

Bacon, Andrew. 2018. *Vagueness and thought.* Oxford: Oxford University Press.

Barker, Chris. 2002. The dynamics of vagueness. *Linguistics and Philosophy*, 25, 1–36.

Barker, Chris. 2013. Negotiating taste. *Inquiry*, 56, 240–257.

Burge, Tyler. 1979. Individualism and the mental. *Midwest Studies in Philosophy*, 4, 73–121.

Caie, Michael. 2012. Vagueness and semantic indiscriminability. *Philosophical Studies*, 160(3), 365–377.

---

[11] If they think credences are mushy, then n here will be a range.

[12] I leave aside the question how best to capture these judgments. I am optimistic that some linguistic theory of vagueness will do better in this regard, since linguistic theories are well positioned to predict that embeddings of indeterminate sentences under modal operators will yield indeterminate sentences—see for instance, Dorr (2003); Rayo (2008); Sud (2018).

[13] I would like to thank Agustín Rayo, Jack Spencer, and the editors of the volume Abrol Fairweather and Carlos Montemayor for helpful comments on earlier drafts.

Dorr, Cian. 2003. Vagueness without ignorance. *Philosophical Perspectives*, 17(1), 83–113.

Fodor, Jerry. 1981. Some notes on what linguistics is about. *Readings in the philosophy of psychology*, 2, 197–207.

Fodor, Jerry. 1987. *Psychosemantics: The problem of meaning in the philosophy of mind.* Cambridge, MA: MIT press.

Kearns, Stephen, & Magidor, Ofra. 2008. Epistemicism about vagueness and meta-linguistic safety. *Philosophical Perspectives*, 22, 277–304.

MacFarlane, John. 2020. Indeterminacy as indecision. *The Journal of Philosophy*, 117(11/12): 643–667.

Mahtani, Anna. 2004. The instability of vague terms. *The Philosophical Quarterly*, 54(217), 570–576.

Rayo, Agustín. 2008. Vague representation. *Mind*, 117(466), 329–373.

Schiffer, Stephen. 2000. Vagueness and partial belief. *Philosophical Issues*, 10, 220–57.

Sennet, Adam. 2012. Semantic plasticity and epistemicism. *Philosophical studies*, 161(2), 273–285.

Smith, Nicholas J. J. 2009. *Vagueness and Degrees of Truth.* Oxford: Oxford University Press.

Smith, Nicholas J. J. 2010. Degree of belief is expected truth value, pp. 491–506 of: Dietz, R., & Moruzzi, S. (eds), *Cuts and clouds: Vagueness, its nature, and its logic.* Oxford: Oxford University Press.

Stalnaker, Robert. 1978. Assertion, pp. 315–332 of: Cole, P. (ed), *Syntax and Semantics 9: Pragmatics.* New York: Academic Press.

Stalnaker, Robert. 1999. *Context and content.* Oxford: Oxford University Press.

Stalnaker, Robert. 2002. Common ground, *Linguistics and philosophy*, 25, 701–721.

Sud, Rohan. 2018. Plurivaluationism, supersententialism and the problem of the many languages. *Synthese*, 1–27.

Williamson, Timothy. 1994. *Vagueness.* New York: Routledge.

PART II

COOPERATIVE AND SOCIAL LUCK REDUCTION

8

Testimony, Luck, and Conversational Implicature

Elizabeth Fricker

1. A Distinctive Epistemic Kind: Testimony

Testimony is the main way in which knowledge and belief are spread across a linguistic community, both at a time and over extended periods of time. In a modern society, with its extensive division of epistemic labour and both epistemic and practical skills, most of what one knows is based on trust in the written or spoken word of others, who possess epistemic skills and knowledge bases that oneself lacks (see Fricker 2006b, 2021a).

When a speaker S testifies that P to an intended audience H in a speech act of telling, she offers her word that P to H. That is to say: by her act she presents herself as assuming responsibility for P's being so, thereby doing so,[1] and she presents herself as suitably authoritative so to do, and in doing this she gives to her audience H her assurance, her guarantee that P is so. This provides to a comprehending hearer H a distinctive basis for knowledge. When the testimony is well-grounded, being an expression of S's own knowledge that P, H can come to know that P through with epistemic propriety[2] trusting the speaker as regards her utterance, accepting her offered word that P, and forming belief on her say-so. When a recipient of testimony believes on this basis, she may aptly respond to the challenge 'How do you know that P?' with a response along the lines 'S told me, and I believe her / I trust her as regards P'. Or she might say '... and S knows about that kind of thing', or some other phrase expressing belief in the speaker's

---

[1] As with other illocutionary acts—things the speaker does in speaking—the recipient's recognising the speaker's intention suffices for it to be achieved, assuming background felicity conditions are in place; in this case, the speaker's being recognised as having suitable status to make such an assumption of responsibility. Small children and the mentally disturbed might not be so recognised. Austin (1975) is the classic source introducing the notion of an illocutionary act, and its felicity conditions.

[2] Fundamentalists about testimony such as Coady (1992), Burge (1993), Graham (2006b) hold that a speaker's word is default credible, and is properly believed in the absence of defeaters. Reductionists like myself (see Fricker 2017a) maintain the recipient should have evidence of the speaker's trustworthiness on her topic, if she believes him. Lackey (2008), Goldberg (2010), and Moran (2018) take intermediate positions. 'Assurance theorists'—Hinchman (2005); Faulkner (2011); McMyler (2011)—distinguish the epistemic position of addressee and onlookers, holding a kind of fundamentalism about the first only. Fricker (2021b) examines the basis for this contrast.

Elizabeth Fricker, *Testimony, Luck, and Conversational Implicature* In: *Linguistic Luck: Safeguards and Threats to Linguistic Communication*. Edited by: Abrol Fairweather and Carlos Montemayor, Oxford University Press.
© Oxford University Press 2023. DOI: 10.1093/oso/9780192845450.003.0008

trustworthiness on this occasion.[3] Knowledge from trust in testimony is thus knowledge at second-hand: the recipient's entitlement to believe invokes the authority of her testifying source, the speaker. So if the testimony to P was not well-grounded—the speaker did not speak from her own knowledge that P—the recipient's belief is also ill-grounded, and she cannot on this basis know that P.[4] We see that testimony is a distinctive epistemic source, where the recipient's entitlement to believe rests on the authoritativeness of her source, the speaker whose word she trusted, together with the fact that this speaker assumed responsibility for the truth of what she testified to.

Various associated normative features surround testimonial transactions. Most crucially, where a speaker has offered her word that P, has by her act overtly assumed responsibility for P's being so, if it turns out that she was not suitably authoritative to give her word as to P—she lacked knowledge that P—then she is liable to complaint from the intended audience of her utterance, and to criticism (though not complaint) from onlookers. This will be so if P is in fact false, and also if P is true, but the speaker did not know this, but only guessed or conjectured it on weak evidence.

2. The Speech Act of Telling

The speech act of telling is the paradigm vehicle for acts of testifying. Tellings are the subset of assertions whose overt conversational aim is to inform an audience presumed in the context actually or possibly ignorant of what is asserted, P. Tellings are only a subset of assertions, since these may be made for various other conversational purposes than to allow belief on the speaker's say-so. For instance, the conversational point of the assertion may be to demonstrate that the speaker knows that P, to an audience whom it is common knowledge already knows whether P, or the assertion may be part of a dialogue aimed at inducing understanding of a proof or argument, so the recipient ends up with her own basis for belief in the conclusion P.

But all assertions involve the speaker by her act assuming responsibility for the truth of what she asserts, P. In theorising assertion, I do not make this feature true merely by definitional stipulation. Rather, I follow the method proposed in Garcia-Carpintero (2018), identifying assertion as that illocutionary act which is the default act effected by utterances of stand-alone declarative mood sentences in English. My thesis is that this is indeed the default significance of such utterances.

---

[3] Fricker (2021b) develops a notion of trust and trustworthiness that fits this role.

[4] The view that for testimony to be well-grounded the speaker must express her knowledge is mainstream, but is challenged by some. See Graham (2006a), Lackey (2008) for challenge; and Fricker (2006a, 2015) for defence.

This initial identification allows the possibility that other linguistic means of communication, and indeed entirely non-linguistic non-conventional means, can effect the same illocutionary act. This thesis is defended in Garcia-Carpintero (2018). In what follows I develop a case against his view, but my argument is not won by a definitional stop that masks the real issues about explanatory communicative kinds. Where needed for clarity, I shall refer to assertions made by utterance of a stand-alone declarative mood sentence which in the context asserts what it literally says, as explicit assertions.[5]

In asserting that P by uttering a suitable declarative sentence, a speaker S presents to her audience a proposition P as the explicit truth-conditional content of her utterance, and she presents P as true, and she moreover presents herself as assuming responsibility to her audience for P's being so. In doing so, S *ipso facto* presents herself as suitably epistemically authoritative to assume such responsibility. In most cases, this amounts to S knowing what she states, P. For tellings— those assertions whose conversational aim is to allow the audience to form belief on the speaker's say-so, this amounts to S offering her word that P to her intended audience: offering them the entitlement to believe that P on her say-so.[6]

Since in any instance of assertion the speaker assumes responsibility for the truth of the proposition she presents, it would seem that one can safely form belief from any well-grounded assertion, on the speaker's say-so. Unfortunately the situation is not quite so tidy. This is because assertions are also made in types of discourse that are not aimed at fact-stating, and where the conversational role of assertions, and the type of epistemic authority claimed in asserting, is somewhat different. For instance, in the context of a philosophy seminar, an assertion makes a claim of epistemic authority re. the asserted proposition apt for that context; but this, I suggest, does not amount to claiming one knows the philosophical proposition one puts forward. The standards for assertion in philosophy are in some respects higher—one must be able to defend what one proposes with arguments— but in another lower. One surely does not claim to know what one puts forward, that would suggest one regards the matter as settled, and not open to further debate—a status rarely, if ever, assumed in philosophical discourse. So it would be a mistake to form belief, taking oneself to have knowledge from the speaker's say-so, from an assertion made in a philosophy seminar. The same may also hold of discourse in other contexts where it is mutually known by participants that knowledge on the topic is not attainable, and is consequently not the operative

---

[5] Explicit assertions do not comprise all assertions on my theory, since I allow that indirect assertions—made by non-literal uses of sentences—are possible. See note 26.

[6] For a fuller statement and defence of this account of telling and assertion, see Fricker (2015, 2023). My thesis is that this definition of assertion picks out a key socio-linguistic-cum-epistemic kind, not that it exactly picks out an everyday concept. However, I maintain that participants exhibit a tacit sensitivity to this category, in how they distinctively respond to utterances that are (perceived as) assertoric.

epistemic standard for making assertions—such as, perhaps, speculative discourse about the future course of share prices.

We can however conclude that all assertions made in the context of everyday fact-stating discourse are proper only when the speaker knows what she asserts—this is the operative epistemic standard; and that one can learn from all of them in the same way that one can from those that are tellings—that is, they are conversationally aimed at allowing belief on the speaker's say-so. Thus a bystander to an oral examination could learn from the candidate's confident answering of questions as to various historical facts by taking her word for what she states, though the point of her assertions is to display her knowledge to the examiners, not to inform them. In what follows I will neglect the complication presented by these special discourse contexts, and treat all assertions as subject to the condition that the speaker must know what she states, and hence as suitable to allow belief-formation on the speaker's say-so: that is to say, all assertions constitute instances of the epistemic source testimony. (So 'assertion' in what follows is to be understood as 'assertions, other than those made in certain special discourse contexts where the sense in which the speaker takes epistemic responsibility for her utterance is not the default one of presenting herself as knowing what she states'.) Assertion, as the illocutionary type associated with a distinctive recognisable syntactic type, the declarative mood,[7] is the more fundamental speech act kind, and tellings are a subclass of assertions.

So speech acts of telling, and assertions more generally, are instances of our epistemic kind testimony. That is to say, knowledge can be acquired from them through a distinctive mechanism characteristic of this epistemic kind. The distinctive mechanism is, as already noted, that the hearer can form justified belief apt to be knowledge *on the speaker's say-so*. This basis for belief is partly individuated by the fact that the hearer can aptly respond to the challenge 'How do you know that *P*?' with the answer '*S* told me that *P*, and I believe her / I trust her as regards her assertion that *P*.' In telling her that *P*, *S* has overtly assumed responsibility for *P*'s being so, thereby offering the entitlement to believe on her say-so, and so *H* can take up this entitlement offered by *S*'s speech act.[8] It is *S*'s act of overtly assuming responsibility for *P*'s being so to *H* that makes available to *H* this basis for belief that *P*. She takes up what is offered, *S*'s assurance that *P* is so. So the possibility of testimonially based knowledge, this epistemic kind, rests on the possibility of such acts of overt commitment by a speaker.

---

[7] Assertion is the default illocutionary significance of the declarative mood. In some special contexts, a non-hedged declarative mood utterance can effect a conjecture or guess, rather than an assertion; but in most situations, the speaker needs to provide a syntactic hedge to indicate she is only suggesting or conjecturing, rather than asserting: 'I believe / I think that the keys are on the kitchen table', rather than the flat-out 'The keys are on the kitchen table'. The flat-out use indicates the speaker speaks from knowledge, and assumes responsibility for what she states being so.

[8] For a testimonial reductionist, she does so with epistemic propriety only when she has evidence that the speaker's word is to be trusted.

3. The Conventions and Social Norms that Enable a Speaker to Assume Responsibility for Truth of a Presented Content

What enables S to do an act in which she overtly assumes responsibility for P's being so to her intended audience H, thereby offering her assurance that P is so to H? S's act must have the performative force of enacting such a commitment by S. That the act has this performative force is a fact about the normative change in S and H's situation that it effects. If a communicative act by speaker S to audience H effects a performance by S of overtly assuming responsibility to H for P's being so, then it has as upshot first, that H acquires an entitlement to believe that P on S's say-so;[9] second, that H acquires the right to complain to S, and S is liable to such complaint (from H) and censure (from H and others), if S's assurance was not well-grounded in her own knowledge that P.

A communicative act by a speaker S can have this kind of performative force and normative power, only when there exists a distinctive perceptible utterance type U such that tokens of U are recognised by practice-participants in a community C and there is a practice in C of making utterances of type U, and where certain conventions and norms govern this practice, which have the effect that an utterance of type U has this performative significance and normative upshot. (For a convention to be sustained regarding U, it must be a distinctive perceptible type, since participants must be able easily to recognise its instantiation, if they are to respond in the ways that constitute its having the significance it does. It need not be syntactically complex, nor linguistic. For instance, in the game of cricket, a certain hand gesture by the umpire has the significance of deeming the player currently batting to be 'out'—that is, his 'innings', i.e. turn at the wicket to attempt to score runs, has ended.)

In the case of assertion, the perceptible (syntactic) utterance type is stand-alone declarative mood sentences, and the conventional performative significance of utterances of such sentences is that the speaker by her act assumes responsibility for the truth of the content P presented by her words.[10] That conventions and norms are in force in C which endow utterances of declarative mood sentences with this performative significance, consists in how participants are regularly determined to regard and respond to such utterances. These participant attitudes

---

[9] More strictly: in every case where S by her act assumes responsibility for P's being so, S offers to H an entitlement to believe on her say-so. On my own reductionist view, H should not take this up unless she has suitable evidence of S's trustworthiness. For a fundamentalist, the offer itself generates a default entitlement to take it up; but one that is defeated if, for instance, H has evidence that S is not trustworthy; or if she already knows that not-P. In cases where the testimony is in fact ill-grounded, there is only an apparent, not a genuine, entitlement to believe offered by the speaker. See Fricker (2015, 2023).

[10] As commented above, this is the declarative mood's default significance; it can be overridden by pragmatic factors in the context of utterance.

are grounded in their knowledge (mainly tacit) of the conventions and norms, and more broadly in their dispositions to hold attitudes to utterances.

So it is a contingent fact about human language use that, when a speaker in a linguistic community C makes an utterance U of a stand-alone declarative mood sentence, and is recognised as doing so, U has the (default) performative force of committing the speaker in the manner described above.[11] It has this force because it is, by participants in the socio-linguistic practice in C, treated as having that force. First, recipients will respond to the utterance as having that force. They may believe what is told on the speaker's say-so, treating her utterance as a suitable basis to give them knowledge; and if a recipient finds the speaker was not suitably authoritative to give her word, she will regard herself as entitled to complain to the speaker, and all will regard her as having been at fault, criticiseable for her defective act. Second, a speaker who makes such an utterance will regard herself as thereby assuming responsibility for the truth of the presented content P, and will be intending to do so, and will expect to be open to complaint, criticism, and censure if it emerges that she was not suitably epistemically authoritative to do so. She will be disposed to withdraw the utterance, if she finds out it is false, or that her evidence was misleading or insufficient.[12]

To summarise: in uttering a stand-alone declarative sentence with explicit content P, S intends to and does present herself to her audience as assuming responsibility for the truth of P, and as being suitably placed to do so. Her act has this force just because it will be received as having that force, and she knows this; and it will be such, because it occurs within a practice governed by a set of norms and conventions which jointly constitute the social fact of its having that force.

Conventional regularities in usage underlie the lexical meanings of the words in the speaker's utterance which, in the context, fix its explicit truth-conditional content.[13] And as we have seen above, there is, crucially, a further convention which fixes the performative significance of an utterance of a stand-alone declarative mood sentence as an illocutionary act of asserting—assuming responsibility for truth of—this content. These are Searlian conventions: rules of the form 'doing X in circumstances C counts as doing Y' (Searle 1996). Where such a rule is in force, it is so just because all participants treat it as being so. This is what it is for a fact to be a Searlian convention. Of present concern, it is a Searlian convention

---

[11] Apparently the distinction of three main syntactic utterance types and their illocutionary significance—assertions, requests, questions—is a linguistic universal (Fogal, Harris et al. 2018, p. 3).

[12] These conventionally constituted facts about the assertoric significance of the declarative mood are parallel to the dispositions to offer and accept as payment for goods and services intrinsically worthless (almost) items that serve as currency in a community. The worth of coins and notes consists entirely in their being treated as having worth.

[13] Pragmatic factors are sometimes also involved in resolving, for instance, the reference of demonstratives and the domain of quantifiers. The explicit truth-conditional content of a declarative utterance is what is *said* in it, as contrasted with implicit not-at-issue content, including presuppositions, conventional implicatures, and conversational implicatures. Only the explicit content is literally presented in the speaker's words. Note 41 below comments on how this line is best drawn.

that a stand-alone utterance of a declarative mood sentence effects an assertion of the presented content.[14] That is to say, it effects an utterance whereby the speaker overtly assumes responsibility for the truth of the presented content. That is to say, utterance of a stand-alone declarative sentence triggers participants' dispositions to have the cluster of normative attitudes described above.

A Searlian convention links the declarative mood with assertion. It is the bunch of participants' attitudes through convention triggered by an utterance of a declarative mood sentence, which constitutes the fact that its speaker assumes responsibility for the truth of the presented content. This bunch of participants' normative attitudes to utterances of declarative mood sentences, i.e. assertions that we have described above, can be summarised in the thesis that assertions (declarative mood utterances) are governed by a social norm: 'One must: assert P only if one has suitable epistemic authority to assume responsibility for P's truth'. In all cases other than the special discourse contexts discussed above, this amounts to a knowledge norm governing assertions: 'One must: assert P only if one knows that P'—henceforth, the **K-norm** for assertion.[15] This norm encapsulates the normative attitudes of recipients and speakers to assertions described above. Participants in C being disposed to have these attitudes to declarative mood utterances is what constitutes the K-norm being in force in C regarding them, which is what makes them have the force of assertions, constituting instances of that speech act.

Assertion as speech act type has the K-norm as constitutive. The corollary of this is that a perceptible speech act type practised in a community C is assertion just if it is governed by the K-norm as a social norm. That is to say, participants' attitudes display sensitivity to the norm as governing it in their practice.[16] The normative consequences of asserting we have noted are part of this. A speaker who asserts P when she lacks knowledge that P is regarded (by others and herself) as having made a defective utterance, and is liable to complaint and censure. And recipients view themselves as acquiring an entitlement to believe P on the asserting speaker's say-so, when she has told them that P.

To summarise: a speech act made by uttering sentence U of syntactic type α with content P, made in community C by a speaker S has the (default) illocutionary force of an assertion, that is it constitutes S's assuming responsibility to her intended audience H for P's being so, only when and because it occurs within a suitable framework of conventions and social norms that govern a practice in C of making utterances of type α. These conventions and social norms are embodied in

---

[14] Of course this default significance of the declarative mood can be overidden, and is so in contexts where the utterance is interpreted as not serious, or not literal—jokes, metaphors, pronounciation practice, etc.

[15] Williamson (2000) is the modern locus classics arguing that assertion has knowledge as a constitutive norm. Fricker (2015 and 2017b) give detailed arguments for this account of assertion's norm.

[16] For a detailed account of this matter, see Fricker (2017b).

the dispositions to have normative attitudes to utterances of type α by participants in the linguistic practice in which S and H are embedded. For U to be an assertion, participants must be disposed to have the attitudes to utterances of type α that constitute these being governed by the K-norm as a social norm in C.

So S's uttering a declarative mood sentence that presents the content P amounts to S asserting that P—that is, her overtly assuming responsibility for the truth of P—just because her act is treated by participants as having that significance, and is made by S in the expectation that it will do so. It is so treated because it is recognised as being of a familiar linguistic type that, in general, has—that is to say, is treated by participants as having—that significance.

So Austin was right, and Strawson in his criticism was wrong.[17] All performative utterances, including the performative move made by assertions, involve Searlian conventions: facts about the move M that an act effects which obtain in virtue of the fact that surrounding attitudes of participants treat it as effecting M. And as part of this, we have seen, the performance effected by an assertion requires the existence in the community in question C of a social norm, the K-norm, governing utterances of the syntactic type that in C realises assertion.

We have seen that the performative force of tellings and assertions more generally is what enables the distinctive basis of entitlement for belief they provide. In an act of asserting, the speaker overtly assumes responsibility for the truth of the explicit content P of her assertion, vouching for P's being so, thereby offering to her audience an entitlement to believe P on her say-so. And we have seen that assertion has this normative performative significance only because it is a socially constituted type of action that conventionally (in the sense explained above) has this significance. That is to say, assertions are made and responded to as having this significance. This is encapsulated in the fact that assertion is subject to the K-norm as a social norm governing the practice of making assertions. So our argument shows how the performative force of asserting can only be constituted within a social communicative practice governed by a suitable framework of conventions and norms, including the K-norm. It follows that acts of asserting, and so of testifying, can only occur via the medium of such a socially recognised utterance type, within a practice governed by conventions and norms that constitute its performative force.

Starting from consideration of the epistemic role of assertions, viz. allowing knowledge to be spread from a knowing speaker to her audience by a distinctive mechanism, we have arrived at an account of assertion as a norm governed social kind. This is a neo-Austinian account of assertion, taking as central J. L. Austin's idea of the conventionally constituted performative force that an utterance type can have (Austin 1975). A very similar account of assertion is proposed in

---

[17] See Strawson (1964); Austin (1975).

Goldberg (2015), also starting from consideration of its epistemic role.[18] There is a huge literature on assertion. (See Fogal, Harris et al. 2018, Pagin and Marsili 2021 for excellent reviews and bibliography; Brown and Cappelen 2011 and Goldberg 2020 are useful collections.) My account contrasts with accounts of assertion as a natural rather than a social-normative kind. Simple Gricean accounts (Grice 1957) in terms of an intended effect on the recipient—whether inducing belief in P, or belief that the speaker believes that P—are subject to counter-example: bald-faced lies are assertions, as is generally agreed. More subtle belief-expression accounts (see Bach and Harnish 1979) can fare better, if a sufficiently refined notion of belief-expression is developed, which allows that a speaker can 'express' a belief she lacks. As they do so, they edge closer to my own account in terms of presenting oneself as believing—or better, as knowing—what one states.[19] It is indeed natural for us to express (in a simple sense) our beliefs in assertions: 'Oh look, there's a goldfinch' one spontaneously cries out to one's companion, as one catches sight of the bird. But the fact that they are naturally used to express belief does not afford an account of what is essential to assertions: the normative epistemic move they effect.

So even if a notion of belief-expression can be refined that extensionally captures assertion—it copes with lies, including bald-faced lies—this notion fails to capture the normative commitment which, I have argued above, is constitutive of assertion, and is essential to its playing the epistemic role it does, allowing a recipient of an assertion to form belief on the speaker's say-so. So I prefer my neo-Austinian account of assertion as a normative social kind to naturalistic accounts.[20]

The arguments first given in Fricker (2012), and revisited below, against the possibility of testifying, or asserting, via non-conventional means, and against the thesis that conversational implicatures are asserted, spring from this account of assertion as a normative social kind suitable for testifying. If a naturalistic broadly Gricean account of assertion were correct, there would be no obvious reason why assertion could not occur outside of any conventional linguistic system. Such a purely naturalistic concept covering instances of communication, including assertions, can perhaps be developed, and the label 'assertion' could be

---

[18] Goldberg and I both approach the topic of assertion with the concerns of epistemology in mind. My only significant difference with Goldberg is over the priority between the performative force of assertion, and the fact that it is governed by an epistemic norm. He thinks the norm is fundamental, and can explain assertion's other features; I hold assertion's performative force to be its most fundamental feature, and its epistemic norm to be a corollary—but this is detail.

[19] Fricker (2023) sets out my account in more detail, including an analytic account of what it is to 'present oneself as F'—a key notion for it.

[20] Pagin (2011, 2020) proposes a minimal naturalistic account that characterises assertion in terms of what one may broadly describe as its functional role. Even if his account captures the extension—which I am doubtful of—to my mind it misses out key normative epistemological features of assertion—something which, as an epistemologist, I regard as crucial. I hope to discuss Pagin's bold and interesting proposal more adequately in future work.

commandeered for it.[21] I maintain that the act distinctively effected by utterances of stand-alone declarative mood sentences, which enables the spread not merely of belief, but of knowledge based on trusting the speaker's word is the normative social kind described above. In the next section I contrast non-linguistic communication, which lacks the force of testifying, with the committing performance of a speaker when she testifies to *P* by asserting *P*.

4. Non-Linguistic Communication Cannot Amount to Asserting and Testifying

The preceding sections developed my account of assertion as a normative social kind governed by the *K*-norm. The *K*-norm being in force in a community regarding utterances of a syntactic type, we saw, is necessary for those utterances to have the performative force of an assertion. To say that the *K*-norm is in force summarises a cluster of normative attitudes that participants are disposed to have to utterances of that type, as was described. Invoking this account of testifying and assertion, I argued in Fricker (2012) that non-conventional communication of a message does not amount to testifying to or asserting it. I also gave reasons why it is not feasible to have, and there does not exist, a practice of treating conversationally implicated content as asserted, subject to the *K*-norm. In the rest of this discussion I revisit and expand upon those arguments, and show how they link to the issue of luck in linguistic communication.

The argument of the previous sections shows that there is no passing on of knowledge via the distinctive epistemic mechanism that characterises testimony, outside of socio-linguistic institutions governed by suitable conventions and social norms. There can be no offering of a person's word, hence no belief through taking it, without exploiting a socio-linguistic act type that supports this performance. Specifically: one can testify that *P* only by asserting that *P*, where assertion is a conventionally constituted linguistic type.

This does not mean that communication, the successful intentional conveying of a message, via recognition of that intent, from sender to recipient, cannot occur outside language. When sender and recipient have a rich enough base of shared knowledge, and the context provides sufficient clues, a recipient can on occasion successfully identify a specific message—or at least a fuzzy set of similar messages—a sender intends to get across to her by her observed act, without resort to the medium of conventional linguistic meanings to fix what that is (see Fricker 2012).

---

[21] Such concepts have existed since Grice (1957) set out his idea of 'non-natural meaning'. The difficulty, as remarked, is to find a naturalistic conception framed in terms of speaker intentions that includes bald-faced lies and similar counter-examples. Turning instead to the idea of the speaker's commitment to the proposition she presents being true copes with this.

But the epistemic mechanism here is different. The sender will not incur responsibility for the truth of her message to the same extent that she does when it is communicated via an explicit telling, an act subject to the K-norm.[22] In such a case, the recipient's basis for belief will be different. It may be something like: S clearly intended by doing act α to indicate to me that P, so (probably) P. For instance, at a dinner party: by kicking me under the table, S intended to let me know that I should stop talking about W—where W is some delicate subject matter. But she cannot rest her belief on S's say-so, her word that P, in the same way as when S explicitly tells her that P. It is up to her what she infers from the fact that S kicked her under the table, even if S intended that she do so. Non-linguistic communicative acts are not subject to the K-norm, this is the 'bottom line' of the fact that the utterer does not present herself as suitably authoritative to give her word as to the intended message. We can illustrate the point with an example adapted from Williamson (2000).

Suppose A and B arrive at the train station, where it is vitally important that B catch a train to a certain destination. Two trains are on the point of departure. A shouts 'That's your train', pointing to one of the two. B runs to the train, and just manages to board before it departs. It is the right train. Suppose A only conjectures that it is the right train. Her utterance is the best thing to do, in the situation; but it is still, *qua* assertion, defective. It presents her as knowing the ostended train is the right one, and she does not know this. Any assertion not issuing from suitable epistemic authority is defective, just as any ungrammatical sentence is defective. In some cases, where very little is at stake, the defectiveness is no more serious than a grammatical error, and there is no moral or prudential wrongness involved. But it is defective, and should be withdrawn, as the asserter will herself recognise.[23] In other cases, the defectiveness of an assertion not based in knowledge is much more serious, where some harm does or may result.

---

[22] In an extended critique of my thesis in Fricker (2012), Garcia-Carpintero (2018) says that qualifiers like 'does not incur responsibility *to the same extent*' or 'does not incur *full-strength* commitment' make my view anodyne and 'acceptable to all' (p. 199). Whether or not acceptable to all, conceiving commitment as a matter of degree, which is less in conversational implicature than in explicit assertion, does not make my thesis trivially true. Commitment and responsibility for truth can be a matter of degree, in that disapprobation and sanctions imposed can be more or less severe. In general, we allow that faults can be more or less bad, and it is coherent to maintain so in this case. The participants' attitudes reported in Mazzarella et al. (2018) vindicate this gradualist approach.

[23] Consider this hypothetical conversation between two people of idle gossip, about celebrities known to them only via the media. A says 'M is getting divorced from N', B responds 'You don't know that, you're just guessing', A rejoins 'I suppose you're right, I shouldn't really have said that'. This is a completely intelligible conversation possibility. A's utterance has no consequential harm or wrongness, nothing is at stake for either A or B; but *qua* assertion it is incorrect, and to be withdrawn, since A does not speak from knowledge, but in flat-out asserting what she did, she presented herself as doing so. The correctness condition for an assertion, as encapsulated in its norm, is that the speaker has suitable epistemic authority to assume responsibility for truth of the presented content. So any assertion where the speaker lacks this is incorrect. In asserting, the speaker presents herself as satisfying the correctness condition for her act. When she is not as she presents herself, her utterance is, in a sense, deceptive—she is not as she presents herself to be.

In contrast, suppose A had simply pointed at the train which it is her best (and correct) guess is the right one. She did the right thing in the circumstances, and there is no sense in which her communicative act is incorrect or defective. She does not, by pointing at it, present herself as knowing that the ostended train is the right one to catch. This lack of fault connects to the feature of non-linguistic communication noted in Fricker (2012), that in fact a specific message, as opposed to a fuzzy set of similar messages, cannot (except perhaps in a few exceptional circumstances[24]) be identified in non-linguistic communication. A is not committed by any K-norm governing her utterance to knowing this is the right train; and this is coeval with the fact that her pointing gesture, even in the situation, cannot be identified as intending to communicate the message—that is definitely your train— rather than the weaker—that is my best guess as to your train. Either would be an aptly relevant message in the situation, so assuming cooperativeness of A's act does not determine the stronger rather than the weaker intended message.

This indeterminacy as to what specific message is communicated via a non-conventional non-linguistic medium of communication, combines with the lack of any social norm governing it,[25] to ensure that the utterer is not committed to an assurance of truth, nor to her own epistemic authority to give this assurance, as regards her intended message. This non-commitment is reflected in the fact that B will have no basis to complain to A, or criticise her, if she finds A only conjectured the ostended train was the right one for B to catch. A did not, by her gesture, represent herself as knowing it was the correct one, so there is nothing to complain about. And even in the situation where A's guess was wrong, B may recognise A's act was the best, given her epistemic position and the overall situation. If B does criticise A, it will (or at least should) be on the ground that her conjecture was poorly based, not that she should not have indicated the train on the basis of a mere conjecture.

Garcia-Carpintero (2018) agrees with my account of assertion as a normative social kind. But, to my surprise, he nonetheless holds that assertions can occur outside of any linguistic conventions and norms.[26] We agree that any assertion is

---

[24] Hawthorne (2012) gives a case where the previous linguistic context (viz. of enquiry to that effect) fixes the topic of a pointing gesture—that the ostended individual came nth in a certain race; and notes that where it is common knowledge between participants that the gesturer knows who came nth, the weaker construal of the gesture's message is ruled out. Cases where the message topic is fixed by the previous and ongoing linguistic context are not instances of purely non-linguistic communication. The second point is, however, well taken. Such situations will, as remarked, be rare.

[25] A social norm must attach (this association of attitudes being conventional) to a repeatable and sufficiently often repeated perceptible utterance type, since this is a causally necessary condition for the attitudes of participants that render the norm in force to come to surround it. This point is further emphasised in my response to Garcia-Carpintero below.

[26] I do not need to disagree with his claim that there can be 'indirect' assertions—cases where a proposition P is asserted which is not the conventional linguistic meaning of the sentence uttered. Irony, hyperbole, understatement, and polite forms of indirection are themselves conventionalised linguistic phenomena, and non-literally conveyed content can be asserted by such utterances.

subject to the K-norm: it should not be made, if the speaker does not know what she asserts, and this means the norm must be in force, that is to say, participants' attitudes must constitute this and other K-norm related normative facts surrounding it.[27] But Garcia-Carpintero maintains I commit a fallacy when I move from the thesis that assertion is governed by the K-norm to the conclusion that it can only occur within the conventions and norms of a language-using practice (p. 200). Admittedly there is a further implicit premiss behind this inference, but the conclusion follows, as the argument of the previous section shows.

Garcia-Carpintero gives an example of a one-off, entirely non-linguistic and non-conventional act which, he says, is clearly an assertion—subject to the K-norm. But for the K-norm to be in force regarding an act, participants must be disposed to have the required cluster of normative attitudes to it, and there must be a knowledgeable expectation by participants of this (it is the knowledge that one's act will be subject to these normative attitudes that constrains speakers' actions). This can be so only if the act instances some recurring perceptible utterance type which triggers, and is expected to trigger, these participant attitudes (see note 25). By definition this cannot be so, with an entirely one-off non-conventional attempt at communication. *Ex hypothesi* there is no utterance type it instantiates such that there is a conventional association, in participants' psychology, of this type with the cluster of attitudes that constitute the K-norm being in force for it.

Garcia-Carpintero's example, taken from a short story by Borges, is of a secret agent tasked with finding out what town is the location of a key facility, and reporting this back to her employers (2018, p. 201). It is stipulated that the only available means she has of attempting to communicate this message is by killing a distinguished sinologist whose surname (Albert) is that of the town; her employers will see the newspaper report, including that the agent committed the murder; she duly kills him. Garcia-Carpintero 'submits' that this murderous act is 'a telling, an assertion' (p. 201). I disagree. First, there is not a determinate message conveyed. Even supposing the agent's employers infer that she is seeking to communicate with them by her action, there are many possibilities here—she could be aiming to convey to them that they should contact someone called Albert to get more information; or it could be interpreted as a signal that she has had enough of the job, and is resigning. The message of her act is certainly indeterminate between 'Albert is definitely the town' and 'Albert may be the town'. Second, and relatedly, contra Garcia-Carpintero, if the agent gives this signal when she has only inconclusive evidence that Albert is the town, she has not violated any norm of communication. Suppose the agent knows she will herself be killed very soon, she has obtained circumstantial evidence and has no chance to get more, then the

---

[27] Garcia-Carpintero (2019) makes much of this point.

best thing for her to do is to try to communicate the town name. Her action—as we are asked to believe—is the best way to try to achieve her task, and so she is not subject to criticism. Her act does not instance an utterance type conventionally associated with the K-norm, and this being so it does not constitute presenting herself as knowing the intended message—which, in any case, is not presented by the utterance, as the explicit content of an assertion is. Garcia-Carpintero acknowledges that for the K-norm to apply to an utterance it is required that 'the speaker manifests the intention of being bound by . . . the norm on the occasion, in ways available to the affected agents' (p. 201). The use of a stand-alone declarative mood sentence signals such an intention on the part of a speaker, and does so because that is its conventional significance. What Garcia-Carpintero misses is that a speaker cannot signal such an intention to her audience without the assistance of such a conventionally signifying utterance type.[28]

Garcia-Carpintero also suggests that conversational implicatures sometimes assert what is implicated. In the following sections I revisit and expand on the arguments in Fricker (2012) as to why this is not so. A practice in which conversational implicatures are treated as asserted is not in principle impossible in the same way that entirely non-conventional communication cannot constitute assertion—implicatures are a recurring utterance type to which normative attitudes can conventionally attach; but, I argue, it is not feasible and is not actual. But first I will say something about presuppositions.

5. Presupposition

We have seen that there is no testifying outside the conventional medium of language, or something like it.[29] It is the conventions and norms governing speech acts that endow them with their performative force. Of present concern, the K-norm as a social norm governing the declarative mood utterances that constitute assertions is the corollary and underpinning of their performative force, that in asserting that P a speaker by her act assumes responsibility for truth of its presented content P. So tellings, and assertions more broadly, are the paradigm vehicle for testifying. But explicit assertion of a content is not the only way in

---

[28] A different version of the story would be: it is pre-arranged between the secret agent and her employers that once she knows for certain the identity of the town, and only then, she will kill a distinguished academic who bears its name. In this scenario it can be maintained that the agent is committed by her murder to knowing the town's name is that of the murdered academic, and her act is an assertion of this. But this is precisely because, in this story, a conventional significance of her act has been arranged in advance by explicit agreement between the parties.

[29] As suggested in the previous note, explicit agreement can set up a convention as to the significance of a one-off signal, for instance that a red lantern placed in the window means the lantern-placer knows that the redcoats are coming, and this allows the signal to amount to assertion of this. That there can be such non-linguistic conventional communication does not threaten my account of assertion and what makes it possible.

which messages are communicated to an intended recipient via use of language. What of other linguistic means of getting a message across? Presupposition, and conventional and conversational implicature are also used by speakers to communicate a proposition,[30] and they are means by which such propositions can get added to the common ground of a conversation.

Which, if any, of these other linguistic means via which a message is communicated also amount to testifying and asserting by the speaker? That is to say, does the speaker present herself as assuming responsibility for the truth of the message, thereby doing so, and present herself as suitably epistemically authoritative to do so—as knowing the proposition made salient as presupposed/implicated by her act—when her message is communicated not by an explicit assertion, but by one of these other means? Only if she does will the same basis for knowledgeable belief—believing on the speaker's say-so—be available to the audience.

On this issue, presupposition is very interesting. To be itself true, an assertion requires truth of its presuppositions, and so it would seem a speaker by her act of assertion commits herself to its presuppositions' truth—and so surely she assumes responsibility for their truth? But that is not how the speaker 'stakes herself' in her utterance.

Exactly how the linguistic phenomenon of presupposition is best characterised and delineated is a complex and much debated matter (see Beaver, Geurts et al. 2021). An approximate fix sufficient for our purposes can be given thus: an utterance of a sentence S asserting P presupposes another proposition Q just if P entails Q's truth, and Q admits of 'projection'—that is to say, Q remains entailed under syntactic embeddings of S, including negation. For instance, 'I'm collecting my sister from the airport this afternoon' presupposes that I have a sister, since to be true it requires the truth of that proposition, and that I have a sister is equally entailed by 'I'm not collecting my sister from the airport this afternoon' (under the salient interpretation of the scope of the negation operator).[31] In uttering a sentence S which in the context asserts a proposition P that presupposes Q, the speaker in an intuitive sense 'presupposes' that Q is already in the common ground of the conversation.[32] Talk of collecting my sister from the airport

---

[30] Or a fuzzy set of similar propositions.

[31] My rough fix covers only semantic presuppositions; re. the broader notion of pragmatic presupposition (see Stalnaker 1974), this is clearly an important phenomenon; but so far as I can see it is hard to draw a line between these and implicatures.

[32] The notion of the 'common ground' of a conversation has become fundamental to linguists' explanations of how conversation works (see Stalnaker 2002). Exactly how it is theorised is debated, but it is unanimous that it includes all propositions mutually believed, or accepted as true, by participants. The thesis of Stalnaker (1978) that the 'essential effect' of an assertion is to add the asserted content to the common ground, and characterisation of an assertion as a proposal to that effect is entirely consistent with the richer characterisation of assertion developed here. While true and fundamental, Stalnaker's thin characterisation does not address the richer normative and epistemological features of assertoric communication; my account supplements it to do so.

builds on the (supposedly known) fact that I have a sister. This suggests that presupposing Q is conversationally apt only when Q is indeed already in the common ground. However, this is not so, due to the widespread phenomenon of presupposition accommodation. In cases of accommodating presupposition, the asserter in effect pretends that Q is already in the common ground. Supposing conversation proceeds smoothly, and her assertion that P presupposing Q is accepted, Q is added to the common ground along with P. In accommodating the presupposition, the audience adds Q to her representation of the common ground along with the accepted asserted content P. Typically this is done as a non-attentional default response, without the audience focussing attention on Q—a precondition for questioning its truth.

Accommodating presupposition is often just an entirely harmless matter of economy in speech—it would be unnecessarily laborious to say 'I have a sister, and I'm meeting her at the airport this afternoon'. But accommodating presupposition is also used in a much more insidious and potentially harmful way: to introduce propositions into the common ground, without them ever being critically evaluated by the hearer, or the speaker being put on the spot to defend them. For instance a speaker who says 'Someone ran into me today, and, guess what, it was another lousy woman driver' presupposes, without focussing the spotlight of attention on it, a fuzzy set of propositions in the range of 'many women are poor drivers'. It should be, one may think, that the speaker assumes responsibility for the truth of such a proposition. But, by presupposing it rather than asserting it, the speaker presents it as part of the common ground, something that 'everyone knows', rather than a disputable claim that she herself is introducing. By presupposing a proposition rather than asserting it, the speaker in such cases (perhaps unconsciously) acts so as to add it to the common ground without it ever being scrutinised, as the explicit content of an assertion is; and without herself assuming responsibility for its being true, or being open to challenge to defend a claim that it is true. She is not staking *her* word on it since, her act posits, it is already commonly known or accepted as true. Relatedly, in responding as a cooperative conversational partner, the hearer will tend simply to add the presupposed content to her belief set, without it ever being a focus of her attention as a proposition to be scrutinised as to its evidential warrant. Presupposition is thus aptly characterised as 'not-at-issue content' (see Stanley 2015, ch.5). Hence, presupposition is a form of communication both suitable and liable to spread prejudices and stereotypical beliefs without the recipient ever realising she is being manipulated into accepting them.

To summarise: though an assertion entails the truth of its presuppositions, the speaker does not present herself as assuming responsibility for their truth, since her act presents them as already accepted as true by all conversational participants. Since it does so, presuppositions will tend to be accommodated without participants noticing that a new proposition has been added to the common ground, and to their background beliefs; hence, without the presupposed contents being scrutinised for evidential warrant before being added. When a presupposition is noticed by the recipient, and questioned, the speaker is held to account for its truth, but doing this is disrupting the flow of conversation, not following conversational rules. One cannot reject a presupposition of an assertion by replying 'No, I don't agree' or 'That is false'; instead, one must say something like 'Hey, wait a minute…'. One first has to make explicit the presupposition on which the assertion builds, in order to then challenge it. This makes presupposition a powerful and dangerous conversational tool for spreading beliefs without them coming under suitable scrutiny, or requiring defence by their propagators.[33]

We have seen that presuppositions are not testified to or asserted, since the speaker does not present them as items that she herself assumes responsibility for the truth of; instead, she presents them as already known by all participants. Accommodating presupposition, we saw, involves a kind of pretence that what is presupposed is already known. If presupposition is governed by a conversational norm enforced by participants as a social norm, this is not the K-norm, but rather:

Presupposition Norm: One must presuppose Q in uttering S, only if Q is already mutually known by conversation participants.

Accommodating presuppositions are excuseable violations of this norm.

The extent to which speakers are in fact challenged and criticised by conversation participants for making utterances with presuppositions that are not in the common ground is an empirical matter; we have seen how the structure of conversation makes it difficult to do this. But if such a norm is indeed in place, then a speaker who presupposes a proposition that is not in the common ground is always liable for such criticism. If what they presuppose is an uncontroversial piece of information—such as that the speaker has a sister—this is properly regarded as unobjectionable. Where it is, for instance, an unwarranted prejudicial stereotype about a particular social category, the speaker is and should be liable to criticism, and her presupposition made explicit and challenged, and then rejected. This does not mean that presupposing is a way of asserting: the norm governing it is different, and a speaker who presupposes a proposition Q does not present herself as assuming responsibility for Q's being so.

---

[33] Langton (2018) explores the importance of, and difficulties in, an audience both noticing and then reacting so as to 'block' presuppositions in speech which embody attitudes and beliefs unacceptable to them.

6. Conversational Implicatures: Their Fragility

The phenomenon of conversational implicature was first theorised by Paul Grice in his (1975), thereby launching the modern field of pragmatics.[34] As Davis (2019) explains, 'What someone implicates is not given to us directly... Hearers have to infer what speakers implicate.'[35] And 'Implicature is indirect because to implicate something is to mean it *by saying something else*' (p. 4; his italics) This inference is mediated by tacit knowledge of the cooperative norms governing conversation first set out in Grice (1975); most significantly in inferring implicatures, the norm that a contribution to the conversation must be relevant to the topic under discussion. Thus, using Davis's illustration, in the following exchange Barbara says (in doing so, explicitly asserting) that she has to work, and thereby, given the context, implicates that she will not be attending the party: Alan: 'Are you going to Paul's party?' Barbara: 'I have to work.'

So, what about conversational implicatures (henceforth simply 'implicatures') of an explicit assertion? Are they asserted and so testified to?—that is, are they treated by participants as asserted? That is to say, do the attitudes of participants to implicatures amount to the speaker regarding herself, and being regarded by recipients, as presenting herself as knowing what is implicated, and assuming responsibility for its truth—so that the speaker is subject to complaint, criticism, and censure if she implicates something she does not know; and so that a recipient has epistemic warrant to believe an implicature on the speaker's say-so, as she can what is explicitly asserted?

One point we must put aside: we saw that the distinctive kind of warrant for belief testimony provides is individuated in part by the type of defence a recipient may aptly offer for a belief so based: 'S told me that P, and I believe her'. So our question is in part about whether this same type of basis for belief, which adverts to the warrant to believe offered by the speaker, is available to the recipient of an implicature: 'S by her utterance implicated that Q, and I believe her.' Unfortunately it is hard to get a grip on this aspect of our question, since although participants certainly have a tacit understanding of implicature, and recover implicated content, the phenomenon of implicature is not explicitly recognised in folk linguistics in the way that telling is. A recipient complaining about a false implicature is thus likely incorrectly to object: 'You told me that Q', and the speaker so challenged is likely to reply by saying 'I never told you that Q, I only said that P'. The fact that a speaker is likely to reply thus (if my empirical claim

---

[34] For introductory reviews and bibliography, see Sperber and Wilson (2005); Potts (2015); Davis (2019).

[35] The contrast in phenomenology, noted in §7 below, between a recipient's grasp of explicitly asserted and of implicated content underwrites the distinction between explicit assertoric content, which is directly perceived and implicated content, which is not and is instead inferred from the perceived content.

here is indeed so) favours my case. But my case against implicatures being testified to will not rest on data concerning what justification for a belief acquired via implicature is typically offered. There is, however, a key difference in the epistemology of explicit assertion and implicature when it comes to how the recipient knows that a particular implicature was intended. This stems from a difference in their phenomenology, as discussed in §7 below.

Whether a speaker regards herself, and is regarded by other participants, as assuming responsibility for the truth of a message implicated by what she asserts is an empirical question about the attitudes of participants that surround the making of implicatures. In Fricker (2012), I made the empirical claim that implicatures are not testified to, and listed several respects in which implicature differs from explicit assertion, which I claimed to underlie and explain this contrast in participants' attitudes.

The differences I pointed out are various aspects or correlates of the greater fragility in the mechanism by which the content of an implicature is recovered, in the context, by the intended recipient. A process aimed at delivering an outcome is *fragile*, I shall say, if it can easily go wrong—fail to deliver the intended outcome. Implicature is fragile: that is to say, when an intended message is successfully communicated by implicature there are many close worlds in which there is miscommunication instead of successful communication. In contrast, a *robust* process is one that does not easily go wrong; one has to go to relatively remote worlds, for it to misdeliver. Communication by explicit assertion is relatively robust. Typically, it goes wrong less easily than implicature.

The fragility of implicature stems from the fact that the successful communication of an implicature requires a rich basis of coordinated belief on the part of speaker and recipient, including higher order beliefs about what the other believes about one's own beliefs. Suppose a speaker S makes an utterance that in the context constitutes an explicit assertion of P, and intends thereby to implicate Q. The mechanism by which she expects the recipient H to recover the implicature, and by which H will recover it, goes something like this: H looks for a reason why S is asserting P to her now; this requires it to be relevant to the current topic (thus conforming to Gricean cooperative norms of conversation), which P in itself is not. Hence H looks for some further proposition such that P is relevant if and only if it is true, and identifies Q, which she accordingly takes S to be intending to implicate.[36]

---

[36] This is the usual way in which implicature works. It is not the only way: Grice's famous example 'Mr. Jones has beautiful handwriting' also works to implicate that Mr. Jones is no good at philosophy via relevance, but it has a more subtle mechanism. Jones's handwriting is irrelevant to the topic at issue: whether he is an able philosopher. The conversational deviance of making this remark signals an unwillingness to say anything relevant, from which it may be inferred that what can be said on the topic is unfavourable. This utterance is not a standard case of implicature, because it is intentionally disruptive, and cannot be rendered relevant.

Suppose at a barbecue party hosted by Sheila and Hannah, Sheila says to Hannah 'We've run out of charcoal', and Hannah responds 'There's a petrol station just down the road'. This fact is relevant to the topic introduced by Sheila's remark only if one can (usually) buy charcoal at petrol stations, or at least at that one. Hence, to render Hannah's statement consistent with Gricean cooperative norms of conversation, including relevance, Sheila infers that petrol stations (often) sell charcoal, or at least this one does, and she will be able (probably) to obtain more charcoal at the petrol station. She accordingly gets her car keys and sets off there.[37]

This process will work only if speaker and recipient have many shared background beliefs. (Most of these are so obvious it is hard to spot them!) For instance, that if the charcoal has run out, then there is a need for more; that if there is a petrol station just down the road, it is possible to get to it and return quite quickly and easily; that it is possible for someone at the party to leave it, and then return having obtained more charcoal—and so on. Without these shared beliefs, the recovery of the intended implicature via relevance is not possible. Most significantly, beliefs about the other's beliefs, including about their beliefs about one's own beliefs, are always involved in the process of recovering an implicature. In our barbecue example, Hannah takes Sheila's statement that the charcoal has run out to indicate she is interested in trying to get more. This requires that Hannah believes that Sheila wants to get more charcoal, to continue the party, and that she believes that Sheila believes that Hannah shares this desire—there would be no point in making the remark to a hostile neighbour who wants proceedings to come to an end immediately. This is a simple illustration of the general fact that many shared beliefs, including higher order beliefs, are involved in the process of identifying via relevance an implicature Q. For instance, Hannah's remark in our example would fail to be relevant, and would be conversationally deviant, in a situation where it is common knowledge between Sheila and Hannah that it is impossible for anyone to leave the venue of the party, or that the specific route to the petrol station is blocked on that day, or that petrol stations do not sell charcoal. Suppose Hannah had said 'There's a chemist just down the road'—this would be deviant, since it cannot be interpreted as relevant, given their background knowledge. It is worth repeating the point: for the implicature to be successfully recovered, it is not enough that each participant have these ground-floor empirical

---

[37] Implicature, at least in cases like this, works very similarly to presupposition. Hannah's utterance is relevant, and so conversationally non-deviant, just if petrol stations (often) sell charcoal, or at least this one does. So in a sense her utterance presupposes that a suitable proposition about petrol stations is already in the common ground; if it is not, her utterance accommodates it to the common ground, to render her utterance conversationally in order. Implicature adds the implicated content to the common ground, because it is required for the asserted content to be conversationally apt in terms of relevance: presupposition, for it to be so in terms of its truth. See Stalnaker (1974).

beliefs about the world; each must believe that the other believes them, and believes that she herself believes them.

For successful communication by any means S and H's relevant beliefs must be aptly coordinated; recovery of the intended message by the recipient turns on this. And, as our illustration above showed, with communication via implicature, the relevant belief set is large. S and H's relevant beliefs about the non-linguistic world must be shared (though these need not be true); and there are many relevant higher order beliefs about what the other believes that must be true. These beliefs, especially the higher order beliefs about what the other believes, can easily be false. This is the main source of the fragility of implicatures.

In contrast, what is explicitly stated in a linguistic utterance is in large part fixed by the lexical meanings of the expression types that occur in it; and, in typical everyday cases of speech within a linguistic community, failure of coordination on beliefs about these[38] is a much less close possibility.[39] It is true that context often plays a role in fixing reference, and sometimes pragmatic factors are invoked in this process. But typically to recover explicit truth-conditional content a much thinner shared belief base is needed, one comprising beliefs that would not easily be false. This is why its recovery is a relatively robust process.

So our question whether implicatures are testified to connects with the topic of the role of luck in linguistic communication. Explicit assertion is a robust speech act type apt to bear the surrounding normative attitudes of participants that constitute its having the performative force of testifying, and does indeed have this force. In contrast, it is argued here, implicature is not apt for this, and does not have the performative force of testifying; and a central explanatory factor (though not the only one) in why it is not apt is the fragility of implicature as a means of communication, in contrast with the robustness of explicit assertion.

The successful recovery of an implicature is a matter of luck in two ways. First: when an implicature Q is correctly recovered by the recipient H from an assertion of P on an occasion, this process will be apt, in Sosa's sense, exhibiting situation-specific safety. Speaker's and recipient's beliefs are suitably coordinated, and so the recipient recovers the intended implicature through deploying her linguistic and pragmatic interpretative skills. She apprehends Q as implicated, and so comes to believe Q. H's implicit belief that Q is the proposition implicated is accurate through exercised competence, and as such is apt,

---

[38] To be more accurate: what is required is that participants have shared dispositions to respond to expressions as having their particular meanings. These are dispositions to form thoughts in response to hearing them, and to use them in certain ways. Explicit beliefs about what expressions mean is not required; and where held, these may not correspond to the meanings the participant's usage embodies.

[39] Where speaker and hearer speak different dialects, and are less than fully aware of this, miscommunication is likely and frequent, however. Any British visitor to the United States will have had many experiences of this. I recall being deeply disappointed when I ordered 'chips' with my meal, only to find what I would call 'crisps', and not what in the US dialect of English are known as 'french fries' arriving.

amounting to knowledge (see Sosa 2011, 2015; Fricker 2019). But this process of recovering the implicature will very often lack higher order safety: quite small and modally close changes in the background beliefs of either sender or recipient, rendering these uncoordinated, would engender the recovery of an unintended message, or of none. The recipient might easily have had different beliefs about what the speaker believed, and in that situation would not have recovered the intended implicature. Or, if the speaker had different beliefs about what the recipient believed, she would not expect her to infer Q as implicature, and so would not intend to achieve this. So the successful recovery of an implicature is typically fragile. Small and modally close changes in the circumstances would disrupt it. When things go well, the recipient of an implicature recovers it, and thereby comes to know it. But that she comes to know it is a matter of luck: things might easily have been otherwise in such a way that would prevent her recovery of the message.

Second: notwithstanding this key role of coordinated background beliefs, it may be that there are some cases where the recovery of a particular implicature is safe—cases where the relevant coordinated beliefs of speaker and recipient are so secure that they could not easily be different, failing to be coordinated. Even in such cases, it is still true that the message is communicated via a type of process that is generically unsafe. Given the role of coordinated background beliefs in recovering an implicature—beliefs which typically could easily differ, failing to be coordinated—communication via implicature is by its nature fragile, liable to misunderstanding and miscommunication. It is likely that misunderstandings of implicatures are relatively frequent, in comparison with explicit assertion.[40] This yields a second sense in which it is lucky if the recipient is able successfully to recover the intended message in a particular case: she receives the message via a type of mechanism that is generically unsafe.

I will refer to the role of relevant background beliefs, including a speaker's beliefs about her intended recipient's beliefs, in light of which she frames her utterance and intends by it to convey a certain implicature; and including the background beliefs, including about the speaker's beliefs, which inform and determine the hearer's recovery of an implicature, as the *epistemics* of implicature.

---

[40] Implicature is intrinsically more liable to misunderstanding than explicit assertion. However, whether misunderstandings are statistically more frequent will depend on how cautious speakers are in their use of implicature. Failure of coordination on relevant background beliefs between speaker and recipient will be more easily the case in some situations than in others. *Ceteris paribus*, it is less likely between two people who know each other very well than between strangers, especially when they come from different social backgrounds. Think of the range of shared references needed for an audience to 'get' a joke, and how attempts at jokes can fail with an audience that does not share one's cultural references! Similar considerations apply to implicature.

7. Four Contrasts in the Epistemics of Implicature versus Explicit Assertion

In Fricker (2012) I noted several contrasts in the epistemics of explicit assertion versus implicature. The contrasting features of implicature mentioned there, plus a new one, are set out below. The basic contrast is that already spelled out above:

(i) **Implicatures typically are fragile, in contrast to the robustness of explicit assertions.**

A much larger set of coordinated background beliefs must be deployed to recover an implicature than is needed for an explicit assertion, and so consequently their recovery more easily goes wrong, and they are more liable to misunderstanding and miscommunication.

The further contrasts are:

(ii) **Iterated knowledge is less frequent for implicatures than for explicit assertions.**

A corollary of (i) is that, while the recipient very often succeeds in recovering an approximate intended message—knows that the speaker intended to implicate something along its lines—iterated knowledge is less frequent. When a speaker tells an audience that P via an explicit assertion—one where what is asserted coincides with what is literally said in the context by the uttered sentence S of their shared language—lexical decoding plus an apt sensitivity to how features of context conventionally fix reference, perhaps also invoking pragmatic aspects of the context, suffice to recover what is explicitly asserted. This is a relatively light computational burden, and a robust process.[41] Hence, typically not only will the recipient know that the speaker intended to tell her that P; she will know that the speaker knows she knows this, and similarly, *mutatis mutandis*, for the speaker's knowledge of her audience's knowledge. That the audience understood the

---

[41] How to theorise what is literally said—the locutionary act—and so what is explicitly asserted is a matter of fierce debate among linguists and philosophers of language, which there is no space to discuss here. I am indebted to the discussion of the issues in Saul (2012). The notion she proposes, which she maintains is apt to capture the lying/misleading distinction, also suits my theoretical purposes. On this view, implicatures and presuppositions are not included in what is said; but what is said has determinate truth-conditional content, including in cases where contextual resolution invoking pragmatic factors is required to fix this—for instance the reference of demonstratives, and domain of quantifiers; as well as 'completions', as in 'S is ready [for some specific activity or event]'. True, pragmatic factors often play a role here: one may, for instance, need to appreciate what speaker intentions are salient in the context in order to fix the domain of a quantifier. But the interpretative burden, in particular the set of background beliefs that must be invoked to recover the intended content, is still light in comparison with that required to recover an implicature. This contrast is considered further in §9.

utterance is normally perceptible from her response in the conversational situation; and this generates this iterated knowledge (see Schiffer 1972, p. 31 ff.).

In contrast, to recover an implicature, it does not suffice to understand the truth-conditional content and the force of the uttered sentence; inference via assumptions about the speaker's beliefs and intentions on the part of the recipient is needed.[42] The recovery of the implicature requires more cognitive processing and invokes more background resources, and consequently its recovery is a more fragile process; and so it is harder for the speaker to know that it has been recovered, and so consequently for the recipient to know that the speaker knows this...etc. Of course, this is true only immediately after the utterance that carries the implicature. Very often, the way the conversation then proceeds will reveal whether the recipient has recovered the implicature—for instance, she may seek clarification as to whether it was intended or challenge it.

Thus the fragile and uncertain epistemics of implicatures are more significant in cases where the interests of speaker and recipient are not aligned, or the speaker's utterance is aimed at probing whether they are aligned, as in Pinker's speeding fine bribe case (Lee and Pinker 2010). A motorist is stopped by a traffic officer, with the looming prospect of being given a speeding ticket; the motorist says 'I'm in a bit of a hurry officer—is there some way we can settle this now, without any paperwork?' This suggests the possibility of bribing the officer not to give him a ticket, but in a way that is deniable if the officer is not receptive (more on deniability below). If the officer is not corrupt, and responds 'I'm afraid I have to give you a ticket sir', then even if she strongly suspects the motorist intended to implicate the possibility of a bribe, she cannot—since she did not take the suggestion up—know this was so; let alone know that the speaker knows that she knows. What one's words as uttered mean is a public matter, even when context is involved in fixing this;[43] but what one aimed to communicate over and above what one said turns on one's intentions, and these are private. More specifically: relevance cannot establish that the motorist intended to offer a bribe. He can respond to such a charge by saying 'I did not have anything specific in mind officer, certainly not a bribe—who do you take me for? I just wondered if there was some procedure available that could be effected on the spot.' Since whether the motorist's utterance was made with, and can only be explained by, the intention to suggest a bribe turns on what exactly he already knows about speeding ticket procedures, and this cannot be publicly proved by the officer, he can get away with this claim about his own beliefs and intentions. This example

---

[42] These inferences are typically non-conscious and automatic; indeed, most ordinary speakers would be unable to articulate the principles, in particular Gricean norms of cooperation, on which they rely. Still it seems right to call the cognitive processing that is undeniably involved a form of inference. See Carston (2002); Sperber and Wilson (2005).

[43] This view marks me as a conventionalist, rather than an intentionalist, regarding how what is said is fixed in cases where context must be invoked. See §9 below.

shows how iterated knowledge of an implicature is hard to attain; and also, how hard it is for the recipient to demonstrate by public evidential standards what the speaker knew and intended, even when she herself knows this. This contrast of a recipient's knowledge about the speaker's intentions and beliefs versus her ability to publicly prove this is what the speaker intended is a key factor in explaining the puzzling phenomenon of deniability, which is discussed in the next section.

(iii) There is a contrast in phenomenology between implicatures and explicit assertions.

A contrast in the phenomenology of explicit assertions versus implicatures is, to my mind, a very significant factor in explaining the difference in participants' attitudes. Competent speakers of a natural language do not hear a speaker as uttering a merely syntactic entity, and infer from what they hear that she intends to render mutually salient a certain proposition conventionally associated with this observed syntactic item. They do not infer from what they hear that the speaker intends to say that P, when she utters a sentence of their shared language suitable to do so, they directly hear her as saying it—they hear the truth-conditional content and force of the words in those spoken words themselves. One who asserts that P is perceived as doing just that, her act is perceived as having that representational content and force. This is a remark about the phenomenology of everyday language use. It is a necessary fact about first-language use (see Fricker 2003).

So it is literally true that when a speaker asserts that P by uttering a sentence apt in the context to do so, she presents a proposition P to her audience, and moreover presents P as true (see Fricker 2015, 2023). In making perceptible her words to her audience, she makes their asserted content a common perceptible between them, the object of their joint attention.[44] In contrast, even in a case where the recipient recovers an implicature of what is said effortlessly and immediately, she does not hear it in the words uttered: it is not perceptually presented to her by the speaker's act. Instead, she infers it from what she perceives the speaker explicitly to state. (Compare: I may conclude effortlessly and immediately from seeing threatening dark clouds that it is going to rain very soon; but I do not see the future rain.) This, I suggest, is why it is so natural, and is standard, to speak of truth-conditional content determined by the words that compose the uttered sentence, and attached

---

[44] This observation is consistent with the fact that, very often, inference from features of context, as well as lexical decoding, is needed to arrive at the truth-conditional content of the utterance. This is effected subpersonally, and the resultant phenomenology is perceptual. Admittedly, there are some cases where the recipient has to think, to work out the reference of the speaker's words. But this case is atypical, and secondary (see Fricker 2003), and anyway once she has done so, she will hear them as having this content. The rich contents of visual perception equally derive from inference-like sub-personal processing. There is no inconsistency between the need for computation and immediate perceptual phenomenology.

to them, as 'explicit' content. It is explicit in the sense that it is right there in the words themselves, presented in them as a joint perceptible between speaker and audience. This contrasts with further content that is only 'implicit'—not presented in the words themselves, but merely suggested by them.

This difference in phenomenology between explicit assertion and implicature makes for a difference in their epistemology. A recipient complaining that a speaker misled her as to P, when P was explicitly asserted, can say 'But you told me that P, I heard you!' Such claims about what was explicitly stated in the context are rarely plausibly deniable. They can be verified by a tape recording.[45] In contrast: 'You implicated to me that Q, I heard you do so!' is not an available basis or justifying defence for a recipient's belief in what (she believes) was implicated. Instead, she must report her inference, saying something like 'You told me that P, I heard you, and so I thought you must mean (to convey) that Q'. For instance 'You knew I needed to get more charcoal, and you told me that there was a petrol station nearby, and so I thought you must mean to indicate that it would sell charcoal.'

That an utterance in which P is asserted was also intended to implicate Q is not something a tape recording can verify;[46] it is an inference made by the recipient, deploying background beliefs that she takes to be coordinated with the speaker's. It may be correct, but it cannot be demonstrated by reference to what was commonly perceived between speaker and hearer, as can what was asserted. A complaint by the recipient that the speaker falsely indicated to her that Q, where this was only implicated, is likely to be met with the response: 'I never told you that Q, I only told you that P.' The speaker here allows that she is responsible for what she told; but not so for what the speaker inferred from the telling that was a common perceptible between them.[47]

---

[45] Sometimes a speaker may attempt denial by maintaining her utterance was not serious—she was joking, or speaking metaphorically or hyperbolically. For instance a murder suspect who was heard saying shortly before the murder that she 'would like to kill X'. But such defences are sustainable only in very limited circumstances. Similar remarks apply to the possibility of lexical or syntactic ambiguity: they provide an epistemic get-out for the speaker only in a very small proportion of cases. (Of course a speaker may craftily construct a sentence to allow such a get-out. There is a club frequented by students in east Oxford called The Library. A student who has failed to submit an essay on time might assure her tutor 'But I was in the library all evening'—thereby uttering a sentence she expects to be interpreted one way, but hoping to avoid the charge of lying if challenged by claiming the alternative interpretation was intended. However such a strategy is transparently deceptive and will surely fail in this case—thereby illustrating the point that exploitation of lexical and syntactic ambiguities will rarely succeed in providing plausible deniability.)

[46] A longer video recording of the entire scene, together with an explanation of the context, including such matters as the power relations between the individuals in question, may however suffice to demonstrate that a certain implication was intended. I understand that a legal test is applied in the USA, of 'what any reasonable person' would infer to be the intention of the speaker in the context; and this can be used, for instance, in cases of claims of sexual harrassment of an employee by her boss. This is very much harder to demonstrate than facts about what words were uttered, and what explicit speech acts were made by their use.

[47] The difference between what is explicitly asserted and what is only implicated by an utterance should not be slavishly tied to compositional semantics. The implicating force of an utterance can itself

This difference in the phenomenology of asserting versus implicating, with the concomitant difference in their epistemology is, I suggest, one among several contrasts that underwrite the difference in attitude of participants to the responsibility of the speaker. Since an implicature is never a common perceptible, but requires an act of inference by the recipient, this makes room for the idea that it is up to the recipient what she makes of what she is told, what she infers from this. It is not the speaker's responsibility, even if she envisages and intends this to occur. The speaker has by her speech act presented the proposition she explicitly asserts, and presented herself as taking responsibility for its truth. She has not by her act presented any implicature to the recipient; *a fortiori* she has not presented one as true and, I have suggested, she does not present herself as taking responsibility for the truth of any implicatures of what she does present that may be inferred via relevance.

So our observation about the phenomenology of language use explains what might otherwise seem an irrational form of assertion fetishism. It is my experience that people are often concerned to avoid lying that Q in a situation, while quite happy to make true assertions whose effect they know will be to mislead that Q. Only by an explicit lie does a speaker present what she knows to be false as true. Envisaging and allowing the other to infer a falsehood from a true statement she makes is not presenting something as true which she knows is false. And so, it can seem, the recipient makes her own inference to the falsehood, it is 'on her'—even though the speaker envisages and intends her doing so.

So the contrast in phenomenology and consequently in epistemology between explicit assertion and implicature is one factor that underwrites and explains the contrast in attitudes that participants have to them. Suppose, to continue our little example, that Sheila drives to the petrol station, but finds they do not sell charcoal. On her return she complains to Hannah, who responds 'I never said they would definitely have charcoal, I just told you about the petrol station'. Hannah takes responsibility for what she stated, but disavows it for the implications Sheila drew from this. That, she suggests, was up to Sheila.

(iv) Indeterminacy: only a fuzzy set of propositions is identified by relevance.

Another aspect of the uncertain epistemics of implicatures is that very often a specific proposition cannot be recovered as implicated, only a fuzzy set of similar propositions. As we have just seen, an implicature of an utterance is not a

---

become conventionalised, and when so may be heard in the words uttered (see Lepore and Stone 2015). Thus, for instance, it is plausible that 'Could you possibly pass me the salt?' is directly heard as a request to pass the salt, and counts as such. And it is plausible that the full content of an 'explicature' is heard in the utterance—for instance, the sentence 'I've already eaten' in suitable circumstances is heard as expressing the proposition that one has already eaten this evening. This counts as what is said, on the account I have adopted—see note 41.

common perceptible presented in the words of the perceived utterance. Implicatures are not presented by the speaker's words, but must be inferred via relevance, and so a unique implicature is recoverable only if there is just one proposition that satisfies the relevance requirement. And this is rarely so. What precisely is implicated is frequently indeterminate. Relevance determines only a fuzzy set of similar propositions. Illustrating with our little example: it suffices for Hannah's utterance to be relevant, that the petrol station might have charcoal. This means that relevance cannot distinguish between 'All/most petrol stations sell charcoal' and 'The nearby petrol station definitely sells charcoal' and 'The nearby petrol station may sell charcoal' as the implicated content. Relatedly, Hannah need not know that the station sells charcoal, she only has to consider it possible for her to consider her utterance relevant and so conversationally proper. Coeval with this is the fact that implicature is not subject, as assertion is, to the K-norm. For the nearby petrol station to be relevant, it only has to be a possibility that it sells charcoal. Hence relevance cannot determine that one should implicate that Q only if one knows that Q. This indeterminacy is one factor that makes it infeasible to have a practice of holding speakers accountable for what they implicate. If there is not a single proposition definitely implicated, *a fortiori* the speaker cannot be held accountable for implicating such a one.[48]

8. Plausible Deniability

These four features of the epistemics of implicature we have noted predict that, and explain why, speakers are not treated as assuming responsibility for what they implicate. In fact these features together engender that it is not feasible to have a practice of holding speakers responsible for implicatures of what they explicitly assert. It is not feasible because indeterminacy, conjoined with fragility plus incorrigibility of the speaker's own claims about her beliefs with respect to which the implicature is fragile have the consequence that implicatures are very often plausibly deniable.[49]

---

[48] Objection: there is a unique weakest proposition that is implicated by relevance. So this can be identified, and the speaker held as committed to that. There is no space to discuss this objection adequately. But I will make two points. First, the implicature must be something the speaker can be plausibly regarded as having evidence for, and this may well be something that entails the weakest proposition, not that proposition itself. Second, there are clear counter-examples. Changing our example a little: suppose at their party, Sheila says to Hannah 'We're running out of booze!' to which Hannah replies 'There's a pub just down the road.' This utterance is relevant only if it is interpreted as intended to implicate a further relevant idea. But this could equally well be either: So someone should go there, buy some more booze, and bring it back here, or: So we should all decamp there and continue to party at the pub.

[49] In an important path-breaking dicussion, Liz Camp (2018) develops an account of plausible deniability, and a theoretical framework that allows explanation of why insinuations of an explicit

This point requires further explanation. There is a growing interest amongst those who work in pragmatics in the phenomenon of plausible deniability: means of getting a message across to a recipient such that the sender can do so, while simultaneously avoiding taking responsibility for it; being able to deny that she intended to convey such a message. This deniability may be to the recipient or to third party witnesses to the exchange. As Camp (2018) observes, the phenomenon is puzzling, seemingly even paradoxical, since in a successful case of plausibly deniable communication the communicative intention succeeds. The recipient knows that the speaker intended to communicate the message,[50] and very often the sender knows that she knows this.

It is easy to see how a message can be plausibly deniable to a third party onlooker, who does not recover the insinuated message at all, or does not know but only conjectures that it was intended to be communicated. This happens when the speaker exploits special knowledge shared only between her and the intended recipient. The phenomenon of 'dogwhistles' exploits such knowledge (see Saul 2018). At the extreme, a secret code or signal agreed between sender and recipient is used. But it can also happen that the speaker can plausibly—that is to say, with incorrigibility—deny to the intended recipient that she intended to convey the implicated message, even though the recipient knows that she did intend it. This is possible due to a contrast between what the recipient knows about the speaker's beliefs and intentions and what she can demonstrate to be so about them, in terms that are publicly irrefutable.[51] An implicature can be denied with some plausibility (plausibility of a denial is a matter of degree) so long as the recipient (or onlooker) is unable to prove her claims as to knowledge of what the speaker believed and intended.

We observed that communication by implicature is fragile. What proposition relevance determines as implicated by an assertion in a context turns on the coordinated background beliefs of speaker and recipient. And so a small change

---

assertion are very often plausibly deniable. She distinguishes between insinuations and implicatures, the first being more indefinite and vague. However there is, as she acknowledges, not a sharp line between the two, rather one shades into the other on a spectrum of indeterminacy and deniability. I have learnt much from her discussion, to which my own is indebted. However I think implicatures are more often deniable than she allows. The reasons for implicatures' deniability are spelled out in what follows.

[50] Our discussion in §6 showed how this is possible despite fragility. The recipient's recovery of the message is apt, though it is not safely apt—it could easily have failed to be so.

[51] Pretty much all existing accounts of knowledge allow for a gap between what someone knows, and what she can demonstrate to a hostile audience that she knows. A reliabilist account in terms of some version of safe or apt belief clearly can do so; but even accounts that also include a justification requirement can allow this. In the case of beliefs about others' attitudes, the knower's justifying explanation (to herself as much as others) of how she knows may invoke her inferential mind-reading capacity: 'I can just tell'; but this is not good enough proof for a hostile audience. The gap between knowing what was implicated and being able to demonstrate this is large, since, as we saw earlier, recipients arrive at knowledge of what was implicated via reliable (adroit), subpersonal, inferential mechanisms that they have little reflective access to.

in these, one which is easily possible, changes what is implicated. This fragility of implicature in itself does not engender deniability; what does so is fragility plus the fact that the background beliefs and intentions with respect to which the implicature is fragile are factors that are relatively inscrutable. That is to say, the speaker can get away with lying about them: lying about what she believed, or what she intended. Her incorrigible lies may be about her relevant background knowledge, or they may be about what she believed about what the recipient believed.

Consider again Pinker's speeding motorist stopped by a traffic police officer, who is about to issue a speeding ticket. He says 'I'm in a bit of a hurry officer, is there a way we can fix this without having to do any paperwork?' A corrupt officer may recognise that he is suggesting a bribe, and a more explicit exchange, including of money, will follow. But suppose the officer, while recognising the offer of a bribe, does not take this up, instead responding: 'I'm afraid I have to give you a ticket sir.' What the officer could not do is to arrest the motorist for an attempted bribe. Relevance determines that the purpose of the motorist's utterance was to offer a bribe, only if there is no other way in which the matter could be dealt with without paperwork. The motorist and officer both know this to be so; but since this concerns the motorist's mental states, specifically his knowledge about traffic regulations and their enforcement, it cannot be demonstrated by the officer that he already knew this; hence, she cannot demonstrate that he intended by his utterance to offer a bribe. Thus if he replies to an accusation of offering a bribe 'Oh no officer, I certainly was not thinking of a bribe, I just wondered if there were some quick on-the-spot way to deal with the matter in accordance with the law', his response cannot be faulted by the officer.

In this case the belief the speaker incorrigibly claims to lack, or to have, is one about the world. But very often it is a belief about what the recipient believed. For instance: flatmate 1 arrives home and announces 'I'm starving, is there anything to eat?' Flatmate 2 responds 'There's some cake in the fridge'. Flatmate 1 eats the cake. It turns out it was flatmate 3's birthday cake, and she gets in trouble. 1 accuses 2 of deliberately tricking her into eating the cake. 2 responds 'Oh, but I thought you'd realise I was teasing you—I thought you knew it was Sarah's birthday cake, and you should not eat it!' Where 2's response is a lie, this illustrates plausible deniability. Where it is true, it illlustrates the fragility of implicature— how easily communication via implicature goes wrong, through one party's mistake about what the other's beliefs are.

Fragility is not sufficient for plausible deniability. Fragility means that there are modally close changes in the context which would engender a miscommunication— non-identity of the message intended with that recovered. But this yields plausible deniability only if it is also the case that the speaker can, exploiting the possibility of this close alternative circumstance, claim that this was actual, and deny that she intended to convey the actual implicature Q. And this requires that the factor that might easily have been different, and which would have yielded a different message, is one that she can get away with a lie about. This is satisfied with implicatures, because amongst the key factors in the context that might easily be different are facts about participants' beliefs, including their higher order beliefs about each other's beliefs. 'If one must lie, then try to lie only about one's own beliefs and intentions' is an excellent prudential maxim to avoid getting caught. A claim that one did not intentionally utter certain words, and thereby make the speech act they are conventionally apt in the context to effect, when one was observed doing so, is rarely plausible.[52] But a claim like 'Oh, I thought you knew/ realised that...' or: 'I never thought that you would think that...' is very hard to refute, even when the recipient is sure it is false.

This basis for deniability is compounded by the fact already noted that often relevance does not determine a unique proposition as intended by the speaker to be implicated, even given participants' coordinated beliefs. But—to repeat the point—even when relevance plus shared beliefs about the speaker's beliefs and intentions does determine a unique implicature, this may often be deniable, since the speaker can disclaim the beliefs and intentions that determine it—that is, they determine it for the recipient via her beliefs about them.

I have given arguments supporting the thesis that it is an empirical fact about human language practice that explicit assertion is the primary and almost[53] sole vehicle for testifying—assuming responsibility to one's audience for the truth of a presented content. Implicatures are not asserted or testified to—that is, they are not treated by participants as testified to. Another related contrast contributing to this difference is that while explicit assertions are added to the conversational record—the representation participants maintain of what contributions have already been made to the conversation—implicatures are not.[54] That is to say: acts of explicit assertion, and their content, are available as a topic for comment, while implicatures and their content are not. For instance, in a version of Grice's classic example: Where *A* has said, in a context of discussion of which students should be nominated for a prize, 'Jones has beautiful handwriting', a response of 'That's not true' would deny he has good handwriting, not that he is no good at philosophy. And it would be deviant to move directly from *A*'s remark to conclude 'Well, we won't nominate him for an award then', without first somehow making explicit in the conversation—putting on the record—the implication that Jones is no good at philosophy. This is another sense in which implicatures and

---

[52] As noted earlier, there is sometimes scope to attempt denial of an explicit assertion. Sometimes ambiguity can serve; or the speaker may seek to deny her words were meant seriously. But scope here is much more limited. If, while understanding them, one intentionally utters words apt in the context to make an assertion, one has done so, and saying one 'did not mean it' does not negate the force of one's act. What force an utterance has is determined by the context, it is not a private matter.

[53] 'almost', since I have allowed that there can be some indirect assertions made by non-literal utterances.

[54] On the idea of the conversational record, see Camp (2018).

insinuations are conveyed, without it being acknowledged by participants that they have been—they are not, as it were, out on the conversational table for comment and further discussion.

How important is this contrast between on-record messages for which the speaker assumes responsibility and off-record ones for which she does not assume it? The contrast between conveying a message through explicit assertion and implicitly through implicature does not always mark a significant divide, either epistemically or socio-linguistically. Politeness is one of several reasons for indirectness in speech. Thus, for instance, one will say 'Could you possibly pass me the salt?' rather than the blunt 'Pass me the salt.' In this case, and others like it, the indirection has itself become conventionalised, so that a speaker who uttered those words will be reported in indirect speech as having asked one to pass her the salt (see Lepore and Stone 2015).

In many low stakes, everyday conversational exchanges between partners whose interests are aligned, and who share a rich base of common knowledge, reasons of communicative efficiency mean that a speaker will leave her intended audience to infer part of what she intends to communicate by implicature. Their rich common knowledge base means misunderstanding is unlikely, and their aligned interests mean that whether the speaker is liable to be held responsible for her message is not going to be an issue of concern. In such circumstances the difference in means of communication between explicit and implicit messages dwindles into insignificance. Indeed, it is a little weird in such situations explicitly to spell out facts that are anyway evident due to relevance in the context.

In more high stakes contexts, and especially in ones where participants' interests are in part antagonistic, the distinction assumes much greater significance. Whether the speaker is liable to answer for the truth of what she communicated becomes of much greater importance, and in some cases communicating a message in a way that allows her to deny she intended to communicate it at all becomes crucial.

I've described several contrasts in the epistemics of assertion versus implicature as means of communication of a message, and I've argued that these features of the epistemics of implicatures I've pointed out, mean it is simply not a feasible practice for speakers to be treated as assuming responsibility for the truth of propositions implicated by their utterances. It is not feasible since, first, relevance often does not determine a unique proposition as implicated; second, even where relevance does determine a unique proposition, frequently the speaker can plausibly deny she intended to implicate that proposition. She can get away with this lie, since it turns on lying about her own intentions and beliefs, often her higher order beliefs about her audience's beliefs, and very often she is incorrigible with respect to such claims. A difference in the phenomenology of assertion versus implicature further enhances this contrast. Asserted truth-conditional content is heard in the utterance itself, while implicated content is not such a common perceptible. It is inferred, not presented, by the speaker in her utterance. These features, I claim, predict and explain the empirical fact that speakers are not treated as assuming responsibility for what is implicated by their assertions. Implicatures are not asserted or testified to.

9. Some Objections Rebutted

My empirical claim that conversational implicatures are not treated by participants as testified to—that is to say, the speaker is not regarded as assuming responsibility for their truth—has been borne out by an empirical study. Mazzarella and others tested whether recipients punish speakers who make a false implicature less than those who make a false assertion, and their results showed that speakers suffer less reputational damage for making false implicatures than for making false assertions. They conclude that

> Our data show that implicating is taken to be less committal than saying...[so that] Implicating allows speakers to get their message across without incurring the same reputational damage as saying [if it is false]...and thus represents a powerful way to minimise drops of trust that result from unreliable testimony.
> (Mazzarella, Reinecke et al. 2018, p. 21)

Despite this empirical support, challenges to my thesis have been raised. The first challenge is that it has been suggested that, even if implicature is not governed by the K-norm as a social norm, as assertion is, it may be subject to a weaker epistemic norm—which would modulate a lesser, but still significant, degree of commitment (see Green 2017).

In considering whether implicature has a proprietary norm, it is important to observe that there is a key sense in which implicature is not a type of speech act. Assertion exists as a speech act type in a community just if there are conventions and norms in force in that community which constitute a particular recurring perceptible act type as having the performative force of asserting (see §§2 and 3). Given the socio-linguistic phenomenon of assertion, plus the Gricean norms of cooperation in conversation, plus normal human cognitive capacities, in particular capacities for mind-reading, the phenomenon of conversational implicatures will then arise. No further conventions or norms are needed to constitute the 'act' of conversationally implicating a content from what is asserted. A recipient with normal mind-reading capacities, and an understanding of what assertion and conversation are, will infer implicatures from an assertion via relevance, and her beliefs about the speaker's relevant beliefs. The phenomenon of implicature is simply a consequence of asserting, together with Gricean norms and recipients' cognitive powers.

Since implicature is a consequential, not a primitive form of speech act, it is not constituted by any special conventions or norms. It does not need and cannot have a constitutive epistemic norm. Still, there might as a matter of contingent social fact be an epistemic norm associated with implicature. This is an empirical matter warranting empirical investigation. But in light of my argument above that a practice of holding speakers responsible for what they implicate is not feasible, due to the indeterminacy and deniability of implicatures, we should not expect there to be one.

If there is no proprietary epistemic norm governing implicatures, then it will be wrong to make a false implicature, or one the speaker only conjectures, just if, in the context, it violates some external norm. It might violate a moral norm, or one of etiquette—be impolite or otherwise socially inept. But there is no *sui generis* type of incorrectness that attaches to a false implicature as such. Thus, in a situation where a speaker implicates a content Q she knows to be false, but where this is the morally right action, there remains no sense in which she has done something incorrect. In contrast, while there are some situations in which the morally right thing to do is to tell a lie, this remains *qua* assertion incorrect. Given the absence of a proprietary norm governing implicatures, any defectiveness of an implicature, or culpability of its maker and criticism she is subject to, will be determined by how the particular facts about how much is at stake, etc., in the context mean that other extrinsic norms, such as moral ones, come into play; not by any general norm associated with the act type as such.

In fact it is plausible that there is a general moral norm that covers falsely implicating. Implicating something one knows to be false is a case of misleading. And it is plausible that, just as lying is *prima facie* wrong, so is misleading. In which case, any knowingly false implicature is *prima facie* wrong. But this is an application of the more general moral norm about misleading—which need not be effected by linguistic means—and the wrongness in question here is moral. This is quite different from a proprietary linguistic norm governing implicature *qua* speech act type, which is not in itself a moral norm. I have argued there is no such norm.

In contrast, any assertion not expressing the speaker's knowledge violates the norm of assertion. In low stakes situations this incorrectness may be scarcely more serious than a grammatical error (see the example in note 23). In high stakes situations, say where someone's life is at stake and one must lie to save it, the intrinsic incorrectness of the lie *qua* assertion remains, while it is the morally correct act in the circumstances. The contrast is illustrated in the following example. One is invited to a party on Saturday. There are compelling reasons why one should not attend, but these cannot be told to the host. She will be upset if her invitation is declined apparently for no good reason. Scenario One: one lies, saying 'I'd love to come, but I'm afraid I'll be out of town on Saturday.' This lie seems morally justified, but *qua* assertion it is nonetheless incorrect. Scenario

Two: One says truly 'I'd love to come, but I'm afraid I'm leaving town on Thursday', implicating via relevance and Grice's maxim of quantity that one will be still out of town on Saturday. This is in fact false, one is returning on Friday. Here, one's utterance is morally justified, and there is no remaining sense in which it is incorrect, since there is no proprietary social norm governing implicatures that one has violated. This is the thesis argued for in this chapter.[55]

The second challenge to my thesis is that it has been suggested that the contrast I suggest between the epistemics of implicature and those of assertion is under-mined by the following two facts about assertion. First, explicit assertions can be hard to recover, when elaborate syntax or esoteric vocabulary is employed (Hawthorne 2012). Second, pragmatic factors about the context must often be invoked to infer the explicit truth-conditional content that constitutes what is said and asserted, for instance resolution of the domain of a quantifier (Hawthorne 2012; Peet 2015; Garcia-Carpintero 2018; Pagin and Marsili 2021, note 10).

On the first point: decoding elaborate syntax and obscure vocabulary may be hard work. But how much cognitive processing it takes to understand an assertion is not the same thing as how large the shared background belief set is that must be invoked correctly to interpret it. Recovering the implicature of a given utterance necessarily always invokes more of the coordinated background beliefs of speaker and hearer than understanding its explicitly asserted content, since recovering the explicit content is just the first part of the route to recovering the implicature. And even if one compares hard-to-process explicit assertions with easy-to-recover implicatures, more of the speaker and audience's shared background beliefs will be involved in recovering the latter—as our examples discussed earlier showed through illustration. Consequently the recovery of implicated content is inher-ently more fragile than recovery of asserted content.

On the second point: this familiar fact was explicitly recognised in Fricker (2012). There are nonetheless significant contrasts in the epistemics of every instance of assertion and every instance of implicature. One contrast is the important difference in their phenomenology described above. What is explicitly asserted is heard in the words uttered, it is literally presented by the speaker to her audience, and is a common perceptible between them. Even when pragmatic factors are invoked in determining what is asserted, this processing is subpersonal, and the asserted content is heard in the utterance itself. A second point, which I can only briefly gesture towards here, concerns the objectivity of linguistically determined utterance meaning. Even when pragmatic factors enter into fixing what is asserted, they do so in accordance with what it is reasonable to take the utterance to say in the context, in light of the conventional lexical meanings of its component words, and the facts of the communicative context; not what the

---

[55] One has, admittedly, violated the Gricean cooperative principle of quantity, since one's utterance is less informative than it could be, but no norm that attaches to implicature directly.

speaker or recipient intends or takes it to say. In this sense, what an utterance strictly says, and so asserts, is a public fact about the meanings of those words of the language in that context. This is why it is possible for someone to assert something by mistake due to linguistic error. Here's an example inspired by the film *Lost in Translation*: suppose an American celebrity on Japanese television, on a chat show. He utters a sentence in Japanese and is greeted with hilarity by the audience. The host tells him 'You just told them you are in love with a giraffe.' In less extreme cases of linguistic error, one can certainly assert something by mistake in one's own language. In contrast, what is implicated by an utterance turns on the particular speaker and recipient's coordinated background beliefs, not on broadly socially determined facts about lexical meanings and how context plays a role in fixing truth-conditions.

Garcia-Carpintero (2016) correctly takes me to hold that someone asserts that *P* by uttering a sentence *S* only when she thereby succeeds in presenting, and securing uptake by her intended recipient of, a specific content *P*. Indeed: unless she achieves this, the question of her assuming responsibility for *P*'s being so to her recipient cannot arise. However, for reasons I have not fully grasped, he maintains that the involvement of pragmatic contextual factors in fixing what is said renders this first condition unattainable. On my requirement, he says, 'almost nothing counts as an assertion' (p. 42). His comment raises foundational issues in meta-semantics that cannot adequately be addressed here. But I will say this much. In my way of seeing things, everyday linguistic communication is not mediated through individuals' possession of imperfectly overlapping idiosyncratic ideolects; it is made possible by exploitation of a shared language, including lexical items with objective public semantic significance. (These semantic facts are socially constituted, but this does not make them fail to be objective.) Individuals speaking a public language aim to be doing just that: using words with the meaning they have in the public language, not in their private ideolect. Thus, so long as the extension an individual would personally ascribe to a word is not way off its actual extension—not a gross misunderstanding—that word in her mouth has the extension it has in the language—there is a kind of gravitational force of the communal meaning of the word which pulls its use in her mouth onto it. This is why, for instance, someone can be wrong about whether something is blue or not: she means by her words to be deploying the public concept attached to 'blue', not an idiosyncratic one of her own. (This approach to how what is said is determined is suggested in Evans 1982, ch.10, and explicitly argued for in Burge 1979. It is an upshot of the exploration of the conditions that ground the normativity of meaning in the celebrated 'rule following considerations' of Wittgenstein 1953.)

It is certainly true that the frequent involvement of pragmatic contextual factors in fixing what is said lessens the sharpness of contrast between the robust epistemics of recovering what is said and the fragile and 'dodgy' epistemics of recovering what is implicated. Peet (2015) gives several convincing cases where the explicit content of an assertion with partly pragmatically determined truth-conditions is deniable with some degree of plausibility by the speaker.[56] (His main case concerns alternative interpretations of the domain of a quantifier.) But a broad general contrast remains.

Even allowing that some assertions have no less fragile and deniable epistemics than some easy-to-recover implicatures, this is entirely consistent with my thesis. I am not committed to the following proposition, about which I can happily remain agnostic: Every case of explicit assertion is cognitively easier to recover, and requires less rich coordinated background beliefs to recover, and is less fragile than every case of conversational implicature. Nor am I committed to the proposition that every implicature is underdetermined by relevance and/or is plausibly deniable. There may be cases of implicature where, given the context, there is a unique proposition determined by relevance, and where it is also epistemically determined for the recipient in her situation, by publicly available facts she can cite, that the speaker has the relevant attitudes, so that it is not plausible for the speaker to deny them.

My claims are, respectively: about explicit assertions that *typically and most frequently* asserted content is easy to recover, and that this process is robust; and about implicatures, that *typically and most frequently* implicature has the 'dodgy epistemics' I have described that enable plausible deniability. These claims underwrite my main thesis: that this generic fact about implicature *qua* type makes it infeasible to have a practice of holding speakers responsible for what they implicate, whereas it is feasible to have a practice of holding speakers responsible for what they explicitly assert; and that correspondingly speakers are not held responsible for what they implicate, at least not to the full extent that they are for what they assert. In short: implicatures are not testified to nor asserted. In addition I have suggested that there is no proprietary epistemic norm governing implicature, neither the *K*-norm nor a weaker epistemic norm.

My thesis about implicature connects to the topic of luck in linguistics, since we have seen it is the fragility of implicature as a means of conveying a message that underlies its plausible deniability, and the consequent fact that a speaker is not treated as assuming responsibility for what she implicates, as she does for what she asserts.

---

[56] Peet's main concern is with deniability. While his article contains much useful argument, it suffers from this mistake: Peet thinks that, for deniability, the recipient must not know what message the speaker intended. If this were so, then whenever a message is deniable, this means it is not asserted, on any assurance account of assertion, including mine, even if it is not in fact denied. But, as we saw above, the requirement for deniability is the easier-to-fulfil one that the recipient cannot demonstrate that the speaker intended the denied message; and this will be so in many cases where she knows perfectly well that this was so—that is, the communicative intent has succeeded.

One final point: there is a current debate as to whether lying is morally worse than misleading (Adler 1997; Strudler 2010; Saul 2012; Berstler 2019). My argument that asserting and implicating are different speech acts makes room for a moral contrast, but it is entirely consistent with the thesis that misleading is no less bad than lying. My analysis does, however, explain the widely held folk belief that misleading is less bad: in a lie, the speaker literally presents as true the asserted proposition she knows to be false, and presents herself as taking responsibility for its truth. This is not so for a false implication of what she asserts.[57]

References

Adler, J. E. (1997). Lying, Deceiving, or Falsely Implicating. *The Journal of Philosophy* **94**(9): 435–452.

Austin, J. L. (1975). *How to do Things with Words*. Oxford, Oxford University Press.

Bach, K. and R. M. Harnish (1979). *Linguistic Communication and Speech Acts*. Cambridge, MA, MIT Press.

Beaver, D., et al. (2021). Presupposition. *Stanford Encyclopaedia of Philosophy*. E. N. Zalta. Stanford, CA, Stanford University.

Berstler, S. (2019). What's the Good of Language? On the Moral Distinction between Lying and Misleading. *Ethics* **130**(1): 5–31.

Brown, J. and H. Cappelen, eds. (2011). *Assertion: New Philosophical Essays*. Oxford, Oxford University Press.

Burge, T. (1979). Individualism and the Mental. *Midwest Studies in Philosophy* **4**(1): 73–122.

Burge, T. (1993). Content Preservation. *Philosophical Review* **102**(4): 457–488.

Camp, E. (2018). Insinuation, Common Ground, and the Conversational Record. *New Work on Speech Acts*. D. Fogal, D. Harris and M. Moss. Oxford, Oxford University Press: 40–66

Carston, R. (2002). *Thoughts and Utterances: The Pragmatics of Explicit Communication*. Maldan, MA, and Oxford, Blackwell.

Coady, C. A. J. (1992). *Testimony: A Philosophical Study*. Oxford, Clarendon Press.

Davis, W. (2019). Implicature. *Stanford Encyclopaedia of Philosophy*. E. N. Zalta, Stanford, CA, Stanford University.

Evans, G. (1982). *The Varieties of Reference*. Oxford, Clarendon Press.

Faulkner, P. (2011). *Knowledge on Trust*. Oxford, Oxford University Press.

---

[57] An earlier draft of this chapter was presented (via Zoom) at the Pacific meeting of the APA in April 2021. My grateful thanks to Abrol Fairweather for arranging this session, and to the audience for many useful comments and questions.

Fogal, D., et al. (2018). Speech Acts: The Contemporary Theoretical Landscape. *New Work on Speech Acts*. D. Fogal, D. Harris and M. Moss. Oxford, Oxford University Press: 1–39.

Fricker, E. (2003). Understanding and Knowledge of What is Said. *Epistemology of Language*. A. Barber. Oxford, Oxford University Press: 325–366.

Fricker, E. (2006a). Second-Hand Knowledge. *Philosophy and Phenomenological Research* 73(3): 592–681.

Fricker, E. (2006b). Testimony and Epistemic Autonomy. *The Epistemology of Testimony*. J. Lackey and E. Sosa. Oxford, Oxford University Press: 225–250.

Fricker, E. (2012). Stating and Insinuating. *Aristotelian Society Supplementary Volume* 86(1): 61–94.

Fricker, E. (2015). How to Make Invidious Distinctions amongst Reliable Testifiers. *Episteme* 12: 173–202.

Fricker, E. (2017a). Inference to the Best Explanation and the Receipt of Testimony: Testimonial Reductionism Vindicated. *Best Explanations: New Essays on Inference to the Best Explanation*. K. McCain and T. Poston. Oxford, Oxford University Press: 262–294.

Fricker, E. (2017b). Norms, Constitutive and Social, and Assertion. *American Philosophical Quarterly* 54(4): 397–418.

Fricker, E. (2019). Knowing Full Well from Testimony? *Episteme* 1–16.

Fricker, E. (2021a). Should We Worry about Silicone Chip Technology De-Skilling Us? *Royal Institute of Philosophy Supplement* 89: 131–152.

Fricker, E. (2021b). Can Trust Work Epistemic Magic? *Philosophical Topics* 49: 57–82

Fricker, E. (2023). An Austinian Account of Assertion. *Analytic Philosophy*.

Garcia-Carpintero, M. (2016). Indirect Assertion. *Polish Journal of Philosophy* 10(1): 13–49.

Garcia-Carpintero, M. (2018). Sneaky Assertions. *Philosophical Perspectives* 32: 188–218.

Garcia-Carpintero, M. (2019). Conventions and Constitutive Norms. *Journal of Social Ontology* 5(1): 35–52.

Goldberg, S. (2010). *Relying on Others: An Essay in Epistemology*. Oxford, Oxford University Press.

Goldberg, S. (2015). *Assertion: On the Philosophical Significance of Assertoric Speech*. Oxford, Oxford University Press.

Goldberg, S., ed. (2020). *The Oxford Handbook of Assertion*. Oxford, Oxford University Press.

Graham, P. (2006a). Can Testimony Generate Knowledge? *Philosophica* 78: 105–127.

Graham, P. (2006b). Liberal Fundamentalism and its Rivals. *The Epistemology of Testimony*. J. Lackey and E. Sosa. Oxford, Clarendon Press: 93–115.

Green, A. (2017). An Epistemic Norm for Implicature. *Journal of Philososphy* 114(7): 381–391.

Grice, P. (1957). Meaning. *Philosophical Review* **66**: 337–388.

Grice, P. (1975). Logic and Conversation. *Syntax and Semantics 3: Speech Acts*. P. Cole and J. L. Morgan. New York, Academic Press: 41–58.

Hawthorne, J. (2012). Some Comments on Fricker's Stating and Insinuating. *Proceedings of the Aristotelian Society Supplementary Volume* **86**: 95–108.

Hinchman, E. (2005). Telling as Inviting to Trust. *Philosophy and Phenomenological Research* **70**(3): 562–587.

Lackey, J. (2008). *Learning from Words: Testimony as a Source of Knowledge*. Oxford, Oxford University Press.

Langton, R. (2018). Blocking as Counter-Speech. *New Work on Speech Acts*. D. Fogal, D. Harris, and M. Moss. Oxford Oxford University Press: 144–174.

Lee, J. and S. Pinker (2010). Rationales for Indirect Speech: The Theory of the Strategic Speaker. *Psychological Review* **117**(3): 785–807.

Lepore, E. and M. Stone (2015). *Imagination and Convention: Distinguishing Grammar and Inference in Language*. Oxford, Oxford University Press.

Mazzarella, D., et al. (2018). Saying, Presupposing and Implicating: How Pragmatics Modulates Commitment. *Journal of Pragmatics* **133**: 15–27.

McMyler, B. (2011). *Testimony, Trust, and Authority*. Oxford, New York, Oxford University Press.

Moran, R. (2018). *The Exchange of Words*. New York, Oxford University Press.

Pagin, P. (2011). Information and Assertoric Force. *Assertion*. J. Brown and H. Cappelen. Oxford, Oxford University Press: 97–136.

Pagin, P. (2020). The Indicativity View. *The Oxford Handbook of Assertion*. S. Goldberg. Oxford, Oxford University Press.

Pagin, P., and N. Marsili (2021). Assertion. *Stanford Encyclopaedia of Philosophy*. E. N. Zalta. Stanford, CA, Stanford University.

Peet, A. (2015). Testimony, Pragmatics and Plausible Deniability. *Episteme* **12**(1): 29–51.

Potts, C. (2015). Presupposition and Implicature. *The Handbook of Contemporary Semantic Theory*. S. Lappin and C. Fox. Chichester, Wiley: 168–202.

Saul, J. (2012). *Lying, Misleading and What is Said*. Oxford, Oxford University Press.

Saul, J. (2018). Dogwhistles, Political Manipulation, and Philosophy of Language. *New Work on Speech Acts*. Oxford, Oxford University Press: 360–380.

Schiffer, S. (1972). *Meaning*. Oxford, Clarendon Press.

Searle, J. (1996). *The Construction of Social Reality*. London, Penguin.

Sosa, E. (2011). *Knowing Full Well*. Princeton, NJ, Princeton University Press.

Sosa, E. (2015). *Judgement and Agency*. Oxford, Oxford University Press.

Sperber, D. and D. Wilson (2005). Pragmatics. *Oxford Handbook of Contemporary Philosophy*. F. Jackson and M. Smith. Oxford, Oxford University press: 486–502.

Stalnaker, R. (1974). Pragmatic Presuppositions. *Semantics and Philosophy*. M. Munitz and P. Unger. New York, New York University Press: 197–214.

Stalnaker, R. (1978). Assertion. *Syntax and Semantics 9*. P. Cole. New York, Academic Press: 315–332.

Stalnaker, R. (2002). Common Ground. *Linguistics and Philosophy* 25: 701–721.

Stanley, J. (2015). *How Propaganda Works*. Princeton, NJ, Princeton University Press.

Strawson, P. F. (1964). Intention and Convention in Speech Acts. *Philosophical Review* 73(4): 439–460.

Strudler, A. (2010). The Distinctive Wrong in Lying. *Ethical Theory and Moral Practice* 13: 171–179.

Williamson, T. (2000). *Knowledge and its Limits*. Oxford, Oxford University Press.

Wittgenstein, L. (1953). *Philosophical Investigations*. Oxford, Blackwell.

9

Linguistic Luck and the Publicness
of Language

Claudine Verheggen

1. Introduction

Donald Davidson wrote, famously: "That meanings are decipherable is not a matter of luck; public availability is a constitutive aspect of language" (1990, 314). Yet Davidson is also famous (or infamous) for maintaining that language possession does not require a speaker to mean by her words what others mean by them. *Prima facie* at least, we seem to have a puzzle here: it might be thought that not meaning by one's words what others mean by them would make communication depend significantly on luck. This thought would be mistaken, however. My primary goal in this chapter is to show that what explains the primacy of idiolects also explains the dispensability of luck. In a nutshell: that meanings are decipherable is not a matter of luck because meanings can be present only if at least some of them have been deciphered; and meanings do not have to be shared by interlocutors in order to be deciphered. Thus the key to solving the "puzzle" is to understand properly the conditions Davidson lays down for the possibility of language possession. I expound these conditions in §2 of this chapter. In §3, I show how Davidson's account of meaning explains why we do not have to rely on luck in order to understand novel uses of language, such as malapropisms and neologisms. I then argue, in §4, that the claim that communication does not rely on luck, given what makes language possession possible, can be used to address the sceptical problem about meaning and rule-following Saul Kripke found in Ludwig Wittgenstein's later writings.

2. Davidson's Account of Meaning

The account, it should be stressed, is supposed to be an account of literal meaning, which Davidson always took to be autonomous, that is, independent of illocutionary forces and perlocutionary intentions. The latter two, though always present in a speech-act, cannot be regimented in the way that literal meaning can be. No systematic theory of force, let alone perlocution, can be given, in the way that a

Claudine Verheggen, *Linguistic Luck and the Publicness of Language* In: *Linguistic Luck: Safeguards and Threats to Linguistic Communication*. Edited by: Abrol Fairweather and Carlos Montemayor, Oxford University Press.
© Oxford University Press 2023. DOI: 10.1093/oso/9780192845450.003.0009

systematic theory of what the expressions of a language mean can be given. Thus, when Davidson says that deciphering meanings is not a matter of luck, he has in mind the deciphering of literal meanings, which often is a necessary step towards deciphering illocutionary forces and perlocutionary intentions, which in turn is needed for full-blown communication. It may well be that luck sometimes plays a role in deciphering the latter two, but these are not what Davidson's claim is about.[1]

2.1. The Beginning of an Account: Radical Interpretation

Reflecting on how to construct a semantic theory for a speaker, a theory that would enable an interpreter to understand any utterance the speaker might produce, was the procedure Davidson initially followed in order to shed philosophical light on the nature of linguistic meaning, that is, in order to provide a meta-semantic theory or foundational theory of meaning.[2] Because he wanted the procedure to be non-question-begging, and because he assumed that all the features belonging to meaning are essentially public, he engaged in the thought experiment of radical interpretation, the interpretation of a speaker whose language and propositional attitudes the interpreter does not know[3] without the help of a bilingual dictionary or of a translator. The idea was that we would learn all there is to know about how meanings are constituted by reflecting on how meanings can be attributed to a speaker from scratch. At this stage, Davidson thought he already had established that the kind of theory that would do the job of yielding an interpretation of any utterance of a speaker is a Tarski-style theory of truth. A recursive theory of this kind is, he thought, formally impeccable, as it can be finitely axiomatized, and can entail, for any utterance of the speaker, a T-sentence, that is, a sentence specifying the conditions under which the utterance is true, which yields the meaning of the utterance.[4] Reflecting on radical interpretation was supposed to tell us how to build a theory of this kind that is also empirically impeccable, that is, a theory that can be "supported or verified by evidence plausibly available to an interpreter" (Davidson 1973, 28).

---

[1] To be clear, Davidson's claim is not that no element of luck is ever needed in order to decipher literal meanings. But, given the systematic way in which these are constituted, significant elements of luck will seldom be needed, whereas the lack of a systematic theory governing illocutionary forces and perlocutionary effects may result in a greater need for luck.

[2] As he makes clear in the introduction to the volume that contains many of his writings on radical interpretation. See especially Davidson 1973 and 1974.

[3] As we shall see, the interpreter has to make some assumptions about the speaker's propositional attitudes, but she does not know them in any detail.

[4] See Davidson 1967. Davidson eventually wondered to what extent Tarski-style theories of truth "can be made adequate to natural languages," but he never doubted that "they are adequate to powerful parts of natural languages" (Davidson 1993, 83–4).

What did the thought experiment teach us? Most importantly, it reinforced an assumption that may be seen to go hand in hand with the assumption that meaning is essentially public, the externalist assumption that features of the environment we live in necessarily determine, at least in part, what we mean by our words. To build a theory of truth that is going to serve as a theory of meaning, the radical interpreter has no choice but to take as evidence the regular connections that obtain between the speaker's responses to the environment she and her interpreter share and features of this environment. Thus, initially she has no choice but to take as evidence the speaker's holding true utterances of sentences in given circumstances and at given times.[5] For instance, if the speaker exclaims "Gavagai" whenever a rabbit is passing by, the interpreter will take this as evidence that the speaker holds true "Gavagai" if and only if she is causally affected by a rabbit at the time she utters it. Next, the interpreter has to start building T-sentences, out of which she will eventually extract the axioms of the theory, axioms which tell us, for every semantic primitive and every mode of combination, how it contributes to the truth-conditions of all sentences of the speaker's language. In order to start building T-sentences, the interpreter has no choice but to assume that the responses the speaker makes to the environment are (at least typically) the responses she herself would make. She has no choice but to apply the principle of charity which, importantly, is holistic. Thus, to begin with, the principle applies not to single beliefs, but to sets of beliefs. This is evident in that no final interpretation of "Gavagai!" could be arrived at until it is uttered in numerously different circumstances, and in the context of numerously different sentences. For initially the speaker could be taken to be talking about an animal, or something fast, or cute, or furry, or dinner! The interpreter should look not just for true beliefs the speaker might express but for coherent ones and justified ones, avoiding the attribution of inexplicable error or ignorance, or, for that matter, inexplicable knowledge. The principle also applies to other propositional attitudes. Thus, the interpreter should try to attribute to the speaker reasonable desires and coherent patterns of preferences. Though the interpreter is looking for matches between her and the speaker's propositional attitudes, the goal is not to maximize agreement between speaker and interpreter, but to maximize intelligibility, and sometimes circumstances will be such as to make disagreement more intelligible than agreement.[6] In short, then, another lesson of the thought experiment is that it augmented the holism implicit in the demand that the theory provide an interpretation of all utterances, actual and potential, of the speaker.

Though Davidson soon made explicit that he thought that language is essentially social,[7] at least in that a socially isolated individual could not have a

---

[5] Evidence which Davidson thought is available to the interpreter before she knows what the utterance means or what belief it expresses.

[6] "The aim of interpretation is not agreement but understanding" (Davidson 1984a, xiv).

[7] See Davidson 1975.

language, not in that one must talk like others in order to have a language, many took reflection on radical interpretation to leave room for an individualistic view, taking the radical interpreter to be a mere dramatic device that may be abandoned once the thought experiment has been worked through.[8] Interpersonal communication was deemed not to be essential to language possession. On the face of it, this was rather baffling, for it is hard to see how the principle of charity, in all its complexity, could be properly applied without the interpreter eventually having linguistic exchanges with the speaker.[9] Be that as it may, as became clear later, with the writings on triangulation, Davidson was bound to think that the interpreter's role is indispensable, for there is a further reason why radical interpretation is not possible without the three-way relation Davidson called triangulation, "the mutual and simultaneous responses of two or more creatures to common distal stimuli and to one another's responses" (Davidson 2001a, xv), and, in particular, without linguistic triangulation, that is, without actual linguistic exchanges between the speaker and the interpreter about features of the shared environment with which they are simultaneously interacting.[10] Indeed, as Davidson came to put it, radical interpretation is just an instance of triangulation.[11] In what follows I explain why this is so, and the basic mechanisms of triangulation. My aim here is not fully to defend Davidson's moves, though I shall indicate their main motivations. It is, rather, to draw attention to those aspects of triangulation that reveal why luck seldom plays a role in assigning literal meanings to a speaker.[12]

2.2. The Full-Blown Account: Triangulation

Reflecting on radical interpretation led Davidson to conclude that "[w]hat determines the contents of . . . basic thoughts (and what we mean by the words we use to express them) is what has typically caused similar thoughts." But eventually a crucial, unanswered question dawned on him: "what *has* typically caused them?" (Davidson 1991a, 201). Obviously, not any cause of a basic response a speaker is giving will do to determine its meaning. The speaker could be mistaken about it, or simply lying, or joking. Equally obviously, basic utterances that are meaningful may not be caused by anything currently present in the speaker's environment. But the typical causes of a speaker's responses to her environment must be isolated

---

[8] As suggested by Lewis 1974 and Glüer 2011. Kathrin Glüer has recently changed her mind about this. See Glüer 2018.

[9] For further discussion of this point, see Myers and Verheggen 2016, ch. 5.

[10] Linguistic triangulation is just a subset of interpersonal linguistic communication. Davidson also thinks that non-linguistic animals may engage in "primitive" triangulation, as when two lionesses stalk a gazelle and cooperate "to corner their prey" (Davidson 2001b, 7).

[11] See Davidson 2001c, 294.

[12] For a more detailed exposition and defence of the triangulation argument, see Myers and Verheggen 2016. For more on Davidson's externalism and the continuity of Davidson's thought from radical interpretation to triangulation, see Verheggen 2017a and 2021.

in order for their meanings to be fixed. How is the interpreter supposed to pick them out? It might be thought that she can do this just by taking the typical causes of the speaker's responses to be what she herself takes to be the typical causes. But there are two problems with this thought. First, it is unclear how, without interacting with the speaker, the interpreter could succeed in picking out some causes rather than others as typical; though some causes could presumably be eliminated just by observing the speaker and her environment, still not all could be. Second, and even more importantly, it is unclear how the typical causes of the interpreter's responses were isolated to begin with. But they must have been, since she does have a language. No foundational account of meaning will be complete until we understand how this was accomplished. Thus started the triangulation argument.[13]

Davidson writes: "without a second creature responding to the first, there can be no answer to the question [what objects or events a creature is responding to]" (Davidson 1992, 119). The problem Davidson initially emphasized was that of determining whether the creature is "reacting to, or thinking about, events at a distance away rather than, say, on its skin" (119), whether, that is, the causes of the creature's reactions are distal or proximal. But he soon came to realize that another problem, to my mind more serious, loomed: the problem of determining what aspect or chunk of the distal cause the creature is reacting to.[14] This problem seems to be more serious because, presumably, the radical interpreter does not face the first problem. Presumably, she can assume that the speaker is responding to objects or events currently present and perceivable in the environment they share. This is after all the only evidence she initially has on which to build her theory of interpretation. But making this assumption is not sufficient to single out particular aspects of these objects and events; indeed, it is not sufficient to determine that the speaker has the very concepts of object and event. Even if the speaker could be described as responding to distal causes, the interpreter could not assign any meanings to those responses, because she could not determine what their particular causes are, as long as she was a silent and passive observer of the speaker's responses. In order to determine what a particular cause is, she must determine to what other causes it is similar. However, as Davidson writes, in answer to the question which causes can be gathered together:

> Since any set of causes whatsoever will have endless properties in common, we must look to some recurrent feature of the gatherer, some mark that he or she has

---

[13] Davidson first mentioned the idea of triangulation in 1982, but did not start seriously developing it until the late 1980s. See Davidson 1991a, 1991b, 1992, 1994, 1999, and 2001b.

[14] What causes a response may be "doubly indeterminate: with respect to width and with respect to distance. The first ambiguity concerns how much of the total cause [what "part or aspect of the total cause"] of a belief [or utterance] is relevant to content…The second problem has to do with the ambiguity of the relevant stimulus, whether it is proximal (at the skin, say) or distal" (Davidson 1999, 129–30). (The new problem is the one Davidson is listing here first.)

classified cases as similar. This can only be some feature or aspect of the gatherer's reactions..., in which case we must once again ask: what makes these reactions relevantly similar to each other?   (Davidson, 2001b, 4–5)

How then is the interpreter to proceed? The short answer is that she must start interacting linguistically with the speaker, for only this will enable her to nail down particular causes. For instance, to stick to a rather simplistic scenario, in order to nail down the typical cause of "Gavagai," she must start asking questions such as "Gavagai?" when a cat passes by or when presented with a rabbit coat.[15] As we shall see, according to Davidson, it is because she herself has engaged in such interactions that she has a language. Thus, in order to answer the question what it takes for a full-blown speaker to understand another from scratch, we must answer the question what it takes for someone to become a full-blown speaker.

Let us accordingly switch to the first person point of view, the point of view of the would-be speaker. Again, the problem she is facing is that of determining which particular features of the world around her she is responding to. These features do not wear any meaning on their sleeves, as it were; they do not label and impose themselves on the agent.[16] Consequently, it is for the would-be speaker somehow to contribute to establishing which features determine which meanings, which causes are similar to which, indeed, which of her responses are correct and which incorrect. This distinction, however, in order to be genuine, has to be objective. It cannot be that whatever response the would-be speaker deems to be correct is the correct one, lest the idea of correctness altogether disappears. Thus the would-be speaker drawing the distinction must have the concept of objectivity. But this is not a concept she can have on her own, for the very reason just mentioned. Thus, on her own, she cannot have the idea of there being an objective distinction between what she thinks is the correct response and what is in fact the correct response. What she needs is a second person with whom to interact, with whom she can have disputes regarding features of the world they are reacting to, and with whom she can resolve the dispute in a consensual way and not exclusively on the basis of what she deems to be the right resolution. Resolving disputes of this kind depends crucially on the interlocutors agreeing on what they are talking about, that is, on what the specific causes, and thus meanings, of their

---

[15] This is simplistic, for Davidson initially thought that unless the interpreter understood the whole language of the speaker, she could not understand any of it. "A T-sentence of an empirical theory of truth can be used to interpret a sentence ... provided we also know the theory that entails it" (Davidson 1973, 139). He claimed to "have subsequently been more restrained on the topic" (Davidson 1993, 80). Still, the point is that only numerous exchanges with the speaker, triangular, linguistic, and otherwise, could enable an interpreter to nail down the causes of the speaker's utterances in such a way that the axioms she would eventually extract would entail the truth-conditions, and hence the meaning, of any utterance of the speaker. Ideally, the interpreter should indeed have a complete knowledge of the theory; only this would ensure a proper understanding of the speaker. In the absence of such complete knowledge, communication will sometimes depend on an element of luck. More on this in §4.

[16] Considered in themselves, as Wittgenstein put it, they are mere "phenomena" (1974, 143).

utterances are. It is through this kind of interaction that they fix the meanings of their words. They do not have to mean the same things by the same words, however. What is essential is that they agree on the meanings of one another's words, that is, that the meanings the speaker assigns to her words are the meanings her interlocutor assigns to the speaker's words, that the speaker is understood in the way she intends to be understood.[17] Of course, and not incidentally, the meanings of many of their words are bound to overlap. What they are talking about in the first place is the world they share, which they perceive and react to in similar ways, and which fulfills similar needs and wishes. But the point is that speaking meaningfully does not require speaking like others. Nor does this entail that being understood requires luck, as I shall shortly elaborate. But first I shall underline the lessons of the triangulation argument.

The triangulation argument spells out at least some of the conditions that are necessary for language possession. But it does not spell out any non-circular sufficient conditions. In effect, it tells us that what is necessary for language possession is linguistic communication, which certainly sounds like a circular statement. The circle is an instructive one, however. Most relevantly to the purposes of this chapter, it shows that using expressions meaningfully essentially depends on having engaged in triangular interactions, that is, on having interacted with features of one's physical environment, and on having shared some of these interactions with other speakers. Significantly, these interactions must be linguistic; one must have understood other speakers and must have been understood by them, in the minimal sense that at least some of the meanings speakers assign to their words must also have been assigned to them by some interlocutors. It is through this shared understanding that they somehow fixed the meanings of their words. I say "somehow" because there is no describing the exact mechanisms through which the gap between having no language and having one is bridged.[18]

---

[17] How do they know they have succeeded? Presumably they have if they get what they asked for—accurate information about the weather, a nice dinner, the best concert tickets. Still, there may be two kinds of cases between which to distinguish here. On the one hand, there are the cases where the speaker is making her first entry into language, where her uses of words literally determine what they mean, and so, not only can she not be wrong about what she means, neither can her interlocutor be wrong about what the speaker means, as the interlocutor facilitates the sharper and sharper focus on aspects of the environment through more and more linguistic back and forth. On the other hand, there are the cases where the speaker has a full-blown language and her interlocutor has had limited linguistic exchanges with the speaker, and so the evidence on the basis of which she understands the speaker may not be strong or broad enough. I shall discuss this further in §4.

[18] As Davidson repeatedly made clear. For instance: "The purpose of this exercise [reflecting on triangulation] is not to explain in detail how the process works, for to do this would amount to reducing the intensional to the extensional. The purpose is to indicate how the triangular arrangement makes the process possible" (Davidson 2001c, 293). This, as he indicates here, is part and parcel of Davidson's non-reductionism, which he advocated from his writings on radical interpretation to those on triangulation. See, e.g., Davidson 1974, 154, and 2001b, 15. For further discussion, see Verheggen 2021.

All we can say at the end is that those who have communicated with others in triangular situations have bridged it.

In short, then, understanding others from scratch requires the same conditions that make possible possession of a language. And, since having a language requires having understood and having been understood by others, it is no wonder that Davidson says that "public availability is a constitutive aspect of language." Publicness is no longer assumed, as it had been initially, but it is vindicated. Meanings are necessarily available because at least some of them must have been shared to begin with, and those that have not been shared are necessarily connected to others that have been.[19] Also, we may surmise that the radical interpreter exploits the knowledge she has of the workings of language when she interprets a speaker from scratch. More importantly, we are now in a position to see how it is possible to understand linguistic uses that are in some respect novel, when these are uses by a speaker with whom we by and large share a language.

3. Linguistic Luck and Novel Uses of Language

One common example of novel linguistic use, made prominent by Davidson, is that of malapropisms. Mrs. Malaprop congratulates the poet on his "nice derangement of epitaphs." Following Davidson, let us suppose that the audience has no trouble understanding that she meant a nice arrangement of epithets by "a nice derangement of epitaphs." Why is this so? Some may say that it is simply because 'epithet' is awfully close to 'epitaph', and given the context it makes sense to think that Mrs. Malaprop was referring to epithets. Some indeed suggest that malapropisms are akin to cases of mispronunciation or other kinds of faulty performance.[20] No doubt, there are malapropisms that fall into these categories. However, my goal here is not to give an exhaustive treatment of malapropisms, but only to indicate how, in light of how the publicness of language is not a matter of luck, some of them can be seen to be easily understood, though this requires assigning the differently used words a new meaning. I shall focus on the above example of malapropism.

Davidson actually acknowledges that the similarity in sound between 'epithet' and 'epitaph' may "tip" the audience "off to the right interpretation." But "similarity of sound is not essential to the malaprop" (Davidson 1986, 90). What may be indispensable to the literal comprehension of the malapropism are elements of

---

[19] For instance, "the contents of the belief that a guanaco is present [may have been] determined, not by exposure to guanacos, but by having acquired other words and concepts, such as those of llama, animal, camel, domesticated, and so forth. Somewhere along the line, though, we must come to the direct exposures that anchor thought and language to the world" (1991a, 197).

[20] See Lepore and Stone 2017.

the context in which it is uttered. Indeed, I believe that Mrs. Malaprop might have been understood just as easily if she had said that the poet delivered "a nice derangement of anagrams." She would have been understood if instances of what she was talking about, namely, epithets, were on the board—say, she teaches poetry and has invited the poet as a guest lecturer and reciter. She and her audience could triangulate on the epithets written on the board, and have further linguistic exchanges about them if needed—Davidson does not say that interpretation of the unexpected use is always immediate.

When Davidson discussed malapropisms, he introduced a distinction between what he called prior theory and passing theory:

> For the hearer, the prior theory expresses how he is prepared in advance to interpret an utterance of the speaker, while the passing theory is how he does interpret the utterance. For the speaker, the prior theory is what he believes the interpreter's theory to be, while his passing theory is the theory he intends the interpreter to use.   (Davidson 1986, 101)[21]

Thus, Mrs. Malaprop's audience is prepared in advance to interpret an utterance of Mrs. Malaprop's 'epitaph' as meaning epitaph, while in the passing theory it interprets it as meaning epithet. As for Mrs. Malaprop, her prior theory, as Davidson usually tells the story,[22] is that she believes her audience will interpret her utterance of 'epitaph' as meaning epitaph, while her passing theory is that she intends her audience to interpret her utterance of 'epitaph' as meaning epithet. According to Davidson, communication rests on the sharing of the passing theory. Communication occurs if the audience interprets Mrs. Malaprop's utterance in the way she intended it to be interpreted. But just how is the passing theory arrived at, how are the meanings of the differently used words fixed in the absence of any opportunity to build holistic connections with other utterances?

In response, two aspects of the passing theory and its connection to the prior theory need to be emphasized. First, for both the speaker and her interlocutor, the passing theory depends upon the prior theory. Though the prior theory may not be sufficient to determine the literal meaning of an utterance and for communication to occur, it is nonetheless typically necessary. Thus, on the speaker's side: "The speaker's view of the interpreter's prior theory is not irrelevant to what he says, nor to what he means by his words; it is an important part of what he has to go on if he wants to be understood" (Davidson 1986, 101). When this is applied to Mrs. Malaprop, there are, I think, at least two cases to be envisaged. On the one

---

[21] As Davidson insists, talk of "theories" here should not be given any special weight. As the quotation suggests, theories here are equivalent to "methods of interpretation," about which neither interpreter nor speaker need have any explicit knowledge. See Davidson 1986, 95–6.

[22] As we shall see below, he occasionally tells it differently.

hand, Mrs. Malaprop's prior and passing theory may coincide, that is, contra what I suggested above on Davidson's behalf, she may have the erroneous view that her audience's prior theory for her includes her meaning epithet by 'epitaph', and that is the passing theory she uses to communicate with her audience (which in turn has to adjust its theory in order to understand her).[23] On the other hand, as Davidson usually seems to have it, Mrs. Malaprop's prior theory may be different from her passing one. She may believe that her audience's theory includes her meaning epitaph by 'epitaph', but intend her audience to interpret her as meaning epithet by 'epitaph', because, say, she is a joker, and knows that her audience knows enough about her to get the joke.[24] What, however, is more important for our purposes is the interpreter's side of what is happening here.

On the interpreter's side, Davidson writes: "Of course, things previously learned were essential to arriving at the passing theory" (Davidson 1986, 103). I take it that those things previously learned include all kinds of facts about the speaker, her habits, preferences, and so forth, but also, crucially, facts about the speaker's previous linguistic behaviour, including what she has previously meant by 'epitaph' and by 'epithet'. The main point is that the interpreter's prior theory for the speaker was essential to arriving at the passing theory.[25] Thus, it is at best misleading of Elisabeth Camp to say that "Davidson's commitment to holism puts him under theoretical pressure to broaden the evidential base of his semantic theory beyond the extreme localism of the passing theory" (Camp 2016, 120). The evidential base is broad from the start, including, as it does, not only the context, linguistic and otherwise, and possibly triangular, of the utterance, but also the evidence on the basis of which the prior theory was arrived at. Precisely for holistic reasons, the passing theory is "extremely local" only in so far as the literal meaning of an utterance might be extremely local. But the passing theory significantly overlaps with a prior theory that could not be extremely local, lest it could not exist to begin with.

Moreover, the interpreter knows what it takes to have a prior theory—she is "at home with the business of linguistic communication" (Davidson 1986, 100), and it

---

[23] Davidson recognizes the possibility of a "malaprop from ignorance" (103). Thus our present Mrs. Malaprop has always meant epithet by 'epitaph', but her audience "who, as we say, knows English,... does not know [her] verbal habits" (104). An interesting question to ask here is how to distinguish malapropisms from ignorance from long-standing idiosyncratic uses.

[24] Joking is only one of a multitude of possibilities, such as mispronouncing, being distracted, temporarily forgetting the meaning, and other ways of displaying local, rather than enduring, ignorance.

[25] The prior theory does not have to be conventional, and seldom is, according to Davidson. Of course, the less we have interacted with a speaker, the more we shall rely on the sociolect that we assume we share; this will be the prior theory we have for our interlocutor, say, a taxi driver at the Singapore airport. See Davidson 1986, 262. That the prior theory does not have to be conventional is missed by Ernie Lepore and Martin Stone (2017). So is the idea that the passing theory is connected to the prior theory. The latter idea also seems to be missed by Josh Armstrong, in so far as he thinks that "triangulation pertains to what is happening at a time, rather than what has happened or what will happen over time" (Armstrong 2016a, 93). No triangular interaction makes sense which is disconnected from other ones or other linguistic exchanges.

is this very kind of knowledge that enables her to arrive at a passing theory. Indeed, and second, the passing theory, as Davidson insists, is

> suited to be the theory for an entire language, even though its expected field of application is vanishingly small...Someone who grasps the fact that Mrs. Malaprop means 'epithet' when she says 'epitaph' must give 'epitaph' all the powers 'epithet' has for many other people. Only a full recursive theory can do justice to those powers.   (Davidson 1986, 100)[26]

Thus, 'epitaph', as used by Mrs. Malaprop, is still part of a systematic theory, which, to repeat, could not be built on the spot. 'Epitaph' must be seen as contributing to the truth-conditions of other sentences in which it may occur. It has all the holistic powers and connections to triangular interactions, and thus to the world, that other words may have, and, in particular that 'epithet' has for the audience. Mrs. Malaprop's audience has no trouble understanding 'epitaph', or 'anagram' for that matter, because, aided by Mrs. Malaprop's gestures and a salient feature of the situation they are in, they promptly understand it as meaning epithet, the understanding of which in turn is the result of holistic connections with other parts of their language. Once one has a language, and is aware, however inarticulately, of its workings, one does not need to establish those connections in order to understand a word whose meaning is new to one.

Now, it might be objected that this kind of understanding works with mala-propisms, "when a word or phrase temporarily or locally takes over the role of some other word or phrase" (Davidson 1986, 103), when in effect we understand a new word that simply is used to express an old concept, a word to express which we can readily supply. But what about neologisms, understood here as words expressing new concepts? Can we understand them on the spot? Here we obviously have no other word that we may supply to understand the concept expressed.[27]

As with malapropisms, my goal is not to give an exhaustive treatment of neologisms. But I believe that two kinds of cases should be distinguished here. There are cases where on the spot interpretation is possible. These are similar to malapropisms. For instance, to borrow an example from Armstrong 2016b, a postman who says "Let me measure the volume of your package with a koba" may have no trouble being understood if he proceeds to grasp the oddly shaped ruler that is on the counter. His interlocutor will again not need to establish holistic

---

[26] I have reverted the last 'epitaph' and 'epithet', which Davidson had in the wrong order.

[27] Davidson writes that "learning to interpret a word that expresses a concept we do not already have is a far deeper and more interesting phenomenon than explaining the ability to use a word new to us for an old concept" (1986, 100). This is more interesting because it is closer to the question how we develop a language to begin with. Thus, it is to be expected that the answer to the question how we understand neologisms will be based on what we learned from reflecting on triangulation.

connections between the present use and other ones in order to understand the postman. He is already familiar with objects that are similar, indeed with rulers, and knows how to talk about them. The same is true of new proper names: they can be understood on the spot. To borrow again an example from Armstrong, if the dog owner, whom I have not met before, tells me, after her dog has jumped on me, "Mupsy loves to greet strangers with a lick," I have no trouble understanding whom she is talking about (provided of course she is not deliberately misleading me, etc.). I know how proper names function, have used a great number of them in a great variety of circumstances. However, not all neologisms or unfamiliar names are that readily understood, which leads to the second kind of case.

These cases also include words that express concepts we do not yet have, but these words, e.g., 'bromance' or 'metrosexual', might not be so easily understood on the spot. The meaning of such neologisms is of course determined, like that of any other word, on the basis of their regular uses in numerous circumstances (unless it is simply stipulated). But in these cases, if we do not have access to at least some of those uses, it is hard to see how we could understand the neologism (unless again its meaning is simply explained to us). This is true of ordinary proper names as well. If a new name is introduced to us with no background whatsoever, we will fail to understand whom the speaker is talking about.[28] This is not to say that we could not get the meaning of the neologism or reference of the proper name without access to some background of use (or an explanation of its meaning). But that would be lucky!

In sum, it is because of what makes meaningful use of words possible, its resting on a shared world with which speakers have sometimes interacted together, linguistically and otherwise, that understanding unexpected or novel uses relies much less, if at all, on luck than it might have been thought.[29, 30] I believe that Davidson can indeed reconcile the claim that deciphering meanings is not a matter of luck with the claim that one does not need to speak like others in

---

[28] We will of course be able to use the proper name if our interlocutors have been using it to talk about its referent, taking ourselves to be referring to whomever or whatever they are talking about.

[29] I think that Davidson's externalist account is in fact superior to other, more orthodox, externalist accounts that make meaning essentially depend on factors of the external world of which speakers are ignorant. Thus, according to Hilary Putnam's physical externalism, what speakers mean by at least natural kind terms essentially depends on the real worldly essences of the kinds these terms refer to. According to Burge's social externalism, what speakers mean by all terms essentially depends on the conventions of the linguistic community they belong to. There is much room here for miscommunication and for luck to play a role if communication is to succeed. See Putnam 1975 and Burge 1979.

[30] Though they understand this claim quite differently from the way Davidson does, Lepore and Stone are right when they say that malapropisms and neologisms "are cases when meaning depends on antecedent regularity that enables interlocutors to coordinate on a meaning." But they have misunderstood Davidson when they suggest that this goes counter to the idea that these cases involve "a speaker creating improvised meaning, and a hearer just recognizing, through processes grounded in, or motivated by, the picture of Radical Interpretation, a match between their own understanding and the speaker's understanding of a situation" (Lepore and Stone 2017, 259). If the process of radical interpretation is properly understood, the match can only be grounded on regularity, including, crucially, as the writings on triangulation make clear, on prior linguistic exchanges.

order to be understood and have a language. According to his foundational account of meaning, what explains what it is for words to mean what they do also explains what it is for us to assign certain meanings to others. This is how it should be. We started by trying to figure out how meanings can be attributed from scratch, in order to draw general lessons about the nature of meaning. We can now apply these lessons to any case of linguistic novelty.

4. Linguistic Luck and Wittgenstein's Rule-Following Paradox

Though he never explicitly used the label, Davidson's theory of meaning is obviously a kind of use theory.[31] As he writes, "it is understanding that gives rise to meaning, not the other way around" (Davidson 1994, 121). And understanding is based, in the first instance, on how speakers use their words in triangular interactions. The most famous inspirer of the use theory is of course Ludwig Wittgenstein. And Davidson can be understood as exploiting some of the remarks Wittgenstein makes in his later writings, though he did not find the idea of triangulation in them. Indeed, what Davidson did, which Wittgenstein never did, is articulate the kind of use in which agents must have engaged in order to speak meaningfully. Accordingly, Davidson's theory can be used to address Wittgenstein's rule-following paradox, and, in particular, the articulation of the paradox developed by Saul Kripke.

Wittgenstein writes:

> This was our paradox: no course of action could be determined by a rule, because every course of action can be brought into accord with the rule. The answer was: if every course of action can be brought into accord with the rule, then it can also be brought into conflict with it. And so there would be neither accord nor conflict here. (Wittgenstein 1953, §201)

When the action is the application of a linguistic expression, the paradox becomes that every application of the expression can be deemed to be correct, or incorrect. And so the very distinction between correct and incorrect applications becomes unintelligible. But, if the distinction is unintelligible, so is the very idea of meaning unintelligible. For expressions whose applications are not governed by conditions of correctness cannot be meaningful.[32]

---

[31] Though this has been disputed by Bridges 2017 and Horwich 2017, among others. For other proponents of my interpretation, see Stroud 2017 and Wikforss 2017.

[32] This "platitude," as it has been called by Wright 1986 and Hattiangadi 2006, though present in Wittgenstein's and in Kripke's writings on meaning and rule-following, was first made explicit by Blackburn 1984. Numerous philosophers followed suit.

This nihilistic conclusion is the conclusion arrived at by Kripke's sceptic; if her reasoning is right, "the entire idea of meaning vanishes into thin air" (Kripke 1982, 22). We certainly take ourselves to speak meaningfully and to communicate linguistically with others, however. Thanks to this, we get all kinds of things done. Most mundanely but crucially, we inform others or get informed about the state of the world—the weather, the contents of the fridge, the various performances of Beethoven's *Tempest*; our wishes are realized—we get the umbrella, a nice dinner, the best concert tickets. Are we being lucky all the time? The sceptic certainly suggests that we may be. For, she asks, what makes me so sure that, for instance, when I request a green shirt, my interlocutor will understand me to mean green by 'green', which is the meaning we seem to have settled on in the past, and that she will not give me a blue shirt because it turns out that she has always taken us to mean grue by 'green' (where, if one means grue by 'green', then "past objects were grue if and only if they were (then) green while present objects are grue if and only if they are (now) blue" (Kripke 1982, 20))? Indeed, what makes me so sure that it is green rather than grue that *I* mean by 'green'? Certainly, I cannot point to my past use of 'green'; this is perfectly compatible with my meaning grue by the word. Nor can I point to some mental image or experience I associate with my use of 'green'; I could mean green by 'green' in the absence of any such image or experience, and, as Wittgenstein emphasized, whatever mental image or experience I may have when I use 'green' could be interpreted as determining a meaning different from green.[33] The same problem arises if I point to an abstract entity I somehow associate with the word; unless it is interpreted in a certain way, it cannot determine one meaning rather than another.[34] Not even invoking a disposition to use 'green' in certain regular ways will do; for either the disposition is characterized in non-semantic terms, in which case it suffers from the same aforementioned interpret-ation problem,[35] or it is characterized in semantic terms, as the disposition to use 'green' to mean green, in which case there arises the question what makes it the case that I have this disposition and that my interlocutors understand me accord-ingly? This is indeed the question that needs answering, and to which Davidson can be seen as providing an answer.

The answer, which stems from the triangulation argument, is this. If I mean green by 'green', it is because I have engaged in triangular interactions with others who have understood me as meaning green. Indeed, my meaning green has been fixed by my agreeing with others to mean green by 'green', agreeing, that is, that greenness is the aspect of objects I am talking about when I use 'green'. Recall that

---

[33] See Wittgenstein 1953, §73.

[34] For a more thorough exposition of what, according to Wittgenstein, I may unsuccessfully point to in the hope of justifying my present use of an expression, see Verheggen 2017c, §3.

[35] For further discussion of this specific problem with reductive dispositionalism, see Myers and Verheggen 2016, ch. 2.

the features of the world that contribute to determining what we mean by our words do not do so on their own. It is speakers interacting with these features who isolate the relevant aspects in the first place. Thus, in the first place, it is, at least in part, what speakers take the causes of their basic responses to be, and so take their words to mean, that determine their meaning. I therefore mean green by 'green' because this is what I have taken 'green' to mean, and what other speakers have taken me to mean. And I mean blue by 'blue' because this is what I have taken 'blue' to mean, and what other speakers have taken me to mean. We have not taken 'green' to mean grue, any more than we have taken 'blue' to mean bleen. The key to the response to the sceptic is that there is no gap, as it were, between what I mean and what I think I mean.[36]

As I suggested earlier, in §2.2, the case of the speaker who has triangulated with others to develop a first language might be different from the case of the interpreter trying to understand a speaker with whom she has had few linguistic exchanges. In the first case, linguistic interactions, triangular and otherwise, have contributed to fixing the meanings of the speaker's words. We may imagine these interactions including utterances expressing beliefs to the effect that blue and green are different colours, that what colour an object has does not depend on the time at which it is observed or described, to cite but two of the beliefs that may contribute centrally to determining what one means by 'green' and 'blue'. However, communication might be less straightforward in the second case. The speaker I am trying to understand may be a Vietnamese, who has only one word to describe green and blue things. Not knowing this, I might be lucky to get a green shirt from her when I ask for one (unless she knows better about how I speak). But, as I keep accumulating evidence about her behaviour, linguistic and otherwise, I may reach a point where I can correct my misunderstanding. As Davidson says,

> [t]he longer we interpret a speaker with apparent success as speaking a particular language, the greater our legitimate confidence that the speaker is speaking that language—that is, that she will continue to be interpretable as speaking that language. Our strengthening expectations are as well founded as our evidence and ordinary induction make them.   (Davidson 1992, 111)

On the basis of the foregoing, Davidson has often been interpreted as maintaining that Kripke's problem is just a version of the induction problem, which is not specific to language. I think that it is better to say, on Davidson's behalf, that

---

[36] As Olivia Sultanescu and I have pointed out, contra Ali Hossein Khani 2017, once it is recognized what it takes for the meaning of a word to be fixed, namely, the contribution of the speaker who takes a certain aspect of the external object or event to be the relevant one, that is, who makes a meaningful judgement to the effect that a certain aspect is the relevant one, the sceptic no longer has any room for maneuver. See Sultanescu and Verheggen 2019, 21.

Kripke's problem has been solved—what in part determine the meanings of our words are the aspects of the environment that we have taken to be the relevant causes of our responses to it. However, even when Kripke's problem has been solved, there may remain an induction problem. This will be more acute the less we have interacted with the speaker and the less we know about her environment as well as her living arrangements and habits. The problem will barely be present, if at all, with our kids and intimate friends. Strictly speaking, only an ideal interpreter, who has all the evidence there is, could be sure never to encounter the problem. But, given what makes language possession possible to begin with, the sharing of the world and our reactions to it, this is an assurance that we may, I think, by and large share.[37]

In sum, then, to the sceptic who asks me what makes me so sure that it is green and not grue that I mean by 'green', I can answer that this is what I have taken my word and been understood to mean in the circumstances in which my meaning was fixed. To repeat, my meaning green by 'green' has been fixed in collaboration with others and the world we share. The latter partner is especially important, lest someone objects that we have lost the distinction between correct and incorrect applications. After all, the objector's thought may go, to fix the meanings of words is to fix their conditions of correct application. Is it not the case, then, that what appears to a speaker, or group of speakers, to be the correct application actually is the correct one, thereby annihilating the idea of conditions of correctness and hence of meaning? The answer is that it is not. For, though speakers contribute to fixing meanings and thus conditions of correctness, once these are established, it is an objective matter whether any given application is correct or not, a matter settled in part by the aspect of the world that, not incidentally, contributed to fixing the meaning of the word in the first place. In other words, the world did provide constraints while the fixing was going on. Indeed, only so could speakers be in a position to have the very idea of there being an objective distinction between correct and incorrect applications.

The resolute sceptic may of course push back at this stage, and insist that there may be a gap between what I think I mean by my words and what I do mean, that is, between what I take to be the causes of my responses to the world around me, which are supposed to contribute to their meaning, and what these causes in fact are.[38] This sceptic is not only resolute but radical. At least she is so if she accepts the externalist theory of meaning that Davidson advocates. For not to know what the causes of my responses are is tantamount to not knowing what I mean by my words. I have been pushed to a position where I cannot even understand the sceptic. I cannot even wonder if it is green or grue that I mean by

---

[37] Thanks to Muhammad Ali Khalidi and Robert Myers for pushing me to address this objection from induction.

[38] This sceptical objection has been suggested by Stroud 1999.

'green'. I have to remain silent.[39] Or I have to come up with an alternative story to explain that it is green that I mean by 'green', but it is hard to see what that story could be.[40]

5. Conclusion

In the end, it is no surprise that, as Davidson put it, the public availability of meanings is not a matter of luck. This is due to the essential role speakers play in determining the meanings of their words, and to that role being played in communion with other speakers, which in turn requires the constraining participation of the world around them. Because speakers, in effect, create the meanings of their words, but can only do this while also understanding and being understood by other speakers, they not only understand their own words, contra Kripke's sceptic, but also have the skills needed to understand novel uses of words. And they know what it takes to convey new meanings; indeed they can intend to convey new meanings only because they know when to expect that their interlocutors will get them. To talk here of "improvised meaning" is misleading at best. No literal meaning can be wholly improvised.[41]

References

Armstrong, Josh. 2016a. "Coordination, Triangulation, and Language Use." *Inquiry* 59–1: 80–112.

Armstrong, Josh. 2016b. "The Problem of Lexical Innovation." *Linguistics and Philosophy* 39: 87–111.

Blackburn, Simon. 1984. "The Individual Strikes back." In Alex Miller and Crispin Wright (eds.), *Rule-Following and Meaning*. Montreal and Kingston: McGill-Queen's University Press 2002.

Bridges, Jason. 2017. "The Search for 'The Essence of Human Language' in Wittgenstein and Davidson." In Verheggen 2017b.

Burge, Tyler. 1979. "Individualism and the Mental." *Midwest Studies in Philosophy*, 4: 73–121.

---

[39] For further discussion, see Myers and Verheggen 2016, ch. 4.

[40] On the one hand, it is hard to see how more orthodox physical externalist theories could do any better. As suggested above, they may even fare worse. On the other hand, internalist theories face the problem of saying, as suggested above in the possible answers to the sceptic, what it is about an internal item that determines one meaning rather than another. No triangulating on internal items is available to remove the ambiguity.

[41] Many thanks to Muhammad Ali Khalidi and Olivia Sultanescu for their comments on an earlier draft of this chapter. Special thanks to Robert Myers for much discussion of some tricky issues, and to Abrol Fairweather and Carlos Montemayor for many stimulating conversations about the chapter.

Burge, Tyler. 1986. "Cartesian Error and the Objectivity of Perception." In Phillip Pettit and John McDowell (eds.), *Subject, Thought, and Context*. Oxford: Oxford University Press.

Camp, Elizabeth. 2016. "Conventions' Revenge: Davidson, Derangement, and Dormativity." *Inquiry* 59–1: 113–38.

Davidson, Donald. 1967. "Truth and Meaning." In Davidson 1984a.

Davidson, Donald. 1973. "Radical Interpretation." In Davidson 1984a.

Davidson, Donald. 1974. "Belief and the Basis of Meaning." In Davidson 1984a.

Davidson, Donald. 1975. "Thought and Talk." In Davidson 1984a.

Davidson, Donald. 1982. "Rational Animals." In Davidson 2001a.

Davidson, Donald. 1984a. *Inquiries into Truth and Interpretation*. Oxford: Clarendon Press.

Davidson, Donald. 1984b. "Communication and Convention." In Davidson 1984a.

Davidson, Donald. 1986. "A Nice Derangement of Epitaphs." In Davidson 2005.

Davidson, Donald. 1991a. "Epistemology Externalized." In Davidson 2001a.

Davidson, Donald. 1991b. "Three Varieties of Knowledge." In Davidson 2001a.

Davidson, Donald. 1992. "The Second Person." In Davidson 2001a.

Davidson, Donald. 1993. "Reply to Jerry Fodor and Ernest Lepore." In Ralf Stoecker (ed.), *Reflecting Davidson*. Berlin and New York: Walter de Gruyter.

Davidson, Donald. 1994. "The Social Aspect of Language." In Davidson 2005.

Davidson, Donald. 1999. "The Emergence of Thought." In Davidson 2001a.

Davidson, Donald. 2001a. *Subjective, Intersubjective, Objective*. Oxford: Clarendon Press.

Davidson, Donald. 2001b. "Externalisms." In Kotatko et al. 2001.

Davidson, Donald. 2001c. "Comments on Karlovy Vary Papers." In Kotatko et al. 2001.

Davidson, Donald. 2005. *Truth, Language, and History*. Oxford: Clarendon Press.

Glüer, Kathrin. 2011. *Donald Davidson: A Short Introduction*. Oxford: Oxford University Press.

Glüer, Kathrin. 2018. "Interpretation and the Interpreter." In Derek Ball and Brian Rabern (eds.), *The Science of Meaning: Essays on the Metatheory of Natural Language Semantics*. Oxford: Oxford University Press.

Hattiangadi, Anandi. 2006. "Is Meaning Normative?" *Mind and Language* 21: 220–40.

Hossein Khani, Ali. 2017. "Review of *Donald Davidson's Triangulation Argument: A Philosophical Inquiry*." *International Journal of Philosophical Studies* 26: 113–17.

Horwich, Paul. 2017. "Davidson's Wittgensteinian View of Meaning." In Verheggen 2017b.

Kotatko, Petr, Peter Pagin, and Gabriel Segal, eds. 2001. *Interpreting Davidson*. Stanford: CSLI.

Kripke, Saul. 1982. *Wittgenstein on Rules and Private Language.* Cambridge, MA: Harvard University Press.

Lepore, Ernie and Matthew Stone. 2017. "Convention before Communication." *Philosophical Perspectives* 31–1: 245–65.

Lewis, David. 1974. "Radical Interpretation." *Synthese* 27: 331–44.

Myers, Robert H. and Claudine Verheggen. 2016. *Donald Davidson's Triangulation Argument: A Philosophical Inquiry.* New York and London: Routledge.

Putnam, Hilary. 1975. "The Meaning of 'Meaning'." In his *Language, Mind and Reality.* Cambridge: Cambridge University Press, 1975.

Stroud, Barry. 1999. "Radical Interpretation and Philosophical Scepticism." In Lewis Edwin Hahn (ed.), *The Philosophy of Donald Davidson.* Chicago and La Salle, IL: Open Court.

Stroud, Barry. 2017. "Davidson and Wittgenstein on Meaning and Understanding." In Verheggen 2017b.

Sultanescu, Olivia and Claudine Verheggen. 2019. "Davidson's Answer to Kripke's Sceptic." *Journal for the History of Analytic Philosophy* 7–2: 8–28.

Verheggen, Claudine. 2017a. "Davidson's Semantic Externalism: From Radical Interpretation to Triangulation," special issue for the centenary of Donald Davidson's birth, C. Amoretti, M. de Caro, and F. Ervas, eds., *Argumenta* 3–1: 145–61.

Verheggen, Claudine, ed. 2017b. *Wittgenstein and Davidson on Language, Thought, and Action.* Cambridge: Cambridge University Press.

Verheggen, Claudine. 2017c. "Davidson's Treatment of Wittgenstein's Rule-Following Paradox." In Verheggen 2017b.

Verheggen, Claudine. 2021. "The Continuity of Davidson's Thought: Non-Reductionism Without Quietism," in Syraya Chin-Mu Yang and Robert H. Myers, eds., *Donald Davidson on Action, Mind and Value.* London: Springer Nature.

Wikforss, Asa. 2017. "Davidson and Wittgenstein. A Homeric Struggle?" In Verheggen 2017b.

Wittgenstein, Ludwig. 1953. *Philosophical Investigations,* trans. G. E. M. Anscombe. New York: Macmillan.

Wittgenstein, Ludwig. 1974. *Philosophical Grammar.* Oakland, CA: University of California Press.

Wright, Crispin. 1986. "Does *Philosophical Investigations* I 258–60 Suggest a Cogent against Private Language?" In Phillip Pettit and John McDowell, eds. *Subject, Thought, and Context.* Oxford: Oxford University Press.

10

Understanding, Luck, and Communicative Value

Andrew Peet

1. Utterance Understanding

'Understanding' has several different uses. First, we can talk of understanding a concept or a topic. This plausibly requires knowing the answer to a certain why question, or perhaps possessing a web of interconnected beliefs regarding a topic. This is not the sense of 'understanding' we will be focusing on here. Secondly, we can talk of understanding a sentence. For example, I might understand the sentence 'Jeg er ikke her' (it means 'I am not here'). This is closer to our topic. Thirdly, we can talk of understanding what is said. That is, of understanding somebody's utterance. It is this third notion of understanding upon which we shall focus.

One can plausibly understand the sentence somebody has used without understanding their utterance. For example, suppose I get home to find a note with the words 'Jeg er ikke her' written on it. I understand the sentence. However, since I do not know who wrote the note, I do not understand the utterance. I cannot grasp what it is saying. Suppose it was written by my wife, but I take it to have been written by my son. Then I have misunderstood the utterance despite understanding the sentence. Consider another example: I am out for dinner with a friend and her steak is undercooked. She complains that her steak is 'raw'. Suppose I take her literally and think she means that her steak is completely uncooked. Then although I have understood the sentence she has used, I have not understood her utterance.

Not only is sentence understanding insufficient for utterance understanding, it is also unnecessary. Suppose I have just had a carpentry accident and managed to get a large splinter stuck in my eye. I am considering whether or not to seek treatment, so I speak to my sister who is a medical professional. She tells me that 'No eye injury is too small to be ignored'. She intends to communicate that no eye injury is small enough that it can be ignored: you should always get an eye injury examined. We both take this to be the literal meaning of the sentence she has uttered. However, we are both wrong. The sentence 'No eye injury is too small to be ignored' really says that no matter how small the eye injury is it can be ignored.

Andrew Peet, *Understanding, Luck, and Communicative Value* In: *Linguistic Luck: Safeguards and Threats to Linguistic Communication.* Edited by: Abrol Fairweather and Carlos Montemayor, Oxford University Press.
© Oxford University Press 2023. DOI: 10.1093/oso/9780192845450.003.0010

So, neither myself nor my sister understand the sentence she has uttered. Yet I plausibly understand her utterance.

Strictly speaking the proposition the speaker intends to directly communicate with an utterance can differ from the proposition they actually express. So, we could further distinguish two forms of utterance understanding—one corresponding to recovery of the speaker's intended proposition, and another corresponding to recovery of the truth conditional content of their utterance. However, in most cases truth-conditional content will correspond to the proposition the speaker aims to directly communicate with their utterance. So, typically these forms of understanding will coincide.[1] My focus here will be on recovery of the speaker's intended proposition. So, I will use 'what is said' to denote the proposition the speaker intends to directly communicate via their utterance. It is also worth noting that understanding an utterance will involve more than recovering the proposition intended by the speaker. It will also involve correctly judging the force of the utterance (i.e. is it an assertion? a suggestion? a sarcastic remark?). I will ignore this complication in what follows. Similar issues to those that arise for content will arise for force, and similar solutions will be applicable.

2. Understanding and Reliability

I will be exploring the prospects for reliability-based approaches to utterance understanding. That is, I will be considering approaches committed to some version of the following:

Reliable Recovery: Understanding requires reliable recovery of what is said.

Many theorists go beyond this, holding that utterance understanding requires knowledge of what is said.[2] However, as we will see, it is hard enough to maintain a mere reliability condition on understanding, let alone a knowledge condition. So, the prospects for knowledge views look dim.[3]

Before going through the arguments for **Reliable Recovery**, it will be helpful to distinguish between two different senses of 'reliable': local and non-local reliability. The distinction between local and non-local reliability comes from epistemology, and corresponds to different ways in which a belief might be reliable. A true

---

[1] See Peet (forthcoming) for an account of the relationship between intended and truth conditional content.

[2] Examples include Campbell (1982), Dummett (1978, 1991); Evans (1982); Davies (1989); Higginbotham (1992); and McDowell (1994); Heck (1995).

[3] For arguments against the knowledge view, see Hunter (1998); Pettit (2002); Fricker (2003); and Longworth (2008, 2009, 2018). And for arguments against the related claim that testimonial knowledge requires knowledge of what is said, see Peet (2018a, 2019). Many of the cases discussed in this chapter are problematic for the knowledge view.

belief is locally reliable if, given the way that very belief was formed, it was not a matter of luck that it was true. Local reliability conditions are often captured in modal terms. For example, it may be thought that for a belief to be locally reliable it must be safe:

Safety: A belief is safe iff there are no nearby worlds in which it is formed in the same way and false.[4]

A belief is non-locally reliable if it is formed in a manner that would yield true beliefs in some range of specific circumstances (that may or may not include the actual circumstances of formation). For example, we might say a belief is non-locally reliable if it is formed in a way that yields true beliefs in normal circumstances.[5] It should be clear that a belief can be locally reliable without being non-locally reliable, and vice versa. Local reliability is typically thought to be necessary for knowledge. Non-local reliability conditions typically feature in theories of justification.

With this said, it should be clear that **Reliable Recovery** is ambiguous. Separate principles could be formulated with respect to local and non-local reliability (or, both could be required). We can get clearer on the precise sense in which utterance understanding requires reliability by considering the arguments for **Reliable Recovery**.

There are a number of potential arguments for **Reliable Recovery**. The first two arguments draw on Longworth's (2018) discussion of the knowledge of what is said condition. As Longworth demonstrates, neither argument provides convincing support for a knowledge condition on understanding. However, they have greater force in support of **Reliable Recovery**.

The first argument starts from the assumption that utterance understanding regularly yields knowledge of what is said. We would typically infer from the fact that somebody understands another's utterance to the conclusion that they know what the speaker has said. If we are to explain the naturalness of this inference we must endorse something like the following: usually, or in normal circumstances, understanding yields knowledge of what is said. This tells us two things. First, it tells us that in normal circumstances understanding yields a veridical judgement about what is said. That is, normally when we understand somebody to have said that p, they will have said that p. So, this already gives us a form of non-local reliability. However, we can go further. When we gain knowledge that somebody has said that p, our judgement must also be locally reliable. That is, it must satisfy

---

[4] **Safety** is widely endorsed, but for influential defenses, see Sosa (1999); Williamson (2000); and Pritchard (2005). I will assume that **Safety** correctly captures local reliability in what follows, although little turns on this.

[5] See Goldman (1986), Leplin (2007), Graham (2016, 2017), and Smith (2016) for versions of this approach.

an anti-luck condition such as the safety condition. So, we also learn that in normal conditions utterance understanding yields a locally reliable judgement about what is said.

The second argument is similar but starts from the observation that utterance understanding serves as a basis for the acquisition of testimonial knowledge. Plausibly, recovery of what is said is essential for testimonial knowledge. If I take you to have said that p, and thereby come to believe p, then unless you have actually said that p I cannot gain knowledge that p from your testimony.[6] So, if understanding underwrites the acquisition of testimonial knowledge (i.e. leads to testimonial knowledge in most cases), it must usually yield an accurate judge-ment about what is said. Moreover, if my recovery of what is said is merely lucky, then this will not be sufficient for knowledge, as my testimonial belief will be Gettiered. Therefore, understanding must yield a safe judgement regarding what is said in the majority of cases.

The two arguments just presented suggest that understanding is reliable in the following ways: First, understanding usually, or in normal circumstances, yields a veridical judgement regarding what is said. Secondly, it usually yields a safe (i.e. non-lucky) judgement about what is said. However, I believe we can go further. There is reason to believe that understanding always yields a non-lucky judgement regarding what is said. There are cases in which an audience fails to understand an utterance despite reaching an accurate judgement about what is said. This failure of understanding is seemingly due to the luckiness of the audience's recovery of what is said. The classic example is presented by Loar (1976), so we will call such cases 'Loar cases':

> **Loar:** Suppose that Smith and Jones are unaware that the man being interviewed on the television is someone they see on the train every morning, and about whom in that latter role, they have just been talking. Smith utters 'He is a stockbroker' intending to refer to the man on the television; Jones takes Smith to be referring to the man on the train. Now Jones, as it happens, has correctly identified Smith's referent, since the man on the television is the man on the train; but he has failed to understand Smith's utterance.   (Loar 1976: 357)

Assuming that 'he' is directly referential, the proposition entertained by Smith is identical to the proposition entertained by Jones. Yet Jones has intuitively failed to

---

[6] Strictly speaking I believe this is false. Testimonial knowledge does not require recovery of what is said or intended. Rather it requires non-lucky recovery of a sufficiently similar proposition. Or, more precisely, it requires that the audience non-accidentally recover a proposition that matches the speaker's intended proposition in truth value. I spell out this view in detail in my (2019). For an alternative approach to the communicative preconditions for the acquisition of testimonial knowledge that also denies that the speaker and hearer must entertain the same proposition, see Pollock (forthcoming). For the sake of simplicity, I will stick with the simpler 'recovery of what is said' condition here. The main points generalize to the less idealized approaches just mentioned.

understand Smith's utterance. Loar concludes that 'he' must not be directly referential. Instead, he holds that interlocutors must coordinate not only on referents but also on modes of presentation in order for communication to yield understanding. However, there is reason to be suspicious of this diagnosis. As Byrne and Thau (1996) note, we can generate similar cases in which the interlocutors coordinate on descriptive modes of presentation. They give the following example:

> **Hospital:** A patient checks into a hospital and is assigned room 101. Tony dubs him "Winston" and the cognitive value she attaches to the name is: the amnesiac in room 101. Alex is thoroughly unaware that Tony has seen the patient, but by sheer chance she also dubs him "Winston" and attaches the same cognitive value to the name. Alex utters "Winston will never recover" in Tony's presence, and Tony forms the belief she would express by saying "Winston will never recover".
> (Byrne and Thau 1996: 147)

Indeed, as I note in my (2019), we can generate similar cases by having interlocutors luckily coordinate on, for example, quantifier domains, the meanings of general terms, or the modal bases for modal claims. In general, understanding will be lacking whenever recovery of what is said occurs in a lucky way. This suggests that understanding always yields a non-lucky judgement regarding what is said. When the audience stumbles upon what is said by luck, they will not have understood the utterance.

So, the considerations adduced so far suggest that there is a local reliability condition on understanding. This is how **Reliable Recovery** will be understood for the time being. In the next section I will consider some counterexamples to the necessity of local reliability for utterance understanding. These challenges force us to take a more nuanced approach when formulating our local reliability condition.

3. Counterexamples to Local Reliability

Despite being well motivated, reliable recovery seems open to counterexample. That is, there seem to be cases of understanding in which reliable recovery fails. This suggests that local reliability is not necessary for understanding. I will consider two forms of counterexample here. The first derives from my (2018). It was originally intended as an example of testimonial knowledge without knowledge of what is said. But it also works as a case of understanding without knowledge that '*S* said that *p*'. The case is as follows:

> **Mad Scientist:** The philosophical mad scientist is at it again. His victim is Sally, a car enthusiast. This time, instead of envating his victim, he has implanted a

special chip in her brain. This chip causes her to sometimes say 'that is a fuel-efficient car', but only when she is in the presence of fuel-efficient cars, and only when she does not intend to do so. It works as follows: whenever Sally is in the presence of a fuel-efficient car it turns on and randomly selects one of two values. If it selects value 1 it switches off and becomes inactive again. However, if it selects value 2 it has the following effect: If Sally doesn't intend, and doesn't gain the intention, to comment on the fuel efficiency of the car, then it forces her to utter the sentence 'that is a fuel-efficient car'. One day Sally and Matt are walking through the city when Sally sees a particularly fuel-efficient car. She considers commenting on its fuel efficiency but hesitates because she doesn't know if Matt has any interest in cars. She decides on a whim to just go for it and says 'that is a fuel efficient car!'. On the basis of Sally's assertion Matt forms the true belief that the car is fuel-efficient. What neither Sally nor Matt know is that this was a case in which the chip selected value 2, so Sally would have uttered 'that car is fuel-efficient' even if she did not intend to.   (Peet 2018: 69)

Two things seem clear: First, Matt understands Sally's utterance. This is highly intuitive. Moreover, he is employing his normal abilities of comprehension, he gained these abilities in a reliable way, the output is fully veridical, and the causal chain leading to his judgement is non-deviant. Secondly though, there is an important sense in which his recovery of what was said is unreliable: his judgement that Sally said that the car is fuel efficient (henceforth 'p') was unsafe.

There are two obvious responses available to the defender of reliable recovery. First, it might be suggested that his 'Sally said that p' judgement was actually safe. That is, it might be claimed that in all nearby worlds Sally did say that the car is fuel efficient. However, in many of these worlds she only said it because the chip in her brain made her say it. Alternatively, it may be suggested that understanding only requires a reliable judgement that 'it has been said that p'. In this case it might be maintained that in nearby worlds Sally does not say that p, but the chip does say that p using Sally as a mouthpiece.

I don't find either response compelling. Saying is necessarily an intentional action. Whilst it is clearly possible that we can say a particular thing by accident (i.e. we can accidentally say p when we mean to say q), it is doubtful that our having said anything at all could be accidental. For example, if I am asleep or under hypnosis, and words escape my mouth without any intention or awareness on my behalf, it seems wrong to claim that I have said something, even if the sounds I produce resemble a meaningful sentence. When the chip sends electrical signals through Sally's brain this causes her mouth to open and certain words to spill out. She has no intention or motivation to make the relevant noises, and the production of the noises is not under her control or guidance. The saying is, thus, in no way attributable to her. Moreover, it makes little sense to claim that the chip says p. The chip is an inanimate object. It can't do things. This can be made even clearer if we alter the case a little and maintain that the chip gained its properties randomly, not through design.

A more promising response would be to modify our modal anti-luck condition so that we only consider nearby worlds at which the speaker said something. That is, we could require that there be no nearby worlds in which both (A) the speaker produced an utterance, and (B) the hearer's judgement that 'S said that p' was mistaken. This allows us to deal with Mad Scientist: After all, there are no nearby worlds in which Sally says 'that car is fuel efficient' and Max fails to recover this proposition. In the few nearby worlds in which she does say that the car is fuel efficient, he reaches the correct judgement.

Unfortunately, this is still not satisfying. First, as Longworth (2008, 2018) notes, young children are able to understand speech. Yet they may not possess the concept of 'saying that'. The requirement that understanding involves a judgement that 'S said that p' seems to over-intellectualize understanding. So, as formulated, our anti-luck condition seems overly demanding.[7] Instead, we can follow Longworth and hold that understanding what is said merely involves the audience's entertaining of the proposition the speaker intends to communicate. In this case we might spell out reliable recovery in terms of it being non-lucky that the proposition entertained by the audience corresponded to the proposition intended by the speaker. That is, we could require merely that there be no nearby worlds in which both (A) the speaker produced an utterance, and (B) the proposition entertained by the audience delivered from the proposition intended by the speaker (for ease of exposition I will continue to speak of 'judgements about what is said').[8]

Unfortunately, this view is also open to counterexample.[9] Consider the following case from Pettit (2002):

German: Imagine that you are travelling in Germany. You are a moderately competent speaker of German, but you come across an unfamiliar word, say, the word 'Krankenschwester'. You see a kindly-looking, elderly German sitting on a bench nearby, and you ask him what 'Krankenschwester' means, hoping that he might know some English. With an air of authority, he smiles and politely replies

---

[7] It may be possible to avoid this problem by only requiring a reliable ability to carve up the space of possibilities in the same way that 'S said that p' carves up the space of possibilities. I will put this possibility to one side in what follows.

[8] This is similar to the condition presented in my (2019) where I require (for the related condition of knowledge-yielding communication) that there be no nearby world in which both (A) the speaker said something, and (B) the propositions intended by the speaker and recovered by the hearer differ in truth value (with some additional caveats).

[9] It is actually open to counterexample along multiple lines. As I point out in my (2019), spelling out the anti-luck condition in purely modal terms also leads to problems as we can generate cases of modally stable luck (also see Lackey 2008 and Broncano-Berrocal 2018). Hyska (forthcoming) raises a similar worry for modal accounts of communicative luck. I resolve this issue by building a 'no-coincidence' clause into the account. I will set this complication to one side here.

in English 'it means nurse' which is indeed what the word 'Krankenschwester' means. Satisfied with his answer, you thank him and go on your way. As a result of this exchange, you are now able to use this previously unfamiliar word correctly and correctly interpret it as it is used by other speakers of German. If a German speaker assertively utters the sentence 'Die Krankenschwester ist nett' for example, you will correctly take the speaker to be asserting that the nurse is nice. Or if you want to say in German that the nurse is coming, you will correctly express this thought with the sentence 'Krankenschwester kommt'. In short, in a familiar sort of way, you have come to understand the word 'Krankenschwester'. However, suppose that, unbeknownst to you, the elderly gentleman—call him Herr Verriickt—is quite senile and doesn't know a word of English. His reply to your question (namely, 'it means nurse') is something he once overheard, but he has no idea what it means or what he is saying when he utters it. In his senility, he has taken to repeating this to tourists, regardless of what he is asked. By sheer coincidence, this was the right answer to the question you happened to ask him. But, had you asked him the location of the nearest postoffice, he would have said the very same thing.   (Pettit 2002: 519–20)

Suppose I am told that 'Die Krankenschwester ist nett'. I thereby have an experience as of the speaker asserting the proposition that the nurse is nice. Plausibly, I understand the utterance. And there is certainly a sense in which my understanding is reliable: in normal circumstances the experience of hearing 'Die Krankenschwester ist nett' and thereby coming to entertain the proposition that the nurse is nice will yield a veridical judgement about what is said. However, it is far less obvious that my judgement is locally reliable. That is, there is a clear element of luck in my recovering the correct proposition. It is, we might imagine, purely by luck that the old man repeats 'it means nurse' to tourists. He could easily have picked some other sentence to repeat such as 'it means chair'. If this had happened, then I would have experienced the speaker as asserting the proposition that the chair is nice. Since this easily could have happened, I don't safely recover what is said. I seem to understand the utterance, yet my recovery of what is said is lucky.[10]

In light of this, we may simply retreat to the claim that understanding requires non-local reliability. However, we are then left with the problem of explaining why understanding is absent in Loar cases. Thus, we have a puzzle. Loar cases seemingly demand a local reliability condition for understanding. Yet cases like **German** seemingly show the opposite.

---

[10] Pettit explicitly focuses on understanding a word or a sentence, rather than understanding an utterance. His claim is that, in this situation, one understands the sentence 'Die Krankenschwester ist nett'. However, it is also plausible that one understands literal utterances of this sentence.

4. A Solution

We must identify a form of luck according to which the audience's judgements in **Loar** and **Hospital** are lucky, but the audience's judgement in **German** is not. To do this we must note a familiar feature of epistemic anti-luck conditions: they are almost always relativized to a method of belief formation. For example, as noted earlier, safety conditions on knowledge hold that an agent's belief, if it is to constitute knowledge, must be true at all nearby worlds in which it is formed in the same way. Without this relativization to methods we would struggle with cases like the following:

> **Old Woman:** Lynn is an old woman. She has a son with severe medical issues: he is often close to dying. He comes to visit her and, upon seeing him in front of her, she forms the belief 'my son is alive'. However, if her son was dead then her younger sister would have come and told her that he was alive. So, she would have believed he was alive even if he was dead.   (Cf. Nozick 1982)

There are nearby worlds in which the old woman's son is dead. And in these worlds, she would still believe that he is alive. However, her belief is clearly not lucky. After all, she can see her son standing right in front of her. Relativizing the safety principle to methods of belief formation resolves this issue: there are no nearby worlds in which her belief is false and formed in the same way.

The key to resolving our puzzle, I suggest, rests in the relativization of our anti-luck principle. The basic idea is that we must hold fixed the 'interpretative base' of the audience's judgement regarding what is said (Peet 2019). That is, understanding will fail whenever there are nearby worlds in which some aspect of the linguistic or interpretative basis of the audience's judgement remains fixed and results in a failure of coordination with the speaker.

It is clear how this deals with Loar cases: in **Loar**, had the man on the train not been the man on the TV, and had Jones reached his judgement in the same way (i.e. relied on the same meaning schemas, drawn the same contextual inferences, etc.), the proposition Jones recovered would have differed from the proposition Smith intended.

However, it is less obvious how this deals with **German**. After all, does the protagonist's trust in the old German man not constitute part of the interpretative base for their judgement? Is the assumption that the old German man was speaking truthfully not part of the basis upon which they reach their judgement? If so, then our anti-luck condition will fail in **German** as well. And that would be problematic. After all, **German** appears to be a case of understanding.

The solution is to carefully delimit exactly which factors are to be included in the interpretative base to which we relativize our anti-luck condition. Should we only include the immediate information drawn upon by the hearer—i.e.

information about word meaning, and judgements about context, etc.? Or should we go further back, and include information about how these judgements regarding context and word meaning were reached?

When we are thinking about knowledge-yielding communication (i.e. the communicative preconditions for the acquisition of testimonial knowledge) it is quite clear that we ought to factor in this wider information. The protagonist in **German** does not, and cannot, gain testimonial knowledge when they are told, for example, that 'Die Krankenschwester ist nett'. Their belief will be luckily true. This is because the basis upon which they acquired their beliefs about word meaning (or, their schemas for application of word meaning in context) was unreliable.

However, as **German** shows, there can be cases of understanding without knowledge-yielding communication. So, it is not obvious that we must factor in this information when assessing whether a hearer has understood an utterance. Rather, I suggest that understanding has a weaker local anti-luck condition: there must be no nearby worlds in which the speaker produces a relevantly similar utterance and the audience's judgement has the same 'direct basis' in which they fail to recover what is said. The direct basis of an audience's judgement regarding what is said will include factors such as their beliefs (or schemas) regarding word meaning, together with the beliefs about context upon which their judgement (i.e. their state of comprehension) is based. It will not include the processes that gave rise to these beliefs about context and word meaning.

In **Loar** and **Hospital** even this weak local anti-luck condition fails: even if we just hold fixed the direct basis of the hearer's judgements, they could easily have been led astray. However, this weak local anti-luck condition is satisfied in **German**: the direct basis for the hearer's judgement did not include any information about the old man. It merely included beliefs such as 'Krankenschwester' means nurse. There were no nearby worlds at which the hearer reached their judgement on such a basis and nonetheless failed to coordinate with the speaker. Thus, I suggest we can resolve our puzzle by requiring that understanding merely satisfy this weaker anti-luck condition.

It is important to note that this form of local reliability is too weak, by itself, to support knowledge of what is said, or testimonial knowledge. When our protagonist first heard 'Die Krankenschwester ist nett' they understood what was said. However, they were not in a position to know what was said and were not in a position to gain testimonial knowledge. So, the considerations adduced so far suggest the following:

1. In normal circumstances understanding yields a safe veridical judgement about what is said—a judgement reliable enough to support knowledge of what is said, and testimonial knowledge.
2. In all circumstances understanding satisfies a weaker local anti-luck condition. However, this condition is not by itself strong enough to support knowledge of what is said, or testimonial knowledge.

This view fits the data nicely. However, it may appear somewhat *ad hoc*. It is natural to wonder at this point why understanding should have an anti-luck condition, especially the specific anti-luck condition I have outlined here. This worry naturally leads on to a deeper challenge for **Reliable Recovery**.

5. Luck and the Value of Understanding

There is a long standing question in epistemology regarding the value of knowledge. Traditionally this problem has been thought of in terms of the value of knowledge over true belief. However, since the emergence of the Gettier problem, focus has shifted to the question of what makes knowledge more valuable than justified true belief. That is, what does the reliability or anti-luck condition add to knowledge? Why is it better to be in a state that satisfies the anti-luck condition than an otherwise identical state that does not?

Linda Zagzebski (2003) nicely illustrates the problem with the following analogy: Suppose we have two coffee machines. One reliably produces great coffee. The other hardly ever produces great coffee. However, on this one occasion, both machines have produced identical cups of coffee. Is the cup of coffee produced by the reliable coffee machine better, just because of the reliability of its source, than the otherwise great cup of coffee luckily produced by the unreliable coffee machine? It is not clear why it would be. So, why should we consider a reliably produced justified true belief to be any more valuable than an unreliably produced justified true belief?

Megan Hyska (2018, forthcoming) has recently argued that a similar problem arises for understanding. Hyska agrees that understanding must satisfy a local anti-luck condition. However, she observes, it is not clear what value this anti-luck condition could add over and above the other conditions on understanding. Other than the reliability requirement, Hyska (2018) thinks of understanding in a broadly Gricean manner, formulated as follows:

An audience understands an utterance (or intentional signal) that p just in case:

1. she entertains that p

2. (a) she entertains that p because of the signal, and (b) it is manifest to her that the speaker intended the signal to cause her to entertain that p.

3. p is (consistent with) the content the speaker intended to get across with the signal. (Hyska 2018: 56–7; cf. Grice 1957)

Why, she asks, would it be better to satisfy these conditions in a reliable or non-lucky way than it would be to do so in an unreliable or lucky way? What does reliability add to the end product?

It might seem that there is a clear answer to Hyska's worry: as observed from the outset, understanding typically supports the acquisition of testimonial knowledge. Usually, when one understands an utterance, this will put one in a position to gain testimonial knowledge (as long as the speaker is reliable and sincere, etc.). If understanding was not necessarily reliable, then it would not be capable of supporting the acquisition of testimonial knowledge. So, assuming that knowledge is valuable, we should be able to resolve the value challenge for understanding.

However, the matter is not so simple. First, as we have already seen, although understanding must be locally reliable, satisfaction of this local reliability condition is not sufficient for knowledge (although it is necessary). Secondly, this answer would render the value of understanding purely epistemic. Yet, Hyska would argue, understanding is a 'signaling achievement'—a communicative achievement, not a purely epistemic achievement.[11]

It is clear that communication often yields knowledge. This is part of why communication matters to us. The spread of knowledge is, in an important sense, one of the functions of communication. However, it is not clear that the *fundamental* goal—the telos of communication—is knowledge acquisition. After all, communication can clearly succeed without knowledge being gained. This is what we saw with **German**: communication was successful, yet the audience was neither in a position to gain testimonial knowledge nor to gain knowledge of what is said.

This is not the place to settle the question of the fundamental goal of communication.[12] I don't think we have to answer this question in order to answer the question of what value is added by reliability.

6. Luck, Credit, and Value

One of the most promising responses to the epistemic value problem comes from virtue epistemology.[13] Virtue epistemologists suggest that knowledge is an achievement—it is something for which we deserve credit. The basic idea is that we can normatively appraise goal directed performances in the following ways:

Success: Does the activity achieve its goal?

Competence: Is the performance produced by an ability to achieve success relative to the goal?

---

[11] Hyska (2018: 78) suggests that the signalling domain is the 'proprietary domain of the value of communication'. She argues that it is, like the epistemic domain, goal directed. But unlike the epistemic domain, the goal is not truth, but rather information transfer.

[12] Although I am sympathetic to Jessica Keiser's (forthcoming) suggestion that the goal of communication is to direct attention. Hyska's suggestion is that communication aims at the transfer of information.

[13] See Sosa (1991, 2011, 2015); Zagzebski (1996); Greco (1999, 2000, 2010); Kelp (2011, 2016, 2019).

Aptness: Is the performance successful in virtue of the agent's competence? (Cf. Sosa 2007)

Ability is standardly thought of as requiring a reliable disposition to succeed at the task in hand. It can also be thought of in terms of the possession of a way of achieving the end that, if employed, would reliably yield success. An agent deserves credit for their success only when their performance is apt. Consider archery: the goal of archery is to hit the target. However, one can achieve success at this practice without deserving credit for it:

Beginner Luck: Suppose a first time archer with absolutely no skill or knowledge of archery hits the target. They succeed in their aim. However, their success is due to luck.

Skilled Luck: Suppose a highly skilled archer fires at the target. Their perform-ance is competent: it is produced by a reliable ability to hit the target in normal conditions. However, conditions are not normal. First, a gust of wind blows the arrow off target. Then another surprise gust of wind blows it back on target. As a result, the target is struck. Although the archer succeeded in hitting the target, and although their performance was competent, their success was due to luck, as their success was not explained by their ability. (Cf. Sosa 2007)

In both cases the goal was achieved in a lucky way. As a result, the performances were not apt, and the agents don't deserve credit for their success. Had the second archer's success been explained by their ability at archery then their success would not have been lucky, and their shot would have been creditworthy.

Skilled Luck is analogous in structure to standard Gettier cases. In Gettier cases an agent competently forms a true belief. The practice of believing aims at truth. So, the agent is successful. However, their success is not due to their competence, so they do not deserve credit for their success.

This provides a natural response to the value problem for knowledge: know-ledge is better than Gettiered true belief because, when a belief is Gettiered, the believer does not deserve credit for their success. Perhaps we could think of the value of understanding similarly? Here are the ways we might assess an audience in a communicative exchange:

Success: Has the audience successfully recovered the intended message?

Competence: Is their state of entertaining a particular proposition produced by an ability to recover intended messages?

Aptness: Is the audience's recovery of the intended message explained by their ability to recover intended messages?

By maintaining that understanding must be apt we are able to explain the value of understanding: it is an achievement, something for which we deserve credit. We are also able to explain why understanding is incompatible with luck: credit-worthiness is inconsistent with luck. Moreover, we are able to explain these matters without making the value of understanding epistemic. Understanding can be thought of as an achievement in the signalling domain.

Unfortunately, the credit approach to the value of understanding faces some major challenges. In order to deal with standard Gettier cases in epistemology the credit theorist has to maintain that the subject's cognitive abilities are the most salient explanatory factor in producing their success (Greco 2003). After all, in typical Gettier cases the subject's cognitive abilities still play *some* role in explaining their success. For example, in typical Gettier cases the subject will employ their perceptual abilities, or their reasoning abilities. The same is true of the communicative credit theory: in order to properly deal with standard Loar cases it has to be maintained that the hearer's abilities are the most salient explanatory factor in their successful recovery of the speaker's intended message. After all, the audience's abilities still play some small role in these cases. For example, the audience's knowledge of the English language, and their general ability to infer what a speaker means by a use of 'that' on the basis of their contextual knowledge both play important roles in Loar's original case. This gives rise to two problems.

First, in typical communicative exchanges the speaker's abilities will be just as important as the hearer's in explaining the success of the communicative exchange. So, if understanding requires that the audience's abilities be the most salient explanatory factor, understanding will rarely be achieved.[14] Secondly, there look to be cases of understanding in which some factor other than either the hearer's or the speaker's abilities is most salient in explaining the audience's success. For example, in **German** the most salient factor in explaining the audience's success is the lucky manner in which they formed their true belief about the meaning of 'Krankenschwester'. Yet this is still a case of understanding.

Indeed, **German** seems to create a general problem for attempts to provide a unified response to the value problems for knowledge and understanding. The problem as it applies to the credit theory is as follows: In **German** the audience understands the speaker, but they are not in a position to know what the speaker has said. If the audience's abilities were sufficiently explanatorily central for them to deserve credit for their successful recovery of the speaker's intended meaning, then they would also be sufficiently explanatorily central for them to deserve credit for their accurate belief regarding the speaker's intended meaning. But if

---

[14] A parallel problem is raised by Lackey (2007) for the credit view of knowledge: in typical testimonial exchanges the speaker deserves as much or more credit for the audience's belief than the audience. There are many responses to this objection, and some of them may carry over to the credit theory of understanding. So I do not want to place too much weight on this objection.

this was the case then they would be in a position to know what was said. Yet, they are not in a position to know what was said. So, the credit approach can't explain both the value of knowledge and the value of understanding.

This point seems to generalize. Any attempt to port over our favoured response to the value problem for knowledge to the value problem for communication will have to contend with the fact that in **German** the subject understands but is not in a position to know what has been said. Suppose that we say that knowledge is valuable because it has some feature F. We would have to say that understanding is valuable due to its possessing F or some closely related feature F^*. Since the subject in **German** is not in a position to know what has been said we will have to deny that their judgement that 'S said that p' has feature F. But since they do understand the utterance it looks like we will have to say that their entertaining of p does possess F, or some closely related feature F^*. This suggests that it will be difficult to find parallel solutions to the value problems for knowledge and communication.

Hyska (forthcoming) frames her challenge as follows: 'understanding bears a relationship to knowledge such that skepticism about the value of knowledge suggests a skepticism about the value of communication' (p. 9). But the considerations raised above suggest that the challenge is more general. Even if we are not sceptics about the value of knowledge there are grounds to worry about the value of understanding.

In the final sections of this chapter, I will explore two alternative ways of responding to the value problem for understanding. I will suggest some problems for the first approach (although these problems are by no means decisive), and I will tentatively endorse the second approach.

7. Representational Calibration

What is the main difference between **Loar** and **German**? Well, in both cases there is a clear sense in which the audience could easily have been led into error. And in neither case is the hearer's success an achievement (at least, not in the sense in which knowledge is often thought to be an achievement). Rather, the difference seems to be that in **Loar**, but not in **German**, the direct basis of the audience's interpretation could easily have led them to error.

In light of this, the following line of reasoning suggests itself: the value of understanding resides at least in part in the relationship between the direct basis of the audience's interpretation and the relevant utterance. But how could the value of understanding derive from this relationship? Here is a suggestion: When we communicate we aim to align our means of representation to those of our community. Successful understanding manifests the calibration of our interpretative mechanisms to our linguistic environment. That is, it manifests the alignment of our means of representation to our community.

This would explain the difference between **Loar** and **German**: In **Loar** the audience's successful interpretation of the speaker does not manifest the calibration of their interpretative mechanisms to their communicative environment. After all, given the direct basis of their interpretation they could easily have gone wrong. However, in **German** the subject's interpretative mechanisms are well attuned to their environment, and their successful recovery of the speaker's intended meaning manifested that fact. This seems promising. However, it immediately raises a new question: Why would such calibration be among the aims of linguistic communication? Why would we not simply aim at, say, information transfer?

There are a few possible answers here. It could be, for example, that there is some special value in our means of representation being calibrated to linguistic practices that go back generations, and that are in some sense definitive of the communities of which we are members. A somewhat less nebulous answer can be found by examining an analogous question regarding epistemic evaluations.

Sinan Dogramaci (2012) observes that we have a practice of negatively appraising certain acts of belief formation even when they reliably track the truth. And we have a practice of praising certain acts of belief formation even when they fail to reliably track the truth. This is puzzling. After all, we aim to form true beliefs. If a method of belief formation reliably yields true beliefs for a subject, then why not hold it in high esteem?

Dogramaci's answer is that we use evaluations such as 'rational' or 'irrational' to influence others' behaviour. When we credit someone with rationality we re-enforce their behaviour. When we criticize someone as irrational, we do the opposite. In doing so, we pressure others to adopt the same patterns of reasoning that we employ. This in turn promotes the coordination of epistemic rules employed within a community. This coordination is desirable, according to Dogramaci, because it allows us to treat others as epistemic surrogates, and thus defer to them unproblematically.

Our question is similar to Dogramaci's. If an audience correctly grasps the proposition the speaker intends to communicate, then why would it matter how they got there? Why do we attribute understanding (a positive evaluation of their performance) only when the audience's success results from the calibration of their means of representation to their linguistic environment? Well, a natural response, following Dogramaci, is that in doing so we re-enforce their behaviour. Our practice of positively evaluating instances of successful coordination specifically when they arise from the calibration of the audience's means of representation to their linguistic environment promotes the calibration of means of representation within the linguistic community. And this, of course, is good for the community in general: it supports smooth successful communication within the community at large.

This response appears promising. Unfortunately, this appearance is deceptive. We are trying to explain why it is better for the various conditions on understanding to be satisfied in a non-lucky way. The suggestion is that when we communicate, we aim for our coordination to manifest the calibration of our means of representation to our environment. And this is supposed to be a good thing to aim for because it promotes the calibration of representational devices within the community. However, if this is right, it is not clear why we would attribute understanding only when our coordination *manifests* the calibration of our means of representation to our environment. Why not attribute understanding whenever the following conjunctive condition is satisfied: (1) The hearer accurately recovers the speaker's intended proposition, and (2) the hearer's means of representation are calibrated to their linguistic environment? This would promote the coordination of means of representation just as well. However, it would also lead to attributions of understanding in cases like **Loar**. After all, **Loar** is the communicative equivalent of a Gettier case. It is a case in which the audience is both successful and skillful. Moreover, their abilities are underwritten by the calibration of their means of representation to their linguistic environment. Jones employs his typically reliable abilities to recover the proposition intended by Smith. However, his success does not manifest his ability. Likewise, it doesn't manifest the calibration of his means of representation to his linguistic environment.

So, the least nebulous way of making sense of the representational calibration response quickly runs into problems. Perhaps these problems can be overcome, or perhaps there are other more promising ways of developing this strategy. But rather than exploring this possibility I'll close with what I consider to be a more promising alternative.

8. Intentional Coordination

So far, we have focused on analogies and disanalogies between communicative and epistemic luck. However, luck also plays a central role in the theory of intentional action: if an agent *s* with the intention of φing, but their φing was lucky, this will often render their action unintentional. Consider an example (Cf. Harman 1976):

> **Unintentional Fulfilment:** Tom intends to kill Pete. He starts driving to Pete's home with the intention of doing so, but on the way, he accidentally hits Pete with his car. Pete dies as a result.

Tom set off with the intention of killing Pete. Moreover, he did kill Pete. So, his intention was satisfied. However, he did not intentionally kill Pete. It was merely by luck that he ended up killing him.[15]

---

[15] Whilst I take this to be the standard interpretation of such cases, there are exceptions. Some, such as Harman (1976) and Roth (2000) hold that the subject's intention is not actually satisfied in such cases.

Communication is an intentional activity. Speakers have communicative intentions: intentions that their audience entertain certain propositions. Moreover, just like any other action, these intentions can be satisfied unintentionally. That is, a speaker's communicative intention can be satisfied (i.e. the hearer can entertain the intended proposition) without the speaker intentionally bringing it about that their intention is satisfied (i.e. without the speaker intentionally bringing it about that the audience entertain the intended proposition). This is just what happens in cases like **Loar**. Smith intended that Jones entertain the proposition that a particular man is a stockbroker. Jones did entertain this proposition. Yet Smith's success is lucky in a way that seems to render it unintentional. Smith did not intentionally bring it about that Jones entertain this proposition. **Loar** seems directly analogous to **Unintentional Fulfilment** in this sense.

So, the following possibility presents itself: we could maintain that an audience understands an utterance only when the speaker intentionally brings it about that they entertain the intended proposition. What about cases like **German** in which there seems to be lucky understanding? Is the speaker's success there intentional? Well, consider the following case:

> **Fire:** Yannick intends to start a fire. In order to start a fire, one must be in an oxygen rich environment. Unbeknownst to Yannick, he has entered an environment in which oxygen levels are typically very low, such that striking a match would not be sufficient to start a fire. However, luckily, and also unbeknownst to Yannick, some oxygen canisters have recently fallen out of a passing airplane and burst, leaking oxygen into his local environment and creating a small island in which the oxygen levels are very high. He lights his match and thereby starts a fire.

There is a clear sense in which Yannick's success is lucky. Nonetheless, his success was still intentional: he intentionally lit the match. What is distinctive about **Fire**? Well, in **Fire** the background conditions for success were established luckily. But once they were in place everything went as it should. Holding fixed the background conditions in **Fire** Yannick's success was not lucky. This sets **Fire** apart from both **Loar** and **Unintentional Fulfilment**. In both **Loar** and **Unintentional Fulfilment** luck intervenes in the process by which the intention is fulfilled. This seems to be inconsistent with intentional success.

Importantly, **German** is analogous in this respect to **Fire**, not to **Unintentional Fulfilment**: in **German** our protagonist is disposed to interpret 'Krankenschwester' as 'nurse'. Their interpretative mechanisms are, in this sense, calibrated to their linguistic environment. The audience's interpretative mechanisms being well calibrated in this way is a background condition against which we typically form our communicative intentions. So, in **German**, like in **Fire**, it is merely a matter of luck that the background conditions for success are satisfied. But holding the background conditions in **German** fixed, it was not lucky that the speaker was successful. So, in **German**, unlike **Loar**, the speaker intentionally brought it about that the audience entertain a particular proposition.

This is promising. Perhaps the value of understanding derives from the fact that understanding is a state intentionally brought about by a speaker. This would explain why it is bad for an audience to recover the speaker's intended proposition in a relevantly lucky way: when recovery occurs in a relevantly lucky way the speaker's success is unintentional. However, a new question immediately arises: why is it better for success to be intentional? In particular, why is it better for the *audience* if the *speaker* is intentionally successful rather than unintentionally successful?

A natural first thought here is that communication is a joint activity. The audience must do their part in interpreting the speaker. So, really, when they understand an utterance, it is not just the speaker's intentions that are satisfied: the audience's intentions (or, perhaps, their collective intentions) are satisfied too. Insofar as we care about our own successes being intentional, this would explain why it is better for the audience to understand the speaker, rather than satisfy all the other conditions on understanding minus the reliability condition.

I think there is a lot to be said for this approach, but I have some worries. First, it is still not entirely clear why it is better to succeed at an activity intentionally rather than unintentionally (unintentional success does not warrant credit, but it is not clear that all intentional successes warrant credit either). Secondly, and more importantly, it is not clear that communication is always a jointly intentional activity. In many paradigmatic cases of utterance understanding the audience is passive. They merely hear an utterance and, without exercising any agency, represent the speaker as having asserted some proposition. For example, if I hear the utterances of a loud passenger on the train, I can understand their utterances despite having no interest in (and perhaps a desire to avoid) doing so. In these cases, it seems odd to describe the audience's interpretative success as intentional. And it is especially odd to describe the interaction between speaker and hearer as jointly intentional. Yet, understanding occurs here just as it does in active conversation.

The aforementioned problems are by no means decisive. However, I believe a more promising approach is available: *ceteris paribus*, when an agent intentionally φs they bear a greater degree of responsibility for φ than when they unintentionally φ. Consider Tom and Pete in **Unintentional Fulfilment**: Tom was clearly responsible for killing Pete. However, had he killed Pete intentionally he would have borne a greater degree of responsibility for Pete's demise. We would consider him blameworthy to a higher degree. It is important to audiences that they be able to hold speakers responsible for the cognitive effects that utterances bring about (new beliefs, consideration of new questions, new plans, etc.). Indeed, the greater the degree of responsibility a speaker bears for the cognitive change their utterance brings about, the better this is for the audience. After all, the greater the degree of responsibility the speaker bears for the audience's cognitive change (e.g. their new belief) the less responsibility the audience bears. So, it will generally be better for the audience if the speaker intentionally brings it about that they entertain some particular proposition than if they unintentionally bring it about that they entertain that same proposition, even if the speaker intends that they entertain that proposition in both cases. If this is right, then we have a neat solution to the value problem for understanding.

9. Conclusion

In this chapter, I have done several things. I started by considering some reasons for and against the claim that utterance understanding must be reliable. There were two reasons for thinking understanding must be reliable. First, understanding typically yields knowledge of what is said, and it typically supports the acquisition of testimonial knowledge. Secondly, there looked to be cases ('Loar cases') in which the unreliability of the audience's judgement seemed to preclude them from understanding an utterance. However, there were also reasons to doubt that understanding had to be reliable: there looked to be cases of lucky understanding. On closer investigation these cases didn't reveal that understanding could be lucky, but they did help us delimit the exact sense in which luck precludes understanding. This set us up for the second half of the chapter in which I discussed the question of why it is better to understand than to satisfy all the other conditions of understanding in an unreliable way. I considered a number of solutions to this problem before tentatively endorsing the proposal that we understand only when a speaker intentionally brings it about that we entertain a particular content.[16]

References

Broncano-Berrocal, F. 2018. Purifying impure virtue epistemology. *Philosophical Studies* 175(2). 385–410.

Byrne, A., & Thau, M. 1996. In defense of the hybrid view. *Mind* 105(417). 139–49.

Campbell, J. 1982. Knowledge and understanding. *Philosophical Quarterly* 32(126). 17–34.

[16] I would like to thank Megan Hyska, my colleagues on Prof. Robbie Williams's GROUNDS project at the University of Leeds, and the audience at the (Mis)communication and Context workshop at the University of Tartu for comments and discussion that greatly improved the quality of this chapter and aided the development of the main thesis. This research was funded by the European Research Council (ERC) under the European Union's Horizon 2020 research and innovation programme (grant agreement no. 818633).

Davies, M. 1989. Tacit knowledge and subdoxastic states. In A. George (ed.), *Reflections on Chomsky* (pp. 131–52). Oxford: Basil Blackwell.

Dogramaci, S. 2012. Reverse engineering epistemic evaluations. *Philosophy and Phenomenological Research* 85(3). 513–30.

Dummett, M. 1978. Frege's distinction between sense and reference. In his *Truth and other Enigmas*. London: Duckworth.

Dummett, M. 1991. *The logical basis of metaphysics*. Cambridge, MA: Harvard University Press.

Evans, G. 1982. *The varieties of reference*. Oxford: Clarendon Press.

Fricker, E. 2003. Understanding and knowledge of what is said. In A. Barber (ed.), *Epistemology of language* (pp. 325–66). Oxford: Oxford University Press.

Goldman, A. 1986. *Epistemology and cognition*. Cambridge, MA: Harvard University Press.

Graham, P. 2016. Against actual world reliabilism: Epistemically correct procedures, reliably true outcomes. In Angel Fernandez Vargas (ed.) *Performance epistemology: Foundations and applications*. Oxford: Oxford University Press.

Graham, P. 2017. Normal circumstances reliabilism: Goldman on reliability and justified belief. *Philosophical Topics* 45(1). 33–61.

Greco, J. 1999. Agent reliablism. *Philosophical Perspectives* 33(25). 273–96.

Greco, J. 2000. Putting skeptics in their place: The nature of skeptical arguments and their Role. In *Philosophical inquiry*. Cambridge: Cambridge University Press.

Greco, J. 2003. Knowledge as credit for true belief. In M. DePaul & L. Zagzebski (eds.) *Intellectual virtue: Perspectives from ethics and epistemology* (pp. 111–34). Oxford: Oxford University Press.

Greco, J. 2010. *Achieving knowledge*. Cambridge: Cambridge University Press.

Grice, H. P. 1957. Meaning. *Philosophical Review* 66. 377–88.

Harman, G. 1976. Practical reasoning. *Review of Metaphysics* 29(3). 431–63.

Heck, R. K. 1995. A sense of communication. *Mind* 104(413). 79–106.

Higginbotham, J. 1992. Truth and understanding. *Philosophical Studies* 65. 3–16.

Hunter, D. 1998. Understanding and belief. *Philosophy and Phenomenological Research* 58(3). 559–80.

Hyska, M. 2018. 'This machine kills fascists: detecting propaganda with formal models of mass discourse structure (and other ideas).' University of Texas at Austin PhD Thesis.

Hyska, M. Forthcoming. Luck and the value of communication. *Synthese*.

Keiser, J. Forthcoming. Language without information exchange. *Mind and Language*.

Kelp, C. 2011. In defense of virtue epistemology. *Synthese* 179. 409–33.

Kelp, C. 2016. Justified belief: Knowledge first-style. *Philosophy and Phenomenological Research* 93. 79–100.

Kelp, C. 2019. How to be a reliabilist. *Philosophy and Phenomenological Research* 98(2). 346–74.

Kvanvig, J. 2003. *The value of knowledge and the pursuit of understanding*. Cambridge: Cambridge University Press.

Lackey, J. 2007. Why we don't deserve credit for everything we know. *Synthese* 158(3). 345–36.

Lackey, J. 2008. What luck is not. *Australasian Journal of Philosophy* 86(2). 255–67.

Leplin, J. 2007. In defence of reliabilism. *Philosophical Studies* 134. 31–42.

Loar, B. 1976. The semantics of singular terms. *Philosophical Studies* 30(6). 353–77.

Longworth, G. 2008. Linguistic understanding and knowledge. *Nous* 42. 50–79.

Longworth, G. 2009. Some models of linguistic understanding. *Baltic International Yearbook of Cognition, Logic, and Communication* 5(26). 1–56.

Longworth, G. 2018. Understanding what is said. *Synthese* 195. 815–34.

McDowell, J. 1994. Knowledge by hearsay. In B. K. Matilal & A. Chakrabarti (eds.), *Knowing from words: Western and Indian philosophical analyses of understanding and testimony* (pp. 195–224). Dordrecht: Kluwer. (Reprinted in his 1998: 414–43.)

Nozick, R. 1982. *Philosophical explorations*. Cambridge, MA: Harvard University Press.

Peet, A. 2018. Testimonial knowledge without knowledge of what is said. *Pacific Philosophical Quarterly* 99(1). 65–81.

Peet, A. 2019. Knowledge-yielding communication. *Philosophical Studies* 176. 3303–27.

Peet, A. Forthcoming. Assertoric content, responsibility, and metasemantics. *Mind and Language*.

Pettit, D. 2002. Why knowledge is unnecessary for understanding language. *Mind* 111(3). 519–50.

Pollock, J. Forthcoming. Content internalism and testimonial knowledge. *Inquiry* 1–22.

Pritchard, D. 2005. *Epistemic luck*. Oxford: Oxford University Press.

Roth, A. S. 2000. The self referentiality of intentions. *Philosophical Studies* 97. 11–52.

Smith, M. 2016. *Between probability and certainty: What justifies belief*. Oxford: Oxford University Press.

Sosa, E. 1991. *Knowledge in perspective: Selected essays in epistemology*. Cambridge: Cambridge University Press.

Sosa, E. 1999. How to defeat opposition to Moore. *Philosophical Perspectives* 13. 137–49.

Sosa, E. 2007. *A Virtue Epistemology: Apt Belief and Reflective Knowledge, Volume 1*. Oxford: Oxford University Press.

Sosa, E. 2010. How competence matters in epistemology. *Philosophical Perspectives*. 24. 465–75.

Sosa, E. 2011. *Knowing full-well*. Princeton, NJ: Princeton University Press.

Sosa, E. 2015. *Judgment and agency.* Oxford: Oxford University Press.

Williamson, T. 2000. *Knowledge and its limits.* Oxford: Oxford University Press.

Zagzebski, L. 1996. *Virtues of the mind: An inquiry into the nature of virtue and the ethical foundations of knowledge.* Cambridge: Cambridge University Press.

Zagzebski, L. 2003. The search for the source of epistemic good. *Metaphilosophy* 34(1/2). 12–28.

11

Luck-Reducing Features of
Lexical Innovation

Samia Hesni

1. Introduction: Lexical Innovation

About halfway into Ingmar Bergman's 1948 film *Port of Call*, a sailor named Gösta responds to a setback by yelling, hurling some chairs across the room, smashing bottles, and overturning a table. He is having what we might call a "mantrum." Whether or not this word I have just introduced makes its way into public discourse will depend on a number of linguistic and social factors, but what I have done is an instance of *lexical innovation*: using a novel expression to communicate successfully. As Josh Armstrong (2016) puts it, lexical innovation involves "cases in which a speaker uses a sentence containing a novel expression-meaning pair, but nevertheless successfully communicates her intended meaning to her audience" (p. 87). I have introduced a new expression: *mantrum*. Its meaning, roughly, is that thing that happens when a man has a tantrum.[1]

Lexical innovation is not restricted to portmanteaus like the one above. Individuals lexically innovate by using familiar words in new ways, such as Busta Rhymes's 2001:

(1)   I'm about to *Picasso* a new picture for you

and sentences like:

(2)   Bea managed to *houdini* her way out of her [prison] cell. (Armstrong 2016)

Lexical innovation can also occur when completely new words are introduced into a lexicon, as frequently happens in fantasy or science fiction:

---

[1] As it turns out, this term already exists in some lexicons, with the same meaning. See Gordon (2015), in an article for the parenting website mom.com: "10 Things to Do When Your Husband Has a Mantrum." Nevertheless, if you are unaware of this, I have engaged in lexical innovation in our particular context.

Samia Hesni, *Luck-Reducing Features of Lexical Innovation* In: *Linguistic Luck: Safeguards and Threats to Linguistic Communication*. Edited by: Abrol Fairweather and Carlos Montemayor, Oxford University Press.
© Oxford University Press 2023. DOI: 10.1093/oso/9780192845450.003.0011

(3) Nassun was in training to become a lorist. (Jemisin 2016)

or in a real-life scenario with technical or unfamiliar tools:

(4) Open the gasper above your airplane seat to increase ventilation.

The phenomenon of lexical innovation, in all its various iterations, was important to Donald Davidson because it showed, to him, that a fully conventionalized account of natural language like David Lewis's (1969, 1975) was inaccurate. According to Lewis, language can be understood as a series of regularities that occur among their users (Lewis 1969, 1975). Davidson challenged Lewis's view of conventionalized language by appealing to lexical innovation. We can and do often use completely novel and made-up expressions to communicate success-fully. So, according to Davidson, linguistic communication can't be fully or fundamentally conventional. Our ability to create new terms and new uses, absent from any convention, challenges a fully conventional account of semantics and communication. Elisabeth Camp (2016) distinguishes between two parts of Davidson's challenge to Lewis: the argument from misuse—speakers can com-municate successfully using the wrong words—and the argument from innovation—speakers can communicate successfully by using expressions in new ways:

> [First], given that speaker and hearer can still converge on a common interpret-ation despite their ignorance, conventional meaning appears to be irrelevant to successful communication. Second, Davidson appeals to cases of 'sheer inven-tion,' such as by authors like James Joyce and Lewis Carroll: since words like 'mimsy' and 'aventried' lack any conventional meaning, it seems obvious that convention can be neither sufficient nor necessary for determining the meaning they do have.   (Camp 2016, p. 115)

Davidson's argument rests on observing different kinds of language use, none of which involve convention, all of which result in successful communication. First are malapropisms, in which a speaker says the wrong word s, intending to communicate x, and the hearer correctly understands the speaker as saying x.[2] On the hearer's part, "the hearer realizes that the 'standard' interpretation cannot be the intended interpretation... The absurdity or inappropriateness of what the speaker would have meant had his words been taken in the 'standard' way alerts the hearer to trickery or error..." (Davidson 1986/2006, p. 252). He goes on:

---

[2] "a malapropism does not have to be amusing or surprising. It does not have to be based on a cliche, and of course it does not have to be intentional" (Davidson 1986/2006, p. 251).

> Malapropisms introduce expressions not covered by prior learning, or familiar expressions which cannot be interpreted by any of the abilities so far discussed. Malapropisms fall into a different category, one that may include such things as our ability to perceive a well-formed sentence when the actual utterance was incomplete or grammatically garbled, our ability to interpret words we have never heard before, to correct slips of the tongue, or to cope with new idiolects.
>
> (p. 255)

A slip of the tongue often won't prevent someone from communicating what they intend, yet conventional meaning is not at play when a hearer correctly interprets a speaker despite the speaker's slip-up. And since there is nothing conventional about malapropisms, conventions can't be the whole story.

Then there is "sheer invention," or the creation of new terms with new meanings, none of which is attached to any previous conventional meaning. According to Davidson, our ability to interpret writers like James Joyce and Lewis Carroll when they use new words establishes "the theoretical irrelevance of conventional meaning" (Camp 2016, p. 116).

Several philosophers have tried to reconcile the phenomenon of lexical innovation with a conventionalized view of language (Armstrong 2016; Camp 2016; Lepore and Stone 2018). Armstrong uses cases of linguistic innovation to motivate a dynamic account of linguistic conventions. On his view, conventionalism can be consistent with the presence of linguistic innovation, so long as we understand linguistic conventions to be *dynamic*: able to rapidly adapt and shift to accommodate new expressions, or to be "revised to shift the meanings of expressions already in circulation" (Armstrong 2016, p. 88). Camp proposes a moderate form of conventionalism that accounts for Davidson's insights without being threatened by them. Lepore and Stone argue that many cases of linguistic innovation and neologism are in fact conventional.

This chapter gives two arguments in defense of a Davidsonian view. The first defends Davidson's objection from a particular line of argument that suggests that linguistic innovation itself can be conventionalized (Camp 2016; Lepore and Stone 2018). The second argument is more particular: it grants that even if some cases of lexical innovation are conventionalized (as Armstrong 2016 argues), it is harder to make the same case for neologisms. Given that my view leaves open the possibility that lexical innovation itself is not entirely conventionalized, I end by considering the question: if lexical innovation is not conventional, then can it avoid being entirely luck-dependent? The beginnings of an answer come from analyzing case studies about the rise of the neologisms 'mansplaining' and 'manspreading' in the early 2010s.

I take it for granted (following Davidson 1986/2006; Camp 2016; Armstrong 2016; and others) that lexical innovation happens and that it challenges a *static* conventionalized view of language. My aims here are to (a) delve a bit deeper into the mechanisms of lexical innovation; (b) argue that some kinds of linguistic innovation cannot be conventional; and (c) explore why and how different kinds of innovation become incorporated into a common lexicon (or, how they "stick"), and how much of this is luck-dependent.

In doing so, this chapter explores the difference between two kinds of lexical innovation: (i) lexical innovation as it pertains to lexical items that are already in use in a given linguistic community (for example, the evolution of the term 'unicorn' to indicate a special person or thing; or using 'Picasso' as a verb); and (ii) lexical innovation that involves the creation of new linguistic items (like the word 'qweet' being used to denote something that is both cute and sweet).[3] I evaluate whether there is a tension between treating the two the same way.[4]

2. Conventionalism and Innovation

According to Armstrong (2016), we *can* give a systematic (dynamic) framework for understanding lexical innovation. This dynamic framework relies on familiar notions of update and accommodation. When faced with an unfamiliar linguistic expression, a hearer "looks to the common ground for an entity appropriate to an expression of that lexical category" (p. 107). Then, the hearer accommodates the expression by affixing it to the entity that best matches the expression given the context.

At this point we should ask what kind of entity Armstrong is referring to and what it is for an entity to be in the common ground. Here is what he has in mind: the common ground is a structure "consisting of a context set, a set of questions under discussion, and an attention state" (p. 107). The context set is a familiar notion: the set of possible worlds compatible with what the discourse participants have said or believe or accept as true. Questions under discussion are also familiar: the context set is divided, roughly, into possible answers to various questions. The attention state is a less familiar feature of common ground: it "specifies a class of entities in a shared perceptual space among the discourse participants" (p. 107). Here is how a common ground model that includes an attention state differs from a common ground that doesn't. Suppose we are walking through an arboretum and admiring the various trees. A common ground model that doesn't include an attention state (say, that consists just of a context set and a set of questions under discussion) will include propositions like "there are beautiful trees here," whereas

<hr>

[3] I thank Jody Azzouni and Mercedes Corredor, respectively, for these two examples.

[4] According to Armstrong, a similar mechanism is going on when we accommodate linguistic innovation of types (i) and (ii). Armstrong proposes a dynamic account of linguistic conventions, motivated by cases of linguistic innovation. He gives an explanation of the mechanism of linguistic innovation as a process of updating the common ground (following Robert Stalnaker 2002 and Craige Roberts 1996, 2004).

a common ground model that includes an attention state will actually include the trees themselves.[5]

When an instance of lexical innovation occurs, for Armstrong, the lexicon of the speakers in the context expands to incorporate the new term-meaning pair. In his example of a postal worker saying:

(5)   Let me measure your package with a koba.

the communal lexicon gets updated once the hearer realizes that the postal attendant is describing a tool that is in the attention state of the common ground, since they can both observe the koba.

> Although this expression was not part of the communal lexicon shared by you and the attendant before your communicative exchange, the attendant's utterance served to update your communal lexicon with a new expression-meaning pair…In these cases, we can say that the innovative use of an expression has resulted in a *lexical expansion* of the language.   (pp. 100–1)

This allows us to establish *new conventions*, and thus a dynamic conventionalism accounts for the successful instance of linguistic innovation. Examples (1) and (2) involve a different kind of conventionalism:

(1) I'm about to *Picasso* a new picture for you;
(2) Bea managed to *houdini* her way out of her [prison] cell.

The second way in which conventions are part of lexical innovation, for Armstrong, is the way in which *background conventions* come into play with certain innovations. For cases like (1) and (2), background conventions and linguistic and social knowledge about Houdini, Picasso, and the use of felicitously turning nouns into verbs all contribute to successful recovery of the innovation:

> the semantic changes in question require a kind of accommodation on the part of audience members. If the audience members do not accommodate the lexical innovation—either because they cannot identify the meaning of the innovation or because they can identify the meaning but reject it—then no update to the background conventions will occur.   (p. 103)

So, in addition to the creation of new conventions, *background conventions* also help us to determine what's going on with linguistic innovation.

---

[5] A model of common ground that doesn't include an attention state might still include the trees themselves insofar as they are included in the possible worlds in the context set, but a model of common ground that includes an attention state would include the trees directly.

Lepore and Stone (2018) say something similar. In their investigation of lexical innovation, they argue that Davidson's motivating cases *do not* in fact involve improvised meaning. They use a central case of the evolution of the term 'bromance' to show the central role that convention plays in meaning change and lexical innovation. Their argument, roughly, is that in cases of malapropisms and neologisms, something *non-arbitrary* must determine how a hearer arrives at the correct (intended) interpretation, despite the speaker doing something unusual with their words. True improvisation, according to Lepore and Stone, is in tension with a non-arbitrary correct interpretation. And so, what is going on is some kind of conventionalism. Here is their argument in more detail:

> The term 'bromance' was "first used by Dave Carnie in the 1990s in an article in his street skating magazine *Big Brother* in recognition of the fact that skaters who spend a lot of time together related to one another with a mix of trust, intimacy, and affection. (Lepore and Stone 2018, p. 13)

As Lepore and Stone point out, the extension of 'bromance' now extends well beyond the skater community. This evolution should be surprising to a Davidsonian, who would ordinarily resolve the meaning of a new term by pointing to the speaker's intention. But 'bromance' and many other neologisms evolve and take on their own meanings as they enter the common lexicon.

> Once the community acknowledges that bromance is a thing, then the community as a whole is implicated in settling what bromance is, in triangulating its nature and delimitations, through processes of discovery ... in a way that accords with their experiences and values. The original speaker, who understood and named the phenomenon, just offers the starting point. In fact, the process can, and often does, lead retrospectively to an understanding of the meaning that *could not have been* attributed correctly to the original speaker.
>
> (p. 14; emphasis added)

The 'bromance' example challenges a Davidsonian objection to conventionalism in three ways. First, it shows that speaker intention is not an integral part of neologism acceptance, which is a counterexample to Davidson's thesis. Second, the evolution and understanding of the term *bromance* rests on background conventions and linguistic knowledge about the terms 'romance' and 'bro', and what it might mean to combine them. Third, and in line with Armstrong's arguments, Lepore and Stone show that 'bromance' has successfully become part of the cultural lexicon. And as such, it is now conventionalized in language. I agree with Lepore and Stone that these three challenges to Davidson's account are successful. However, Lepore and Stone take it that cases like these generalize. In the next section, I give an argument against this generalization.

3. Innovation without Convention

3.1. Short-Lived Innovations

Lepore and Stone are right that cases like the introduction and evolution of the term 'bromance' involve conventions. There is a history that can be traced from the term's origin to its current popular usage, including (as they note) a split between the intentions of the term's originator and its current meaning. I take it that Lepore and Stone have successfully shown that *some* cases of lexical innovation can be conventionalized.

But I am more interested in what is happening in the specific moment where the innovation is occurring, as was Davidson's original interest. An analogy to innovation in other contexts is useful here. Jazz music, especially before recordings, is famously improvisational. Musicians play a base chord pattern, and perhaps a standard melody, and then a soloist improvises over those chords and the melody: often they use alternate notes, rhythms, sometimes changing tempo, sometimes introducing themes from elsewhere in the piece, or other pieces entirely. Once recordings came along, certain solos did *become conventionalized* (or 'codified').[6] It is now standard for musicians to (a) recognize and (b) learn to play particular solos, like Miles Davis's *So What?*. So there is now a sense in which that specific solo has become part of the musical lexicon of jazz musicians and aficionados. The solo *eventually* gets conventionalized, but at some point, at first introduction, it was an innovation. And if we were arguing over whether music was fully conventionalized, that innovation would show that it wasn't.

So, to return to lexical language: I'd like to focus on instances of a new word-meaning pair that in the moment is spontaneous and innovative, but cease to become part of our conventionalized lexicon down the line. I think (with Davidson) that this is a common part of language usage, and offer the following example:

Bear or Dog

You and I are on a hike, and we come across some dark, dried scat. This is very exciting, because it might indicate bear presence in the area. I point to it and ask, "is it bear?—or just dog?" You say, "I don't think it's dog, it's really dark and fibrous." I'm convinced: "Good point, it must be bear!"

That's the end of our conversation. It's clear to both of us that we're not talking about actual bears or dogs, and there is no prior established convention of calling

---

[6] As an aside: there was a long and controversial debate over whether to record jazz solos for this very reason. See Porter 1985, Solis 2004, and Berliner (2009) for some histories and ethnomusicographies of jazz recordings and solo improvisations.

any particular scat by its originating animal's name. But maybe I want to be polite, or mindful of the fact that you're eating a snack, or I'm feeling a bit playful and want to emphasize the bear and not its dropping. Either way, I've done something innovative: I've introduced a new expression-meaning pair. And you've picked up on it easily.[7] Unlike *bromance*, it's not going to stick. Later that day when we're walking the dog and I hand you a poop bag, I don't ask you to pick up 'the dog'. Contra Lepore and Stone and Armstrong, the innovation has not made it into our lexicon, nor has it become conventionalized. Yet, it was successful.

This example generalizes. Any instance of a one-off usage of a new meaning-expression pair that does not eventually make its way permanently into a lexicon is an instance of non-conventionalized lexical innovation. A possible objection to this argument is that in the example I gave, the innovation is locally conventionalized: in the few sentences during which I introduced 'bear' and 'dog' as new terminology (by pointing, or by taking advantage of the fact that the object of discussion is in the common ground via our shared attention states), we developed a new, short-lived convention of using animal terms to refer to their fecal matter.[8] I think we can respond by just imagining that the observation didn't develop into a full-fledged conversation. Suppose that after I asked "is it bear, or just dog?" you said "I don't know," and changed the subject. I've still successfully communicated my question to you using a new expression-meaning pair, you have understood me, and we have not developed any new conventions around the term. In fact, as I mentioned earlier, it would be strange to try to resume this nomenclature pattern in a different setting (like when walking the dog).

Some innovations aren't meant to be around forever—or even longer than a few seconds. There's a temporal gap between successful interpretation (what Armstrong calls 'recovery') and entry into a lexicon (like *bromance*). What happens in that case need not involve convention; but it does involve successful communication using novel term-meaning pairs.

3.2. Unusual Objects

Armstrong's (2016) account of dynamic conventions differs slightly from Lepore and Stone's. While they are interested in what happens *after* a neologism becomes conventionalized, Armstrong also discusses the ways in which interpretation can itself be convention: for example, by drawing on preexisting conventions around language use and linguistic knowledge. In his example:

---

[7] One might suspect that this example is an instance of synechdoche, where a part of the object is standing in for the whole. To this worry, we can amend the example to one where we are pointing out animal tracks (although this might be conventionalized in some circles) or scratches on tree bark. I thank Elizabeth Fricker for this point.

[8] This objection is in keeping with Armstrong (2016) on localized conventions.

(2)   Bea managed to *houdini* her way out of her cell

familiarity with Houdini and with prison cells helps us understand that the speaker is telling us that Bea escaped from a prison cell, and probably impressively.

But not all cases of lexical innovation are going to be like this. It's more likely that new usages of preexisting terms and portmanteaus (or other neologisms that incorporate familiar words) will draw on this kind of conventionalism. Sentences like

(3)   Nassun was in training to become a lorist
(4)   Open the gasper above your airplane seat to increase ventilation

place the hearer on less familiar ground. That is, without knowing about lorists or gaspers antecedently, I'm not going to know what you mean by (3) or (4) without additional context. And crucially, that context need not be conventionalized. In the first case, I need to keep reading the fantasy novel to learn that a lorist is someone who studies the history and lore of stones. To learn what a gasper is, I might first watch you demonstrate opening yours, and then infer that my gasper is the small vent above my own seat.

I think this highlights a crucial distinction between lexical innovation of familiar and unfamiliar terms. I take familiar terms to encompass both preexisting terms used in new ways, and new twists on preexisting terms (such as portmanteaus and neologisms that involve identifiable old words). Perhaps Davidson erred in assuming that all lexical innovation could not be accounted for with conventionalism. But we should not then conclude that all (or most) instances of lexical innovation are conventionalized. We should recuperate some of Davidson's original insights that there are some kinds of lexical innovation that are purely unconventional.

Further work might examine the sorts of psychological states one has when encountering a new term versus new uses of an old one (like Bambini et al. 2013). Work on language acquisition will prove instructive here, as well as empirical work on the evolution of certain terms. In the next section, I examine some such empirical work.

4. What Makes Some Innovations Stick?

This section examines *anti-luck conditions* for lexical innovation.[9] What makes some lexical innovations, like 'bromance', persist, and others fall by the

---

[9] Thanks to Carlos Montemayor and Abrol Fairweather for suggesting this locution.

wayside?[10] Two questions about luck are relevant here: (1) If it's not convention that determines when and how linguistic innovation works its way into a lexicon, then is it luck? (2) If it's not convention that determines successful interpretation of a lexically innovative speaker by a hearer, then is it luck? This section will focus mostly on answering question (1), though I suspect that a Davidsonian answer to the second question is no. Our ability to glean the meaning of (2) has to do with our ability as speakers to understand each other extra-linguistically, and our ability to take apart speaker meaning from word meaning. Knowledge of back-ground information about the context, as well as knowledge about the speaker and the speaker's intentions, dispositions, and linguistic habits will also be determin-ants of this ability. For example, many kinds of lexical innovation are playful, and knowledge of whether one's conversational partner is being a particular kind of silly or witty will help determine successful recovery of an innovation, as opposed to leaving a hearer confused. This is not unlike the ability to determine whether someone is being sarcastic, or making a deadpan joke, and this ability is often aided by familiarity with the speaker (or further knowledge of the context).[11]

So what about the luck around when a new term actually becomes part of a lexicon? For example, what happens in between the first time the term is used or introduced and its canonization in the *Oxford English Dictionary*? A full story is beyond the scope of this chapter and would require engaging with literature on language change (see Eckert 2016). Here I explore one feature of one hypothesis: the social features around the use of a given neologism influence its uptake into a given lexicon. For this hypothesis, I think it's instructive to look at one case study where social media seems to have played a significant role in getting it off the ground.

In the decade between 2008 and 2018, the term 'mansplain' went from being a nascent neologism (traced back to writer Rebecca Solnit's 2008 blog post, 'Men Explain Things to Me') to a common characterization of what happens when someone explains something pedantically or patronizingly. As Ursula Lutzky and Robert Lawson (2019) explain: "Solnit's post swiftly led to the coining of the term *mansplaining* to describe an explanation, usually offered by a man, which is patronizing, condescending, or ignores women's experience and knowledge" (Lutzky and Lawson 2019, p. 3).

Using a corpus of 20,803 English tweets collected from November 2016 to April 2017 on the social media site *Twitter*, Lutzky and Lawson analyzed instances of

---

[10] For a long time, I tried to convince those in my linguistic communities to adopt the expression 'feeling crow' to denote the desire to get from one place to another, as the crow flies, without making any stops in between: e.g., "I don't want to go to the grocery store on my way home from work; I'm feeling crow." My efforts have been largely unsuccessful. Thanks to Katy Meadows for being a notable exception.

[11] One distinction to explore further is the suggestion that Davidsonian luck reduction is ability-related while Lewisian-based luck reduction is more closely related to coordination, and rule following. Thanks to Abrol Fairweather and Carlos Montemayor for this interesting observation.

the term *mansplaining* in conjunction with other neighboring terms and concepts to learn more about the term and its rise in popularity. Lutzky and Lawson give us quite a few reasons to be interested in social media from a linguistic perspective: there's lots of innovation happening not just around terms, but around the use of "memes, Graphic Interchange Formats, emojis, orthographic variation, and more" (Lutzky and Lawson 2019, p. 2).[12] Hashtags, the process of affixing a word or phrase to the "#" (hash) sign, are doubly instructive. They have their own interesting linguistic features, but they also enable researchers to track *metadata*:

> ...the # symbol indicates that what follows is metadata. It signals a distinction between "two orders of meaning," between tagged and untagged language use in tweets and thus highlights the special status of hashtags as metadiscursive material...Not only do hashtags provide information about a tweet, they also embed these tweets in wider discussions on the same topic.   (2019, p. 2)

This allows researchers to track the usage of the term through "retweets," as well as quantify the instances of the term over time.

In their study, using the above methodology, Lutzy and Lawson conducted a corpus analysis of all instances of *#mansplaining* in English tweets over six months, and contrasted the term with similar findings for *#manterruption* and *#manspreading*. I want to focus here on two of their findings to help respond to our question about stickiness: first, the results about relative popularity of each term. Second, the *keyword clusters* they found associated with each.

Lutzky and Lawson (2019) found that of the three terms, "#manterruption was the least frequent hashtag with 210 instances compared to #manspreading's 3,838 and #mansplaining's 16,755" (p. 4). They hypothesize that

> This suggests that there is more cultural awareness and recognition of *mansplaining* as a concept, potentially due to the fact that this term is the oldest of the three...*manterruption* and *manspreading* are relatively new additions to the lexicon and therefore do not yet seem to have the wider social distribution that *mansplaining* has.   (p. 9)

Two features of their findings and analysis are that (a) they posit a close link between concept recognition and term use; and (b) they note that temporality can be a proxy for social distribution and recognition. We might further investigate the relationship between (a) and contemporary work in epistemic injustice (Fricker 2003; Dotson 2011). That is, according to Fricker (2003), there was a conceptual lacuna for 'sexual harassment' until the term was finally coined. To test

---

[12] See also North (2007) and Blommaert (2015).

Lutzky and Lawson's hypothesis, we might try to ascertain whether a rise in the acceptance of the *concept* of sexual harassment translated into a rise in its usage.[13] This would tell in favor of concept-formation as part of an anti-luck condition for linguistic innovation.

Their second finding, related to keyword clusters, was that each term was typically used in conjunction with several other words, or keywords. That is, #*manspreading* occurred most frequently with terms like 'transit', 'seat', and 'legs' (p. 5). #*Mansplaining* co-occurred with 'explain', 'women', and 'tell'. #*Manterruption*, the least frequently used term, also had the sparsest cluster (including words like 'app', 'interrupt', 'interrupted', and, mysteriously, 'Paulo').[14] That is, the neologisms that were used *more* frequently were *also* used in conjunction with many of the same cluster words: or they had tighter keyword clusters. This could also support a tight connection between concept recognition and term use, if we think that co-occurrence with the same few words suggests a closer cultural or public concept associated with the term.[15] Another reason to think this, especially with newer terms, is that when there is ambiguity and variation about usage, the term might just fade out of existence due to a lack of coordination.[16] This could suggest a possible reconciliation of Lewis and Davidson, following views like Camp's (2016). Davidson would be right about the innovation, but we can have a Lewisian explanation of what sticks; the greater the coordination on the meaning, the more people can use it to communicate, the more the term sticks around.[17]

From this study, we can take away that (a) concept recognition and (b) social distribution are important. Maybe this is just obvious, and what we're looking for is what goes on to enable both (a) and (b). For now, I'll say, following Soraya Chemaly (2018), that, especially when it comes to language that describes the social world in ways like the ones above, some combination of social events, activism, influence of the term's originator, and the people who pick it up all contribute. Recall that at the point of her writing, Rebecca Solnit was a well-known published author. Accountability for sexual and gender-based harassment and violence was in the air. Public consciousness around sexism was relatively high.

---

[13] See Grossman and Noveck (2015) for suggestions on blending historical linguistics with experimental work.

[14] Less mysteriously: one particularly visible campaign, "Woman Interrupted," originated in São Paulo.

[15] Another possible explanation is that "manterruption" rolls off the tongue less easily than "mansplain" and "manspread," suggesting that phonetics, aesthetics, or general 'catchiness' could partially explain this discrepancy as well. Thanks to Rachel Rudolph for this observation. In this case, luck could be a determinant as it connects to the randomness of how certain words sound. This could be further investigated by looking at cross-linguistic lexical innovations involving similar concepts. If terms with similarly tight keyword clusters were used less often depending on their natural language, this could be a point in favor of the phonetic hypothesis.

[16] See Lepore and Stone (2018) on the evolving use of *bromance*, for example.

[17] Thank you to Rachel Rudolph for helpful conversation about Lewisian coordination.

This is all to say, extra-linguistic events helped the rise of the term's popularity.[18] Further, many people were finding solidarity and voices in platforms that were a stark contrast to the ways they were *not* listened to outside of social media contexts. Future work can look at terms that did *not* gain traction, as well as examples of linguistic innovation that are not as explicitly social or political.[19]

In this chapter, I have given two arguments in defense of a Davidsonian understanding of lexical innovation. These arguments rest on a distinction between lexical innovations that become conventionalized in a given lexicon, and one-off innovations that do not "stick" around. I have examined some anti-luck features of large-scale lexical innovations related to language and social activism, and offered a hypothesis that in at least some of these cases, concept-formation is closely linked to the successful conventionalizing of lexical innovation. This still leaves many questions open. Crucially, what about lexical innovation in the time of Davidson, Lewis, and everyone else who predated Twitter? And what are the factors, linguistic and not, that enable a new expression-meaning pair to enter a lexicon? Perhaps some of it is luck; in the meantime, I hope that I have gone some way into showing some of these features.[20]

References

Armstrong, Josh. 2016. 'The Problem of Lexical Innovation'. *Linguistics and Philosophy*. 39: 87–118.

Bambini, V., M. Ghio, A. Moro, and P.B. Schumacher. 2013. 'Differentiating among Pragmatic Uses of Words Through Timed Sensicality Judgments: Metaphor, Metonymy and Approximation'. *Frontiers in Psychology* 4.

---

[18] Also, as Lutzky and Lawson hypothesize: "Neither *manspreading* nor *womanspreading* had been included in the *Oxford English Dictionary* by the time of writing this article. However, they do appear in the *Urban Dictionary* with the earliest entry for *manspreading* from December 21, 2014, and the earliest one for *womanspreading* from March 27, 2015. They were thus first recorded in this dictionary around the same time as MTA's Courtesy Counts campaign was introduced. A further extra-linguistic event leading to increased discussion of the topic on Twitter occurred in November 2016. It was then that BuzzFeed featured a video on its website which reported the experiences of three women who tried *manspreading* for a week (Boyajian, 2016). They deliberately took up as much space as possible on public transport as well as in other everyday life situations and commented on this experiment in short video diary sequences" (Lutzky and Lawson 2019, p. 8).

[19] Among these are not just #*manterruption*, but also #*womanspreading*. Lutzky and Lawson (2019) quote two such Tweets: "29. #feminist [sic] complain about #manspreading, but what about #womanspreading? Seriously though, #idc. Just pointing out we all do it. 30. All this talk from @BuzzFeed about #manspreading, but #womanspreading is the real epidemic. #truth" (p. 7). I think it would also be interesting to look at the short-lived #Wakandathevote trend, in which the proper noun Wakanda (the mythical African homeland of the superhero Black Panther) was turned into a verb to encourage young Black voters to the polls in 2018 and 2020 (Lockhart 2018).

[20] For helpful comments and conversations, I am grateful to Jody Azzouni, Mercedes Corredor, Megan Hyska, Elizabeth Fricker, Justin Khoo, John Perry, Rachel Rudolph, and audiences at the 2021 Pacific APA meeting. Special thanks to Abrol Fairweather and Carlos Montemayor for written comments on the final version.

Berliner, Paul. 2009. *Thinking in Jazz: The Infinite Art of Improvisation*. University of Chicago Press.

Blommaert, Jan. 2015. 'Meaning as a Nonlinear Effect: The Birth of Cool.' *Aila Review* 28(1): 7–27.

Boyajian, Melissa. 2016. 'Women Try Manspreading for a Week'. *Buzzfeed*. Published November 22. https://www.buzzfeed.com/melissaboyajian/women-try-manspreading-for-a-week

Camp, Elisabeth. 2016. 'Conventions' Revenge: Davidson, Derangement, and Dormativity'. *Inquiry*. 59:1: 113–138. DOI: 10.1080/0020174X.2015.1115277

Camp, Elisabeth. 2006. 'Contextualism, Metaphor, and What is Said'. *Mind and Language* 21(3): 280–309.

Chemaly, Soraya. 2018. *Rage Becomes Her: The Power of Women's Anger*. Atria Books.

Clark, Eve and Herb Clark. 1979. 'When Nouns Surface as Verbs'. *Language* 55: 767–811.

Davidson, Donald. 1986/2006. 'A Nice Derangement of Epitaphs'. in *The Essential Davidson*. Oxford University Press: 251–265.

Davidson, Donald. 1984. 'Convention and Communication'. *Synthese* 59(1): 3–17.

Dotson, Kristie. 2011. 'Tracking Epistemic Violence, Tracking Practices of Silencing'. *Hypatia* 26(2): 236–257.

Eckert, Penelope. 2016. 'Variation, Meaning, and Social Change', in N. Coupland, ed., *Sociolinguistics: Theoretical Debates*. Cambridge University Press: 68–85.

Fricker, Miranda. 2003. "Epistemic Injustice and a Role for Virtue in the Politics of Knowing." *Metaphilosophy* 34: 154–173.

Fricker, Miranda. 2011. *Epistemic Injustice: Power and the Ethics of Knowing*. Oxford University Press.

Gordon, Meredith. 2015. '10 Things to Do When Your Husband is Having a Mantrum'. *Mom.com*. Published June 3. https://mom.com/kids/20049-10-things-do-when-your-husband-has-mantrum

Grossman, Eitan and Ira Noveck. 2015. 'What Can Historical Linguistics and Experimental Pragmatics Offer Each Other?' *Linguistics Vanguard* 1(1): 145–153.

Jane, Emma A. 2017. '"Dude... Stop the Spread": Antagonism, Agonism, and #Manspreading on Social Media'. *International Journal of Cultural Studies* 20(5): 459–475.

Jemisin, N.K. 2016. *The Obelisk Gate*. Orbit.

Lepore, Ernie and Matthew Stone. 2018. 'Convention before Communication'. *Philosophical Perspectives* 31(1): 245–265.

Lewis, David. 1969. *Convention: A Philosophical Study*. Harvard University Press.

Lewis, David. 1975. 'Languages and Language', in K. Gunderson, ed., *Minnesota Studies in the Philosophy of Science*. University of Minnesota Press: 3–35.

Lockhart, P.R. 2018. '#WakandaTheVote: How Activists Are Using Black Panther Screenings to Register Voters'. Published February 21, 2018. https://www.vox.com/policy-and-politics/2018/2/21/17033644/black-panther-screenings-voter-registration-wakanda-the-vote

Lutzky, Ursula and Robert Lawson. 2019. 'Gender Politics and Discourses of #mansplaining, #manspreading, and #manterruption on Twitter'. *Social Media and Society* 1–12.

North, S. 2007. 'The Voices, the Voices: Creativity in Online Conversation'. *Discourse Analysis Online* 2: 1–19.

Porter, Lewis. 1985. 'John Coltrane's "A Love Supreme": Jazz Improvisation as Composition'. *Journal of the American Musicological Society* 38(3): 593–621.

Rhymes, Busta. 2001. *Genesis*. Studio album. Flipmode Records and J. Records.

Roberts, Craige. 2004. 'Context in Dynamic Interpretation', in L. Horn and G. Wards, eds., *The Handbook of Pragmatics*. Blackwell.

Roberts, Craige. 1996. 'Information Structure: Towards an Integrated Formal Theory of Pragmatics', in J.H. Yoon and A. Kathol, eds., *OSUWPL*, Volume 49: *Papers in Semantics*. Ohio State University: 1–53.

Solis, Gabriel. 2004. '"A Unique Chunk of Jazz Reality": Authorship, Musical Work Concepts, and Thelonious Monk's Live Recordings from the Five Spot, 1958'. *Ethnomusicology* 48(3): 315–347.

Solnit, Rebecca. 2008/2014. 'Men Explain Things to Me', in *Men Explain Things to Me*. Haymarket Books: 1–18.

Solnit, Rebecca. 2012. 'Introduction to "Men Explain Things to Me."' *Guernica Magazine*. https://www.guernicamag.com/rebecca-solnit-men-explain-things-to-me/

Sperber, Dan and Gloria Origgi. 2012. 'A Pragmatic Perspective on the Evolution of Language', in D. Wilson and D. Sperber, eds., *Meaning and Relevance*. Cambridge University Press: 124–131.

Stalnaker, Robert. 2002. 'Common Ground'. *Linguistics and Philosophy* 25: 701–725.

12

We Forge the Conditions of Love

Georgi Gardiner

This essay is not about what love is. It is about what self-ascriptions of love do. People typically self-ascribe romantic love when a nexus of feelings, beliefs, attitudes, values, commitments, experiences, and personal histories matches their conception of romantic love. But what shapes this conception? And (how) can we adjudicate amongst conflicting conceptions? Self-ascriptions of love do not merely describe the underlying nexus of attitudes and beliefs. They also change it. This essay describes how conceptions of love affect romantic experience. I limn distinctions between love and obsessive infatuation and explore ways language can cultivate queer romantic preferences. Since conceptions of love are shaped, often implicitly, by terms available in one's linguistic community, the resulting nexus of concepts and conceptions manifests linguistic luck. I suggest ways we might sculpt the language of love to better understand—and change—ourselves. Love can help us flourish and so can our "love" language.

1. Love or Confusion?

Terry is a fan of Sam Seder, host of the political analysis show *The Majority Report*. Terry has listened for years. He finds Seder charming, funny, astute, and handsome. Terry admires Seder's sense of style, moral judgement, and interpersonal conduct. He is sexually aroused by Seder. But, more than that, watching the show makes Terry deeply happy. He feels Seder is on his wavelength. Terry has never met Seder nor attended a live show.

> "I'm in love with Sam Seder," Terry tells his friend Laura. "Don't be silly," Laura replies. "You can't be in love with someone you've never met. You just have a celebrity crush. You're enamoured, maybe infatuated. But you can't be in love with him." "No," Terry insists, "Celebrity crushes are superficial. This isn't a mere crush. I've watched the show for years. I know him well and my feelings run deep. I'm in love with him."

Terry and Laura have different conceptions of romantic love. One's conception of love is one's personal implicit theory about what love is. Laura's conception

Georgi Gardiner, *We Forge the Conditions of Love* In: *Linguistic Luck: Safeguards and Threats to Linguistic Communication.*
Edited by: Abrol Fairweather and Carlos Montemayor, Oxford University Press. © Oxford University Press 2023.
DOI: 10.1093/oso/9780192845450.003.0012

precludes Terry's attachment from qualifying. She has a nexus of ideas, thoughts, assumptions, experiences, and linguistic interpretations that—to some degree— mutually cohere and allow her to communicate, describe reality, navigate social spaces, and make sense of her experiences. This nexus includes (or entails) that love requires bilateral communication. Terry has a similar network of ideas and experiences. It helps him navigate the social world, describe reality, and so on. But Terry's conception allows that one can be in love despite unidirectional communication.

Relationships with unidirectional communication are increasingly common in media, elite sport, and celebrity culture. They are characteristic of hierarchical occupations, including politics, research, and the arts.[1] We also have a kind of unidirectional relationship with deceased public figures, including dead authors, actors, and musicians. We receive their assertions, but they cannot receive ours. Given that relationships of unidirectional communication are commonplace, Laura's more restrictive conception excludes far more potential objects of love.[2]

§2 avers that, despite their disagreement, it is possible that neither Terry nor Laura is wrong.[3] There is no fact of the matter about whose conception is correct because the reference of "love" in "in love with" is not fully determinate. The term's reference has permissive flexibility. §3 illustrates how a person's idiosyncratic conception of romantic love can—in some cases—shape underlying feelings, values, beliefs, relationships, and experiences in feedback loops that lead to maker's knowledge. §4 extends this to conceptions of sexuality. §5 argues that— since conceptions can be incomplete, mutable, and confused—the ability to inhabit rival conceptual schemas is a valuable cognitive skill.

The looping effects of self-ascriptions raise questions about language-based cultural engineering. By manipulating language, conceptions can be steered to promote individual and collective flourishing. §§6 and 7 illustrate by showing how language can help cultivate a more queer society.[4]

§§8 and 9 explain why differences in conception manifest linguistic luck. Small, contingent quirks of the linguistic environment can lead to large, stable, consequential effects. Finally, §12 posits transformative conceptual shifts, in which

---

[1] Such communication can be starkly asymmetrical, but not strictly unidirectional. Celebrities and social media influencers contact fans.

[2] Terry's conception might be more restrictive in other ways. Perhaps Terry's, but not Laura's, includes that romantic love requires sexual attraction, for example.

[3] This claim is stronger than that their disagreement is reasonable. In reasonable disagreements, at least one party's belief is false.

[4] Jenkins (2017, 2018, 2020) also notes that conceptions of love are influenced by, and influence, society. Recognizing same-gender attachments as romantic love buttresses those relationships, for example. Jenkins motivates ameliorative conceptual engineering towards non-monogamic conceptions of LOVE. Many theorists claim the meaning of "love" exhibits permissive flexibility and—under various guises—motivates love-focused conceptual engineering. See, for instance, Lee (1973); Neto (1993); Hooks (2000); Armstrong (2003); Murdoch (2003); and Earp and Savulescu (2020: 50).

acquiring or revising conceptions in the neighbourhood of love profoundly shapes one's conception of—and experiences with—love. I illustrate this by examining how conceptions of limerence affect conceptions of love.

Some preliminary clarifications: Firstly, I follow the convention of using SMALL CAPS for concepts and quotation marks for words. Secondly, throughout this essay, by "love" I refer to romantic love, focusing on the idea of *being in love with*. I largely set aside other kinds of interpersonal love and attraction such as *philia*, the platonic love amongst some friends and kin. I focus on contemporary conceptions of romantic love in English-speaking cultures. Thirdly, I contend that ROMANTIC LOVE is itself best understood as a cluster of distinct interlocking subcategories that are often conflated owing, in part, to impoverished linguistic resources. The English language would be improved by including more distinct terms. This contention supports §5's claims that conceptions of love are mutable, incomplete, suboptimal, confused, and sometimes inapt: Given that English speakers cannot avoid using the term "love," this linguistic inadequacy undergirds the term's permissive flexibility. But I largely set this contention aside.

This essay isn't about the nature of love. It's about how conceptions of love affect self-ascriptions of love, which in turn affects the underlying clusters of attitudes, emotions, dispositions, beliefs, intentions, attention, values, relationships, and commitments that those self-ascriptions aim to describe. Wherever possible, this essay is agnostic about the nature, limits, and metaphysics of love. For this reason, whether any specific example exemplifies love or the word's permissive flexibility is relatively unimportant. If you find my examples uncompelling, amend the example. Suppose you think Terry is clearly wrong, for example: He cannot be in love with someone he has never met. You can adjust the example so that Terry has met Seder a few times. Or if Laura's conception seems implausibly demanding, imagine instead Terry's affections are further from paradigmatic romantic love, such as towards a historical or fictional character.

2. Permissive Flexibility

"Love" is messy.[5] People disagree about which nexus of feelings, values, beliefs, commitments, intentions, experiences, relationships, and personal histories fall under the extension of "love." Some of these disagreements concern matters of degree, such as how intense, enduring, or arresting feelings must be to qualify as love. These differences in conception resemble differing thresholds for how loud a crowd must be to qualify as rowdy; individual thresholds differ. (These thresholds are often vague, but vagueness doesn't always eradicate disagreement.)

---

[5] So, I'm told, is love.

But for fraught, mysterious, complex phenomena—like love—some disagreements in conception are not merely a matter of degree. And these differences can concern relatively central features of love. Divergences include whether love is consistent with disliking the person or finding them repulsive, dull, or morally abhorrent. Is love consistent with abusing the person or not caring about their interests? Is it possible to be in love at first sight or without reciprocation? Can a prepubescent person be in love? Can an adult be in love with a child, animal, group, place, or cartoon character?

For some such disagreements, one disputant is simply wrong. A person cannot be in love with a number or a rock; one can be in love with someone of the same gender. If a person's conception of love says otherwise, they are confused or mistaken. But for some disputes, the term "love" exhibits permissive flexibility. The boundaries aren't determinate. There are no biological, psychological, or social forces—especially authoritative or dispositive forces—that chisel the meaning of "love" to determine a unique communal answer. This differs from terms like "adult" or "number," for which fiat, social pressure, or metaphysical natures carve sharper boundaries.

The permissive flexibility of LOVE subsumes relatively central, consequential features. Disagreements about whether love requires liking the person, for instance, are central to love's nature. Whether Terry can love Seder despite never meeting him is peripheral in one sense: If it is romantic love, it isn't prototypical. But attachment to public figures can be a central aspect of one's life. Perhaps Terry never feels such affinity towards acquaintances, but feels ardent towards celebrities. Given that romantic self-ascriptions affect underlying attachments, these differences in conception can have profound effects.[6]

Adjudicating between Terry and Laura—if it can be done—does not depend on facts about love or a public meaning of the term "love." Instead whether one conception is better can depend on whether either conception clashes with the individual's various beliefs, experiences, or other concepts, or proves more apt for communicating or understanding the world. This means that if either conception is superior, this can stem from contingent, shifting features of one's community and which *other* concepts the individual has.

We each have an idiosyncratic network of concepts and conceptions. If Laura's overall network stymies her understanding of intense affection for celebrities, or if Terry's lacks any way to mark differences between his attitudes towards Seder and those arising in reciprocal, committed relationships, these inabilities might count against their respective conceptions of love. But these hermeneutical inabilities aren't objections to conceptions of love without consideration of a broader network of concepts. This generates "deep coherentism" about whether beliefs

---

[6] Setiya (2022) discusses whether love without acquaintance is possible. See also Harrington and Bielby (1995), Eaglehawk (2019), Tukachinsky (2021) on parasocial attachment to public figures.

and perspectives are epistemically good; coherence affects whether *what the person's thoughts mean* is epistemically good. Terry's belief that he loves Seder might be epistemically impaired if he lacks the concept ROLE MODEL, for example, even if Seder isn't his role model.

Some further clarifications: Firstly, not all disagreements about love are disagreements in conception. If one person says *X* loves *Y* and the other demurs, they can be disagreeing about, for example, the depth of *X*'s feelings. Disagreement can also stem from, for example, what is psychologically possible, rather than the conditions delineating love. Perhaps Laura believes it isn't psychologically possible to develop the required levels of affection and commitment without acquaintance, for example. But many disagreements about love stem from differences in conception. Since "love" evokes a heady mess of concepts and conceptions, Laura and Terry cannot easily adjudicate which kind of disagreement they have, even if they comprehend the distinction between concepts, conceptions, and possibility conditions.

Secondly, some person-level changes—such as increased energy, smiling, and spending—can be seen as evidence for love and causally connected to love without appearing in a conception of love. Thirdly, conceptions are not wholly propositional and so, unlike beliefs, aren't the kinds of things that can be true or false. Conceptions—ways of thinking about what constitutes love—can instead be *confused* or lacking in other ways, such as by being inapt, unhelpful, damaging, or incomplete.

3. Maker's Knowledge: Interpretive Feedback Loops of Love

Differing conceptions of love—and their resulting categorisations and self-ascriptions—can affect one's underlying nexus of feelings, beliefs, values, and experiences.[7]

This can happen over time. Let's stipulate that Terry's conception is not misguided. It is possible to be in love with someone you've never met: Either Laura's conception is too narrow or the borders of LOVE are silent on the matter and so both conceptions can be apt. (Whether the conceptions are in fact apt depends, in part, on their conceptions of neighbouring phenomena.) Terry's conception of himself as falling in love influences his interpretation of his own feelings, values, and dispositions. It can affect his intentions, commitments, and conduct. In some cases, Terry's interpretation of his underlying emotions changes his emotions in a feedback loop.

---

[7] See Barrett (2017) on constructed emotions and Hacking (1995) on looping effects generated by conforming to mental health diagnoses. Thanks to Jon Garthoff, Renee Jorgensen, and Will Fleisher for discussion.

Consider a cluster of Terry's sensations, values, beliefs, and commitments. These might include gratitude for Seder's role in his life, appreciating Seder's nature, and believing him uniquely special. Note this underlying cluster of attitudes does not reduce to the most fundamental substratum conditions or neurochemical correlates of affection. If Terry is open to the idea of falling in love with Seder, this receptivity can itself nurture those underlying feelings and attitudes. He embraces the warmth, which kindles it. Feeling positively about his fealty towards the podcaster can itself bolster that commitment. Judging loving admiration as warranted strengthens that admiration. Self-ascriptions of love have an attentional draw, and attention fuels emotions. This cycle boosts Terry's attitudes, including those—like profound gratitude—that distinguish love from mere crushes.[8] And so Terry's conception of love can, over time, help make it true that he loves Seder.

Applying his conceptual framework to himself, furthermore, helps corroborate the framework. Terry's conceptual scheme includes that one can love non-acquaintances. And self-ascribing love helps make sense of his experience; the framework seems to fit. Indeed, given the stipulation above, it does fit. Despite being partly self-fulfilling, Terry's experiences support his framework. Using the conceptual framework to make sense of reality both creates and fits that reality. We forge LOVE.

This is a kind of bootstrapping: Applying the conceptual schema itself provides reason to think it matches reality; applying a different conception might have supported a different schema. But, despite the spectre of circularity or speciousness, this process can nonetheless provide legitimate support because it is how some conceptions work. Social concepts and conceptions change behaviour, and so reality changes to fit conceptions. Acquiring the concept FUCK BUDDY can help cause those arrangements. One's conception of FUCK BUDDY can affect, for example, whether the amatory pals go on dates. Emotion concepts can be similar. Terry exemplifies how concepts and conceptual schemes can affect attention, interpretation, internal narratives, and self-explanations, and thus change the underlying nexus of values, attitudes, and emotions.

Consider another person, Mark. His initial underlying cluster of attitudes towards Seder resembles Terry's but his conception of love, like Laura's, precludes his being in love with Seder. In some cases, as a result Mark doesn't implicitly nurture those feelings, beliefs, and values as loving ones and so they don't develop in that direction. By interpreting his experience as a mere celebrity crush, he thereby shifts his attitudes towards shallower ones. Mark develops and bolsters other conceptions in the neighbourhood of love to categorise relevantly similar feelings. This might include infatuation, celebrity crush, lifestyle lust, or being

---

[8] I stipulated above that romantic love without acquaintance is possible. This stipulation makes more plausible that features like gratitude distinguish love from crushes. This is because romantic love cannot be, given the stipulation, delineated by bilateral interpersonal features.

enamoured or smitten. Mark might see himself as simply an admiring fan or cast Seder as a role model. Mark categorises his feelings as non-love, which can itself support his restrictive conception of love. Like Terry, Mark can aptly describe his experience and by doing so also steers that experience.

Maker's knowledge is distinctive insight about the way something is because the knower themselves makes it so. Typical examples include an artisan's knowledge of their products' intentionally created properties. It also includes, for example, knowing the coffee is sweetened after adding sugar. Maker's knowledge includes some self-fulfilling beliefs, such as a traditional couple's belief that the wife does the cooking.[9]

Knowledge of love, including self-ascriptions, can be maker's knowledge. But it exemplifies an unusual kind. In standard examples of propositional maker's knowledge, the relevant propositional content is determinate. The believer-maker changes the world to match particular propositional content. Conception-based maker's knowledge is different; the meaning of "I love" is also created. Two people start with small, diffident divergences in interpretation of terms in their linguistic environment. These differences grow and entrench as the people observe and create confirming instances. They thereby shape the world—including themselves—to conform to those evolving conceptions. Emotions and conceptions can (sometimes!) mutually adjust to make one's judgement true. Terry can make it true that he is falling in love; Mark that he is not. We make love.

It is worth emphasising that I merely claim self-fulfilling, cyclical self-ascriptions are possible and occur in at least some borderline cases. I don't claim that all self-ascriptions of love have significant or self-fulfilling effects. And, of course, self-ascriptions are often mistaken.

The Seder example raises questions. Terry's conceptual schema categorises his initial feelings as love, and Mark's categorises comparable initial feelings as not love. It's possible that neither is mistaken. Their overall conceptual schemas can both be apt, albeit different. Suppose Mark's conception of love changes over time. In 2020, Mark's conception entails he doesn't currently love Seder. Mark's later conception of love entails that back in 2020 he loved Seder. Is Mark wrong at one of those times? Perhaps not. Perhaps Mark's beliefs, though seemingly incompatible, were correct at both times, given what he meant by "love."

A child who calls every black bird a raven is simply confused about what "raven" means; "raven" isn't flexible. But judgements with conceptions that yield permissive flexibility are common. Suppose Clerk the birdwatcher has an expansive conception of CHARMING, such that many birds count as charming. This expansive categorisation—seeing more birds as charming—in turn helps him appreciate charming features of more birds. Clerk thus enjoys birdwatching more.

---

[9] Hintikka (1974: 80); Langton (2009); Flòridi (2018).

Kristina's conception of charming is more restrictive; fewer behaviours count as charming. Must one of them be wrong? A serene monk categorises few behaviours as "grating." As a result, he is irked by fewer behaviours. Given the permissive flexibility of GRATING, the monk's categorisation can be apt. Given its effects, it might be prudent. So, what constrains the appropriateness of conceptual engineering of emotions? This question is vast, of course; I cannot hope to answer it here.[10] I simply motivate that some conceptual engineering of emotions is feasible, valuable, and ineluctable.

4. The Constraints of Thinking Straight

The example of Terry and Mark is developmental. It happens over time. The reality-sculpting power of conceptions also happens synchronically. To see this, compare two college freshmen, Ali and Belle, who join the basketball team. They each develop a comparable cluster of attitudes and dispositions towards their coach, Pat Summit. They have the same slight degree of heightened arousal and nervousness around Pat. They both view Pat as charming, funny, and pretty. They want to impress Pat and enjoy her company. Ali sees herself as queer. Belle sees herself as straight. As a result, Ali interprets her attitudes as being—to some degree—romantic or sexual attraction to Pat. Belle doesn't. In *some* cases, this interpretation, which is grounded in their self-conceptions as either queer or straight, can be self-fulfilling. Ali is sexually or romantically attracted. Belle is not. In some cases, both are correct, and it is maker's knowledge.[11]

Several forces underlie this. Firstly, attention is powerful. Belle may downplay or fail to notice her kernel of sexual arousal around Pat, and so it dies out. Secondly, some experiences of emotion include one's attitude to, and perspective on, those very experiences. Part of falling for someone, or being sexually aroused, can include relaxing into the sensation.[12] Thirdly, sensations are affected by one's

---

[10] I lack space to argue this here, but moral reasons favouring one conceptual schema above another are not best understood as moral encroachment. Moral encroachment concerns the narrow question of whether particular propositional content is justified by a given body of evidence, not which interpretative schemas are better. Gardiner (ms) contrasts moral encroachment's specificity with epistemic normativity's breadth. Finocchiaro (2022) theorises the related epistemic value of conceptual fidelity. But fidelity concerns "carving at the joints," which seems inadequate for assessing rival conceptions of love, given that "love" has permissive flexibility. Epistemology's normal battery of tests for evaluating epistemic value are inadequate for epistemically assessing rival conceptual schemas.

[11] Some such beliefs aren't knowledge. They can be false, poorly grounded, unreliably formed, evidence-resistant, insensitive, or unsafe. But permissive flexibility complicates these properties. How should we define safety, for example, when modally nearby sources of error are the person's developing a different conception, classificatory schema, or cluster of concepts.

[12] Not always. A person can become romantically attached whilst trying to not; and consider a teen with unwanted or inconveniently timed sexual arousal.

perspectives on them. Belle may have internalised homophobia and so feel nauseated by any kernel of sexual arousal around Pat. If Pat makes Belle nauseated, it can be harder to detect or foster budding romantic or sexual attraction. Thus if Belle isn't receptive to romantic or sexual feeling, she may overlook those feelings or interpret them as platonic. Suppose Belle feels butterflies or is clumsier around Pat. Given Belle's self-conception as straight, she might interpret this as platonic admiration of Pat's basketball prowess or jitters about impressing her coach.

Contrasting two people indicates how one's interpretation, perspective, and conceptions can synchronically affect occurrent attitudes and feelings. The effect need not be developmental. A particular base cluster of values and attitudes can qualify as romantic or sexual attraction for one person, and not for another. Those classifications can affect the cluster in synchronic interpretive feedback loops. In *some* cases, through lifelong repetition, these forces make it true that Ali is queer and Belle is straight.[13]

The potency of interpretation isn't limited to same-gender attraction. Everyone experiences borderline cases of attraction. One can feel mildly sexually or romantically attracted to a person. In some such borderline cases, seeing one's own attitudes as either platonic or non-platonic can be apt. And, through feedback loops, either judgement can be self-reinforcing.

These feedback loops don't rely on the conceptions' permissive flexibility. But permissive flexibility adds richness to the epistemology of self-fulfilling self-ascriptions. Epistemic assessment is not simply a matter of whether the concepts "carve at the joints"—sometimes there aren't determinative joints—or whether these judgements match reality. Judgements can steer reality. Neither is it simply a crude prudential matter of which conceptions have better practical outcomes.

Sometimes people are simply wrong, of course; self-ascriptions can be mistaken. Error stems from inapt conceptions, self-deceptive mental blocks, and failures to notice or properly interpret emotions. Indeed many people initially miscategorise themselves as straight and later realise they are not. Given this, it is particularly ironic that teenagers who "come out" as queer are frequently disbelieved or told they're mistaken. If anything, it is self-ascriptions of heterosexuality that should be treated with suspicion. When compared to non-heterosexuality, self-ascriptions of heterosexuality typically have less evidence and are susceptible to genealogical debunking. People are liable to assume they are straight—even when false and despite counterevidence—because of cultural heteronormative

---

[13] Perhaps gender identities can similarly be maker's knowledge. Perhaps in some cases, a cis person is cis partly owing to their conception of gender and resulting gender conformism, for instance, yet nonetheless they know they're cisgender.

assumptions. Heterosexual ascriptions (for self and other) are more frequently wrong or recanted. This makes heterosexual ascriptions, including self-ascriptions, harder to know, even if true.

Ali and Belle illustrate how conceptions can affect an underlying nexus of attitudes and underwrite synchronically self-fulfilling self-ascriptions. Occurrent interpretative feedback loops also occur within one individual. To explain how, we turn to the nature of conceptions.

5. Conceptual Tourism and the Interpretive Traveller

Conceptions are psychological structures that aid one's ability to apply concepts to cases. They steer categorisations and help individuals adjudicate principles involving the concept.[14] A person's conception of CHAIR allows them to sort chairs from non-chairs and adjudicate whether, for example, chairs can be impulsive. (They cannot. They are the wrong kind of thing.) But conceptions are not merely the thinnest, least information-heavy structures needed for these sorting and adjudicating capacities. Conceptions are implicit theories of what the thing consists in or what the concept is of. They "flavour the contents of conscious states and influence the direction of thinking."[15]

Conceptions are how one conceives of what X is. This differs from, for example, their full set of beliefs about X. A person might know love's common physiological effects or believe nobody has fallen in love on Mars, but these don't feature in their conception of love. Conceptions also differ from the full set of associations with, attitudes to, or emotions about X. A widow might feel wistful whenever she thinks of love, for example, but this lies outside her conception. Conceptions also differ from concepts. Concepts are the bare feature of thought in virtue of which one is able to refer to Xs at all.[16] Possessing a concept or conception doesn't require strict definitions or necessary and sufficient conditions.

Conceptions can be personal and idiosyncratic. My conception of love is a different mental entity from yours and likely includes different content. Conceptions can be incomplete, internally inconsistent, confused, and—especially at the margins—wrong. They aren't always reflectively accessible. Consider an elegant Georgian sofa with formal embroidered upholstery and ornately carved, rolled armrests on either side.

---

[14] Burge (2003: 383). Thanks to Jon Garthoff and Claire Dartez for insights throughout this section.
[15] Woodfield (1991: 550). See also Rey (1985); Peacocke (1992, 1998); Margolis and Laurence (2021); Isaac (2021).
[16] Concepts and conceptions play different functional roles and might be different metaphysical kinds. The main functional role of concepts is enabling reference (i.e., getting onto the world). The main functional role of conceptions is explanation (i.e., understanding the world).

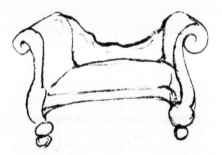

Figure 1

The archetypal chaise longue has only one armrest. A person's conception of chaise longues might be silent or mistaken about whether this symmetrical furniture item can be a chaise longue. She might never notice whether her conception entails, precludes, or is silent on this.

Conceptions evolve. They update in response to new experiences, insights, and beliefs. They also shift to make room for newly acquired concepts and to accommodate changes to other conceptions in the network. A child who acquires the concept LAKE might accordingly adjust their conception of ponds to exclude larger bodies of water. This more discerning conception of ponds makes room for the newly acquired LAKE concept to pick out a distinct thing; and shifting POND helps make sense of why there is a separate term "lake." Such shifts can refine overall understanding.

Suppose a child acquires the concept PUPPY LOVE and thinks of puppy love as superficial, fleeting, or morally facile. This concept acquisition can affect their conception of fully-fledged adult love. They might consequently conceive of adult love as more stable, enduring, or serious.

This process can be distorting. Suppose "puppy love" is a misleading categorisation. Perhaps youthful love is not different from adulthood love, for example, because they're equally fleeting, enduring, facile, or serious. Perhaps the term stems from an envying dismissal of youth. If so, acquiring the concept PUPPY LOVE may degrade the child's overall conceptual schema, including their conception of love. Perhaps their subsequent conception of love wrongly excludes youthful attachments or incorporates properties, like durability, it ought not.

Conceptions' operative features can vary by context. A parent might categorise adolescent attachments as mere puppy love when considering their adolescent children's relationships, yet deem comparable underlying emotions as constituting "proper" love when remembering their own adolescent attachments.[17]

Given these features of conceptions, Terry might be able to tap into a conceptual schema according to which he qualifies as being in love and one in which he

---

[17] These features of conceptions are formidable challenges to developing artificial intelligence. See Camp (2017, 2019) on trying on different interpretative perspectives.

doesn't. In the second schema, love requires bidirectional communication. Belle might similarly be able to flick between interpretations according to which she is straight and not, and thereby experience her feelings as either platonic or not. Belle's arousal might be platonic jitters or a romantic crush. If she can transition amongst interpretations then, through self-fulfilling interpretive feedback loops, maybe both can be true.[18]

People might lack this cognitive control. Perhaps the most one can do deliberately is gradually steer oneself between cognitive perspectives. But there is distinctive epistemic, moral, social, and prudential value in being able to try on and adopt different perspectives, especially for terms like "love" that exhibit permissive flexibility. One can inhabit Laura's perspective, according to which Terry's state cannot be love, and Terry's, wherein it can. Adopting different conceptual schemas enhances understanding of ourselves and others. It helps us appreciate virtues and limits of rival conceptual schemas and so hone, adapt, and assess those schemas. Conceptual travelling—like geographical travelling—enriches perspectives and lives.

This epistemic value is not well theorised as gaining evidence or evidence-acquisition capacities. It is the cognitive capacity to switch amongst perspectives. Given the permissive flexibility surrounding romantic, sexual, and affective concepts, conceptual explorers need not adopt conceptions or beliefs they consider inapt. Ali and Belle need not believe claims about their sexuality they deem false, for example. They can instead question what "straight" and "queer" mean or what kinds and degrees of affection or excitation qualify as romantic. Conceptual explorers might also reasonably take up a flawed perspective for various epistemic reasons, such as gaining concepts and skills, seeing things anew, or better understanding other people.[19]

Ali and Belle can experimentally reinterpret ambiguous unease, or ease, they feel around their coach. This cognitive skill is empowering. Many young people are prone to mistakenly regard themselves as amorously attracted to coaches, bosses, and teachers because this is one natural interpretation of the nervous excitation educed by authority figures. This misinterpretation can be self-fulfilling. "Pick-up artists" use negging and similar tactics to leverage the common conflation of nervous energy, stress, and romantic attraction to manipulate "targets" into misattributing their reactions as attractions. Owing to the reality-shifting power of interpretation, targets can thereby become attracted to the pick-up artist.

---

[18] One way to understand this possibility is if apparently conflicting claims feature different concepts and so concern different propositional content. They aren't inconsistent; it is akin to believing both "I'm attracted to S" and "I'm not very attracted to S." Alternatively, the claims can feature the same concept, and so be incompatible, but tap into different conceptions. And thinking about each claim sufficiently changes the underlying attitudes, such that this thinking itself changes whether the person satisfies the content. It is similar to thinking "I have a headache" immediately causing a headache. Perhaps thinking "I am [not] enamoured" can similarly shift one's state. Or one might deny compositionality.

[19] Cf. Simion (2018) and Podosky (2018) on conceptual engineering and "epistemic loss."

Culture influences the availability and salience of concepts, conceptions, and interpretative frames. Socio-linguistic practices thus steer conceptions to enhance (or hinder) flourishing. Through language, we conceptually engineer emotions. This raises questions about which concepts and conceptions are missing or suboptimal.

6. Cunning Linguistics and the Gay Agenda

Suppose it is better if more people are queer. By "queer" I mean attracted to more than one gender; that is, neither exclusively homosexual nor heterosexual.[20] Call this value judgement BMQ. BMQ differs from the less controversial claim that it's better if queer people aren't closeted, repressed, or in denial. It is bolder: BMQ concerns the underlying prevalence of queerness in a culture. Given that sexual and romantic preferences are partially influenced by social forces, perhaps it is better if social conditions encourage queerness to prevail in more people. The relevant social conditions include economic and political conditions, queer acceptance, and education.[21] These social conditions also include the terms in common use.

Society could evolve so that subsequent generations gradually incline towards queer preferences. Consider the declaration: "I am a soldier so my son can be a shop-keeper, so his son can be an artist."[22] A contemporary man might declare, "I will think of men as graceful, so my son can think of them as beautiful, so his son can fall in love with them." Over generations, he aims to free cognition from the shackles of heteronormativity.

Ineluctably cultures embed assumptions, values, and schemas. (Consider the default heterosexuality embedded in most children's TV shows.) Given this, one should interrogate what these values are and whether better ones are available.

---

[20] Historically "queer" is pejorative in many cultures but has been largely reclaimed. My (mildly stipulative) definition excludes homosexuality, which appears to match an emerging meaning of "queer." But this emerging linguistic trend is hard to measure, because—owing to increased gender-queer visibility and decreased biphobia in LGBT (lesbian, gay, bisexual, and transgender) spaces—people who formerly would have identified as homosexual might now self-ascribe abrosexuality or another continuum preference, and thus fall under this emerging conception of "queer." Thanks to Alex Fitzgerald for discussion.

[21] One might endorse BMQ but deny that social forces influence sexual preferences. (Consider the comic trope of the lonely gay man bemoaning the prevalence of heterosexuality.) But, in response, effects of social context on operative sexuality are evidenced by, for example, cross-cultural differences in prevalence of queer activity and attraction (Baumeister, 2004; Rupp, 2006; Potki et al., 2017). For similar reasons, many LGBT rights advocates object to grounding LGBT acceptance in "born this way" rhetoric (Bindel, 2014; Walters 2014, Grzanka et al., 2019). Sexual preferences are fluid and differ from sexual behaviour and self-ascriptions, making them hard to measure (Albury, 2015); Ghaziani and Brim, 2019); Compton et al., 2018; Finocchiaro, 2021). Thanks to Patrick Grzanka for helpful insight.

[22] This expression evolved from John Quincy Adams's, "I must study politics and war that my sons may have liberty to study mathematics and philosophy."

This differs from "conversion therapy," which targets specific individuals. Gradual evolution need not aim to change the existing sexuality of any particular individual, especially after puberty. BMQ-motivated cultural interventions aim to expand the gender range one is potentially receptive to; conversion therapy, by contrast, hopes to stifle or contract it.[23] The claim that culture influences sexual preference does not entail, and is distant from, the claim that sexual preference is an individual choice. Cultural contexts shape sexuality over the course of generations, even if sexuality is not voluntary.

I sketch three categories of motivation for BMQ. Firstly, moral reasoning about human nature. Secondly, benefits accruing to individuals. Thirdly, interests of groups, communities, or cultures. The applicability of some arguments for BMQ depends on sexuality, gender, and social context.[24] Given space constraints, these are truncated summaries of arguments. I am sympathetic to BMQ, but the arguments below are oversimplified.

Firstly, exclusive heterosexuality or homosexuality might encode inappropriate or morally inferior ways of viewing people. Perhaps, like many racialised sexual preferences, it responds to the wrong features of a person. Or perhaps gender-based *tendencies* are morally copacetic, but flatly excluding individuals from romantic or sexual consideration based on gender—especially before meeting them—is prejudiced.

Perhaps it is better to be attracted to wit, intelligence, grace, or moral character, rather than to appearance. Plausibly these characterological features are closer to the core of what matters about a person and responding to these features "gets it right" or manifests better values. Character-based preferences might be more inclusive of people, such as burn victims, who depart from social norms about physical appearance. Similarly, they might nurture better, healthier, and more concordant relationships, especially as people age or physiologically change. Character-dominated preferences plausibly cultivates character virtue—in the judge, judged, and third-parties.

Attraction-relevant physical features are probably more gender dimorphic than attraction-relevant character traits. Breasts are more gender dimorphic than creativity, for example. And so perhaps dispositions of attraction that respond to a person's "core" features (such as characterological features, rather than body shape), will tend towards all genders, not just one. To see this, consider friendship: Friendships are typically built more on character traits than body shape. Accordingly, people have friends of various genders. It seems "off"—perhaps sexist—to exclusively have friends of one gender, especially if that gender exclusivity is decreed before meeting new potential friends. Maybe romantic and sexual liaisons are similar.

---

[23] Compare also lesbian separatism.   [24] Thanks to Ray Briggs for discussion.

As noted above, this reasoning is overly simplified owing to space constraints. For one thing, character traits can also be gendered; and queer attraction also responds to gender dimorphic body shape.[25]

I turn now to benefits accruing to individuals. Perhaps if society has a higher prevalence of queer people, finding *simpatico* lovers is easier. To illustrate, suppose men prefer casual sex and women prefer romantic dating.[26] These preferences are more easily satisfied if many people are queer. Or consider a young man with marginalised, stigmatised hobbies in a small town. These interests shape his life and values and are the basis for wonderful friendships. But few women participate. Consider, for example, stereotypes about games like Warhammer. Openness to romantic relationships with men could engender a more fulfilled life. These (oversimple) examples motivate evolution towards less gendered social structures, including relationship structures.[27]

Benefits arise from experiencing diverse ways of relating. Suppose relationships with men differ from relationships with other genders, for example, or some sexual activities are gendered. Experiential diversity is valuable. Consider the value of travel, a broad education, trying new things, exposure to ideas, and wide-ranging friendships with diverse people, including across age gaps. This variety might have intrinsic value; and additionally one thereby acquires new perspectives, skills, and ways to communicate, bond, and relate. This doesn't entail having many lovers is better than few. But variety has value, at least for many people. It can enhance virtue, understanding, and flourishing, and strengthen future relationships.

Society benefits from a higher prevalence of queer people. There is value in epistemic diversity. Queer people help others understand aspects of sexual, romantic, or social flourishing that are occluded by heterosexual norms. Hermeneutical progress occurs in online queer spaces, for example, that benefits heterosexual people.[28]

A higher prevalence of queer people would improve norms for signalling romantic interest. Many heteronormative societies rely on systems like assuming members of the same gender are not interested and being more judicious or guarded around members of the so-called "opposite" gender, including especially similarly aged single people. This system could be improved.

---

[25] Thanks to Richard Eldridge and Kevin Ryan for discussion.

[26] Open non-monogamy is most common in gay-male partnerships (Coontz, 2020). Consider also heteropessimism—disillusionment about one's own heterosexuality based on feeling that men and women are incompatible (Seresin, 2019).

[27] Cultivating queer proclivities might help avoid unwanted pregnancies and sexually transmissible health conditions.

[28] See Crimp (1987), Berlant and Warner (1998), Coontz (2020), Ward (2020), and Andler (2022) on importing queer insights into heterosexual contexts. Consider LGBT-driven innovations about consent and kink; and disabled people's insights about sexual flourishing, such as co-masturbation techniques, which others benefit from.

This ends the brief survey of motivations for BMQ, the claim that it is better if more people are queer. To forestall two concerns: Firstly, BMQ doesn't imply people are unethical for being exclusively heterosexual or homosexual. To compare: Suppose it's better if people work less, partly because working less manifests and cultivates virtue. This doesn't mean individuals are unethical for overworking or workaholism. Given socio-economic conditions, some people have no choice; and work attitudes are culturally shaped. Gradual shifts towards working less can be valuable even if no individual is morally wrong for overworking.

Secondly, detractors might claim that romantic desires are immutable. In response: Firstly, desire is shaped by forces like advertising. Consider recent trends of revulsion towards women's body hair, for instance. Consumerism encourages people to treat one's own current preferences as fixed and to change the external world to match their preferences, typically through purchasing. It is often wiser to steer one's own preferences instead. The capacity to appreciate things—like artworks or exercise—is often a cultivatable skill; attention is a powerful force for this. Perhaps romantic desires are, to some degree, similarly mutable: The media manipulates sexual attraction. Arguably such preferences, including racialised and slenderness-based sexual preferences, can be unlearnt. Steering one's own preferences is empowering. Secondly, recall that BMQ-inspired evolutions are multi-generational and so need not change any individual's existing sexuality.

7. Curious or Queer?

Recall that conceptions sometimes affect self-ascriptions, which affects interpretation of occurrent emotional states, which, in turn, affects those states.[29] The concepts and conceptions suggested—and made salient—by one's linguistic community can thus influence sexual preferences.[30] Given this, are some linguistic patterns better?

Compare the terms "bi-curious" and "queer." The term "bi-curious" suggests a centre of gravity towards, or default of, straightness. In widespread conceptions a "bi-curious" person is straight or almost entirely straight. Many dictionaries define "bi-curious" as a subset of heterosexual behaviour.[31] Wikipedia's entry for "bi-curious" begins "Bi-curious is a term for a person, usually someone who is a heterosexual, who is curious or open about engaging in *sexual activity*" (emphasis added).

[29] Studies suggest exposure to conceptions of sexuality as fluid or gradable increases queer self-ascriptions (Morandini et al., 2021).

[30] I focus on sexuality. Dembroff (2020) posits gender identities that depend on conceptions, such as conceptualising the gender binary as "to be resisted."

[31] Examples include the Collins, Macmillan, and Oxford dictionaries (Holleb, 2019: 43), and *Academic Dictionaries and Encyclopedias*. See also Wilson and Rahman (2008).

Being "bi-curious" is commonly contrasted with bisexuality. The term "bi-curious," unlike "bisexual," implies a temporary phase of activity, rather than a stable orientation or preference.[32] The exploration is usually seen as purely sexual, rather than relationship-forging emotional intimacy. The term culturally evokes "straight girls kissing" at parties and "petting" rather than "full" sex. Sociologists document how:

> [S]traight college students today can make out with women and call themselves "bi-curious" without challenge to their heterosexual identity... Straight women can be... "bi-curious"... but too much physical attraction or emotional investment crosses over the line of heterosexuality.   (Rupp and Taylor, 2010)

> The emergence of terms such as heteroflexible and bi-curious... possibly signalled a shift... among *straight* people who have same-sex desires... [B]y not adopting the label 'bisexual' those youths also signalled that their sexual interest in both women and men need not transfer them out of the *heterosexual category*.
> (Carrillo and Hoffman, 2018: 93; emphasis added)

The term "bi-curious" is associated with the idea that one needs relevant sexual experience to qualify as bisexual.[33] The term "queer," by contrast, suggests a non-straight centre of gravity. It is not a way of being straight. "Queer" isn't associated with mere activity. It is instead associated with romantic attachment, emotional investment, and relationship-building.

In English-speaking cultures, the term "bi-curious" was relatively common during formative years of Gen X and Millennials. It since receded, and terms like "queer" are increasingly popular. Recall Ali and Belle, who each felt ambiguous admiration of, and arousal around, their coach. A young Gen X or Millennial with a kernel of potential sexual or romantic feeling might, owing to terms prevalent in her linguistic community, categorise herself as bi-curious and so see herself as fundamentally straight. Given that self-ascriptions affect one's experience of underlying emotions, these conceptions can be self-fulfilling. Heteronormative concepts can be a cognitive straitjacket. A Gen Z youth with comparable initial underlying emotional dispositions, by contrast, might instead characterise herself as queer and thereby implicitly nurture that kernel of desire towards women. She interprets her feelings as emotionally invested, enduring, and manifesting her stable sexuality, rather than as a temporary exploratory stage. This too can be self-fulfilling.

---

[32] Sexualities can be fluid throughout one's life, but this differs from heteronormative "just a phase" associations of the term "bi-curious."

[33] See Bi-Curious in *Academic Dictionaries and Encyclopedias*; Smith (2019). See also Essig (2000) and Thomas (2019) on the term "bi-curious" contributing to bi-erasure and bi-phobia.

Comparing "bi-curious" and "queer" is just one illustration, but it is suggestive of avenues for linguistically sculpting concepts and conceptions. Alterous attraction is desire for emotional closeness, which is neither wholly platonic nor non-platonic, quoiromanticism is not experiencing strong distinctions between romantic and non-romantic attraction, greysexuality is experiencing sexual attraction rarely or with low intensity, abrosexuality is characterised by long-term shifts in sexual and romantic dispositions, whilst sexual fluidity is situation-dependent flexibility. Possessing these concepts can affect self-ascriptions, which can affect underlying emotions and relationships.[34]

Concepts are not necessarily apt, useful, or good, of course, and some conditions of concept acquisition impede flourishing. Consider contexts of concept acquisition that encourage ascribing demon possession, wandering womb, or multiple personality disorder, for instance. Perhaps some self-ascriptions of quoiromanticism stem from inept introspection, for example, and for some people possessing the concept impedes self-understanding.

8. Linguistic Luck: The Happenstances of "Love"

A person's conceptions affect whether they categorise underlying feelings, experiences, values, fealty, commitments, and shared histories as love or something else, such as platonic devotion. These categorisations, in turn, affect those underlying conditions. Practices of self-ascription, concept use, and interpersonal communication shape—by affirming, challenging, or honing—those conceptual schemas.

These feedback loops are infused with linguistic luck. Two hallmarks of luck are—firstly—small, fluky differences in initial conditions that lead to large downstream effects. Things could easily have been different. A person is lucky to spot a hawk, because by chance they looked up as it flew past. With small changes in initial conditions, they would have missed it.[35] Secondly, typically outcomes are good or bad, rather than neutral. Although we might call correctly guessing a card from a deck when nothing is at stake "lucky," typically the term "luck" implies valanced outcomes.

The linguistic contingencies that shape conceptions of love exhibit these characteristic features of luck. Compare three children. The first, A, reaches 18 without hearing the term "puppy love." The second, B, hears it once on TV at 9 years old.

---

[34] Thanks to Ray Briggs, Héctor Carrillo, Patrick Grzanka, Nate Parsons, and Delia McDevitt for discussions that greatly improved this section.

[35] Pritchard (2005). The term "luck" sometimes refers to good (or bad) circumstances, even if they are modally secure. The duke of Westminster, Hugh Grosvenor, is "lucky" to be wealthy, for example, but given his multiple lines of extreme inherited wealth, not easily could he be otherwise. Plausibly these uses of "lucky" pick out a different concept, such as BEING FORTUNATE. Thanks to Steve Grover for the example.

The third, C, hears it often. Their parents are dismissive of teenagers and use the term to denigrate teenage relationships. As a result of this linguistic exposure, Child C is prone to develop a conception of puppy love as immature and distinct from adult love. They might well interpret their own feelings, relationships, and potential through this conceptual lens, which can be self-fulfilling. They might treat their early romantic affections and relationships less seriously, for example, which limits their potential. Child A doesn't form a conception of puppy love—his linguistic environment doesn't seed it—and so he interprets his youthful affections as full-blown love. This too can be self-fulfilling. Child B fleetingly hears the term. He might ignore it or not incorporate it into his conceptual lexicon. If Child B takes it up, the contours of his conception are notably underdetermined by the linguistic stimulus. He might embed PUPPY LOVE in a conceptual framework according to which puppy love is a species of "proper" romantic love, for example, or one in which they are mutually exclusive kinds.[36]

These initial contingent differences can be small, fluky, and easily reversed. Child B's conception of puppy love might hinge on minutiae like the actor's intonation. But over time his conception embeds in a broader rational framework. Once ensconced, it is harder to upend. This illustrates another aspect of linguistic luck: One's nexus of concepts and conceptions could have been configured in other ways. One could have never received the concept or interpreted it differently. But once embedded, intransigence develops; established meanings are hard to adjust or remove. They become rationally anchored to other concepts and beliefs. Accordingly, rational assessment of conceptions is initially relatively limited. Acquisition can be chancy and rationally underdetermined. As Dolores Durkin (1976) notes, "Language is as much caught as it is taught." Entrenched conceptions are more rationally assessable. We might ask whether a conception is properly situated within the broader conceptual nexus, for example, and whether appropriate inferential links have been forged.[37]

Conceptions, misconceptions, and conceptual lacunas are consequential. Suppose Holly meets Manny on holiday. They romantically and sexually liaise that week. Holly possesses the concept HOLIDAY ROMANCE.[38] Her implicit conception includes that holiday romances are brief, even if the rapport feels precious. The term "holiday romance" offers a social script: Interactions are romantic, not merely carnal, and the timeframe is circumscribed. Holly categorises their relationship as a holiday romance. She is accordingly more prone to understand her

---

[36] Other options are available. Perhaps only some instances of puppy love are "proper" love, for example.

[37] Cf. irrelevant influences on beliefs (Vavova, 2018). But the factors discussed here influence which conceptual frameworks, including interpretive taxonomies, one has, rather than which propositions one endorses.

[38] Consider also HOLIDAY FLING, HOLIDAY ROMANCE, and SUMMER FLING. Contrast with "comet lover" and "holibae," for which the time periods are brief, but recurrent.

feelings as largely arising from situational features, including especially its evan-escence: The relationship was less likely to develop if they lived near each other because they likely would have been more cautious about rapidly expressing romantic interest. Aided by her conception of holiday romances, Holly is less inclined to centre Manny's unique traits in her implicit understanding of their interactions or view Manny as irreplaceable or a potential long-term romantic partner.

A person lacking the concept might (mis)take the same underlying nexus of feelings and experiences as indicating a deep connection to Manny, owing to Manny's unique traits, and see potential for enduring connection. They subsequently—owing to cognitive feedback loops—feel those underlying emo-tions differently. These differing interpretations, which are steered by differences in conceptual framework, affect expectations and conduct. The latter person might pine for Manny or lament their geographical distance. Holly might, by contrast, underestimate their long-term romantic potential. Indeed, since one shouldn't pursue or lament every potential good long-term romantic partner, the concept HOLIDAY ROMANCE may have prudential value in encouraging this underestimation.

Holly illustrates how *which* concepts a person possesses can matter. The contours of conceptions and the configuration of concepts within an interpretive schema are also significant. Suppose Terry conceives of love as being stable. On Terry's con-ception, once love roots, it takes substantial force or time to dislodge. This contour may partly stem from contrasting LOVE with PUPPY LOVE. Terry's affections for Sam Seder might thereby endure longer, in virtue of Terry's conceptual scheme accord-ing to which love is durable and he qualifies as being in love.

9. In the Neighbourhood of Love

The terms "puppy love" and "holiday romance" may seem like unconvincing examples of linguistic luck because they are common in English-speaking cultures. One might think that if Child B didn't hear "puppy love," or misunderstood it, on that occasion it would later be rectified. So it isn't a matter of luck that their conceptual scheme includes PUPPY LOVE; not easily could it have been otherwise. In response, firstly, plausibly it's indeterminate whether puppy love is a species of "proper" love. If so, his conception cannot be "corrected"; it wasn't wrong. It can merely be changed. And even if Child B's possessing the concept is not chancy, the conception's contours are. Slight variations in acquisition conditions can shape conceptions in path-dependent ways. The actor's slightly condescending tone can have substantial downstream effects on Child B's conception, for example.

Secondly, my illustrations used familiar concepts within Western culture. But real-life linguistic luck arises for arcane concepts in the neighbourhood of romantic love.[39] Consider less well-known ideas such as companionate love, which is intimate, non-passionate, long-term committed attachment. Long-term commitment distinguishes companionate love from typical close friendship.[40] Romantic friendships are intense intimate friendships. Squishes are platonic crushes, typically characterised by yearning to be closer friends.[41] A "work spouse," "work husband," or "work wife" is a colleague with whom you have "a special, platonic friendship...characterised by a close emotional bond and high levels of disclosure and support."[42] A comet relationship is an intense, intimate romantic relationship with someone who passes through your life intermittently. The term "Eintagsleibe"—based on the German for "mayfly"—translates as "one day's love" and refers to an intense, brief loving relationship.[43] "Carrying a torch" is undisclosed, unrequited long-term romantic fondness, typically towards a former partner. In my conception, the attachment is mild but entrenched. Limerence is obsessive infatuation characterised by intrusive thoughts about, and overestimation of, another person.[44] Yandere is a Japanese archetype in which intense lovesick devotion leads to violent, controlling, and possessive conduct. Trauma bonds are intense positive attachments an abused person feels for their abuser. Stockholm syndrome is a (disputed) phenomenon in which kidnapping victims develop strong attachments to their kidnappers.[45]

Some of these phenomena are subcategories of romantic love. Some are compatible with romantic love. Others might be incompatible. Their presence in one's conceptual schema can stem from linguistic luck. It can be lucky (or unlucky) that a person's linguistic community or subculture has a term for the idea. And it can be a matter of chance that one encounters the term.[46] §12 illustrates how acquiring these concepts affects conceptions of love.

10. Limning Limerence

Luck does not end with concept possession. These concepts are fraught, complex, and difficult to calibrate interpersonally. People's conceptions vary considerably.

---

[39] Thanks to Jef Delvaux, Blake Stannard, and Alida Liberman for examples. Special thanks to Ray Briggs for many insights.

[40] See also "holibae," "zucchinis" in "queerplatonic relationships," and varieties of erotic friendships (Kearney, 2015).

[41] See also alterous attraction.   [42] Quoting the Wikipedia entry.

[43] Prest and Kaboli (2015).

[44] Cf. Maslow's (1954) distinction between D-love (deficiency-love) and B-love (being-love). The former is grasping, possessive, dependent love.

[45] Dutton and Painter (1993).

[46] Some communities, such as queer online forums, create and feature a wider variety of such terms. See §6 on epistemic benefits of queer communities.

Recall limerence—infatuation characterised by intrusive thoughts. There is scant academic research on limerence, but it is enthusiastically discussed in internet forums, podcasts, blogs, and popular media.[47] Call the collection of scholarly research, media, and forums the "limerence discourse."

There is broad agreement on how limerence characteristically sets in.[48] An initial spark, known as a "glimmer," of perceived reciprocal romantic interest is closely followed by confusion or doubt about the relationship's nature or future. This doubt is typically caused by perceived "mixed signals." The flirtation-confusion sequence is accompanied by an attentional magnet. This attentional magnet is often a situational feature that means pursuing the relationship would be particularly consequential.[49] Perhaps it would constitute an adulterous, first, workplace, student-teacher, boss-employee, or May–September relationship, for example, or a relationship between flatmates or close friends. The relationship might challenge one's perceived sexuality, religious convictions, or social status. Perceiving someone as "damsel-in-distress" is an attentional magnet for many limerents.

According to the limerence discourse, the early onset of confusion or doubt leads to mentally replaying past interactions. Since that activity is enjoyable—it happens early, during the glimmer—thinking about the person causes a dopamine hit. The attentional magnet and dopamine hit reinforce this thought pattern. If repeated often in a short timeframe, the limerent becomes cognitively conditioned towards thinking of the person. At its most extreme, this process disrupts normal dopamine regulation and becomes a debilitating addiction to thinking about the person.[50]

Abnormally high levels of mentally replaying early flirtatious interactions—the first step towards limerence—can also stem from anxiety, loneliness, or escapism. Stress, mid-life, introversion, and adversity are risk factors for limerence because they amplify the allure of reverie. The uncertainty endemic to ambiguous, text-based, online communication engenders limerence. Limerence research pioneer Dorothy Tennov notes that emotionally intimate discussions, particularly during psychotherapy, can seed limerence.[51] I return to this.

Scholars and laypeople debate relationships between limerence and love, including whether limerence is a species of love, a precursor to love, or incompatible with it.[52] Some claim that early stages of limerence and falling in love are

---

[47] Wakin and Vo (2008) and Wolf (2017). The word "limerence" is sometimes used for ordinary affective states of falling in love. This (arguably mistaken) usage departs from Tennov's neologistic definition and the subsequent limerence discourse.

[48] Tennov (1979: 201) and L (2020). Cf. Ortega y Gasset (1957: 53); Stendhal (1975); Armstrong (2003: 71f).

[49] Reconsider Romeo and Juliet, for instance.

[50] L (2020: ch. 3, "The Neuroscience of Limerence").   [51] Tennov (1979: 203).

[52] See, for example, Wakin and Vo (2008); Sack (2012); Willmott and Bentley (2015); Nguyen (2021). Almost no philosophers distinguish between love and limerence, perhaps because limerence is obscure. Lopez-Cantero (2022) is an exception. See also Velleman on "blind, romantic love" (1998: 351) and Ortega y Gasset (1957) on falling in love.

close cousins that evolve differently. Some researchers claim few people experience limerence; others claim limerence is widespread but miscategorised as love. I won't summarise these debates. This essay is relatively agnostic about what, if anything, constitutes limerence. I instead focus on how people *conceive* of them. For this reason, I describe ways the limerence discourse differs from mainstream conceptions of love.

Firstly, limerence discourse focuses on pragmatic strategies for "coping with" and "recovery from" limerence. It describes "deprogramming" through Pavlov-inspired deconditioning strategies. Authors advise imagining limerence as a monster inside your mind, known as the "limerbeast." This differs from typical discourse about romantic love.

The admired person is called the limerent object, usually rendered "LO." This term is largely viewed as appropriate because the limerent attends to an idealised, constructed version of the person. During a phase of "crystallisation" the limerent perceives their limerent object as literally flawless. This idealisation is, limerence theorists claim, a kind of objectification.[53]

The addiction described by the discourse is not to interacting with the person. It is to *thinking* about them. Tennov (1979: 18) explains "Limerence is, above all else, mental activity. It is an interpretation of events, rather than the events themselves." Limerence is thus viewed as a maladaptive attentional habit. Two features of this mental activity are emphasised: Incessance—the thoughts are constant—and lack of cognitive control. Therapeutic manuals bluntly deny limerents can intentionally stop thinking about the limerent object. Tennov writes "In summary, limerent fantasy is, most of all, intrusive and inescapable. It seems not to be something you do, but something *that happens*" (40; emphasis in original).

I cannot overstate these two features of the discourse. Forum posts continually cast suicide as the only escape. Accordingly, perhaps the starkest testament to the thematic dominance of incessance and inescapability is the album title *Post-Suicide Limerence*. Truly, then, ineluctable.[54]

Explanations for the attachment, even those offered by limerents themselves, decentre the LO's traits. Explanations instead emphasise situational features, neurochemicals, the limerent's character and "pathologies," or clinical psychological theories, like attachment theory. The terms "limerent brain" and "limerbrain" are commonplace in the discourse. The non-centrality of the limerent object's traits can be so pronounced that people claim limerence for strangers,

---

[53] L (2020: 33).

[54] L (2020: 33). The limerent addiction is to thought patterns, not a person. This explains why limerence is particularly hard to control or to intentionally end. It is possible—albeit difficult—to wholly break from (or externally restrict) extrasomatic entities like drugs, gambling, food, and social media. One strategy is displacement—doing other things in other places. But if the addictive activity is thought itself, then cessation and displacement won't work. Thinking is constant. And thought is associative; it connects topics. In extreme cases, sufferers think of all topics *by* thinking about the limerent object (Tennov 1979: 34–5), and so limerent thinking cannot be displaced.

fictional characters, and acquaintances they dislike. In the rare cases where the LO's traits or conduct feature in causal explanations, they often impute ill will or manipulative behaviour to the LO. This differs starkly from discourse about love, where causal explanations typically recount the beloved's admired qualities.

Researchers claim limerence is characteristically undermined by better familiarity, and fuelled by lack of contact, because limerence is a "completely unilateral relationship to the idea of someone else."[55] With its emphasis on fantasy, rather than reality, limerence is described as a way of *avoiding* becoming close to people. Love, by contrast, is characterised as bringing people closer. Some writers claim that limerents do not truly care about their limerent object's interests. For these reasons limerence, but not love, is often characterised as solipsistic or narcissistic.

For limerence, but not love, researchers clinically describe average durations and factors that exacerbate duration. Unlike love, limerence seldom exceeds a few years and—absent suicide—is almost never lifelong. Again, this differs from love.

Many forum contributors claim to have platonic, alterous, and non-sexual limerence.[56] Alterous attraction, recall, is desire for emotional closeness itself, which is neither strictly romantic nor platonic attraction. Indeed the Wikipedia entry on limerence begins "Limerence is a state of mind which results from romantic *or non-romantic* feelings for another person" (emphasis added). Many forum contributors describe their limerence as contiguous with, or identical to, non-romantic obsessive thoughts about persons, such as a self-ascribed obsessive need for approval from authority figures or platonic fixation on teachers. A common platonic theme is yearning to discuss deep emotional topics and personal histories with the person. §12 returns to these themes.

Following Tennov's seminal work, two rival academic views developed. Focusing on negative features, Wakin and Vo (2008) aim to categorise limerence as a mental disorder. They write,

> Love and limerence are not interchangeable terms or concepts . . . Neither is a subset of the other . . . Limerence is an involuntary condition that is necessarily negative, problematic, and impairing, with clinical implications. . . . The profile of limerence seems to resemble that of OCD and substance dependence . . . Most importantly [future research] should concentrate on diagnosis, prognosis, and treatment interventions. (Wakin and Vo, 2008)

Willmot and Bentley (2012, 2015) posit positive roles for limerence, including precipitating building a self-narrative that reintegrates one's past and present, and helping the person create or find meaning. I return to this.

---

[55] Molotkow (2018); see also Arabi (2022).
[56] See also Tennov (1979) and Willmott and Bentley (2015).

11. Seeding Conceptions

The above summary synthesises my interpretation of scholarly research, self-help resources, and forum posts. Given the term's obscurity, there is a good chance many readers hadn't heard of limerence before reading this essay. My description has shaped your conception.

I could have centred different themes from the discourse. Neurochemical descriptions foreground the limbic system's flight or fight response, which differs from the neurochemical correlates of love. Psychological explanations centre on introversion and attachment styles, which I mentioned only fleetingly. Emotional facets include mood swings, fear of rejection, and acute longing for reciprocation. More extreme emotional themes include profound confusion, psychic collapse, and a sense of disintegration of the self. Not seeing the person's flaws and vastly overestimating reciprocated romantic interest are striking epistemic features. Another common theme is erratic conduct, stalking, violence, self-destructive behaviour, and imprudence. Foregrounding these features instead would steer your newly seeded conception, which could influence your experiences differently.[57]

Were I developing a philosophical analysis of limerence, I would centre on attentional addiction and the epistemic error of idealisation. People claim to have limerence without various other common features, but these two features seem to be core features.[58]

I could have instead offered a sceptical, debunking appraisal of limerence discourse: Firstly, the broad, multifarious "risk factors" collectively describe most life stages and social contexts. The so-called "pathway to limerence" describes almost all flux flirting. That is, flirtation with a trajectory. (By contrast, "fleeting flirting" involves fugacious interactions amongst strangers and "fixture flirtation" involves reliable, unchanging, script-like interactions amongst firmly platonic acquaintances.) If the putative "explanation" for limerence describes most romantic attraction, it cannot explain a distinctive phenomenon. Secondly, people are susceptible to speciously self-ascribing psychological conditions. Purported symptoms for multiple personality disorder are feelings that many people have to some degree, leading to vast overdiagnosis, especially for self-ascriptions.[59] The concept LIMERENCE seems similarly risky. Thirdly, academic research is scarce. And so limerence forum contributors—typically people at the height of infatuation; and self-anointed limerence experts, who sell limerence self-help products and therapy—dominate the discourse. These groups may overstate

---

[57] These themes are ubiquitous, but see especially Tennov (1979); Reynolds (1983); Sack (2012); Eaglehawk (2019); L (2020); and Delacruz (2021).

[58] Lopez-Cantero (2022) defines infatuation, but not limerence, as "unreasonable." I disagree.

[59] Hacking (1995).

the phenomenon. Emphasising debunking explanations could steer readers towards viewing limerence as simply a crush or "New Relationship Energy" (NRE).

Possessing different concepts and conceptions in the neighbourhood of love can affect an individual's perceptions of their own attachments, which can—owing to interpretative feedback loops—affect those attachments. Do you see your own infatuation as rooted in your character, situational features, and/or the beloved's perceived traits? Should you understand your enthrallment as escapism or a coping mechanism, rather than as a profound valuing of another?

Recall that limerence discourse emphasises situational risk factors, such as stress, adversity, and student-teacher relations. Without an unusual attentional magnet or perceived immediate need to resolve confusion or doubt, flirtatious ambiguous "glimmers" don't tend to cause disproportionate early replaying. Thoughts about the person evolve—growing or dissipating—at a more ordinary rate, which deflects limerence. Notice the similarity to HOLIDAY ROMANCE: Both ideas downplay the other person's character traits and instead emphasise context-ual features. Studies indicate that some people are more susceptible to limerence than others. But the same applies to holiday romances: Some people are predis-posed towards or against holiday romances. Yet contextual features are nonethe-less central explanations for occurrences of limerence and holiday romances.

The limerence discourse, unlike "holiday romance," is not a linguistic term. It is a diffuse, variegated discourse conveying a package of ideas, associations, theories, and advice. The word "limerence" is largely unknown. But ideas about limerence *could* be conveyed by everyday terms, like the ideas conveyed by terms like "puppy love," "celebrity crush," "old flame," "high school sweetheart," and "frenemy." This exhibits linguistic contingency: Just as "holiday romance" conveys ideas about the causes, expectations, and conditions of holiday romances, a language could feature terms embedding purported features of limerence. Echoing Attentional Deficit Disorder (ADD), Vare (2011, 2012) dubs her love addiction "Affection Deficit Disorder." And recall the portmanteaus "limerbeast" and "lim-erbrain." Other potential neologisms include "cress" for a crush that arises from, or distracts from, stress; and "Limerent Attentional Limbic Affliction" (LALA) for love-lost daydreaming in la-la-land. Perhaps such terms would help people understand, or even steer, their affections.

Researchers claim that learning of limerence can pre-empt limerence-induced confusion and reduce dangerous effects, like stalking, violence, and suicide.[60] But caution is needed. Recall that acquiring inapt concepts, like MULTIPLE PERSONALITY DISORDER, can have costs.[61] Acquiring the concept LIMERENCE might cause people to speciously self-ascribe limerence, see themselves as mentally ill, or behave in destructive limerence-congruent ways.

---

[60] Wakin and Vo (2008) and Delacruz (2021).
[61] Hacking (1995). Thanks to Jon Garthoff and Renee Jorgensen for discussion.

12. Transformative Conceptual Shifts

Recall that conceptions shift in response to acquiring or adjusting nodes in one's conceptual schema. Acquiring the concept LAKE can affect how a child conceives of ponds; acquiring LIMERENCE can affect LOVE. These shifts can be transformative.[62]

A transformative experience changes one's point of view and core values. And the only way to know what it is like is to undergo the experience yourself.[63] A transformative conceptual shift radically changes how you interpret the world, including how you interpret your own thoughts and feelings. This too can shift your values. And given the richness of conceptual interpretive webs—and how they frame thinking of other topics—arguably the only way to fully appreciate a conceptual schema is inhabiting it.

This section provides three illustrations of transformative conceptual shifts about love and limerence. They exemplify how conceptual transformations can occur; I do not claim they are apposite.

i. Attention and Polyamory

Discourse about love emphasises its attentional qualities. Ortega y Gasset (1957: 48–50) wrote vividly—and disparagingly—about how falling in love captivates attention: "'Falling in love', initially, is no more than this: attention abnormally fastened upon another person ... Consciousness contracts and is occupied by only one object. The attention remains paralyzed: it does not advance from one thing to another. It is fixed and rigid, the captive of one person alone." And people morally owe romantic partners cognitive attention; neglecting to think of people can attentionally wrong them.[64]

Suppose Marianne's conception of love foregrounds attention. The attention must be of a particular kind, of course. Terror preoccupies but differs from love. And a parent can romantically love her spouse but think of her children more often.[65] Attention is competitive: Thinking about one topic can crowd out others. On some conceptions of attentional dispositions, this suggests a monogamic conception of romantic love. If romantic love is partly characterised by an attentional hierarchy, and *if* only one person can occupy its summit at once,

---

[62] Conversational podcasts allow real-time observation of such shifts. During *Multiamory*'s episode on limerence, for example, acquiring LIMERENCE influences discussants' understanding of love and "New Relationship Energy" (NRE).

[63] Paul (2014).

[64] Thanks to John Parker Epps for discussion. Gardiner (forthcoming, ms) discusses attentional demands of love and friendship. On love and attention, see also Stendhal (1975); Brümmer (1993: 39f); and Murdoch (2003).

[65] Note that falling in love differs attentionally from established love. Thanks to Jon Garthoff for helpful discussion.

then a person can only romantically love one person at a time.[66] On this conception, loving more than one person simultaneously is precluded by love's attentional hierarchy. This differs from the weaker claims that romantic polyamory is rare, difficult, or psychologically unavailable to some individuals.

Suppose Marianne later learns of limerence. Attentional patterns are a core feature of limerence and, according to the discourse, limerence's attentional effects are extreme. Tennov writes, for instance,

> [T]he perpetual presence of LO in your head defines all other experience in relationship to that presence. If a certain thought has no previous connection with LO, you immediately make one.   (Tennov 34–5)

> In his limerence, Larry's preoccupation was almost 100 percent...It was near torture to wrench his mind free of Margaret in order to deal effectively with his work.   (Tennov 36)

Perhaps, then, limerence—not love—is a monomaniacal attentional phenomenon. And so *limerence* is monogamic: One can only be limerent for one person at once. (This claim is widely endorsed by limerence researchers.)

Learning of limerence could subsequently make space for Marianne to characterise love as constituted by different features, such as truly knowing the person, caring for their interests, and long-term commitment. These things, unlike attention, are not competitive. And so they are less apt to underwrite a monogamic conception of love. Thus learning about limerence, and seeing limerence as monogamic, could allow room in Marianne's conceptual schema for polyamorous romantic love.

ii. Is Love Good?

Suppose Daphnée had bad experiences with ardent admirers. Infatuated ex-boyfriends stalked and harassed her. She became cynical about love. Daphnée later reads about limerence in a magazine. The article associates limerence with violence, obsession, and mental prostration. As a result, Daphnée conceives of limerence as pathological, narcissistic, and inimical to flourishing or intimacy.[67] She views limerence (accurately) as an individual's state, not a shared bond. And she (perhaps implicitly) sees limerence as essentially different from love. (Daphnée might see limerence as incompatible with love or as simply not entailing it.) As a result, Daphnée might now recategorise obsessive infatuations from her past as

---

[66] Not all competitions have a unique first place, of course.   [67] Keller (2011).

limerence, rather than love. Lacking an alternative, she previously labelled them as love. Now she doesn't.

As a result, Daphnée's attitudes and associations about love become more positive. And her conception of love can also shift. She understands what love is differently. Her conception of love becomes more infused with positive assessment. It moves towards the *Corinthians* ideal: *Love is patient, love is kind. It does not envy...* The LIMERENCE category siphons away some destructive, obsessive emotional states, which creates room in Daphnée's conceptual schema to understand love as a profound appreciation of a person; a valuable bond that both nurtures and constitutes flourishing.

Similarly, understanding limerence as involving unrealistic idealisation of the limerent object "makes room" for love to involve accurate appraisal and deep knowledge. In Daphnée's subsequent schema, *limerence* is blind; love is not.

Put slightly differently, suppose Daphnée conceives of limerence as characterised by debilitating cognitive ruts and a distorted, idealised perception of the person. No matter how much these features are dialled up, the attachment does not thereby become love, on Daphnée's conception, because love is characterised by different features.[68]

Ortega y Gasset contemned falling in love because, he claimed, attention is monomaniacally focused on the beloved. He dismissed it as "a relative paralysis of the life of our consciousness," "psychic angina," and "an inferior state of mind, a form of transitory imbecility" (1957: 44, 49, 51). But perhaps if Ortega y Gasset came across the idea of limerence, and viewed it as a distinct phenomenon, he would have viewed falling in love more positively.

iii. Addiction, Rumination, and the Unmet Need

Lastly a person whose conception of limerence is shaped by discourse that emphasises addiction science, neurochemical pathways, or behavioural conditioning might accordingly conceive of limerence as primarily an addiction. The addiction is to thought patterns, rather than external drugs or behaviours like cocaine or gambling. They might thus understand limerence as contiguous with non-romantic cognitive or attentional addictions, such as maladaptive daydreaming, compulsive rumination, cognitive stimming, mental perseveration, and compulsive suicidal, violent, argumentative, or sexual ideation.[69] Consider also habitually thinking in the form of dialogue or social media posts or compulsively doing mental maths, art, or music.

---

[68] On some such conceptions, love and limerence are incompatible. Suppose they require accurate and inaccurate appraisal, respectively, for example. On others, a person with limerence might also be in love—they aren't incompatible—but not in virtue of the same features constituting their limerence.

[69] Rumination is mentally imagining or replaying conversations. Perseveration is the continual involuntary repetition of a thought or behaviour.

Some of these mental habits—not all of which are deleterious—are ways of processing emotions, especially at times of distress or upheaval. Perhaps limerence can serve a similar cognitive role.

There are suggestive consilient links between limerence and reinterpreting one's life experience into a new personal narrative. Tennov (1979) notes therapy is a situational risk factor. Limerent self-help manuals warn that deep introspective conversations precipitate and sustain limerence. Limerence is associated with periods of reassessing core values, such as mid-life crises. A reoccurring forum theme is alterous, non-sexualised attraction and the longing for emotional intimacy, especially including discussing personal histories. Research suggests the characteristic crux of limerent fantasies is emotional intimacy, not sexual activity, and sexual content is avoided because it "contaminates" limerent fantasy.[70] Most explicitly, Willmot and Bentley (2015) view the turmoil, confusion, and rumination of limerence as a process for reintegrating life experiences into a more coherent self-narrative. And Eaglehawk (2021) writes,

> limerents have a strong desire to collate their journey into a coherent story...a limerent focus can be any source of inspiration ruminatively analysed and, often obsessively, revisited... [We can] envisage limerence as...a highly common emotional and cognitive state of active manifestation, motivation, inspiration and transformation. For with empowerment comes healing...   (Eaglehawk, 2021)

With this background exposure, someone might conceive of limerence primarily as obsessive rumination—running conversations in your head—as a tool for deep emotional processing. According to the discourse, establishing limerence requires an attentional magnet with an attendant dopamine hit. And for most people, amorous glimmers can provide this. But for some people, alterous or platonic attention is captivated by teachers, bosses, virtuosos, or celebrities. On this conception, sexual and romantic aspects recede into the background; limerence is at core platonic. It is a tool for understanding oneself.

Perhaps then limerence—like many addictions—ultimately arises from unmet needs. Perhaps three central clusters of unmet adulthood interpersonal needs feed a tripartite clustering of limerence kinds: The need for romantic companionship or to feel desirable, which corresponds to romantic limerence. The need for approval, especially from authority figures, which commonly underwrites limerence for teachers and bosses.[71] And the need for emotional processing, leading to limerence for therapists and alterous limerence.

In the resulting conceptual nexus, perhaps love is—at least in its most ideal instantiations—a way to bond, connect, and structure a life. Limerence is a way to think. It is characterised by one-sided mental conversations, but always with the

---

[70] Tennov (1979) Willmott and Bentley (2015); and various forum posts.
[71] Limerence for authority figures is a common forum theme.

same "listening" persona. Limerence is often characterised as hellacious and destructive. Instead, conceiving of one's limerence as a valuable therapeutic tool for emotional processing could be self-fulfilling.

Thus acquiring and transforming conceptions in the neighbourhood of love can affect conceptions of love. Crucially, a transformative conceptual shift, unlike a transformative experience, does not require experience. A person might simply come to realise that their existing conceptions should—or did—shift. Perhaps there was an internal tension which is resolved by, for example, altering one's conception of love.[72] These shifts in conceptions can, in turn, affect feelings, values, commitments, affections, interpretative schemas, self-ascriptions, and relationships. This, ultimately, shapes flourishing, community, happiness, and the core of who we are.

13. So, What...? So What?

I have not said what I think love is. Nor limerence, infatuation, puppy love, bi-curiosity, or lust. I have only described what they could be and how conceptions can affect self-ascriptions. And how, in turn, those self-ascriptions affect the underlying nexus of values, emotions, commitments, and beliefs with which we build relationships. The contours of one's conceptual schema matters, but usually the values, emotions, and relationships matter more.[73]

References

Popular Media

Ambrosino, Brandon (2016) 'I Am Gay—But I Wasn't Born This Way'. *BBC Future*, June 28.

Arabi, Shahida (2022) 'Love or Limerence? 11 Signs You're in a Fantasy Relationship'. *Thought Catalog*, January 28.

[72] Consider Kuhnian paradigm shifts.

[73] This research benefitted from feedback at three workshops: The SoGro Research Group, the University of Tennessee's Epistemology Research Group, and Northeastern University's Ethics & Epistemology Workshop, I am grateful to those participants, especially Amy Flowerree, Cat Saint-Croix, Sophie Dandelet, Anna Brinkerhoff, Alexandra Lloyd, Sophia Dandelet, Catherine Rioux, Arianna Falbo, Elise Woodard, Linh Mac, Paige Greene, Donnie Barnett, Chad Lee-Stronach, Kay Mathiesen, Renee Jorgensen, Sam Berstler, Marcello Di Bello, Rafal Urbaniak, and Will Fleisher.

This essay benefitted from many wide-ranging conversations. I am grateful to Richard Eldridge, Kevin Ryan, Jef Delvaux, Alasdair Murray, Alex Fitzgerald, John Parker Epps, Elle Benjamin, Quill Kukla, Steve Grover, Blake Stannard, Alida Liberman, and Jen Steel for helpful comments; and to the many people who shared their stories, secrets, words, and insights with me, including through my anonymous messaging site. Thanks to Patrick Grzanka, Héctor Carrillo, and Laurie Essig for guidance about sexuality terms. Special thanks to Ray Briggs, Claire Dartez, and Jon Garthoff for many valuable insights and comments throughout this research.

This research was supported by an ACLS Fellowship from the American Council of Learned Societies and by the University of Tennessee's Office of Undergraduate Research and Fellowships. Special thanks to Nate Parsons and Delia McDevitt for excellent research assistance.

Coontz, Stephanie (2020) 'How to Make Your Marriage Gayer?' *New York Times*, February 13.

Delacruz, Nollyanne (2021) 'Limerence Sparks Dysfunctional Relationships'. *Daily Titan*, September 28.

Eaglehawk, Wallea (2019) 'Limerence: Persona as face—Persona as Fantasy' *Medium Revolutionaries*.   https://medium.com/revolutionaries/limerence-persona-as-face-persona-as-fantasy-e739639d7e97

Eaglehawk, Wallea (2021) 'Limerence: A Longing for Love' *Medium 'Revolutionaries'*, January 5.

Essig, Laurie (2000) 'Heteroflexibility'. *Salon*, November 15.

Frankel, Valerie (2010) 'The Love Drug' *Oprah.com*, July 26.

Hirji, Sukaina and Meena Krishnamurthy (2021) 'What is Romantic Friendship?' *The New Statesman*, November 2.

Kearney, Jayne (2015) 'Between Love and Tinder: Investigating the Erotic Friendship'. *Archer Magazine*, June 24.

Keller, Kristine (2011) 'Limerence: When Is It More than Heartbreak?' *Psychology Today*, September 23.

Lindgren, Jase, Emily Matlack, and Dedeker Winston (2021) '320—Limerence and NRE: The Dark and Light Sides of the Force'. *Multiamory Podcast*, May 4.

Molotkow, Alexandra (2018) 'New Feelings: Crush Fatigue'. *Real Life Magazine*, August 1.

Nguyen, Julie (2021) 'What Is Limerence? 5 Signs You're Experiencing It (Not Love!)'. *Mind Body Green*, October 11.

Prest, Kaitlin and Mitra Kaboli (2015) 'The Hurricane'. *The Heart Podcast*, March.

Sack, David (2012) 'Limerence and the Biochemical Roots of Love Addiction'. *Huffington Post*, June 28.

Smith, Erika (2019) 'What Does It Mean to Be "Bi-Curious"?' *Refinery 29*, August 19.

Thomas, Brooklyn (2019) 'Stop Calling Yourselves "Bi-curious"'. *An Injustice Magazine*, November 10.

Vare, Ethlie Ann (2012) 'Love Addiction: You Might Be a Love Addict If . . .'. *HuffPost*, April 11.

Forums

https://limerence.net
https://discord.gg/t2V59gs4
https://www.reddit.com/r/limerence/
https://livingwithlimerence.com
https://limerence-recovery.tumblr.com
https://thestateoflimerence.tumblr.com

Academic Resources

Albury, Kathy (2015) 'Identity Plus? Bi-Curiosity, Sexual Adventurism and the Boundaries of "Straight" Sexual Practices and Identities'. *Sexualities* 18(5–6):649–664.

Andler, M. (2022) 'Nonbinary Design: Making Dating Apps Queer'. *Boston Review*. https://www.bostonreview.net/articles/nonbinary-design-making-dating-apps-queer.

Armstrong, John (2003) *Conditions of Love: The Philosophy of Intimacy*. Norton.

Banker, Robin *Socially Prescribed Perfectionism and Limerence on Interpersonal Relationships*. ProQuest Dissertations Publishing.

Barrett, Lisa Feldman (2017) *How Emotions Are Made: The Secret Life of the Brain*. Houghton Mifflin Harcourt.

Baumeister, Roy (2004) 'Gender and Erotic Plasticity: Sociocultural Influences on the Sex Drive'. *Sexual and Relationship Therapy* 19(2):133–139.

Berlant, Laura and Michael Warner (1998) 'Sex in Public'. *Critical Inquiry* 24(2):547–566.

Bindel, Julie (2014) *Straight Expectations: What Does It Mean to Be Gay Today?* Guardian Books.

Brümmer, Vincent (1993) *The Model of Love: A Study in Philosophical Theology*. Cambridge University Press.

Burge, Tyler (2003) 'Concepts, Conceptions, Reflective Understanding: Reply to Peacocke in Hahn and Ramberg (eds.)'. *Essays on the Philosophy of Tyler Burge*. MIT Press.

Camp, Elisabeth (2017) 'Perspectives in Imaginative Engagement with Fiction'. *Philosophical Perspectives* 31(1):73–102.

Camp, Elisabeth (2019) 'Imaginative Frames for Scientific Inquiry: Metaphors, Telling Facts, and Just-So Stories'. *The Scientific Imagination*, ed. Godfrey-Smith and Levy. Oxford University Press, 304–336.

Carrillo, Héctor and Amanda Hoffman (2018) '"Straight with a Pinch of Bi": The Construction of Heterosexuality as an Elastic Category among Adult US Men'. *Sexualities* 21(1–2):90–108.

Compton, D'Lane, Tey Meadow, and Kristen Schilt (2018) *Other, Please Specify: Queer Methods in Sociology*. UC Press.

Crimp, Douglas (1987) 'How to Have Promiscuity in an Epidemic'. *October* 43:237–71.

Dembroff, Robin (2020) 'Beyond Binary: Genderqueer as Critical Gender Kind'. *Philosophers' Imprint* 20(9): 1–23.

Durkin, Dolores (1976) *Teaching Young Children to Read*. Allyn and Bacon.

Dutton, D. G., and S. Painter (1993) 'Emotional Attachments in Abusive Relationships: A Test of Traumatic Bonding Theory'. *Violence and Victims* 8(2):105–120.

Earp, Brian and Julian Savulescu (2020) *Love Drugs: The Chemical Future of Relationships*. Stanford University Press.

Finocchiaro, Peter (2021) 'How to Project a Socially Constructed Sexual Orientation'. *Journal of Social Ontology* 7(2):173–203.

Finocchiaro, Peter (2022) 'Seek the Joints! Avoid the Gruesome! Fidelity as an Epistemic Value'. *Episteme* 1–17.

Flòridi, Luciano (2018) 'What a Maker's Knowledge Could Be'. *Synthese* 195:465–481.

Fraser, Rachel (2018) 'The Epistemology of (Compulsory) Heterosexuality'. *The Bloomsbury Companion to Analytic Feminism*. Bloomsbury, 329–354.

Gardiner, Georgi (forthcoming) 'Attunement: On the Cognitive Virtues of Attention'. *Social Virtue Epistemology*, ed. Alfano, Klein, and de Ridder. Routledge.

Gardiner, Georgi (ms) 'Against the New Ethics of Belief: The Morass of Moral Encroachment and Doxastic Partiality'.

Ghaziani, Amin and Matt Brim (2019) *Imagining Queer Methods*. NYU Press.

Grzanka, Patrick, Katherine Zeiders, and Joseph Miles (2019) 'Beyond "Born This Way?" Reconsidering Sexual Orientation Beliefs and Attitudes'. *Journal of Counseling Psychology* 63(1):67–75.

Hacking, Ian (1995) *Rewriting the Soul: Multiple Personality and the Science of Memory* Princeton University Press.

Harrington, C. L., and D. D. Bielby, D. D. (1995) *Soap Fans: Pursuing Pleasure and Making Meaning in Everyday Life*. Philadelphia, Temple University Press.

Haslanger, Sally (2000) 'Gender and Race: (What) Are They? (What) Do We Want Them to Be?' *Noûs* 34(1):31–55.

Haslanger, Sally (2012) *Resisting Reality*. Oxford University Press.

Hintikka, Jaakko (1974) 'Practical versus Theoretical Reason—An Ambiguous Legacy'. *Knowledge and the Known: Historical Perspectives in Epistemology*. D. Reidel, 80–97.

Holleb, Morgan Lev (2019) *The A–Z of Gender and Sexuality: From Ace to Ze*. Jessica Kingsley Publishers.

hooks, bell (2000) *All About Love: New Visions*. Harper.

Isaac, Manuel Gustavo (2021) 'Which Concept of Concept for Conceptual Engineering?' *Erkenntnis* 1–25.

Jenkins, Carrie (2017) *What Love Is and What It Could Be*. Basic Books.

Jenkins, Carrie (2018) 'All Hearts in Love Use Their Own Tongues: Concepts, Verbal Disputes, and Disagreeing About Love', ed. Martin, *Routledge Handbook of Love in Philosophy*. Routledge, 72–82.

Jenkins, Carrie (2020) 'When Love Stinks, Call a Conceptual Plumber'. *Philosophy by Women*. Routledge, 44–53.

Knox, David (1970) 'Conceptions of Love at Three Developmental Levels'. *Family Coordinator* 19(2): 151–157.

L, Dr. (2020) *Living with Limerence: A Guide for the Smitten*. Lwlonline.

Langton, Rae (2009) 'Speaker's Freedom and Maker's Knowledge'. *Sexual Solipsism*. Oxford University Press.

Lee, John (1973) *The Colors of Love.* New Press.

Lopez-Cantero, Pilar (2022) 'Falling in Love'. *Philosophy of Love in the Past, Present and Future.* Routledge.

Margolis, Eric and Stephen Laurence (2021) 'Concepts'. *Stanford Encyclopedia of Philosophy.* Stanford University Press.

Maslow, Abraham (1954) *Motivation and Personality.* Harper.

Morandini, James, Liam Dacosta, and Ilan Dar-Nimrod (2021) 'Exposure to Continuous or Fluid Theories of Sexual Orientation Leads Some Heterosexuals to Embrace Less-Exclusive Heterosexual Orientations'. *Scientific Reports* 11: 16546.

Murdoch, Iris (2003) *The Sovereignty of Good.* Routledge.

Neto, Félix (1993) 'Love Styles and Self-Representations'. *Personality and Individual Differences* 14(6):795–803.

Ortega y Gasset, José (1957) *On Love: Aspects of a Single Theme.* The World Publishing Company.

Paul, Laurie (2014) *Transformative Experience.* Oxford University Press.

Peacocke, Christopher (1992) *A Study of Concepts.* MIT Press.

Peacocke, Christopher (1998) 'Implicit Conceptions, Understanding and Rationality'. *Philosophical Issues* 9:43–88.

Podosky, Paul-Mikhail Catapang (2018) 'Ideology and Normativity: Constraints on Conceptual Engineering'. *Inquiry*, https://doi.online.org/10.1080/0020174X.2018.1562374

Potki, Robabeh, Tayebe Ziaei, Mahbobeh Faramarzi, Mahmood Moosazadeh, and Zohreh Shahhosseini (2017) 'Bio-Psycho-Social Factors Affecting Sexual Self-Concept: A Systematic Review'. *Electronic Physician* 9(9):5172–5178.

Pritchard, Duncan (2005) *Epistemic Luck.* Oxford University Press.

Rey, G. (1985) 'Concepts and Conceptions: A Reply to Smith, Medin and Rips'. *Cognition* 19(3):297–303.

Reynolds, Sarah (1983) '"Limerence": A New Word and Concept'. *Psychotherapy* 20(1):107–111.

Rupp, Leila (2006) 'Everyone's Queer'. *OAH Magazine of History* 20(2):8–11.

Rupp, Leila and Taylor Verta (2010) 'Straight Girls Kissing'. *Contexts* 9(3):28–32.

Seresin, Asa (2019) 'On Heteropessimism' *The New Inquiry*, October 9.

Setiya, Kieran (2022) 'Other People'. *Rethinking the Value of Humanity*, ed. Buss and Theunissen. Oxford University Press.

Simion, Mona (2018) 'The 'Should' in Conceptual Engineering'. *Inquiry* 61:8:914–928.

Stendhal (1975) *Love.* Penguin.

Tennov, Dorothy (1979) *Love and Limerence.* Stein and Day.

Tukachinsky, Riva (2021) *Parasocial Romantic Relationships: Falling in Love with Media Figures.* Lexington Books.

Vare, Ethlie Ann (2011) *Love Addict: Sex, Romance, and Other Dangerous Drugs.* Health Communications, Inc.

Vavova, Katia (2018) 'Irrelevant Influences'. *Philosophy and Phenomenological Research* 96(1):134–152.

Velleman, David (1999) 'Love as a Moral Emotion'. *Ethics* 109(2):338–374.

Wakin, Albert and Duyen Vo (2008) 'Love-Variant: The Wakin-Vo I. D. R. Model of Limerence'. *Challenging Intimate Boundaries. Inter-Disciplinary—Net. 2nd Global Conference.* Sacred Heart University.

Walters, Suzanna Danuta (2014) *The Tolerance Trap: How God, Genes, and Good Intentions are Sabotaging Gay Equality.* NYU Press.

Ward, Jane (2020) *The Tragedy of Heterosexuality.* NYU Press.

Willmott, Lynn and Evie Bentley (2012) *Love and Limerence: Harness the Limbicbrain.* Lathbury House Limited.

Willmott, Lynn and Evie Bentley (2015) 'Exploring the Lived-Experience of Limerence: A Journey toward Authenticity'. *The Qualitative Report* 20(1):20–38.

Wilson, G. and Q. Rahman (2008) *Born Gay: The Psychobiology of Sex Orientation.* Peter Owen.

Wolf, Noah (2017) 'Investigating Limerence: Predictors of Limerence, Measure Validation, and Goal Progress'. Master of Science Thesis, University of Maryland, College Park.

Woodfield, Andrew (1991) 'Conceptions'. *Mind* 100(4):547–572.

Index

For the benefit of digital users, indexed terms that span two pages (e.g., 52–53) may, on occasion, appear on only one of those pages.